LEGITIMACY AND FORCE

Volume Two

LEGITIMACY AND FORCE

Volume Two

National and International Dimensions

Jeane J. Kirkpatrick

Transaction Books
New Brunswick (U.S.A.) and Oxford (U.K.)

Library of Congress Catalog Number: 87-13789
ISBN: 0-88738-100-6
Printed in the United States of America

Library of Congress Cataloging in Publication Data

Kirkpatrick, Jeane J.
  Legitimacy and force.

  Contents: v. 1. Political and moral dimensions—
v. 2. National and international dimensions.
    1. United States—Foreign relations—1981-
2. United States—Politics and government—1981-
3. World politics—1975-1985.   I. Title.
E838.5.K57   1987   327.73   87-13789
ISBN 0-88738-099-9 (v. 1)
ISBN 0-88738-100-6 (v. 2)
ISBN 0-88738-646-6 (pbk. : v. 1)
ISBN 0-88738-647-4 (pbk. : v. 2)

To and for

José
Chuck
Carl
Ken
Alan
Allan
Jackie
Dick
Bill
Harvey
Louise
Shannon
and the USUN Team,
1981-1985.
R.I.P.

Contents

List of Documents

Introduction

The United Nations is a fascinating environment in which to work. It is also deeply disturbing. In the UN, majorities claim the right to decide what is legitimate and what is illegitimate, what is true, what is false, what is Zionism, what is self-determination, what is fair, what is permissible, what is liberation, and what is aggression.

No assumptions concerning politics, society, and government are shared by all. All moral and epistemological assumptions are challenged in UN debate. All questions are settled by votes, and votes are settled by factors that have little to do with the merits of the case. Reasoned debate has a role inside the United Nations. But its role is much less to persuade than to justify. Votes are decided in capitals by governments' judgments of their national interest, and/or in New York by interactions within blocs. They are decided, that is, by considerations of power.

Serving as U.S. Permanent Representative to the UN from January 1981 to April 1985 gave me ample time to think about the United Nations, and ample data on the relations among nations in and out of that institution. The first problem in thinking about the United Nations is to understand what it does, what actually goes on in its council rooms and great halls. This is not easy. It is a complex institution and little has been written on its actual dynamics: how it works, why it works that way, what are the consequences, how we might influence events. Much of what has been written about it is misleading formal legal analysis that begins with the hopes of the founders and proceeds by analyzing official documents and tables of organization. Through most of its life the UN has been protected against scrutiny and description by the silence of its participants and the reverence of observers.

Observing what is actually said and done in UN bodies reveals the first fact about the UN, namely that few of its activities even aim at the peaceful resolution of conflicts, or promotion of human rights or economic development. The UN is a place where representatives of governments state demands, make declarations, cast votes concerning the legitimacy of other governments' actions, the distribution of resources, the causes of problems, and the nature of things. The principal products of the United Nations are groups, speeches, resolutions, declarations, and bureaucracies. Its principal activities are the composition of the resolutions and declarations, and the majorities that support them. These decisions and declarations are offered in the name of the "world community."

The UN is an institution whose majorities claim the right to decide—for the world—what is legitimate and what is illegitimate. If you believe, as Plato, Augustine, Rousseau, Mosca, Weber, and Lasswell did (and as I do), that societies, governments, and civilizations are grounded on a conception of legitimacy, then it is clear that UN debates and decisions should not be dismissed as "merely" verbal exercises. The definitions of reality and morality are at stake. Every opinion is possible and no conclusion is too far-fetched to be defended by some representative of some government. No shared assumption concerning politics and society serves as the grounds for this extraordinary assemblage.

It is true that the UN, like the U.S., was built on an idea of stable democratic world order as embodied in its Charter, which, like the U.S. Constitution, serves—in principle—as the authoritative statement of the organization's purposes and basic rules of procedure. But the Charter is a misleading guide to the UN. United Nations members are not united as the Charter says they should be in promoting peace and security, national independence, respect for sovereignty, human rights, democracy, and development—in part because they do not agree about what these good things are and in part because some members are committed to quite different political principles.

The principles of the UN Charter that theoretically unite the members forbid aggression and permit self-defense. But what is aggression? What is self-defense? Is the Soviet invasion of Afghanistan aggression, as it seems to Americans and to most of the world, or is it self-defense as Soviet spokesmen assert? Was the U.S. action in Grenada aggression, as a UN majority insisted, or collective self-defense, as the U.S. and the OECS believed?

The Charter affirms the right to self-determination—but what is self-determination? How can we tell if it exists? Do the people of Afghanistan or Latvia enjoy self-determination? Or Puerto Rico? How can we decide? And what of human rights—what are they?

No "ought" is universal enough or mundane enough to escape contradiction. The result of the continuing clash of incompatible ways of thinking, valuing, being, is less tolerance than cynicism that simultaneously limits the sincerity of human relations and the seriousness of political interactions. The chasm across which delegates relate to one another is wide and deep. It is, as diplomats say, "deniable"—but it is probably not bridgeable.

A continuing political struggle is waged to control the definitions of key terms, descriptions of reality. What are human rights? Who is guilty of human rights abuses? Who is abused? What is aggression? Who is the aggressor and who is the victim? What is a national liberation movement—who is liberated, who is subjugated? When is force legitimate, when is it illegitimate? All are "decided" by majority vote. Whether events deserve the attention of the world is decided by majority vote.

In the UN the most basic questions of morality and reality are translated into questions of political power. What happens to an issue before the Security Council or General Assembly is determined by who controls the necessary votes—or vetoes.

In considering these facts and their implications four points need to be emphasized:

1. There is no consensus among UN members about values or standards of valuation, cause and effect, ends and means, about what is real or un-real, or how to decide. In this system, epistemology and ethics are determined neither by convention, revelation, nor empirical evidence, but by majority vote.
2. In making these determinations the Soviet client states constitute solid blocs of solid votes, while other states, especially the democracies, are divided.
3. This practice of making conceptions of reality dependent on politics is, obviously, more consistent with Marxism than with Western conceptions of science, truth, and logic.
4. Key terms, redefined by majority vote, are incorporated into an ideology then presented as the view of the "world community."

The votes that determine meaning and morality are more a function of organizations than of argument and evidence. Blocs are the principal arenas of decisions. Almost all members of the UN (except the United States, Japan, and Israel) are members of one or more overlapping, interlocking blocs that regularly provide majorities for the Soviets and their friends. The existence of these majorities has a profound effect on the agendas and decisions of UN bodies. Once a decision is made in a bloc it is extremely difficult to unmake the decision. Decisions of the blocs are made by consensus. Since a single member can block a decision, all members are considered to be bound by a bloc's decisions. As in most organizations, all members are not equal. More active, stronger members have more influence in the decision of the group.

The Western democracies are not among the most active and influential. They do not determine the meanings of terms, the agendas, or the decisions. Normally the Western democracies participate energetically in discussions and debates about the nature of things and the requirements of legitimacy only where their own government is directly involved.

For reasons that are not wholly clear, Western nations lost their appetite for defending democratic values in UN arenas after the influx of new nations into the world body in the 1960s. Opposing the Soviet Union and its eastern European satellites was one thing. Opposing their former colonies was another. Perhaps because of guilt, perhaps because colonial elites had learned too well the arguments and vulnerabilities of their former colonial masters, perhaps because of fatigue, perhaps because of deep ambivalence about their own societies and allies, Western governments including the U.S. lost their zest for explaining and defending Western values and developed instead a habitual reticence and disdain for what more and more was called "confrontational" or "ideological" responses. They developed the habit of participating in debate narrowly and only when their own government was directly involved. This left the new nations of the Third World and the Soviet bloc free to impose their understandings on the work of the United Nations.

In the absence of an active Western role the perspectives and priorities of radical Third World nations came to dominate the UN agenda and UN debate. The change was more radical than is generally understood. The UN Charter reflects the assumptions, values, priorities, and practices of democracy, but after the influx of the sixties, the UN has been dominated by governments that do not share democratic assumptions and goals.

Since in the UN the most basic questions of morality and reality are treated as questions of political power, the relative inactivity of the democracies affects conceptions of truth and error, justice and injustice, war and peace.

The UN today is the place to discover the meaning of cultural diversity. It is also the place to study relations between language and power. Zionism, the historic doctrine of the Jewish people, was redefined by vote of a majority of the UN on November 10, 1975, as "a form of racism and racial discrimination." This is perhaps the most dramatic, succinct example of the relation between power and ideology inside the UN. But examples abound of the transvaluation of values, the radical inversion of the values, expectations, identifications, and demands characteristic of Western liberal societies and politics.

The votes depend less on the merits of the issue than on the structure of the blocs. Because Libya can count on majority support (from the Soviet bloc as well as portions of the Arab group and the nonaligned states, and the African group), Chad gets no help in defending itself against Kaddafi's invasion. Because Lebanon and the PLO have the votes, Israel is condemned for returning fire across the border, but Lebanon and the PLO are not condemned for firing. Because Syria has the votes no mention is made of withdrawing Syrian troops from Lebanon, while maximum pressure for withdrawal is put on Israel, which lacks the clout to protect itself. Because nations that use terror as an instrument of state policy (Iran, Syria, Libya, the U.S.S.R., among others) are linked to the powerful blocs—the Islamic Conference, the nonalignment movement—and enjoy the support of the Soviet bloc, there can be no action against terrorism. Because the Soviet Union has the votes it is not asked by name to remove the troops from Afghanistan, but because it lacks the votes, the U.S. is repeatedly requested to revise its foreign policy around the world—to cease, for example, providing economic and military aid to Israel.

Because the Soviet Union has clout inside the UN and the U.S. lacks strength, the U.S. is criticized repeatedly for failing to assist less developed countries and the Soviet Union is never mentioned even though the economic and technical assistance offered by the U.S. to the Third World greatly exceeds that offered by the Soviet Union.

Because it lacks power and powerful connections in the UN and is the object of a "national liberation movement," El Salvador is the target of resolution after resolution condemning its human rights practices. And because it has powerful connections, Nicaragua is never mentioned in human rights proceedings. Because of the cumulative impact of attacks by the "world community," small struggling nations like El Salvador are demoralized and seek the cover of silence. Because they can count on the support of interlocking blocs of "nonaligned" states, the Nicaraguan government grows confident and bold with success. Because governments and people dislike being attacked and dislike losing, governments avoid associating with the losers (us), avoid defending unpopular positions, and avoid opposing the arguments and positions of the stronger inside the UN system.

There is no "automatic majority" at the disposal of the Soviet Union. The proof of this fact is that each year a large majority of UN members vote for resolutions which, even though they do not name the offending parties clearly, call for Soviet withdrawal from Afghanistan and for Vietnamese withdrawal from Cambodia. In these votes only absolutely reliable client states vote with the Soviet Union. However, the affinity between Third World ideology and Marxism/Leninism gives the Soviet's preferred positions a majority on many issues. To reinforce this alliance the Soviet Union, like the Chinese, has a longstanding practice of voting with the Third World majority on matters in which its interests are not involved. It is not nearly so easy for the U.S. to join the majority because we and our interests are so often the target. Many resolutions explicitly attack American interests or principles.

There developed in the United Nations a new ideology which Carlos Rangel has called the Third World ideology. That is as good as any other name. The ideology is not shared by all Third World nations, but it is supported by virtually all of them in the UN context. New symbols of identification have emerged, new demands have been articulated. The perspective embodied in the "Third World ideology" is revolutionary in the technical sense that it postulates new identifications, expectations, and demands. The "world community" or "international community" replaces national and ethnic symbols of identification. Associated expectations emphasize that everyone and everything is part of a world community, that all persons are "fellow citizens" in the global community and share a "common heritage." From the concept of a "world community" comes such related conceptions as the "world's wealth," the "world's protein," and the "world's energy" and the "common heritage of mankind."

To the doctrine of global citizenship is added a socialist doctrine of property, a belief that if property is not theft it is something very like it, that redistribution of wealth is the key to improved standards of living in the Third World, and that the United Nations is the governing body of the "world community" and the custodian of the "world's resources." As always with socialism there is more concern with distribution than production. Little attention is paid to who has produced the "world's" resources, or how. More attention is paid to who has a "fair" and who an "unfair" share of the "world's wealth."

A good many of those who purvey this ideology are explicitly hostile to the United States. Cubans charge us with spreading dengue fever, the Ethiopians charge us with genocide, the Syrians charge us with massacring civilians, the Ghanians charge us with pillage and exploitation, the Zimbabweans charge us with racism and imperialism, the Chinese charge us with hegemonism. Americans who dismiss such charges imagine they do not matter. They are wrong. As "might" cannot long endure unless it is transformed into "right," "right" defined by United Nation majorities has important cumulative consequences for power distributions, and power distributions then determine the viability of values and institutions. Governments whose legitimacy and policies are subject to constant assault are weakened in the process—even if they do not understand that it is happening to them.

I believe it is very important for the United States to participate seriously and energetically in the debates and discussions of the United Nations. I believe we should take its proceedings seriously, and should insist that issues be considered on their merits even when we know that power will finally decide. We at the United Nations between 1981 and 1985 tried to do this at the same time that we worked in other ways as well to enhance the American position. This collection reflects various stages of that effort.

Most of the speeches in this volume were delivered at the United Nations or inspired by our situation or our experiences there, in the period between December 1980 when I was appointed U.S. permanent representative to the United Nations and April 1985 when I resigned from government. They were written in response to events taking place in the UN or as part of an ongoing effort to understand the activities and processes of the international body in the context of the goals and assumptions of the Reagan administration. The content of the speeches is therefore heavily influenced by the UN agenda. That agenda does not resemble the front pages of the world's newspapers. Often, the UN marches to a different drummer—its own.

The statements delivered in the United Nations are official statements. The positions stated in them were those of the Reagan administration. Although most of the texts were not "cleared" through a formal bureaucratic process, they were carefully coordinated with the State Department and with other parts of the U.S. government as appropriate. Relevant bureaus of the State Department sometimes provided data incorporated into speeches, but the presentation—the speeches themselves—were written in New York. I wrote most of the speeches included here. However, other members of the U.S. Mission to the UN drafted part or all of a statement. Carl Gershman and I worked most closely on the preparation of my speeches.

The speech on the International Court of Justice delivered before the American Society of International Law, for example, was a joint product. We consulted with two distinguished scholars in international law, Professors Myres MacDougal and Justice Arthur J. Goldberg, and their views shaped certain key formulations. Carl Gershman did the original draft of one part of the speech, Allan Gerson another, I another. I wrote the final draft, as I regularly did for the speeches which I delivered.

Many of the speeches were prepared under great time pressures. I wrote some of the statements under the "right to reply" in intense debates in the Security Council or General Assembly. Some of them were drafted and delivered in the middle of the night.

I was, for example, in Marrakesh, Morrocco, for a few days vacation when KAL-007 was shot down. I was called back by the secretary of state, and arrived in Washington 24 hours before the Security Council hearings. After a day of intensive briefings about what had occurred, and conversations with persons preparing the videotape of the Soviet pilot's comments as he targeted and destroyed the plane, I worked until late into the night on the speech I would give the next day. In the morning, I checked my descriptions with experts most knowledgeable about what had transpired, then flew into New York shortly before the speech and presentation of the tape.

The initial speech on Grenada was also prepared rapidly in close consultation with Secretary of State Shultz, Undersecretary Lawrence Eagleburger, and, especially, with Deputy Secretary of State Kenneth Dam who supervised the preparation of the legal case. The emphasis on the unique nature of the circumstances leading to U.S. participation in the Grenada landing reflected Dam's concern that the Grenada case be treated—legally and politically—as a discrete case.

Some of the speeches were written without specific consultation with anyone, either because there was no time or no need. But regular participation in the National Security Council, the National Security Planning Group, and the Cabinet gave me a clear sense of the content and rationale of most policies. This in turn enabled me to speak with confidence that I was correctly reflecting the president's views concerning U.S. policy. Where there were new issues, complexities, or doubts about the U.S. position, I checked at top levels of the government to determine the authoritative position.

There is a great demand in a democracy for public discussion of policy. Because I believe in the importance of public discussion of public issues, I tried earnestly to articulate my understanding of the administration's premises and policies. With regard to the United Nations, particularly, I thought that there had been too little frank discussion of how the institution actually functions. I also found there was a great deal of public interest in the subject. I believed the treatment of Israel in the UN was in special need of greater public airing. In 1981 the way had been prepared for denying Israel participation in UN bodies much as South Africa had been denied participation in 1974. There was very little public understanding of the campaign of delegitimization that had already led to Israel's being declared an "international outlaw" and "not a peaceloving state." Defeating the campaign, I quickly concluded, required action by the Congress, and that in turn, required public support. I therefore discussed the issue and described the campaign in a number of speeches.

Most of the speeches were delivered before general audiences. All were written with the understanding that, regardless of the number of disclaimers I included, the public speeches of a member of an administration are not taken as the statement of private views. Speeches of public officials necessarily differ in the style and level of discourse from academic speeches. Most of these speeches mix advocacy with analysis. A few of the speeches included here—especially the speech to the Republican Convention—are highly partisan. Even these, however, reflect my understanding of the issues treated and my understanding of what the president intended.

Many go beyond the discussion of the issue at hand to more basic issues of legitimacy. In the United Nations there are no widely-shared views about what is legitimate. Therefore, the most basic questions of legitimacy are always open. None of the speeches deal with the issues raised in the depth that I would have liked.

Part I
THE MIDDLE EAST IN THE UNITED NATIONS

1
Delegitimizing Israel

THE LOSS OF SADAT

Mr. President, on behalf of the host country, I should like to read a statement which was given today by our President, Ronald Reagan, who said:

"Today the people of the United States join with the people of Egypt and all those who long for a better world in mourning the death of Anwar Sadat.

President Sadat was a courageous man whose vision and wisdom brought nations and people together. In a world filled with hatred, he was a man of hope. In a world trapped in the animosities of the past he was a man of foresight—a man who sought to improve a world tormented by malice and pettiness.

As an Egyptian patriot, he helped create the revolutionary movement that freed his nation. As a political leader, he sought to free his people from hatred and from war. As a soldier he was unafraid to fight. But—most important—he was a humanitarian unafraid to make peace. His courage and skill reaped a harvest of life for his nation and for the world.

Anwar Sadat was admired and loved by the people of America. His death today, an act of infamy—cowardly infamy—fills us with horror. America has lost a close friend, the world has lost a great statesman and mankind has lost a champion of peace.

Nancy and I feel that we have lost a close and dear friend. And we send our heartfelt sympathy to Mrs. Sadat and to his children who were here with us such a short time ago."

Mr. President, to this statement of President Reagan's, I desire to add only that Anwar Sadat was an authentic hero, a man who demonstrated that the classical virtues of reason, courage, charity, vision, and honor are

Address before the 36th United Nations General Assembly, October 6, 1981.

3

as relevant to our times as to past ages. His death is a tragic loss not only to the people of Egypt but to the whole world.

DISHONORING SADAT

The death of Anwar Sadat was an event that may significantly alter the shape of the world. Sadat was a man whose life had profoundly affected events and alignments in a region that is crucial to other areas dependent upon its strategic resources. His death introduces one more element of potential instability into a region that for some time has borne a disturbing resemblance to the Balkans just prior to World War I.

Let us be clear. Egypt's political system has shown a reassuring capacity to cope in an orderly, constitutional fashion with the succession crisis; and Sadat's chosen successor, Hosni Mubarak, has plainly stated his commitment to continuing Sadat's policies—specifically the peace process rooted in the Camp David accords. Secretary of State Alexander Haig has forcefully warned other nations against attempting to take advantage of Sadat's assassination to provoke or profit from increased instability. Nonetheless, during the period in which Mubarak establishes his leadership and consolidates power, Egypt will feel the trauma of Sadat's brutal murder and his sudden removal. Because leaders embody collective identity and aspirations, the violent destruction of a powerful leader is felt as a threat throughout a polity. Discussion of the possible policy consequences of a tragic event like this one is inevitable.

Such discussion began even before Sadat's burial. "For American policy in the Middle East, can there be life after Sadat?" an American journalist wrote, and answered, "Yes, of course, but that policy can succeed only if we finally learn not to tie policy wholly to the survival of strong men." It has been said repeatedly that the death of Sadat resembles the fall of the Shah, because once again a powerful leader, important to the U.S., whose government rested upon personal power, has been abruptly removed from the scene. And, in fact, the death of Sadat, like the fall of the Shah, underscores the vulnerability of policies that depend—or seem to depend—on a single individual. Some commentators, like the one quoted above, rush to the conclusion that the U.S. should not rely on policies that depend on men. But in the Middle East, as in various other parts of the world, the realities

The New Republic, November 11, 1981.

of politics force us to rely heavily upon relations with individual rulers. Such regimes are characteristic of the area. The tradition of paternalistic authority is strong in the Middle East. It rests on firm, authoritarian, patriarchal family structures. Khomeini's fundamentalist theocracy is no less dependent on his personal leadership than the Shah's preceding monarchy was dependent on his. Presidents Qaddafi and Nimeiry, Kings Hussein and Khalid differ in their goals, their policies, their methods, and their styles, but they all head regimes that depend heavily on their individual leadership.

The truth is that we cannot control the governments of the area or choose the rulers. We cannot structure their institutions or transform their beliefs. We have no magic wand to turn the Moslem states that stretch from North Africa to South Asia into replicas of modern, secular, democratic nations living harmoniously with one another. We must deal with them as we find them: authoritarian, traditional, deeply religious, subject to the kinds of instabilities characteristic of personal autocracies. These last include periodic rebellions, chronic succession crises, and complicated, personal rivalries, all of which have culminated repeatedly in war. To the traditional sources of instability and conflict have been added modern weapons and ideologies, secular education, communication, transportation, oil, Israel, and the Soviet ambitions. These new elements have exacerbated rivalries and conflicts, extending both their scope and intensity. They are the conditions and the limits for our relationships with the region and the nations that comprise it.

It is easy to infer from the reality of Arab identity—based on what my Georgetown University colleague Michael Hudson terms "ethnicity and religion"—an assumption that there is unity among Arabs. Nothing could be more mistaken. Arab nations remain profoundly divided among themselves and frequently within their own borders as well.

Iraq is enmeshed in a seemingly endless war with Iran. *Libya's* Qaddafi has stepped up his violent campaign to spread Islamic radicalism through North Africa and the Middle East, has invaded Chad outright, and is involved in a criminal assault against the Sudan. *Syria*, whose 25,000 troops more often disturb the peace in Lebanon than enforce it, is threatened internally by pressures from fundamentalist Sunni Moslems and also by intense hostility from Iraq. *Lebanon*, meanwhile, has almost succumbed to the complicated and violent struggles among Maronites and Moslems, Syria and Israel, the PLO and the Haddad forces protecting the Christian and Shiite enclave in the south. The government of *Morocco* is challenged by the violent demands of the Polisario. In 1979, the regime in *Saudi Arabia* was the object of an attempted coup by an unholy alliance of religious extremists and political radicals. Even more than Saudi Arabia, the government of *Jordan* has felt the destabilizing effects of radical politics introduced into the area under the cover of Palestinian nationalism. Although Jordan expelled Palestinian guerrillas after the conflict of 1970-71, the effects of Palestinian radicalism on Jordan's politics remain strong. Nearby, *Iran* teeters on the brink of anarchy; the fanatical theocrat who replaced the Shah has managed to hold onto power in the midst of a mind-boggling carnage. Executions, bombings, and war have devastated Iran's polity and economy. But still the Ayatollah Khomeini hangs on, snuffing out lives like the mad Queen of Hearts in *Alice in Wonderland*. And of course the threat of Soviet expansion hangs over the entire region. Soviet armies on the borders of Iran, like Cubans in "Democratic" Yemen, threaten the independence of all nations in the region.

In sum, war, assassinations, coups, ethnic separatism, religious fundamentalism, secular revolutionaries, and the Soviet appetite disturb the peace of the Arab world. And we have not even come to Israel.

In need of a unifying factor—beyond language and religion—around which peoples of the region can coalesce, many Arabs have associated themselves with the cause of radical Palestinian nationalism. This cause is closely related to, but not quite identical with, hostility to the state of Israel.

"It is difficult to emphasize sufficiently the importance of the Palestine issue for the politics of legitimacy in the Arab world," Michael Hudson wrote in his book *Arab Politics*. Most scholars would agree. In the decades since the establishment of Israel, the Palestine issue has undergone a subtle change. A myth has been built on the foundation of the genuine problem of Palestinian refugees: the myth that the Palestinian problem is the barrier, in Hudson's words, "to the integration of the Arab homeland." Alongside this myth has developed the extraordinary belief that *only* the presence of Israel stands in the way of achieving Arab unity and integration, and peace and stability in the Middle East.

Although this is patently false, it is not surprising that Israel should have become a special object of hostility in this region filled with hostilities. Israel is modern in the midst of traditional societies; democratic in the midst of authoritarian societies; egalitarian in the midst of class-based societies; Jewish in the midst of Moslem cultures. And its ties to the United States and the West stand as both a problem and a provocation to Soviet appetites in the region.

In this Arab world where faith and politics are linked, traditionalists and radicals, Saudis and Libyans can unite in hostility against the state of Israel—whose right to exist they deny, whose very existence they refuse even to acknowledge, whose name they refuse to utter, calling Israel instead the "Zionist entity" or the "deformed Zionist entity." Not only has Palestinian nationalism become centrally identified with pan-Arab nationalism, but the PLO, using fair means and foul, has won wide acceptance as *the* spokesman for Palestinian rights and interests. The PLO preaches a brand of Palestinian nationalism and radical politics that links the struggle for the destruction of Israel to the triumph of violent, Soviet-sponsored revolutionaries in Nicaragua, El Salvador, Africa, the Middle East—indeed, everywhere. Moreover, the PLO has linked the destruction of Israel to the Soviets' global agenda. No wonder the Kremlin has now added to its supply of military hardware for the PLO the prize of full diplomatic status.

The PLO wins acceptance from modern Arab nations because their leaders have been persuaded that the link between faith and politics calls for the destruction of Israel, and the PLO is the group most militantly dedicated to that cause. The PLO is more than an instrument of Palestinian nationalism: it not only declines to recognize Israel, it is committed, as it reaffirmed in 1980, "to liquidate the Zionist entity, politically, economically, militarily, culturally, ideologically." The ideological appeal of *jihad*—which provides a certain sense of Arab unity—is reinforced by terror, selectively, effectively, and ruthlessly employed. The ideology that links faith, politics, the destruction of Israel, and Palestinian nationalism is continually reinforced by violence and fear. Note, however, that the same linkage covertly commits traditional Arab rulers to strengthening the radical forces, which are carriers of revolutionary politics hostile to their own survival. The PLO thus enlists traditional Arab rulers in their own destruction. Never has the dialectical "cunning of history" operated more clearly to enlist the powerful in the struggle for their own undoing.

This brief overview of the dynamics of Middle East politics makes clear, I hope, not only that there are multiple political and military problems in the region which are unrelated to the PLO or the Israel/Arab problems, but also that there exist at least three urgent major problems for U.S. policy to address:

First, an appetite-control problem: preventing Soviet belligerence from leading—on the model of Afghanistan—to the straightforward invasion or occupation or incorporation by other means of additional Moslem lands into the Soviet empire.

Second, strengthening regimes friendly to, or at least compatible with, U.S. interests—for their sake and ours. Reinforcing moderate Arab governments should enhance regional order and help prevent the transformation of such regimes into hostile ones. This problem is *not* identical with discouraging Soviet expansion. The Ayatollah Khomeini is neither a client of the U.S.S.R. nor a friend of the U.S.

Third, protecting Israel against its sworn enemies. The U.S. is tied to

Israel by many factors: by security interests (it is the only state in the region that *welcomes* U.S. bases); by common values (it is the only functioning democracy in the area); by honor (we have repeatedly sworn to protect its rights to survive); and by the fact of membership in a single ancient community of values. Protecting our civilization's values and institutions commits us to protecting Israel. Failure to do so would compromise the moral basis of our foreign and national security policy.

American policy must be based on the fact that the primary obstacle to peace has been the refusal of Arab governments to recognize the right of Israel to exist. This was the issue that separated Sadat from his "rejectionist" Arab brothers. This was the issue that separated Sadat from the PLO. And, of course, this is the issue that Israel cannot compromise and that no friend can ask it to compromise.

The political importance of Anwar Sadat was that he pointed the way to positive answers to all these problems. A devout Moslem, a revolutionary leader, and a friend of the United States *and* of Israel, Sadat embodied a solution to all these major policy problems confronting the U.S. Because he was also a man of extraordinary personal courage, honor, and vision, his message was all the more powerful. Anwar Sadat demonstrated, with dignity and grace, an alternate way of being a serious Moslem dedicated to the Arab cause and committed also to a solution to the Palestinian problem.

He reminded us that the cause of the Palestinians is not identical with the cause of the PLO Sadat honored the one, rejected the other. He understood that dealing with the PLO cannot lead to a solution of the Palestinian problem, because such an approach was not compatible with a stable regional order. Finally, Sadat established that to be a good Moslem it is not necessary to be hostile to Israel. He illustrated to a disbelieving world that it is possible simultaneously to be a good friend of the U.S., to live at peace with Israel, and to remain a modernizing, revolutionary, nationalist Moslem leader.

This alternate model of nationalist Arab leadership may have cost Sadat his life. Certainly the peace process initiated by Sadat, Menachem Begin, and the United States constitutes a threat to the war process from which our common adversaries profit. But the bullets that can kill men cannot kill visions. Sadat's vision—and ours—is of regional order based on respect for the independence and security of all nations.

Sadat's enemies loved to pretend that he had betrayed "the" Arab cause when he made a separate peace; and, reinforced by confusion, fanaticism, anti-Semitism, and terror, this charge was potent enough to produce a diplomatic boycott that stretched from Morocco to the Soviet border. In fact, Sadat never abandoned the Palestinian cause.

If the Camp David peace process is to move forward, if peace compatible with Israel's security—indeed her survival—is to be had, it is crucial to be clear about what Sadat did and intended. Sadat struck an extraordinary deal. It involved Israel's returning all occupied Egyptian land, including Sharm el-Sheikh and its naval base, the three strategically important airfields in eastern Sinai, and the oil fields developed by Israel—all in return for what? For the acceptance through normal diplomatic relations of Israel's right to exist and survive. Nothing more, nothing less. For this Sadat was ostracized. For this, Arab nations broke diplomatic relations with Egypt, boycotted Sadat's funeral, and—in the case of many—rejoiced at his death.

The issues that divided Egypt and Israel were thorny; those that divide Israel and her other neighbors are thornier still. As we set about advancing peace in the post-Sadat era, it is vital that we bear this in mind.

Anwar Sadat struck out in new directions. But to his dying day he insisted that his separate peace did not imply indifference to Palestinian aspirations and well-being. He insisted that the PLO was not the custodian of Palestinian aspirations; that Israel's existence was not incompatible with Arab self-fulfillment; and that frank friendship with the U.S. was the route to regional order, national independence, and economic development in the Middle East. What is most needed now is that other Arab leaders match Sadat's courage, originality, and tolerance.

It is shocking that, so soon after his death, influential Americans should be proposing solutions that would take us down the pathway Sadat scorned. It is especially shocking that they should suggest negotiating with the deadliest enemies of peace in the area. These individuals should be aware that the path they propose will only add to the Soviet Union's capacity to foment troubles. Powerful forces hostile to U.S. interests and Israel's survival are at work today diminishing Sadat's legacy. It is the job of all who honor his achievements to remember well and think clearly about his example.

AN UNRELENTING ASSAULT*

With Allan Gerson

Both Israel and the United Nations have their origins in the immediate aftermath of the war against Nazism. Indeed, the widespread support which the United Nations enjoyed at its founding derived in no small measure from a nearly universal conviction that what happened during World War II must never be permitted to recur. Who, then, would have believed, in the wake of the war against Nazism, that the United Nations would eventually become deeply implicated in an assault against the very state which serves, more than any other, as haven for the survivors of Nazi persecution? Who would have thought, in the wake of the war against Nazism, that the United Nations would eventually single out that state for a malicious, relentless campaign of vilification and obloquy and would accuse that state of Nazi-like crimes? And who would have dared to imagine, in the wake of the war against Nazism, that United Nations resolutions would serve to legitimize anti-Semitism? Surely, when the United Nations was founded, these were unthinkable thoughts. And yet today, thirty seven years after the founding of the United Nations, all of these seemingly inconceivable, seemingly unimaginable developments have in fact come to pass.

The obsessive quality of the United Nations' campaign against Israel is readily demonstrable. Over 150 anti-Israel resolutions have been adopted by the Security Council, the General Assembly and the Commission on Human Rights subjecting Israel to endless vilification and calumny. At least 50 percent of the time of the Security Council and 25 percent of the time of the General Assembly have been devoted to the sound and fury of anti-Israel diatribes. In 1981, the Security Council met 60 times, but failed to deal even once with the Soviet invasion of Afghanistan, with Vietnam's invasion of Cambodia, with Iraq's invasion of Iran or with Libya's invasion of Chad. Instead, 21 of its 45 meetings devoted to substantive issues dealt with complaints by Arab states against Israel.

The unrelenting assault against Israel has even spilled over into the specialized UN agencies. Supposedly non-political agencies like UNESCO, the World Health Organization, the International Labor Organization, the World Meteorological Society, the United Nations Conference on Women,

Address before B'nai B'rith International, Toronto, Canada, October 18, 1982.

the International Atomic Energy Agency and the International Telecommunication Union have been transformed into anti-Israel platforms. Functional bodies whose entire *raison d'etre* is to help nations transcend their political differences by focusing on our common humanity, and by addressing our common needs, have become politicized and degraded. "Israel is a state that belongs nowhere because it comes from nowhere." That statement, uttered by a spokesman for the Arab League at UNESCO in 1974, has become the watchword of a campaign to delegitimize Israel, a campaign waged by the "automatic majority" at the United Nations in utter disregard of the purposes for which it was founded, and the ideals upon which it is based.

But the politicization of the UN's humanitarian agencies constitutes only the first stage of the campaign to delegitimize Israel. Israel's enemies have not been content merely to transform Israel into a pariah-state; they have sought to brand it an international outlaw as well. On November 10, 1975, their efforts were crowned with success when the General Assembly—in perhaps its single most indecent act—declared Zionism "a form of racism and racial discrimination." That vote, as Henry Kissenger has observed, was "a moral condemnation of the State of Israel and not simply an abstract vote on Zionism." It was meant, in other words, to subvert the moral basis of Israel's existence. A British writer and social critic, the late Goronwy Rees, was present in the General Assembly the day its Third Committee adopted the Zionism-Racism resolution. "There were ghosts haunting the Third Committee that day," wrote Rees, "the ghosts of Hitler and Goebbels and Julius Streicher, grinning with delight to hear not only Israel, but Jews as such, denounce in language which would have provoked applause at any Nuremberg rally."

If the ghosts of Hitler, Goebbels, and Streicher are grinning any less delightedly today, it is only because the obscene anti-Israel rhetoric has lost some of its novelty, has become, as it were, virtually institutionalized at the United Nations. Since 1975, numerous UN resolutions, documents, and statements have referred approvingly to the "Zionism equals racism" formulation and have explicitly linked Israeli policies to those of Nazi Germany. In February, 1976, for example, the UN Commission on Human Rights found Israel guilty of nothing less than "war crimes" in the occupied territories. In April, 1976, a General Assembly committee document likened Israeli measures on the West Bank to Nazi atrocities in World War II. "The sealing of a part of the city of Nablus," this document declared, "is a violation of basic human rights ... reminiscent of the ghettos and concentration camps erected by the Hitlerites." Speaking before the General Assembly on October 1 of this year, Soviet Foreign Minister Andrei Gromyko blandly accused Israel of perpetrating "genocide" against Palestinian

Arabs. The Soviet representative to the Security Council, meanwhile, speaks glibly of the "Israeli new-Nazis," while some of his Arab colleagues refer to the "Judaeo-Nazis of Tel-Aviv."

The equation of Zionism with racism constitutes an attempt by the "automatic majority" at the United Nations to deprive Israel of its ideological legitimacy. A parallel effort to deprive Israel of its historical legitimacy is also underway at the United Nations. On November 10, 1975—the same day that it declared Zionism a form of racism—the General Assembly also established a Committee on the Exercise of the Inalienable Rights of the Palestinian People. This so-called Palestine Committee, composed of 23 members, 19 of which have no relations with Israel, has become the Palestine Liberation Organization's (PLO) principle instrument at the United Nations. In 1977 it persuaded the General Assembly to create a Special Unit on Palestinian Rights within the heretofore neutral UN Secretariat. Under the imprimatur of the Secretariat, the special unit has held numerous conferences, and published numerous documents purporting to provide an objective, scholarly account of the history and origins of the Arab-Israeli conflict. All of these documents, without exception, are obnoxious compilations of falsehoods, slanders, and highly tendentious analyses, whose sole purpose is to undermine Israeli statehood by distorting its history. As Professor Leo Gross, one of America's foremost international legal scholars, has observed, "Never before has the Secretariat been asked to perform what may best be described as a public relations job on behalf of an organization which is bent on the destruction of a member of the United Nations, and is in the meantime engaged in terrorist attacks on Israel and moderate Arabs."

Now that Israel has been transformed into a pariah at the United Nations and its specialized agencies, now that she has been systematically excluded from every UN organ on which she'd previously served, now that her ideology and her history have been systematically distorted, now that her every action is routinely equated with those of Nazi Germany, and now that the PLO enjoys a position of singular importance and influence within the UN system, Israel's enemies have begun their final offensive: a bid to oust Israel from the General Assembly altogether.

Israel's ouster from the General Assembly was first proposed at a meeting of the 92-member non-aligned Conference held in Cuba in the late summer of 1979. Responding to the PLO's bidding, the non-aligned's "Final Declaration of Havana" demanded "Israel's exclusion from the international community." It also demanded a study of what political, diplomatic and economic measures should "be taken against countries that support the Zionist racist regime."

The next step in the drive to oust Israel from the General Assembly was taken on September 20, 1980, at the 42-member Islamic Conference in Fez, Morocco. It resolved to press for Israel's removal from the UN. In January, 1981, the Islamic Conference, meeting in Taif, Saudi Arabia, endorsed a "holy war" (jihad) against Israel. And at an Arab League meeting held in Tunis on February 13, Arab foreign ministers decided to take "all the necessary measures to expel Israel from the UN and its specialized agencies."

A week before that Tunis meeting, the groundwork for Israel's expulsion was already being laid. On February 5, an emergency session of the UN General Assembly produced an unprecedented resolution which called upon "all member states to cease forthwith, individually and collectively, all dealings with Israel in order totally to isolate her in all fields." No country, not even South Africa, had ever been subjected to such a massive ban by the UN. The vote, by the way, was 86 to 21, with 34 abstentions.

The ban was accompanied by a judgment which is unique in the history of the UN Israel was formally declared to be not a "peace-loving state." Since Article IV of the UN Charter stipulates that UN membership is open only to peace-loving states, the ultimate purpose of the resolution was apparent. It is worth noting, by the way, that according to statistics compiled by Dr. William Korey, the 86 countries which decided that Israel is not a peace-loving state contribute only 22 and three quarters percent of the total UN budget. This is less than what the U.S. alone contributes. Conversely, the countries which voted against the resolution declaring Israel a non-peace loving state provide nearly 70 percent of the UN budget.

At a second special emergency session of the General Assembly, which began on April 22, several of the more militant Arab states, led by Syria and the PLO tried to carry the campaign to oust Israel from the General Assembly another step forward. They prepared a draft resolution which instructed the 37th Session of the General Assembly "to review Israel's status." A vigorous U.S. campaign against this draft resolution, along with behind-the-scenes efforts by UN Secretary General Perez de Cuellar, and the opposition of a number of Third World nations, forced the Arabs to revise their draft. Nevertheless, on April 28, by a vote of 86 to 20, with 36 abstentions,, the General Assembly once again declared that Israel "is not a peace-loving member state," and "has carried out neither its obligations under the Charter nor its commitment under General Assembly Res. 273 of 11 May, 1945." Coming only two days after Israel had demonstrated its commitment to peace by completing its withdrawal from the Sinai—a withdrawal which, in its magnitude and scope, has no precedent in the history of the twentieth century—the vote constituted nothing less than a political and moral obscenity.

In the wake of recent events in Lebanon, efforts to expel Israel from the

General Assembly and the specialized agencies of the UN have intensified. On September 24, the General Conference of the International Atomic Energy Agency violated its own constitution by voting to reject Israel's credentials, thus precipitating a U.S. walkout from the conference. The International Telecommunication Union is currently considering an Algerian draft resolution calling for Israel's expulsion from that agency. And on October 8, the Arab group in the General Assembly announced that it would mount a challenge to Israeli credentials at the current session of the General Assembly. Thus, the campaign to delegitimize Israel continues, gathers momentum, and appears to go from strength to strength. . . .

Israel's deteriorating position at the UN can be attributed to the bloc politics which goes on at the UN. For all intents and purposes, the Arab and African blocs have entered into an alliance. In return for Arab support on questions relating to South Africa, the Africans have pledged their support on questions relating to Israel. The combined votes of the Arab, African, and Soviet blocs constitutes that "automatic majority" which, in the words of Israel's permanent representative to the UN, Ambassador Yehuda Blum, "has trampled under foot every provision of the Charter that it perceives as inimical to its bloc interests, and in particular those provisions designed to safeguard the rights of the minority within the organization."

Despite the immense power wielded by the "automatic majority" at the UN, serious obstacles stand in the way of any attempt to oust Israel from the General Assembly. The UN Charter permits suspension or expulsion only "upon recommendation of the Security Council." And in the Security Council, ouster of Israel is certain to be vetoed. But legal principles have not always prevailed at the United Nations. In 1974 an extra-legal challenge to South Africa's credentials led to the unseating of the Pretoria delegation. After a Security Council veto, the president of the Assembly nonetheless ruled that the South African delegation was not to be seated. When challenged by the U.S. and the UK, he was upheld by an overwhelming majority, 91 to 22.

In a speech which I delivered before an Emergency Session of the General Assembly on February 5, 1982, I warned that the resolution declaring Israel a non-peace loving state "is a profoundly serious matter, filled with ominous portent. Questions of membership in this body and its associated agencies," I continued, "should not, indeed, cannot be settled by majority passions. The United Nations or any similar organization can only exist if the principle of majority rule is balanced by respect for minority rights."

It is sometimes argued that what goes on at the UN should not be taken very seriously. After all, it is said, the United Nations is merely a 'talkshop,' its deliberations have little resonance outside its chambers, and its resolutions are of no practical consequence to the world at large. In fact, however, what goes on at the United Nations matters a great deal precisely because the United Nations is a "talk-shop" or, rather, a forum where certain ideas are both expounded and legitimized. When these ideas are defamatory, when crude, obscene lies receive the imprimatur of international approval, then we have every reason to be extremely alarmed. For as the great Jewish theologian Abraham Joshua Heschel once said, "Of all the organs with which the body is endowed, none is as dangerous as the tongue. The Holocaust did not begin with building crematoria; it began with uttering evil words . . . it began with defamation."

The fact of the matter is that words do matter; ideas have consequences. And if the idea of Israel's illegitimacy is allowed to take hold within the international community, the ideological groundwork for Israel's ultimate annihilation will have been laid. With that in mind, I repeat this evening what I have often said in the past, and what President Reagan has often said in the past. The U.S. will not participate in, and will withhold its fundings from, any UN body which illegally excludes the state of Israel. This is neither a threat nor a warning. It is a simple statement of fact. The simple fact is that we will not acquiesce in the delegitimization of a fellow democracy. We will not acquiesce in a travesty of minority rights. And we shall never, never stand indicted of the crime of silence.

Israel as Scapegoat*

*With Carl Gershman

It is a great pleasure for me to be here tonight with the Anti-Defamation League of B'nai B'rith. I have long admired the ADL for its leadership in the field of civil rights, its effective and persistent opposition to all forms of prejudice and discrimination, and its commitment to an open society and the democratic way of life. It has been said that the price of liberty is eternal vigilance. The ADL pays this price day after day, year in and year out. It exemplifies the kind of involvement and commitment by private organizations that has made American society strong and free, diverse but at the

Address before the Anti-Defamation League, Palm Beach, Florida, February 11, 1982.

same time unified, a model of ethnic and institutional pluralism that knows no equal anywhere in the world.

I have a special reason for feeling close to the ADL. We are, after all, neighbors; and in our part of town over at Turtle Bay, we don't take a friendly neighbor for granted. Indeed, we at the United States Mission derive a certain comfort in knowing that the ADL building stands just a block away. With its name boldly emblazoned above First Avenue, the Anti-Defamation League of B'nai B'rith serves as a constant reminder to the self-contained world of the United Nations that there is, in fact, another world out there.

But it is about the self-contained world of the United Nations that I would like to speak tonight. I have been at the United Nations for more than a year now, which is already longer than a good many of my predecessors served. I have been able to observe the organization at close range and from a rather special vantage point. And I have concluded that some aspects of the United Nations work very well in ways that would make us all proud. For example, the refugee program, which last year won the Nobel Prize. Some of the other technical and humanitarian agencies of the United Nations, the so-called specialized agencies, do marvelous work in the world eradicating disease and sustaining unfortunate peoples. Obviously, we want to offer generous support to those activities. But these activities do not diminish our conviction that the United Nations is an organization that is in a profound and deepening crisis.

Nothing reveals the nature and the scope of this crisis more clearly than the manner in which the United Nations has dealt with the Arab-Israeli conflict. The Arab-Israeli conflict (or more specifically the campaign against Israel) is the focus of controversy at meetings that are—or should be—totally unrelated to this question. Thus a women's conference is suddenly transformed into a forum for the denunciation of Zionism—and it will be solemnly announced by the assembled delegates of what is euphemistically called the "international community" that, having carefully studied the problem, the conclusion has been reached that the biggest, most important obstacle to the realization of women's full enjoyment of equal rights in the world is Zionism. The opening of an African refugee conference is delayed as a result of efforts to bar Israel from participating. An international conference on Kampuchea becomes engulfed in controversy when the Israeli ambassador is suddenly disinvited from a dinner for all participants. A meeting of the International Atomic Energy Agency becomes so absorbed in negotiations and debate over a resolution to suspend Israel from membership that it almost forgets to worry about nuclear nonproliferation.

The General Assembly itself deals with the issue over and over and over again. When the Assembly debates the issue of Afghanistan, which is one of the most important questions facing the world today, it adopts a single, straightforward resolution and then moves on to other matters. When the Assembly adopts a resolution on Kampuchea, it does so, once it gets over the question of Israel's participation at dinner, and then moves on to other matters. This is not so with respect to Israel and the conflict in the Middle East. Six anti-Israel resolutions may be adopted under the report of the Special Committee to Investigate Israeli Practices in the Occupied Territories only to be followed by what is called "The Question of Palestine," when six more resolutions are adopted. And it is only at that point that we get to the item on the agenda entitled "The Situation in the Middle East" and the adoption of still more, always predictable, resolutions. They are called, around Turtle Bay, ritual denunciations.

If all this furious activity actually contributed in some way to bringing about peace in the Middle East, one could say that it served some useful purpose. But quite the contrary is true. In fact, it has now become standard practice for the General Assembly to denounce the one agreement that actually *has* contributed tangibly to peace between Israel and her Arab neighbors. That agreement, of course, is the Camp David Accords, which ended the long conflict between Israel and Egypt.

It is instructive, in fact, to contrast the way the Arab-Israeli conflict was approached at Camp David and the way it is dealt with in the interminable debates at the United Nations.

Three factors were responsible for the success of the Camp David approach. First, it was oriented toward the achievement of practical results. In this respect the negotiations were marked by a pragmatic, non-ideological, incrementalist approach to solving the problem. Second, participation in the negotiations was limited to those parties seriously committed to reaching a settlement with each other, namely, Israel and Egypt. And finally, the parties were assisted in working out their differences by a mediator who had credibility to both sides. The mediator, of course, was the United States.

At the United Nations, none of these factors are present. First, the debates are intensely ideological, as are the resolutions that are ultimately adopted. The objective is never to find some common ground of agreement with Israel. The objective is instead to isolate and denigrate Israel and ultimately to undermine its political legitimacy. A related objective is to isolate those countries friendly to Israel, above all the United States. The only compromises made during negotiations on resolutions concerning the Middle East are not with Israel and certainly not for the purpose of promoting a peace settlement. Instead, compromises are negotiated within the majority for the sole purpose of enlarging the anti-Israel vote. In these respects the approach taken toward the Arab-Israeli conflict at the United Nations has nothing to do with peace, but is quite simply a continuation of the war against Israel by other means.

Second, participation in the debate is globalized, and the initiative is generally seized by those with the strongest ideological antagonism toward Israel. A decisive role is played by the Palestine Liberation Organization, which, far from being prepared to reach a settlement with Israel, is committed in its National Covenant to the view that the establishment of Israel is "fundamentally null and void" (Article 19) and that the goal of "liberation" can only be achieved through armed struggle (Article 21). The process of polarization is aided and abetted by the Soviets since it offers them a good anti-Western, anti-United States propaganda weapon and allows them both to divert attention from issues like Afghanistan and to pose as an ally of the Third World. Many African countries have joined the anti-Israel majority in order to obtain Arab support for their own campaign against South Africa and because they are frequently subjected to considerable economic and political pressures. That obnoxious phrase "Zionism Is Racism" symbolizes the alliance between the Arab and the African countries in the United Nations. Thus, the waters at the United Nations are not only muddied but churned up by the participation of parties that have no direct interest in settling the Arab-Israeli conflict and, in many instances, are committed precisely to its perpetuation and intensification.

Given its failure to take a balanced approach to the Arab-Israeli conflict and its loss of credibility with Israel, the United Nations has been effectively eliminated as an effective world mediator. The time when a Ralph Bunche could work on behalf of the United Nations for peace between Israel and the Arabs is long past. As a result, a valuable mediator has been lost, and the cause of peace has suffered a significant setback.

It is sometimes believed that despite what happens in the General Assembly and in some of the specialized agencies, the Security Council of the United Nations remains a citadel of reason and balance. Unfortunately, the Security Council itself has not been unaffected by the overall politicization of the United Nations. The recent prolonged debate over the question of Israel's extension of its civil law over the Golan Heights is a depressing illustration of this point.

Throughout this debate—which began in the middle of December and didn't conclude until last Friday—it was assumed that Israel's action, the extension of her jurisdiction over the Golan Heights, alone constituted a threat to international peace. Our government made clear at the outset that we opposed Israel's legislation because it purported or appeared to alter unilaterally the international status of the Golan Heights. We therefore joined in the initial Security Council resolution, in December, which both called upon Israel to rescind the legislation and declared that it was without international legal effect.

Yet this, as we pointed out in our statements, was hardly all there was to say about the problem. The state of relations that existed between Israel and Syria before the passage of Israel's Golan Heights legislation was far from peaceful. A cease-fire had been in effect since 1973 based upon Security Council Resolution 338. This resolution called upon the parties to "start immediately" to negotiate the implementation of Security Council Resolution 242, which was passed after the 1967 war. It was Resolution 242 which established the only valid and enduring framework for negotiating peace between Israel and its Arab neighbors, namely, the withdrawal of Israel "from territories" it had occupied, in exchange for the recognition of Israel's existence within "secure and recognized" borders.

The central threat to peace which the Security Council should have addressed in December was the lack of progress in implementing Resolution 338's mandatory call for immediate negotiations in the framework of 242. But the Security Council would not reaffirm or even recall or even note Resolution 338 or Resolution 242. The facts are that Syria has refused to negotiate with Israel and her refusal has been and remains the chief obstacle to peace. Yet the Security Council took no note of these facts. Instead it ignored its own resolutions, ignored the facts, and directed its attack solely against Israel's Golan Heights legislation.

This pattern did not change even after December 29, when, with a little prodding from the United States, Israel submitted a letter to the secretary general reaffirming its readiness to enter into unconditional negotiations with the Syrians over the international legal status of the Golan Heights. At that point the only constructive role for the Security Council to play was to facilitate such negotiations in accordance with Resolutions 242 and 338. Instead it entered into more than two weeks of what is euphemistically called debate, during which a floodtide of invective flowed through the council, sweeping away whatever prospects might conceivably have existed for reason and compromise.

The Syrian delegate had already set the tone by declaring during the first Golan debate that it was necessary to turn the tide of "Israeli aggression which began long before 1948, with the arrival of the first colonists." This is the same Syrian delegate who frequently refers to Israel as a crusader remnant and suggests ominously that just as the crusades were defeated and the crusaders were driven out of the Middle East, the last crusade will be as well. The Syrian delegate opened the new round of debate by saying that peace, in his government's view, did not mean anything "identical to or remotely resembling the structural or institutional injustices inherent in the Camp David Accord." Cuba, entering the debate, described Israel's letter of December 29 as "an insolent rebuff of the council and the international community" and called on the council to "halt Zionist arrogance, which is one of the greatest threats to world peace." The PLO, which had been invited to participate in the council proceedings as if it were a member state (in clear violation of the council's own rules of procedure), praised the Soviet Union as "a great nation with a profound knowledge of what it takes to crush fascism," that is, Israel. This knowledge was relevant to the present discussion, according to the PLO, because Israel had "the same militaristic, expansionist, and racist motives and aims as the fascists the Soviets fought in World War II." Nicaragua joined the chorus by attacking the United States for what it called our policy of support "for repressive regimes hostile to Israel's neighboring states." It accused us of trying to impose "the law of the jungle" in the Middle East as well as in Central America. Not to be outdone, the representative of Jordan reminded the council that Arnold Toynbee had once described Israel as "a fossil of Assyriac civilization."

The Syrian delegate was given another turn before the vote, which he used to praise Vietnam as a "heroic country" because it "broke the back of the United States and Israel." Just to make sure we got the point, he went on to praise Cuba, which, he said, "has defied the entire system that was imposed upon it by the United States of America." "Israel," he said, "was imposed by the United States of America on our region to destroy our life, to control us and a strategic route to the region, and also to control our oil and our wealth."

I found these remarks so illuminating about the thinking of the Syrian delegate that when he finished I took the floor for the first and only time in the debate to thank him "for his very useful clarification of the issues," at which the Syrian delegate demanded to know what I meant. I was violating his right to understand, he asserted, citing a "right" new even in the United Nations' exhaustive list. Was my statement "constructive ambiguity or merely an example of imperialist obfuscation?" he demanded. I told him later that I thought it was an example of imperialist obfuscation but I wasn't sure.

The resolution before the council was consistent with the debate that had preceded it. It did not seek to promote negotiations for a peaceful settlement but rather to impose sanctions to punish Israel. In explaining our vote, I pointed out that the resolution constituted "an aberration, even a perversion of the very purpose which the Security Council is called upon by Chapter VII of the United Nations Charter to perform." That responsibility is to prevent "an aggravation of the situation," when the situation may be dangerous to peace. Far from doing that, the resolution before the Security Council would have itself become a source of aggravation of a dangerous situation. In spite of our best efforts, nine positive votes were accumulated for the obnoxious resolution. Therefore, exercising our constitutional right as a permanent member of the Security Council, the United States vetoed this harmful resolution, which opened the way for what is called a Uniting for Peace resolution. It might better be called a Uniting for Mischief resolution given the way it is used these days.

Under a Uniting for Peace resolution, an emergency special session of the General Assembly may be called when one member has vetoed a majority vote in the Security Council. Yehuda Blum, the Israeli ambassador to the United Nations, later noting the repetition of the special session, commented, "Some emergency!" as people made the same speech for the fourth time. The session provided an occasion for the adoption of a fourth resolution on Israel's Golan Heights action that was much more extreme than the one presented to the Security Council. The most recent one, passed only last Friday, is the most objectionable and dangerous of all. The resolution called for comprehensive sanctions against Israel and for Israel's total isolation in all fields. It also harshly criticized us, by the way, for supplying military, economic, and technical support to Israel and for exercising our veto in the Security Council. Basically that resolution denies the legitimacy of the veto in the United Nations and the legitimacy of Israel's membership in the United Nations because it raises a serious question about whether Israel is "a peace-loving member state," which is charter language describing the requirements of membership. You have to be a peace-loving member state like Syria in order to be eligible for membership in the United Nations. The Golan Heights resolution suggests that Israel is in violation of the charter and of the resolution under the terms of which it was admitted. This unique action against a member state laid the groundwork for an attack on Israel's membership in the United Nations. It did not itself seek to expel Israel, but it lays the legal groundwork for an expulsion or suspension.

What did we do? We did what we always do in those situations, but a bit more effectively this time. We worked very hard to stimulate opposition to this resolution, which we pointed out to everyone was unprecedented in the seriousness of its attack. We lobbied in New York, in Washington, and in capitals, and we were actually only defeated by 4 to 1, which by United Nations standards is something of a victory. In December the vote was 127 to 2, and last week it was only 86 to 21. Last week also our European allies and the other democratic nations voted with us against that resolution against Israel. All the Latin American nations except those tied to the Soviets abstained, and that is good by the United Nations standards. Fiji was the only full-fledged member of what is known as the Third World to vote against that resolution. There should be a special fund for Fiji.

What happened? What happened there was one more example of what goes wrong at the United Nations. This organization, which was developed out of a vision of how to build a better world, how to replace violence with reason, how to contain conflict, how to resolve differences peaceably, has been transformed. Instead of being an effective instrument for conflict resolution, it serves all too often as an arena in which conflict is polarized, extended, and exacerbated, in which differences are made deeper and more difficult to resolve than they would otherwise be.

What can we do about that? We ought to do something, I think that's quite clear. We ought to do something because we know that the "ritual denunciations" that took place over the last six weeks do in fact take their toll. They take their toll because words matter. Words can destroy. What we call each other ultimately becomes what we think of each other, and it matters.

What can we do about this organization to which the United States contributes more than $1 billion annually? We can, first of all, take it seriously. We can face the fact and let everybody else understand that we believe that what happens there matters, that we know and we care. That's our slogan at USUN: "We take the United Nations very seriously."

Second, we can make certain that when we speak we are serious and credible. It is important to let countries around the United Nations understand that when we say that destructive exercises and attacks like those of the last six weeks matter to us, we mean it. It is important that the other nations understand that when we say that attacks on the membership of Israel or her right to participate matter, we mean it. We try very hard at the U.S. Mission to establish that kind of seriousness, and I believe we have. David Broder, *Washington Post* columnist, said that the president reminded him of Horton the Elephant. Horton, you may recall, was the Dr. Seuss elephant who faithfully sat on the egg till it hatched. Horton's slogan was: "I meant what I said and I said what I meant; an elephant's faithful 100 percent." We try at the United Nations to be faithful 100 percent and to be sure that everybody understands that we said what we meant. We try also to answer attacks against our own country and against our friends when those attacks are unfair and unjust. We try to be fair, balanced, and reasonable but also vigorous in our response to attacks against us and our friends and our principles.

Finally, I think what we can do and should do is pursue a consistent policy over time, letting our actions demonstrate that we are, indeed, serious people who notice and who care and who distinguish between actions and between countries who behave like friends and supporters of democratic institutions and freedom—and those who do not. If we do not act consistently, we cannot protect ourselves, our friends, and our principles.

I should like to emphasize that the policies we carry out at the United Nations are the policies of a president who is a very good friend of Israel and of Secretary of State Haig, who is another very good friend of Israel. Right now, in Geneva, Michael Novak and Richard Schifter, two other good friends of Israel, are very busy defending our principles and our friends and ourselves at the United Nations Human Rights Commission. There are a good many of us throughout the administration, beginning at the top. It is important for all of us to know that when we stand for ourselves, our friends, and our principles, there are organizations devoted to freedom and democracy and fidelity who, like Horton the Elephant, are standing with us.

ANTI-HISTORY*

With Allan Gerson

Nowhere is the United Nations' departure from the ideals and principles which attended its birth more clearly in evidence than in its dealings with the Arab-Israeli conflict. Here, instead of upholding truth, rendering justice and maintaining peace, the United Nations has all too often served as a vehicle for legitimizing the most hate-filled anti-Israeli positions. The United Nations has increasingly become the principal forum of a concerted worldwide campaign against Israel.

The implications of this campaign go way beyond the Arab-Israeli conflict itself. It is symptomatic of the United Nations' ill health and of the decline—the perhaps unnecessary decline—of Western power.

The United Nations has become pathologically obsessed with the question of Israel. In no small measure this is due to the alarming growth of PLO power and influence at the UN. Examples of this pathological obsession abound, but let me cite just a few. Last July, at the opening of the conference on the continuing Vietnamese occupation of Kampuchea, the question of Israel came up. In a move of astounding hypocrisy, Israel was disinvited from a dinner given for all the conference participants, while the representative of the murderous Pol Pot was allowed to be present. We

Address before the Yeshiva University, New York, New York, December 13, 1981.

urged other Western countries to boycott the affair unless the invitation to Israel was restored, but only Canada joined us in choosing not to attend.

In August the UN debated the South African incursion into Angola. Israel was held responsible for the South African attack because it was argued that Israel had established the principles of preemptive attack—as though there had never before been a preemptive attack by other nations, as though Libya had not this year invaded Chad, or the Russians Afghanistan, or the Vietnamese Kampuchea.

Let me mention just one more example of this obsession with Israel. Last year the Security Council met 77 times. As you will recall, 1980 was a year of momentous events in Afghanistan, Iran, Poland and other places, but in the Middle East it was a year of relative peace and stability. Still, of the 77 meetings of the Security Council, 38 of them were held on Middle East issues—most of them in one way or another an occasion to assault and to isolate Israel.

This condemnation of Israel at the UN is not, of course, a new phenomenon. In one way or another this has been going on since Israel's inception in 1948. But 1975 marks a new watershed in that campaign.

As you know, on November 10, 1975, at the 30th session of the General Assembly, the United Nations branded Zionism "a form of racism and racial discrimination." This theme has since been so repeatedly reaffirmed and embellished that I fear its slow corrosive effect on world public opinion has now become evident. Numerous United Nations resolutions have repeated the Zionism equals racism formulation. Perhaps most disturbing of all, however, is the institutionalization, within the UN itself, of organs dedicated to reinforcing that theme. The same 1975 resolution which condemned Zionism as racism also established a UN committee termed "The Committee on the Exercise of the Inalienable Rights of the Palestinian People." This committee is composed of 23 members, including Cuba, the German Democratic Republic, Hungary, the Ukraine, and Yugoslavia. Participating as observers on the committee are Jordan, Libya, Iraq, Syria, the PLO, Mauritania, Egypt, and the Arab League. None of the Western countries and none of the Latin American states, except Cuba, was willing to serve on the committee. Only four states on the committee have diplomatic relations with Israel.

It is hardly surprising then that the committee has become a PLO base and an organizer of such events as Palestinian Solidarity Day held two weeks ago at the UN. This event included graphic displays, marked as the product of joint committee-PLO efforts, that were mounted in the visitors' entrance to the UN. Photographs showed disabled babies and dead children under the caption "Because they were Palestinians," with reference made to U.S.-supplied F-16 fighters used by Israel over Lebanon. At the opening of this Solidarity Day, the PLO unfurled a huge flag of Palestine in the corridor outside the Trusteeship Council and hung a map of the Middle East which showed a Palestinian state within all of Israel's borders and without any mention of Israel.

While it was not surprising, given the composition of the Committee on Palestinian Rights, that it has become a springboard for the PLO, what is somewhat surprising, and much more disturbing, is that the Secretariat of the UN should have permitted itself to become equally corrupted by PLO influence. In 1977 the committee persuaded the United Nations to establish within the UN Secretariat a supposedly nonpartisan international civil service body, a branch called the Special Unit on Palestinian Rights. Its function has been to turn out pamphlets and other items of information which carry the imprimatur of the United Nations and the appearance of evenhanded objectivity. In fact, they distort the historical background and current dimensions of the Arab-Israeli conflict. Evidence is cleverly marshalled to make Israel appear as an international criminal and the PLO to be its victim, a victim whose use of terror and dedication to the destruction of a member state of the UN must be overlooked or condoned.

Let me illustrate. Within the last three years, the United Nations Special Unit has published seven pamphlets on the Arab-Israeli conflict: in 1978, its opening "study" on "The Origins and Evolution of the Palestinian Problem;" in 1979, "An International Law Analysis of the Major UN Resolutions on the Palestine Question," "The Status of Jerusalem," "The Question of the Observance of the Fourth Geneva Convention of 1949 in Gaza and the West Bank including Jerusalem," "The International Status of the Palestinian People," and "The Question of Palestine." In 1980 it published "Israel's Policy on the West Bank Water Resources" and "The Palestinian Question: A Brief History."

This last study is particularly intriguing. Like the others, it provides in its introduction that it has been "Prepared from and under the guidance of the Committee on the Exercise of the Inalienable Rights of the Palestinian People." What differentiates this one from the rest, however, is that it is "intended for younger readers." As such, it provides a synopsis of the ideas more fully developed in the other larger studies. In one of the opening chapters, entitled "Conflicting Promises to Palestine," the theme is developed that the Balfour Declaration was in direct contravention of Britain's earlier McMahon Letter of 1915 in which Palestine was ostensibly pledged to the Arabs. The study states: "The controversy (over whether Palestine was included in the Ottoman areas pledged to the Arabs) continued until 1939 when the British Government conceded that, in 1917, they were not free to dispose of Palestine." No source is given for the quotations. Omitted is any reference to the famous statement of McMahon himself, printed in the *Times* of London on July 23, 1937, which stated: "I feel it is my duty to state, and I do so definitely and emphatically, that it was not intended by me in giving this pledge to King Hussein to include Palestine in the area in which Arab independence was promised."

The younger reader is left with the altogether inaccurate impression that Britain itself had repudiated the legitimacy of its right to issue the Balfour Declaration.

But this is only the beginning. In its treatment of the 1948 Arab-Israel War, the 1967 War, and the failure to reach a peaceful solution to the conflict, perspective is distorted through manipulation or omission of the true facts. Here is how the attack against the new born state of Israel in 1948 is described: "As the last British troops ceremoniously departed the following day (May 15, 1948), troops from bordering Arab countries entered the areas allotted to the Arab state, and the first Israel-Arab war began." As if Egypt's entry into the Negev—the territory allocated to the Jewish state by the 1947 Partition Plan—was allotted to the Arab states; as if Jordanian-Iraqi-Syrian entry into the Western Galilee and the West Bank was not undertaken, as those armies themselves professed, to destroy the nascent state of Israel. The pamphlet then states, "By the time the United Nations Security Council effected a cease-fire, Israeli forces had established a decisive superiority." What is conveniently not mentioned is that the invading Arab states rejected early Security Council calls for a cease-fire while they were gaining ground.

The 1967 War is described as follows: "In the war of June 1967, Israel expanded and occupied the rest of the Arab territory of Mandated Palestine, including Jerusalem. It also took control of and occupied the Golan Heights of neighboring Syria and the Sinai of Egypt." Never mentioned in the study are any of the developments that precipitated the hostilities in 1967: The closing of the Straits of Tiran and passage through the Gulf of Aquaba; the ejection of the United Nations Emergency Force and the resulting development of strong contingents of Egyptian forces along the frontier; the signing of joint defense pacts by the Arab states on Israel's frontiers and the subsequent mobilization of Arab forces on all of Israel's frontiers and the "sabre-rattling" war fever generated in the streets of Cairo and other Arab capitals. These events were put in perspective at the time by a leading Arab journalist and nonofficial government spokesman who wrote on May 26, 1967: ". . . the march of events during the 10 great days which changed the situation and balance of the Middle East—[as] one calculated and effective move followed another—created a situation where Israel has to reply now. It has to deal a blow. Then it will be our turn to respond as effectively as we can." This passage is quoted not out of any desire to get into the judicial niceties of responsibility for that war but simply to point out to what one would have thought was clear: that in 1967, Israel acted defensively.

The pamphlet's treatment of events since the 1967 War is equally pernicious. No mention is made of the 1973 War. Referring to the quest for peace, the UN Special Unit's pamphlet for young readers on "The Palestine Question" tells us that "Israel refused to withdraw from occupied territories without a general peace settlement encompassing all the elements of Resolution 242. It maintained this position despite repeated calls by the United Nations General Assembly for Israeli withdrawal." But, Security Council Resolution 242, as made clear by subsequent Security Council Resolution 338—a resolution never mentioned in this pamphlet—calls for withdrawal in the context of a negotiated peaceful solution.

No mention is made of the refusal by the Arab states, other than Egypt, to negotiate peace with Israel. Instead the PLO is accorded glowing treatment. Its right to self-determination is demanded, even though as formulated by the PLO, exercise of that right would extinguish another peoples' right to self-determination. The PLO's endorsement of terror-armed struggle directed against innocent civilians is, the Special Unit pamphlet tells us, something which needs be condoned. After all, we are told, the PLO's "resort to violence—claiming justification from the General Assembly's affirmation of the legitimacy of the people's struggle for liberation from . . . foreign domination and alien subjection by all available means including armed struggle (Resolution 0070 of November 30, 1973)—(has) focused world attention on the plight of the Palestinians and on their determination to regain their rights."

These examples are illustrative of the distortions of fact and glorification of the PLO which mark the work of the UN Special Unit on Palestinian Rights. They demonstrate that the independence of the UN Secretariat has been severely compromised in its nonpartisan standing by allowing the Special Unit to continue to function with it. The question remains: What do we do about it?

We have tried to influence our Western and South American allies and friends to recognize the danger the Special Unit poses to the independent functioning of the UN Secretariat and the search for a peaceful solution to the Arab-Israeli conflict. However, we have so far met with little success. Just a few days ago, on December 8, when the UN Fifth Committee considered funding of the Committee on Palestinian Rights and the Special Unit, the U.S. made sharp statements opposing these expenditures and argued that the money could be better spent on humanitarian activities. The vote on the resolution calling for the Special Unit to be provided "with the necessary additional resources to accomplish its tasks" was 75–4 with the U.S., Israel, Canada, and Australia voting "no" and 18 states abstaining.

One million dollars was allocated outright to the Special Unit, with an additional $2,140,400 set aside for consideration under "conference servicing requirements." Incidentally, one such conference entitled the "Inalienable Rights of the Palestinian People" was held in September of this year in that great capital of human rights—Havana. The opening session was chaired by the head of the International Relations Department of the Cuban Communist Party and the conference heard a message from Yassir Arafat who pledged continued armed struggle as "the only language understood by the racist occupiers." I am proud to say that because of its awareness of the destructive role played by both the Committee on Palestinian Rights and the Special Unit, the U.S. Congress has provided in the Foreign Relations Authorization Act of 1978, and in subsequent reenactments of this act, for the withholding of funding to the committee and unit as part of the U.S. assessed contribution to the UN budget.

The growth and increased funding of the Special Unit and the Committee on Palestinian Rights reflect the increasing strength the PLO has assumed within the United Nations, and sadly enough, the attenuation of Western power and influence. Although it has only observer status, the PLO nevertheless participates in the Security Council with special privileges, as if it were a full member.

It has also been officially invited as an observer to such UN specialized agencies as the International Telecommunications Union, the Universal Postal Union, the International Civil Aviation Organization, and UNESCO—all of which have, or should have, almost nothing to do with Middle East–related issues.

The U.S., under this administration, has undertaken firm steps to blunt the edge of the anti-Israel campaign. We have routed attempts to exclude Israel from the United Nations itself or its specialized agencies.

We have let it be known simply and firmly that if Israel were expelled or suspended, the United States would find it impossible to participate and would withhold its contemplated major contributions. These advance warnings were not just threats, but a statement of clear purpose.

Secondly, we have regularly opposed the politicization of United Nations bodies and the scapegoating of Israel at the United Nations. For example, when the UN Human Rights Commission made a point last February of denouncing Israel for "war crimes," the U.S. response was no longer to register the politic, pro forma opposition when such statements were made under the Carter administration.

The Reagan administration's new appointee to the Human Rights Commission, Michael Novak, expressed his outrage at hearing "so much hatred, so many lies, such squalid racism, such despicable anti-Semitism—all in the sacred name of human rights."

In March of this year, the Security Council considered the issue of the killing of two Nigerian members of UNIFIL—the United Nations Interim Force in Lebanon—by the Christian forces of Major Haddad. Although 29 UNIFIL soldiers had died in action since its establishment in 1978, the Security Council had never shown such concern when UNIFIL troops died at the hands of the PLO, even though a majority of the UNIFIL soldiers killed in action died at PLO hands. The United States refused to join in a statement which criticized Israel without criticizing other parties to the violence in Lebanon—namely Syria and the PLO. It took four days of hard negotiation before the Council agreed to an impartial statement. In the end, however, the U.S. position prevailed: Israel was not singled out for censure in the final approved Security Council statement.

To cite one other example, on November 12, we blunted—by obtaining 34 abstentions—an effort to enlarge the June 1981 Security Council action regarding the Israeli strike on the Iraqi nuclear reactor by now terming it an act of "aggression." In my speech before the General Assembly on that day, I stated that "aggression" is "a legal term scrupulously avoided by the Security Council in its deliberations on this matter last June." I stated: "the United States Government objects strenuously to the use of that term and insists that such actions must be viewed in their total context, which in-cludes Iraq's refusal to accept the international consensus formulated in Security Council Resolution 242 and 338 and its refusal to make peace with Israel."

These examples demonstrate that although often the United States can only measure its victories at the United Nations by our limitation of damage and do no more than simply voice our opinion and urge others to vote with us, we can also score small but significant successes by taking firm stands.

The pathological obsession with Israel and the acquiescence in the PLO efforts at distorting history leave the task of making peace in the Middle East all the more difficult and endanger the very raison d'etre for the UN's existence. Yet this struggle for fairness and peace leaves both the U.S. and Israel a little stronger.

THE DEHUMANIZATION AND DENIAL*

*With Allan Gerson

Simon Wiesenthal has for me, as for so many in the world, become synonymous with the struggle of right against wrong, of conscience against apathy and indifference. Most people refused to face the horrors of the Holocaust's mass murder even while this tragedy was occurring. Even afterwards, they have been all too eager to forget the awful crimes of the Nazis and their collaborators.

Simon Wiesenthal, concentration camp inmate, Jew, citizen of the world, worked nearly single-handedly to assure that the world would remember. In so doing, he not only affirmed justice but, in restoring responsibilities, he restored the moral meaning the Nazis sought to deny. Ben Franklin once said that eternal vigilance is the price of liberty. Simon Wiesenthal has prodded and insisted that we know and remember that accountability is a necessary ingredient of moral meaning.

The dehumanization of the Jews and the denial of moral responsibility for their murder proceeded side by side. "I must emphasize here that I have never personally hated the Jews," said Rudolf Hess, the commandant at Auschwitz, in his wooden, self-serving memoir. "It is true that I looked upon them as enemies of our people," wrote Hess. Jews were not people, they were enemies of the people not to be treated like normal people, with empathy, with feeling. "The emotion of hatred is foreign to my nature," wrote the man who organized the murder of two million Jews at Auschwitz. "The reason behind the extermination program seemed to me right. I did not reflect on it at the time. I had been given an order. I had to carry it out. Whether this mass extermination of the Jews was necessary or not was something on which I could not allow myself to form an opinion," wrote Hess, "for I lacked the necessary breadth of view." "What is right and what is wrong?" wrote the most monstrous executioner in history.

Simon Wiesenthal's passionate search affirmed the moral meaning of the Holocaust. It holds the perpetrators responsible, relentlessly refusing them the escape into relativism that would excuse and forget even genocide. The fact that today courts of law and ministries of justice in Germany, France, The Netherlands, Israel, and the United States continue to investigate,

Address before the Simon Wiesenthal Humanitarian Laureate Dinner, New York, New York, April 17, 1983.

indict, prosecute, and punish those responsible for the attempted genocide of the Jewish people, and the murder of countless others as well, is in very large part a tribute to Simon Wiesenthal's commitment, tenacity, and courage.

Wherever an Eichmann and a Barbie are confronted in courts by their crimes, Hess's question is confronted, too. "What is right? What is wrong?" "This," civilized world says in its confrontation with the killers of Europe's Jews, "is wrong." No statute of limitations can run on a deed so wrong.

For Jews, these last few days have been the Days of Remembrance. As President Reagan said last week, during his appearance before the Gathering of the Jewish Holocaust Survivors in Washington: "Ours is the only nation other than Israel that marks this time with an official national observance." Ours is the only nation other than Israel that will soon have a Holocaust Memorial Museum. Last Thursday, two federal buildings not far from the Washington Monument, were designated to house a permanent memorial to the six million Jews slain as part of Hitler's final solution. There, surrounded by other monuments and museums testifying to the greatness of Western civilization, will be a permanent reminder of its failure, its humiliation and the utter perversion of its values which Auschwitz represents. There should never be a question that the United States remembers and cares.

Of course, the state of Israel remembers and cares. Its existence and vitality give meaning to the oath—Never Again, "What is right? What is wrong?" What do they remember, how much do they care? What lessons have they learned, have we learned? What lessons are there to be learned? I raise these questions as the chief United States delegate to the United Nations, a body rooted in World War II, that global catastrophe integrally linked with the murder of European Jews. That body proclaims in the first sentence of its charter its purpose—"to save succeeding generations from the scourge of war which twice in our lifetimes has brought untold sorrow to mankind." The United Nations is also the one world body in which the word genocide is probably most frequently spoken today.

A few weeks ago I had the great pleasure of visiting Israel for the first time. Escorted by Gideon Hausner, the man who prosecuted Adolf Eichmann, I was on my second day there and was taken on a tour of Yad Vashem. My schedule was tight. My next appointment was with Prime Minister Begin, whom I did not intend to keep waiting, but I found it difficult to go beyond the first exhibit. There in black and white for all the world to see were copies of German ordinances imposing heavy, discriminatory taxes on Germany's Jews, eliminating religious freedom for Germany's Jews, restricting movement, abridging fundamental civil rights, and even calling for the construction of concentration camps. Amazingly most of these laws were promulgated not in 1939 or '40 or after World War II had broken out, not after the Final Solution was underway, but six years earlier. Clear warnings of the impending disaster were there, but the words and the ideology which they represented were either ignored or rationalized by their contemporaries as only words. Many Jews who still had the opportunity to flee viewed these words and the associated wave of oppression as just another "pogrom" which, too, would pass. Many non-Jews who might have helped, shrugged as they turned away, denying empathy and vision. They were only words.

Just as the warning signs of impending doom for the Jews were clear, so too were the signs of impending German aggression against its neighbors and all of Europe also clear. Yet they, too, were ignored, rationalized, shrugged off. A generation ago the American people felt like many others in the Western world. They felt that they could simply ignore the expanding power of a totalitarian ideology or that they could afford to give it every benefit of the doubt. Winston Churchill wrote after the war in the first volume of his memoirs, *The Gathering Storm*, of "how easily the tragedy of the Second World War could have been prevented." He attributed the fact that it was not to "the malice of the wicked . . . reinforced by the weakness of the virtuous." Thus, "The councils of prudence and restraint became the prime movers of mortal danger (and) the Middle Course adopted from the desires for safety and a quiet life led directly to the bull's-eye of disaster."

What lessons can be drawn from this sad story of wishful, shallow, misguided thinking and of sentimental optimism that led to death, material ruin and moral havoc the likes of which had never darkened the imagination or the reality of former centuries? The first lesson which I think we all must draw is that words have consequences. Their meaning can be ignored only at the peril of all of us. Often the words of those who would perpetrate the most awful crimes against peace and humanity clearly express their intent even as they veil the horror that they propose. Thus, the Nazis did not say outright in the beginning that their aim was the extermination of Jews, though that clearly was their aim. As the documents at Yad Vashem established, they planned extermination of Jews on a worldwide basis, even in the United States. Yet, first, murder had to be rendered "acceptable." For this purpose, the Nazis devoted time and energy to redefining the victims as subhuman, as non-people, outside the universal pale of human beings. The myth had to be created as to the Nazis' superiority to justify their calls for the extermination of the unfit. "I must freely confess," Hess wrote, "That I almost came to regard humane consideration and feelings toward the Jews as a betrayal of the Fuehrer."

The second lesson from this history is that totalitarians test the ground for more sustained aggression and persecution by beginning with minor oppressions and calculated violence. Thus, the Nazis began their systematic degradation and oppression of the Jewish population more than six years before Germany's entry into World War II. Similarly, they tested Western resolve for about an equal period of time to see whether it would oppose German rearmament in violation of the Versailles Agreement and blatant aggression in the Rhineland and against Czechoslovakia. Only after they discovered the relative acquiescence of European powers and the United States did the Nazis feel sufficiently emboldened to embark upon the Final Solution, the destruction of the Jews and the conquest of Europe.

A third lesson is the need for concerted action between the United States and its allies to ensure that the totalitarian forces of anti-freedom and dehumanizaiton do not prevail.

Unfortunately, however, these lessons have not all been learned, nor are their implications universally shared. Unfortunately, at the United Nations we see not only the frequent perversion of that organization's moral *raison d'etre*, but we hear a systematic, totalitarian assault on language and meaning, the tools with which we understand the world. Palestinian Arabs are redefined as "the Jews of the Arab world," living in the "Diaspora," longing to be restored to Jerusalem. The Israelis are redefined as Nazis. The pattern of such talk, inspired by the Soviets, elaborated upon by Arab speakers hostile to Israel and now freely used by anti-Israel militants, is so common at the United Nations that often our good friends chide me at being concerned. "It's only UNery," they counsel. Never mind that despotic governments are called democratic, that policies intended to incite war are deemed "peaceful," that measures imposed by terror are termed "popular," that reactionary tactics are called "progressive." Never mind that the word genocide is used most often to describe Israeli practices on the West Bank and Gaza. "It's only UNery; they're only letting off steam," they say. Be assured, however, that as the representative of the United States in the United Nations, I do mind and I will go on minding.

If anyone had serious doubts that these words have consequences, his doubts should have been dispelled at the last session of the General Assembly, when the so-called rhetoric against Israel came to a head in a move to expel Israel from that body on the grounds that all the anti-Israeli resolutions passed had conclusively established that Israel, of all the nations in the United Nations, was not a peace-loving state. The United Nations Charter provides that UN membership is open to peace-loving states. Accordingly, this became the redefinition to force Israel out of an organization in which Vietnam, the Soviet Union, Nicaragua, and Libya, to name but a few, are all defined as "peace-loving" states. This view held that once Israel was isolated, humiliated by expulsion, and determined to be an international criminal unworthy of membership in the community of nations, further encroachments upon Israel's rights and prerogatives as a sovereign state would be possible. These would be justified by a myth, not too different from the one the Nazis initially used against the Jews in Germany. That massive deprivation of the Jews' fundamental rights and, indeed, their murder, was considered "acceptable" because the Jew was mutant, an *untermensch* or subhuman as the Germans put it, not a normal entity.

Thus the myth is nurtured that Israel is not a real nation, not a normal nation; it is often called a "Crusader remnant," "an unnatural growth rejected by the body unto which it is transplanted." That is the language with which Israel is frequently described.

Concomitantly with this process of delegitimization of Israel at the UN, the unique legacy of the Holocaust of the Jewish people and Israel has been subjected to systematic destruction or, perhaps more accurately, to theft. The PLO, with the acquiescence if not the complicity of the Soviet and the nonaligned blocs, has sought to ride on the coattails of the true Jewish experience of discrimination, exile, oppression, and murder. Let us be clear. The Holocaust was unique to the Jewish people. What occurred was not, as some now contend, one more episode in a long line of anti-Semitic, ostensibly church-inspired, collective violence. The Holocaust was fundamentally different. Collective violence is used to lash out at a scapegoat, to put or keep that scapegoat in its place. Genocide aims to eliminate the scapegoat; it is calculated, planned, purposeful, and total in its intent. To use the term "Genocide" against Israeli actions is the worst possible outrage. It is a sacrilege against the dead and an attempt to deprive their death of any meaning and to deprive the state of Israel of its rightful history.

Another lesson I draw from the Holocaust and the rise of Nazi Germany is, as President Reagan recently put it, that "Those who gloss over the brutality of tyrants are no friends of peace or freedom." This lesson, too, is too often honored in the breach at the United Nations. The Soviet Union has extinguished the torch of freedom in Afghanistan and deprived its Jewish population, as well as other ethnic groups, of their most fundamental human rights under the UN Charter and the Universal Declaration of Human Rights: The right to leave their own country so that they might at least enjoy liberty elsewhere. The suppression of human rights in Poland, in Afghanistan, suppression of the rights of Soviet Jews—these are never considered proper items for Security Council consideration. We have more important items to deliberate about: the now twice "imminent invasion" of Nicaragua by the United States; the imminent U.S. invasion of Libya's international waters at a time when our ship, the *U.S.S. Nimitz,* did not in fact even approach the area the Libyans claim to be within their territorial jurisdiction; and the alleged case of Israeli poisoning of Arab schoolchildren on the West Bank, or, as the PLO put it in its most recent letter to the Security Council president, the Israeli "genocide" on the West Bank. These items, together with the consideration of Libya's invasion and occupation of Chad, which produced a non-conclusive Security Council statement, are the items that, during the last month or so, have been the focus of our attention in the Security Council. The really important questions have not even come to our agenda.

Is it really much wonder that the aggressors and tyrants feel encouraged to go ahead in furthering their aggression and their tyranny? Is it any wonder that "peace-loving" states like Libya and Iran, and a national liberation movement like the PLO, operate in concert and plan their worldwide deprivation of freedom? It is only a wonder that, with the experience of the Holocaust and the tragedy that was World War II so recently behind us, so many in the United Nations so quietly acquiesce in these obscene practices.

I believe that the experience of the tragedy of Nazism and the hard experience of Israel's 35 years of history have given us all a higher sense of reality and a sharper sense of the consequences of its denial. I believe that the affirmation of that reality is the most important task that we as citizens of the United States, citizens of the world, persons concerned about the well being of Israel, must take as our own. I believe, like Simon Wiesenthal, that we must insist that human behavior is essentially moral, that responsibility is an irreducible dimension of human behavior and of human life, that it cannot be avoided, that illusion will not be permitted to prevail over fact, murder will not be permitted to prevail unpunished, horror will not be permitted to persist unacknowledged.

Like Simon Wiesenthal, we insist on moral meaning. We take seriously the United Nations Charter's call for saving succeeding generations from the scourge of war and the untold sorrow which befell this generation.

By the grace of God, we shall prevail.

THE UNITED STATES AND ISRAEL IN THE UNITED NATIONS

This evening I propose to talk with you briefly about some of Israel's continuing problems in the United Nations.

It is easy there to lose sight of the forest for the trees. One can readily imagine that a debate is really about the so-called principle of "non-acquisition of territory by force" or "self-determination of all peoples," as some of Israel's adversaries claim. In fact, in almost all discussion of the Arab-Israeli problem at the United Nations the issue is the legitimacy of Israel itself.

The United Nations was founded, to quote the language of the preamble of its Charter, "to save succeeding generations from the scourge of war which twice in our lifetime has inflicted untold sorrow on mankind." How tragic that the United Nations has allowed itself to pervert the meaning of that phrase by becoming a forum for the pursuit of war by other means.

In 1948, ten Arab states surrounding Israel launched a war against Israel in an attempt to frustrate implementation of the resolution calling for the establishment of an independent Arab and Jewish state in Palestine. Thirty-five years later, General Assembly Resolution 181-II has still not been accepted by all. Of course, four wars have since reshaped the grounds of the territorial dispute.

Inside the United Nations also, the debate has been reshaped by the emergence of the blocs, and the system of bloc politics.

Four major blocs dominate UN politics: the African bloc, the Arab bloc, the Soviet bloc, and the Non-Aligned Movement. The first three together control some 90 votes—about 60 percent majority—and the Non-Aligned Movement bloc can control individually up to 97 votes. Each bloc contains moderates and extremists. Each requires a unifying issue. For the African bloc, it is opposition to South Africa; for the Arab bloc, opposition to Israel; for the Soviet bloc, Soviet interests. For the Non-Aligned Movement, by its nature less cohesive than others, its hostility to both South Africa and Israel acts as a unifying force.

The interaction of the blocs explains a good deal of the politics of the United Nations. Thus, the African and Arab blocs agree to support each other on their respective unifying issues, in a kind of trade-off. The obnoxious slogan—Zionism is racism—reflects this alliance. The Soviet bloc agrees to support both of them in order to buy influence and divert attention. The Soviets use their influence to encourage extremism wherever

Address before the Alliance Israelite Universelle, June 6, 1983.

possible and to turn the Arab and African blocs as much as possible against the West and against the U.S. in particular. Generally this kind of politics goes under the rubric of opposing imperialism, Zionism, neo-colonialism, and racism.

Against this background, it is not too hard to see why the Soviets, the PLO, and the radical Arab states are able to use the UN not as a place for conflict resolution, but as a forum for the pursuit of the war against Israel by other means. Thus, anything Israel does or can be suspected of doing is characterized as criminal, while real crimes committed by others are totally ignored or even justified.

Because there is not a comparably effective Western bloc able to muster a United Nations majority, truly delinquent actions by the United Nations members receive little attention.

Thus, Libya's deep involvement in the promotion of international terrorism and subversion of its neighbors goes unnoticed. But Israeli excavations of archeological sites in Jerusalem are a source of great outrage and become the subject of resolutions adopted by appropriately large majorities. The Soviet effort to absorb the people and country of Afghanistan into its empire has been accompanied by unspeakable atrocities, including the destruction of literally hundreds upon hundreds of villages, the depopulation of whole regions of the country, the creation of the largest refugee population in the world, the use of chemical weapons in violation of international law, massacres of innocent civilians, and the destruction of a whole culture. Yet such behavior arouses nothing like the uncontrollable rage that is set loose when Israel is accused of wrong-doing.

So far, I have described the actors in this continuing warlike campaign against Israel, and how they have been able to use the bloc system at the United Nations for their purposes. The campaign has been more effective than most people think. It has succeeded, in perhaps its most notorious act, in equating Zionism with racism; a 1975 resolution of the General Assembly attests to that. It has succeeded in formally characterizing Israel, on at least one occasion, as "a non-peace loving state." It has, to an extent, succeeded in isolating Israel within the community of nations and through a barrage of rhetoric and resolutions at the United Nations, established the Jewish state as a sort of pariah among nations.

I call this the delegitimation of Israel. I choose this word carefully—delegitimation. What it means, quite simply, is that the political assault upon Israel at the United Nations is intended to completely isolate Israel internationally and to deny it any legitimacy whatsoever in international law and world opinion. This cause has nothing to do with human rights, peace, and self-determination. Yet at the United Nations these cherished ideals are enlisted for this very destructive purpose.

Inside the United Nations, the U.S. resolutely opposes the efforts at delegitimation of Israel and the doctrines through which this is attempted:

1. The doctrine that Zionism equals racism;
2. The doctrine that Israel is an outlaw state, without the right to membership in UN bodies.
3. The doctrine that Israel, as an outlaw state, is fair game for all and lacks even the right to self-defense against terrorist attacks.

We have insisted on calling lies and calumny against Israel by their name, believing that freedom requires defending with truth; believing, too, that lies left unnamed are terribly dangerous.

Outside the UN the U.S. government has worked and is working to help create peace in the region under conditions that will provide security for Israel. We have reaffirmed UN Resolutions 242 and 338, which remain, we believe, the framework for stable peace in the region. We have remained loyal to the approach called Camp David which we believe remains the only realistic, fair basis for peace in the Middle East. President Reagan reaffirmed both in his speech of September 1, 1983.

This is exactly the approach followed by Secretary Shultz in his efforts to consummate the agreement between Israel and Lebanon, an agreement that we hope will lead eventually to the withdrawal of all foreign forces—Israeli, Syrian, and PLO—from Lebanon. If this agreement ultimately achieves its objectives and reestablishes respect for Lebanon's territorial integrity and independence, it would constitute an enormous step forward in the effort to bring peace to the Middle East.

There are some people who have a simple formula for achieving peace in the Middle East. Just increase the pressure on Israel, tighten the screws, and a settlement will be reached. This approach is based upon a number of false assumptions, among which are the view that a proud and vigorous state like Israel will allow itself to be subjected to such crude pressure, as well as the view that it is in the United States' interest to weaken Israel.

The Reagan administration does not accept either of these views. Israel is not a burden or an inconvenience to the United States. It is a cherished democratic friend and a valued ally. It has also emerged as an important power in a region of immense strategic significance. It does not serve American interests to undermine the position of such a friend and such a power. It harms those interests. Similarly, it does not serve the cause of peace to seek to impose a settlement upon Israel or upon any of the other parties to the conflict. A peaceful settlement is possible only among those who wish it and will it. Our job is to help bring those parties together and to facilitate the peace process.

The past year has been a momentous one in the history of the Middle East and in the history of United States relations with Israel. Some commentators have interpreted the inevitable differences between the United States and Israel on one or another issue as a sign of crisis in U.S.-Israeli relations. In fact, the events of the past year have demonstrated the durability of U.S.-Israeli relations, even during the most difficult periods. This durability, as should now be perfectly clear, is based fundamentally upon two elements—common values and common interests. The common values of democracy and freedom provide the moral underpinning of a sustained relationship between Israel and the United States. The common interests of peace and security provide the strategic underpinnings for such a relationship. These common values and interests are shared not just by Israel and the United States, but by all countries committed to democracy and peace. It is within this democratic framework that Israel occupies a secure and valued position, one that cannot be effectively challenged or—indeed— delegitimized by any resolution of the United Nations.

ZIONISM IS RACISM:
AN ASSAULT ON HUMAN RIGHTS

There is probably not much new that can be said about that most obnoxious resolution considered here today. When Daniel Patrick Moynihan was our nation's chief representative to the United Nations, he described that terrible day in vivid language. He asserted that what we have here today is a lie, a political lie of a variety well-known to the 20th century. Through that lie, he asserted, the abomination of anti-Semitism has been given the appearance of international sanction.

Why should we say more about this obscene resolution, about which there has been a good deal of talk already today? Although it has been nearly a decade since it was passed in the General Assembly, its effects are very much with us. Like a terrible bacillus, it has spread its poison literally worldwide.

The answer to why we should continue to speak about it today lies in both the past and in the future. We must continue to speak about the

Address before a conference co-sponsored by B'nai B'rith, World Jewish Congress and the World Zionist Organization, and U.S. Department of State, December 10, 1984.

resolution as long as the vicious campaign it symbolizes against the state of Israel continues. I am here today from the General Assembly to tell you what you already know, that the campaign continues, in full force, this very day.

It has become very clear in the years following the passage of the Zionism is Racism resolution that it is less a slogan than a program, a program for the delegitimization and disappearance of the state of Israel. The Zionism is Racism resolution has special significance in the campaign of destruction and delegitimization of Israel. First, it symbolizes the alliance of the African and Arab blocs inside the United Nations with regard to all questions concerning the Middle East. That alliance, not written on paper, clearly stipulates that African nations will vote against Israel on questions involving the Middle East, and Arabs will vote with Africans on all matters concerning South Africa. That alliance plus the Soviet bloc, which can always be counted on to join a vendetta, provides the famous automatic majority which is available for all resolutions against Israel. The alliance provides the stable structural base for anti-Israeli actions inside the body. It is very important to understand this because support for anti-Israel resolutions in the UN is independent of any particular circumstances, it is available regardless of Israel's policy, or the merits of any particular case. It is as permanent as the blocs on which it is based. That alliance has cracked in the last two years largely under U.S. pressure, and some Africans have been persuaded to distinguish their interests from those of Arab nations. But the alliance is still very much alive, and it provides a permanent structural base for anti-Israel resolutions of all kinds.

Second, that Zionism is Racism resolution constitutes a direct attack on the moral foundations of Israel. It is not simply an attack on the ideology of Zionism, it is not even primarily an attack on the ideology of Zionism. To appreciate the full meaning and the power of this assault on the moral functions of Israel, it is necessary to understand that inside the United Nations, adversaries of Israel wholly identify the state of Israel with Zionist ideology. They refuse normally to call Israel by her name, referring to her instead as the Zionist entity.

It is important to remember also that inside the United Nations racism is the ultimate crime. In the United Nations context, states which are designated as racists have no rights whatsoever. They have only obligations. Their very existence is considered to be a form of aggression, and anything which calls itself a national liberation movement can act against a racist state.

When Israel is designated a racist state the word is out, that Israel is fair game for every would-be aggressor in the world. Speech after speech, resolution after resolution inside the United Nations, reams of official propaganda produced inside the United Nations by the Committee on Palestinian Rights and all other committees associated with it, describe the founding and existence of Israel as aggression. It is very important to understand that by defining the foundation of Israel as aggression, the intention is clear: to brand Israel's very existence as a crime against international law.

Resolution after resolution describes Israel as guilty of genocide. Any attack against the state and the people of Israel is justified. Any Israeli effort to defend herself against attack is defined as unjustified aggression against the attacker. PLO firing into Israeli villages is ignored or justified as the legitimate right of a national liberation movement. But Israelis firing back is a serious threat to international peace and security, a crime against civilized society. This sounds like exaggeration; it is not exaggeration. It is necessary only to listen and to read the speeches and the resolutions of the United Nations in order to understand the extent to which the campaign of delegitimization against Israel dominates that organization.

One rather stunning case was that of the terrorist, Abu Ein, who was charged with setting off a bomb in a crowded Israeli supermarket which killed two persons and wounded scores. Abu Ein was treated in a whole panoply of speeches as a hero. Israel, for seeking to bring him to trial through due process of law, was mercilessly excoriated for violations of international law. And the United States was berated for extraditing Abu Ein after he had exhausted some two- and-one-half years of full protection of our court system. In the same resolution that condemned the United States for extraditing Abu Ein, the General Assembly voted 75 to 21 with 43 abstentions, to "reaffirm the legitimacy of the struggle for independence, territorial integrity and national unity and for liberation from colonial and foreign domination by alien subjugation by all available means." This could not be clearer. The PLO has a right to set off bombs in crowded supermarkets—that's struggle by any and all means. Israel has not even the right to try the bomber in a court of law with full legal protection.

It is difficult for persons who have not lived at the United Nations and witnessed it first hand to understand the ferocity and the perversity of the assault on Israel inside the United Nations. I sometimes am very hesitant about actually quoting speeches attacking Israel inside the United Nations because they sound so extreme, so violent, it almost seems like a breach of good taste or reason even to quote them. And that kind of reticence— which is very widely felt—compounds the problem of understanding how intense the feeling is against the state of Israel.

When Israel—a state that was founded in the ashes of the Holocaust—is routinely accused of nasty practices and genocide, we know that we are facing moral double speak. Not just moral double speak, but a kind of moral double bookkeeping in which Israel can do no right and her detractors can do no harm. No crime literally is to indecent for Israel to be thought guilty of. Thus, in a letter to the Security Council, in March 1983, the permanent representative of Iraq, charged that, "Israeli terrorism has now reached the point of the implementation of schemes for the collective poisoning of Palestinian students and inhabitants." The representative of Jordan in another letter the same day described, "the collective poisoning of nearly 1,000 schoolgirls in the West Bank," and the PLO asserted, the same day in a letter to the Security Council that, "without question, a new phase in Israel's campaign of genocide against the Palestinian people has now been launched."

When investigations conducted by the World Health Organization and the International Red Cross at the behest of the Secretary-General could find no evidence of poisoning, the matter was simply dropped. No one apologized. It is difficult to grasp the obsessive quality of the campaign against Israel, where literally any occasion can be turned into an assault, where no one really expects that Israel will receive fair treatment. I felt sad at the thought of my new Israeli colleague, Ambassador Benjamin Netanyahu, encountering the treatment of Israel at the United Nations. I felt certain that he did not understand, as indeed virtually no one understands, how bitter and intense the assault against Israel is, and how widespread the expectation is inside that body that Israel will not receive fair play.

This very week the General Assembly is addressing a package of resolutions on the occupied territories, the so-called question of Palestine, and the situation in the Middle East. All these resolutions are unbalanced and unfair. The worst is offered under the title of the "Situation in the Middle East." It is a reiteration of the obnoxious Golan Heights resolution which calls down upon Israel a kind of anathema that no other nation in the history of the United Nations has ever been subjected to. In that resolution there is reiterated the finding that of all the nations of the world, Israel is not a peace-loving member state, "that it has persistently violated its obligations under the Charter, that it has carried out neither its obligations under the Charter, nor its commitment under the General Assembly resolution 276 of 11 May 1949." That resolution calls for Israel's total isolation. It calls on all states to end all economic, financial, technological, military assistance and cooperation with Israel. It calls on all states to sever diplomatic, trade and cultural relations with Israel. Clearly, this resolution portends more efforts in U.N. bodies seeking Israel's expulsion. That resolution is co-sponsored by Bangladesh, Cuba, India, Indonesia, Jordan, Malaysia, Pakistan, Vietnam, and Yugoslavia. That resolution will pass. Neither fairness nor evidence will matter; that resolution will pass.

It is not as though we have very high standards for nations inside the United Nations either. We do not have very high standards for sovereignty. The Ukraine can sit in the Security Council and Byleorussia and Mongolia are full members of the General Assembly. We do not have very high standards for peace-loving qualities either. Libya, who commits aggression on a regular basis against her neighbors, sits as a peace-loving state; Vietnam and the Soviet Union, both of whom currently occupy neighboring countries, sit as peace-loving states. It is not that we have very high standards; it is that we have double standards. There is one standard for Israel and another for everyone else. These resolutions have no positive purpose, but that does not mean that they are devoid of content. They intend to destroy.

Senator Moynihan, when he was Ambassador Moynihan, observed that we should reflect on the fact that if the General Assembly did not exist, that Zionism is Racism resolution would not have passed. That of course is true. It is also true that if the General Assembly did not exist, we could not reaffirm on a continuing basis the resolutions which are so revolting. A kind of crowd psychology described by Sigmund Freud takes over in these circumstances and nations which have no problem with Israel—no Jews, no Arabs, no Moslems, no Palestinians—join in a kind of seizure of mob psychology in the vote against Israel. It is a dismal thing to watch. The fault is not the General Assembly. Ambassador Meir Rossene and I were just exchanging some comments about this. The problem is not the General Assembly; the problem is the members of the General Assembly. The problem is not with the Secretariat; it is with the members of the United Nations. It is the members who offer the resolution, and it is the members who vote for the resolutions, and it is the members who lend themselves to a campaign of delegitimization and destruction of the state of Israel. At the same time, they also lend themselves to the perversion of the institution by falsifying language, falsifying concepts like sovereignty, law, self-defense, and collective self-defense, and by perverting the instruments of peace. They lend themselves to the campaign for the destruction of Israel.

It is my solemn opinion and most serious judgment that Israel would have already been expelled from the United Nations had it not been for the laws on our books making clear that if the state of Israel is denied participation in any body of the United Nations, the United States will withdraw also and will withhold all financial contributions until Israel's right to participate has been restored. Were it not for that law—and were it not for the vigor with which we have campaigned to prevent the expulsion of Israel—I believe that Israel would already have been expelled from most UN agencies. The campaign has so far been mounted in the International Atomic Energy Agency, in the International Telecommunications Union, in the World Health Organization, in the General Assembly itself, and so forth. As it is turned back, the campaign is only stopped temporarily.

Last year the Iranians devoted a tremendous amount of effort and worldwide lobbying to the campaign for the expulsion of Israel from the General Assembly. They visited countries which no representative of the Ayatollah ever visited, seeking votes for the resolution to deny participation to Israel. They attempted to raise donors' cartels, whose purpose would be to donate the money that the UN would be deprived of if the United States left. They worked very hard at this effort and we have some grounds for believing that they have already gone to work on the same effort for next year.

Because of the perversion of language and law that is associated with the campaign against Israel, the General Assembly and the United States is unable to do a good many of the constructive tasks which we might otherwise do. We cannot act against terrorism because terrorism is defined in terms of national liberation movements which are defined as having all rights when they act against illegitimate regimes such as the state of Israel. What difference does it really make anyway? Why should we bother? Why does it matter?

I think we have already seen in our times the tragic consequences of the refusal to face unpleasant truths. We have permitted lies to go unchallenged, which are then transformed into policies, and policies to go unchallenged which are then transformed into murder. Examples abound. In *Mein Kampf,* for example, we all know that Hitler stated in the most unambiguous terms his views about the hatred and contempt he felt for Jews. If the Final Solution is not spelled out clearly in *Mein Kampf,* it is clearly foreshadowed. Almost no one heeded the clear warnings that were present, not even when that hatred was translated into policies—into attacks on Jewish stores, and into discriminatory legal declarations, and discriminatory legislation requiring the Star of David to be worn, forbidding Jewish lawyers to practice before German courts or excluding Jewish children from German schools.

The predisposition to shrug off horrible facts is powerful in our time. All of us would rather not face the truth, either about the hate around us, or the silence of others in the face of hate, about unfairness around us, or the likelihood that the unfairness will prevail. That is almost un-American. We Americans are supposed to look on the bright side and we 20th century Western citizens are optimists.

Lies which go unchallenged are mistaken finally for the truth. I think that the lie that Zionism is Racism has already spread far, and damaged many. That lie will only be expunged when it is pursued, not only with the purpose of demonstrating that as to the facts it is incorrect, but to demonstrate that its consequences are deadly for all of us and for the institutions through which we would like to make peace and improve our society.

The challenge is enormous. I do not believe we can forget that lie as long as it circulates in the world. It is the political and moral responsibility of all of us to refuse to ignore it and to insist on calling attention to just how revolting and obscene it remains.

ZIONISM, RACISM, AND THE UNITED NATIONS

Obviously, I am very pleased to be here today. I would have no other reason whatsoever to be here because, like Connor Cruise O'Brien, I represent only myself here today and only my commitments and whatever views I have developed, above all in the last five years, about these problems.

Ten years ago, when the "Zionism is Racism" resolution passed the General Assembly of the United Nations, it was, as almost everyone understood, tantamount to declaring the state of Israel an illegitimate state based on an illegitimate philosophy. It was the first organized attack—and let us be clear, it was organized, highly organized—it was the first highly organized attack on world Jewry since the defeat of Hitler's armies. It has already been mentioned today that by an almost unbearable coincidence, the Zionism is Racism resolution was passed on the anniversary of Kristal Nacht, November 10, 1938, when Nazis smashed the windows of Jewish stores and Jewish homes in cities all over Germany, announcing to the world that Germany's Jews were marked for destruction. And 37 years later, in the very institution established to eliminate violence from international life, another announcement was made—the announcement that now the Jewish state was marked for destruction.

More than any single act, I believe the passage of the Zionism is Racism resolution on November 10, 1975, symbolized the death of the dream of the United Nations as an institution dedicated to reason, democracy and peace. It symbolized the triumph of forces of unreason, hate, violence and war in the very palace built to celebrate the opposite values.

The resolution had very special significance for the United Nations for

Address before the conference on Zionism, Racism and the United Nations, United Nations, New York, New York, November 10, 1985.

another reason. It was the first time, though God knows not the last time, that a majority of the UN—made up almost exclusively of non-democratic states—decided to arrogate to themselves the right to declare a democratic member state illegitimate. They decided to arrogate to themselves the power to decide what is legitimate and what is not legitimate. That is the reason, in my opinion, that it is so very important that this conference be held today and that discussions of these issues take place in our country, here in the United States, in Israel and, indeed, in the world, because legitimacy matters. Rousseau was not the first and certainly not the last to point out that might cannot long endure unless it is first transformed into right. And states do not long endure if their moral foundations are sapped and destroyed through the corrosion of lies and violence. That is, I believe, what is at issue in the attack on Israel in the United Nations.

Everyone here appreciates the significance of those terms in the UN context. You understand that racism in the UN syntax is the ultimate political crime. It is the ultimate violation of human rights. A state based on racism is an outlaw state unworthy of membership in what is euphemistically called "the family of nations." A racist state in UN terminology has no rights at all. It has no right to exist. It has not even a right to defend itself.

What was underway in the passage of this resolution was what Nietzsche called a transvaluation of values, an effort to turn literally upside-down the understanding of what is legitimate and what is illegitimate; who has a right to exist and to defend themselves and who has no such right at all.

Adolf Eichmann, in writing his own diaries as he awaited trial in Israel, wrote that he had never really felt personal animosity toward the Jewish people; that he had never acted out of personal hatred; that he had simply not thought much about whether it was right or wrong for he was, after all, simply trying to find effective ways to do what was asked of him by his head of state. He ended this passage by saying, "after all, what is right and what is wrong."

That is the power that the General Assembly of the United Nations claimed on the day they passed the Zionism is Racism resolution. They claimed the power to decide for politics in the world in our time what is right; what is wrong; what state deserves to live; what to do die; what is legitimate; what is illegitimate. It could not be more incompatible with and opposite to our own American conceptions of legitimacy than it is.

It is, after all, our Declaration of Independence that declares very clearly, at the very act of our founding, what makes a state legitimate. Our Declaration of Independence says, we hold these truths to be understood by all men at all times: men are created equal; that they are endowed by their Creator with certain rights to life, liberty and the pursuit of happiness; and to protect these rights, governments are instituted among men, deriving their just powers from the consent of the governed.

What makes a government legitimate? The protection of the rights of people. What kind of government is legitimate? A government based on consent of the governed because it protects those basic rights. There was in this resolution a very explicit, not just rejection, but inversion of the meaning of good and evil, and also of the doctrine of legitimacy on which the United States is based.

I believe it is important to note that in the same day that the General Assembly of the United Nations passed the Zionism is Racism resolution, they also affirmed the legitimacy of the PLO, endowed the PLO with the rights of a member state, and established a permanent committee with a very large budget to promote the interests of the PLO within the United Nations and within the world. Henceforth, after this declaration of the illegitimacy of Israel and the legitimacy of the PLO, the use of force against Israel by the PLO would enjoy the support of the same majority of the member states of the United Nations. And the use of force by Israel to defend herself with the rights granted by the Charter of the United Nations would be treated and characterized as aggression. That follows from the Zionism is Racism resolution and the declaration of the PLO as a national liberation movement—as the sole representative of the Palestinian people. That is what it meant then and that is what it means today. It was tantamount to declaring an open season on the state of Israel, and to declaring Israel's self-defense an act of aggression. That is a shocking, appalling, dreadful fact. It has consequences. And while there may be some positive consequences, as Connor Cruise O' Brien has suggested, there are certainly many negative consequences.

The most important of those negative consequences is confusion—confusion among many people in the world, some of whom have no experience with Israel, no experience with Jews, no experience with Arabs, who could not find the country on a map. Ambassador Netanyahu has described one African country which I visited—a country without Arabs, without Jews, without Moslems—feature on its national day a large banner proclaiming "Zionism is Racism." We hear only this week the political head of state of an important friend and allied nation articulate the same kinds of confusion when that person described the right of the PLO to undertake an armed struggle for its territory. The right to an armed struggle is rooted, we were told, in the historic right of people deprived of their homeland to resort to violence. How much confusion is involved in such an argument? The same historic tradition, which was alluded to in that discussion, suggests that if a nation seeks peace, as Israel has sought peace from the moment of her founding, and is denied peace by persons who continue to make war on her—who make war in the name of war; and state objectives which are quite clear and those of war—that such people do not have that right of armed struggle. Our tradition is quite clear. The right of armed struggle is the right of people subjected to conquest, like Afghans, in a condition where they have never, never, never relied on violence against their neighbors, and where they seek only peace and peaceful coexistence.

I think that there is terrible confusion engendered by the categories of Zionism and racism and aggression. And this confusion continues inside the United Nations, particularly, to result in the unfair treatment of Israel. There are many ways in which the state of Israel is routinely mistreated inside the United Nations—so routinely it is not even noticed anymore—for example, the denial to Israel of membership in a regional group. Israel is not a member of any regional group. And Israel today, I would wager, would not be admitted, could not find a regional group which would accept her as a member. And because Israel is denied membership in a regional group (those regional groups have a very important influence on the agenda, for example, and the debate and the outcome of UN affairs), Israel is routinely denied that important dimension of participation inside the United Nations.

Israel is routinely made the object of demands which are made on no other nation. For example, the demand is made on Israel that she submit to an international conference, made up of the United Nations, to settle her borders. There is, I will wager, no nation in the United Nations which would be willing to submit the determination of its borders to a conference of the United Nations. But the fascinating thing is, no other nation is asked to submit the settlement of its borders to the United Nations. And when last year, in the debate in the General Assembly on a resolution which is as least as destructive as the Zionism is Racism resolution, I suggested that perhaps those countries who had voted in favor of the resolution would like to have their own border disputes brought before the international conference, this was regarded as unduly provocative. A great many telegrams were received by the State Department concerning this provocation.

Israel is submitted to name-calling at a level and of a quality which no other nation in the world is submitted to. Israel is called genocidal and neo-Nazi. There is a lot of talk of Judeo-Nazis of Tel Aviv. And, of course, Israel is regularly described as the racist, Zionist Entity. The demand is made on Israel by the General Assembly through repeated resolutions that she be isolated in the world, that trade and aid of any kind whatsoever and diplomatic representation and all kinds of relationships with all other peoples and all other countries in the world be terminated. No other country in the world is made the object of such demands. I believe, after having reflected a good deal on my experience of the past four years at the United Nations, that there are many specific things the United States should and should not do with regard to Israel. Some of those I have spelled out on another occasion in another place and some of them I will spell out on some other occasion in some other place, but they could all be summed up basically in two simple principles: That if we Americans desire to be fair to the state of Israel and to disassociate ourselves utterly from the calumnies heaped on Israel in this body than we should resolve never to judge Israel by standards which other nations in the United Nations are not judged by—never, not on any issue, not under any condition; and never, under any circumstances, at any time, any place, to make demands on the state of Israel that are not made on other member nations. That is what I recommend. Thank you.

Harsh Truths

My relationship with the state of Israel goes back to my own girlhood. I vividly remember the bells on the Riverside Church ringing on the day in 1948, the establishment of Israel, I was in a philosophy class, at Barnard, Harry Truman had taken a strong and marvelous stand. The United States had played the catalytic role. And it seemed like the end of a long nightmare, marking not only the realization of age-old dreams and prophecies, but also the end of the nightmare of the Holocaust, the horror of war and genocide, and the birth of a new democracy. It was exciting as well as gratifying, and very much to be celebrated.

My relationship with the organized Jewish community of the United States—and, I discover when I travel, of the world—is not nearly so long-standing. It is an artifact of my four and one-fourth years at the United Nations. It is a byproduct of the obsessive anti-Israel campaign that so dominates the agenda and proceedings of the Security Council and the General Assembly. It is, above all, an artifact of our shared concern that the state of Israel receive fair treatment—nothing more, nothing less, than fair treatment—inside United Nations' bodies. I have sometimes said that my highest goal for the United States in the United Nations was that we be treated as well as any small, poor Third World nation. You think that's a joke. That is also my hope for Israel. But I may say, I know it to be utopian.

Address before the conference of Presidents of Major Jewish Organizations, New York, New York, April 19, 1985.

Israel is not likely to get fair play in the United Nations, no matter what her policies, her style, her efforts. That is a harsh fact about these times, that place, our world. It is a harsh fact, difficult to accept, doubted and denied by many Americans and most others.

You know, we Americans take optimism and boosterism almost as articles of faith. We all think it's important to believe that we can in some significant measure control how others treat us, that we can determine the way they respond to us. We think that how they treat us depends on how we treat them. It's important to almost all of us to believe that. It's important to believe others' behavior towards us is a *response*. It's important to believe that if they are hostile to us, it is because we have behaved badly; or because there's a misunderstanding. In that case, we can affect that hostility and deal with it. If it's hostility in response to our bad behavior, we can improve the way we behave. If it's hostility due to a misunderstanding, then we can get together, talk it over, explain away the misunderstanding. We can make things right. It is terribly important to us to believe that by our efforts and our good faith and hard work, we can make things right.

That belief is a basic tenet of the creed of contemporary civilized Americans, and, I think, of civilized Westerners generally . . . that is the reason we have such difficulty understanding and accepting that some people may in fact simply hate us. The reality of hate is very difficult, I think, for any of us, contemporary American and Westerners, to perceive, understand and accept. It is, in the most literal sense, *incredible.*

That is the reason that neither Europe's Jews nor almost anyone else believed in the reality of Adolph Hitler's intentions. Who could believe such a thing? Such a thing was, literally, incredible, even though Adolph Hitler and his Nazi colleagues' intentions were manifest in *Mein Kampf;* and in the many speeches that followed upon *Mein Kampf;* even when those speeches became policies—who could believe what was played out before their very eyes?

We all know that in *Mein Kampf,* Adolph Hitler states in the most unambiguous terms his view, his hatred, his contempt, for the Jews. And if the "final solution" was not wholly spelled out in *Mein Kampf,* it was very clearly foreshadowed. Yet almost no one heeded the warnings that were present, not even when that hatred was translated into a tax on Jewish stores, into discriminatory legal declarations and discriminatory legislation—decreeing, for example, that because of what you were, not what you did, you wear a *Star of David*; that you could not practice law; that you could not work for the government; that you could not be admitted to public schools.

The inclination to shrug off horrible facts is surely one of the most important, basic defining characteristics of modern, Western, liberal, democratic civilization.

All of us would rather not face horrible truths. We would also rather not face the indifference of others in the face of horrible truths. We would rather not face the unfairness around us or the likelihood that unfairness may prevail. I want to be clear; when I say "we," I mean "we." I would also rather not face these things. The truth is that the civilized Western mind rejects the horrible and the hate and the reality of hate that provokes and accompanies the horrible.

The United Nations is like a cram course in the horrible when dealing with the Middle East. It is difficult to believe what one hears in Security Council hearings and in General Assembly debates about Israel. It is impossible, however, not finally to realize, through the endless succession of 'immorality' plays acted out in the Security Council and the General Assembly, that what is rejected is Israel itself—not its policies; its existence. The speeches make painfully clear that the stakes here are not disagreement with policies but contempt for the people who make the policies.

I didn't know that before I went to the United Nations. I learned it at the United Nations, listening to those Security Council hearings, listening to that General Assembly, listening to the talk in the corridors. I should like to emphasize that, of course, it isn't the institution of the UN, it's the members that cause these problems, but its members, of course, in that context *comprise* the institution.

Israel, a state founded in the ashes of the Holocaust, is routinely accused of genocide, and when that happens, we know we are in the presence of a kind of doublespeak that is almost literally incredible because Israel is *not* guilty of genocide. There is no limit to the crimes of which Israel is accused. No crime is too indecent for Israel to be thought guilty of it. I shall never forget the hearing that took place in March, 1983, on the question of mass poisonings of schoolgirls on the West Bank. In a letter to the Security Council in March, 1983, the permanent representative of one moderate Arab country charged, "Israeli terrorism has now reached the point of the implementation of schemes for the collective poisoning of Palestinian students and inhabitants." On the same day the representative of another "moderate" Arab nation asserted: "The collective poisoning of nearly 1,000 Palestinian schoolgirls in the West Bank is intolerable." And the PLO asserted in the Security Council: "Without question, a new phase in Israel's campaign of genocide against the Palestinian people has now been launched." That's only a sample of the rhetoric.

The speeches given on this and comparable occasions are so extreme, so violent, that it is almost a breach of good taste even to quote from them.

Our reticence to quote from such violent and scurrilous attacks compounds the problem of understanding how intense the feeling is against the state of Israel inside the United Nations.

May I remind you that when the investigations of Arab schoolgirl poisonings conducted by the World Health Organization and the International Red Cross at the behest of the Secretary General could find *no evidence of poisoning whatsoever*, the matter was simply dropped. No one apologized. No one said that they had been wrong. It was just dropped.

I have said before that I felt badly thinking about my colleague, Ambassador Benjamin Netanyahu's arrival in New York, thinking that it was going to be very difficult for him to face the irrational, obsessive campaign against Israel and against Israel's people, that he would encounter there.

I felt sorry that he would learn the harsh truth that his nation, virtually alone among nations in the world, could not expect fair play in the United Nations. There is a name for contempt for the people of Israel and those who identify with them, and that name is anti-Semitism. It is difficult to face and accept, also, the existence and the extent in that world body of real, authentic anti-Semitism . . . bold, unashamed, revolting. It is manifest almost any time Israel is discussed and that is all too frequently.

I personally might have believed that Israel brought some of these problems on herself had I arrived in the United Nations in 1982 instead of 1981. But by the time of the Galilee Operation, I had already learned that Israel was an object of vitriolic attack, even for defending herself against the military attacks of the PLO. No matter what Israel did, that nation became the object of an incredibly violent, bitter, hateful, hate-filled attack.

I've said it before; I will doubtless say it again. I was never quite certain which was more horrible—the violent attacks and the unfair abuse of Israel, or the silence and passivity of almost everyone in the face of that violent and unfair treatment.

I came to believe in a way more concrete and meaningful than ever before in my life, that acquiescence in injustice makes one a kind of accomplice to it. I read again about the Holocaust and realized that silent acquiescence in the face of unfairness, victimization, incarceration, and finally, the slaughter of Jews, was almost as much a problem as the perpetration of those acts.

I came to believe very deeply that in systematically treating a nation and a people unfairly, in applying to them standards that have never been reached by any nation in human history, in applying to them definitions, which do not fit the ordinary practices of nations—such as the attack on Israel as a violator of the Geneva Conventions only two weeks ago—that in such attacks, the ground is laid for even greater unfairness, injustice, and victimization.

It is terribly important to remember the victimization of the Jewish people. It is terribly important to remember the Holocaust. These days of memorial are profoundly important. We need to remember because to forget is to dishonor the victims. Some say we have remembered enough, and we have learned enough. But, of course, we have not remembered enough, and we can never remember enough or learn enough from that terrible human catastrophe.

The fact is that hate and victimization and, yes, anti-Semitism, is not a problem to be solved once and for all. It is not a battle won on a single battlefield in a single war, it is a struggle that must be continued day after day, week after week, month after month, year after year. The organized American Jewish community, represented here, has a terribly vital role in that ongoing struggle. It is for you to mobilize, for you to work, alongside some of the rest of us, to remind the world, in this country and elsewhere, that something ultimately horrible happened and that it happened because people did not care enough, remember enough, struggle enough. The fact is, we are not all equally guilty. We are not all equally dangerous. We are not all equally victims.

Though I lived through the Holocaust as a high school student, and understood, because I was in New York, and met survivors, as they straggled out of Europe, something of the horror of the Holocaust, it was not until my four years at the United Nations that I understood the extent to which the drama—the victimization of the Jewish people—continues to this very day. Having learned that lesson, I believe it is very important never to forget it. And I say to you now, it is impossible to overstate the importance of the organized American Jewish community to the well-being and the survival of the state of Israel.

A FAIRNESS DOCTRINE FOR ISRAEL

I want to thank the Jabotinsky Foundation for this extraordinary honor by which I am very honored and very grateful. I should like to note that I was looking at the roster of previous winners, and I noticed my friend, the former prime minister of Israel, Menachem Begin, and my very good friend and mentor, the late Scoop Jackson, my former colleague with whom I worked long on just the problem we are discussing tonight.

Address before the Jabotinsky Foundation, New York, New York, October 30, 1985.

What I did with regard to Israel at the United Nations seemed to me my simple duty. And I should be remiss if I did not note that every vote I cast was cast with the full approval of President Ronald Reagan. There should be no doubt about that.

I did not expect or hope for Israel anything more than I hoped for the United States: that was that Israel should be treated fairly, granted the same rights and courtesies and the same respect as any member state. That seems obvious. But, inside the United Nations, Israel is regularly denied courtesy—the same respect and courtesy awarded to the world's most aggressive and least worthy states. No charge is too wild and no rhetoric too harsh, no procession of accusers too long, no treatment too discriminatory for Israel to be submitted to inside the United Nations.

Armed terrorists attacks on Israel are met with silent indifference. Armed retaliation by Israel is treated as an act of aggression, as if Israel did not enjoy the right of self-defense guaranteed by the United Nations Charter to all governments. And, in fact, doctrines have developed which assert just that: that Israel does not have the right to defend herself because she is a racist state—because Zionism is racism, and racism is the basest crime in the UN lexicon, and those who practice racism are outlaws, and outlaws have no rights.

Israel, it is asserted, is itself intrinsically illegitimate. Why? Because, it is argued by some of our "distinguished colleagues" at the United Nations, the very act of founding Israel was an act of aggression, and therefore an illegitimate act. As one "distinguished colleague" from a neighboring state of Israel's put it, "Aggression against the Arab nation began, not in 1948 with the founding of Israel, but with the arrival of the first settlers in Palestine."

After the defeat of the Arabs in 1967, Israel's enemies have turned to the United Nations and turned the United Nations into a place where war is continued by other means.

Because the enemies of Israel are well placed inside the Arab bloc, the Islamic Conference, and the Soviet bloc, they are able to make the very survival of Israel a continuing item on the agenda of UN bodies. The first Security Council meeting with which I dealt in 1981 concerned Israel. The last issue with which I dealt, before leaving in 1985, concerned Israel. Both of them gave me practice in saying "No."

In the more than four intervening years, I came to understand and care a good deal about the effort to delegitimize and destroy Israel. I thought a good deal about how to defend against this effort inside the United Nations and I would like to share with you some of my reflections and conclusions about how a friend and ally of Israel such as I trust the United States will always be, might conduct itself with regard to the relentless attacks against

Israel in the United Nations. I speak here as an American citizen reflecting on my own experience to share with you my views about how an American ally might be expected to behave with regard to the state of Israel in the United Nations—regardless of who is president, or secretary of state, regardless of which party is in power, regardless of who is permanent representative of the United States Mission to the United Nations.

The first and the most obvious point is that the United States should follow inside the United Nations the same principles and policies which our government adopts outside the United Nations. That may not sound like much, but it is. The UN context has a corrosive and powerful effect, and it has more than once happened that policies adopted by our government are in fact substantially altered in their application in the United Nations by ambassadors and foreign service officers anxious to please their UN colleagues.

Second, I would emphasize that the United States should not agree to UN resolutions or presidential statements which are not consistent with U.S. policy with regard to Jerusalem. As a former permanent representative and Supreme Court justice and distinguished international lawyer, Arthur Goldberg reminded us, the United States government has never included East Jerusalem as part of the occupied territories—a term which is normally applied to the West Bank. President Reagan, in his initiative of September 1, 1982, said, "Jerusalem should remain undivided; its final status should be decided through negotiation." He did not incorporate Jerusalem into the category of occupied territories. That means, specifically, that the United States should not accept resolutions or formulations which apply to "occupied Arab territories including Jerusalem." That is a very common formulation which was once accepted, but has never been again accepted. Also, settlements should not be characterized as illegal. President Reagan has explicitly refused to so-characterize settlements, though he has appealed for a moratorium on new settlements. United States policy and the Reagan administration's policy is quite clear on this issue; so should our policy be in the United Nations.

Third, we should never accept resolutions or statements of any kind that include language drawn from Chapter VII of the United Nations Charter. Chapter VII is the part of the Charter that applies to the use of sanctions against a country. Resolutions should be rejected if they include such terms as "threats to international peace and security," "acts of aggression," or "armed aggression." Such language and such terms raise some very troublesome legal questions, prejudge issues, and invite later problems. They are always cited when a case is being made to brand the state of Israel an international outlaw.

We should vote "No" on any resolution or statement that characterizes

Israel as "not a peace-loving state," which condition is a prerequisite for membership in that not so exclusive body. I think we should always vote "no" on any attack on the United States relationship with Israel because it constitutes an unwarranted and intolerable interference in the internal affairs of the foreign policy of our countries. We should accept no resolution that includes any call for the isolation of Israel—military, economic or diplomatic. Moreover, it is not enough to vote "No" in these cases. It is important to explain why these terms and formulations are unacceptable.

In citing and affirming resolutions 242 and 338 as a basis for U.S. policy and for a settlement in the Middle East, it is important to explicitly affirm *all* their parts, including the requirement for direct negotiations among the parties and for secure boundaries for all parties. This brings us to the question of war and peace and Israel in the United Nations. I think it is worth noting again and again and again, when the question of Israel's peace-loving or nonpeace-loving nature is at issue (it is at issue all the time in the United Nations), the evidence on Israel's will to peace, because the contrary is continuously urged.

The fact that Israel's neighbors have refused to resolve the war with Israel has confronted Israel with a kind of permanent double bind inside the United Nations as well as outside it. Because, at the same time *they* refuse peaceful negotiations, if Israel undertakes a policy appropriate to an occupier in an occupied territory, then Israel is immediately accused of unilateral, arbitrary, illegal acts. So, for example, one finds resolutions like the Golan Heights where Israel is denied peace, yet expected to live as though at peace with her neighbors existed even though it is perfectly understood those neighbors deny peace to Israel. This matters in UN language because an incursion into Lebanon during war is not an act of aggression in war. Yet, it is systematically treated as an act of aggression inside the United Nations. Thus, Israel is expected to act always as though she were at peace while being denied peace. Obviously we should never accept the characterization of an act of retaliation as an act of aggression. It is not enough that an act of retaliation should simply be described as part of a cycle of violence, though even that is never achieved in UN resolutions. It is, in fact, not simply part of a cycle of violence. An act of retaliation against prior violence is an act of self-defense and should be stated as such.

Obviously countries in the United Nations should not sit silently while unreasonable obscene attacks like those involved in the resolution on Zionism is Racism are made, or the perversion of conferences like that of the Refugee Conference, the Kampuchea Conference or the perversion on the Decade of Women are introduced. I have, as a woman, always resented the notion that, after weeks of preparation and debate and millions of dollars spent, the conferences at Copenhagen and Mexico City finally decided that the greatest obstacle to the full realization of women's opportunities and rights was, of course, Zionism.

Obviously no nation should acquiesce in efforts to deny Israel the full rights and benefits of membership. Our country now has on its books a law which states that in case Israel is denied full rights of participation in any United Nations body, the United States will immediately withdraw our own participation and withhold any financial support for that organization. That law should be enforced; and it should be, in my opinion, elaborated simply to make clear that in case such an outrageous act of exclusion should occur, then not only should financial support be denied, but it would never be reimbursed once the problem is worked out. That is a loophole that still exists in that law and some interested citizens should take an interest in it.

Obviously no country should sit silent in the presence of anti-Semitism. No country should be cowed by the mores of the United Nations into silence in the face of rank anti-Semitism. We should not accept an interpretation of the UNIFIL mandate that is prejudiced in its implementation against Israel, nor should we accept practices that contribute to creating and preserving bitterness among Palestinian refugees through the UNRWA program. Obviously we should not fund the PLO and its activities against Israel or indeed in any activities at all.

I think it is just as obvious that we should not attempt to enforce against Israel standards and practices which are not invoked against other nations. The Fourth Geneva Convention is an example of this. Because some U.S. administration at some time on some occasion acquiesced in a formulation, that should not bind all succeeding U.S. administrations on all succeeding interpretations. Just because a mistake was made, there is no reason we should transform it into a precedent and then honor it.

The points I have made are so far are relatively obvious. It is just as clear that the United States should always guard against slowly, subtly acquiescing in the double standards to which Israel is regularly submitted. We should never seek to require Israel to negotiate with those who do not negotiate in good faith, nor should we pretend that good faith exists when it does not, nor should we ever take part in a process which submits Israel into an unreasonable demand to which if she acquiesced her security would be endangered. That is another kind of double bind which contributes eventually to the characterization and branding of the state of Israel as an international outlaw. Above all, I think we should work never to be affected by the cumulative corruptions and corrosive temptations and pressures of majority opinion in the United Nations nor of bloc politics.

We should insist on fair play for the state of Israel as well as for the

United States and all other nations. This is more difficult than one who has not lived in that body might imagine. But the rewards are enormous.

I should like to end by saying that to remain silent in the face of an outrageous injustice is to make oneself an accomplice. The consequences are demoralization for oneself and injustice for the victim. To take part in a righteous struggle is an exhilarating reward. It is reward enough. I have made new friends, found new purposes and have thoroughly enjoyed my part in the struggle. This prize is an absolutely unanticipated, and utterly delightful, welcome *embarras de richesses.*

2
Variations on a Theme

CONDEMNING ISRAEL: THE IRAQI REACTOR

Let me begin by congratulating our current president, the distinguished ambassador from Mexico, who has acquitted himself with distinction in carrying out his difficult responsibilities, showing so keen a sense of the importance which the international community attaches to these deliberations. May I also congratulate the distinguished ambassador from Japan, who last month earned the esteem of the entire Council by managing our affairs with singular deftness.

The issue before the Security Council in the past week—Israel's attack upon the Iraqi nuclear reactor—raises profound and troubling questions that will be with us long after the conclusion of these meetings. The Middle East, as one prominent American observed last week, "provides combustible matter for international conflagration akin to the Balkans prior to World War I," a circumstance made all the more dangerous today by the possibility that nuclear weapons could be employed in a future conflict.

The area that stretches from Southwest Asia across the Fertile Crescent and Persian Gulf to the Atlantic Ocean, is, as we all know, torn not only by tension and division, but also by deeply rooted, tenacious hostilities that erupt repeatedly into violence. In the past two years alone, one country in the area, Afghanistan, has been brutally invaded and occupied, but not pacified. Afghan freedom fighters continue their determined struggle for their country's independence. Iraq and Iran are locked in a bitter war. And with shocking violence, Libya, whose principal exports are oil and terror, invaded and now occupies Chad. Lebanon has its territory and its sovereignty violated almost routinely by neighboring nations. Other govern-

Address before the Security Council, June 19, 1981.

59

ments in the area have, during the same brief period, been the object of violent attacks and terrorism. Now comes Israel's destruction of the Iraqi nuclear facility. Each of these acts of violence undermines the stability and well-being of the area. Each gravely jeopardizes the peace and security of the entire area. The danger of war and anarchy in this vital strategic region threatens global peace and presents this Council with a grave challenge.

My government's commitment to a just and enduring peace in the Middle East is well-known. We have given our full support to the efforts by the Secretary General to resolve the war between Iran and Iraq. Our abhorrence of the Soviet Union's invasion and continued occupation of Afghanistan—against the will of the entire Afghan people—requires no elaboration on this occasion. For weeks, our special representative Philip C. Habib has been in the area conducting talks which we still hope may help to end the hostilities in Lebanon and head off a conflict between Israel and Syria. Not least, we have been engaged in intensive efforts to assist in the implementation of the Egyptian-Israeli treaty, efforts that have already strengthened the forces for peace in the Middle East and will, we believe, lead ultimately to a comprehensive peace settlement of the Arab-Israeli conflict in accordance with resolutions 242 and 338 of the Security Council.

As in the past, United States policies in the Middle East aim above all at making the independence and freedom of people in the area more secure and their daily lives less dangerous. We seek:

- The security of all the nations and peoples of the region;
- The security of all nations to know that a neighbor is not seeking technology for purposes of destruction;
- The security of all people to know they can live their lives in the absence of fear of attack and do not daily see their existence threatened or questioned; and,
- The security of all people displaced by war, violence and terrorism.

The instability that has become the hallmark and history of the Middle East may serve the interests of some on this Council—it does not serve our interests and it does not serve the interests of our friends, be they Israeli or Arab.

We believe, to the contrary, that the peace and security of all nations in the region is bound up with the peace and security of the area.

It is precisely because of my government's deep involvement in efforts to promote peace in the Middle East that we were shocked by the Israeli air strike on the Iraqi nuclear facility and promptly condemned this action, which we believe reflected and exacerbated deeper antagonisms in the region which, if not ameliorated, will continue to lead to outbreaks of violence.

However, although my government has condemned Israel's act, we know it is necessary to take into account the context of this action as well as its consequences. The truth demands nothing less. As my President, Ronald Reagan, asserted in his press conference:

> . . . I do think that one has to recognize that Israel had reason for concern in view of the past history of Iraq, which has never signed a cease-fire or recognized Israel as a nation, has never joined in any peace effort for that. . . . it does not even recognize the existence of Israel as a country.

With respect to Israel's attack on the Iraqi nuclear reactor, President Reagan said: ". . . Israel might have sincerely believed it was a defensive move."

The strength of U.S. ties and commitment to Israel are well-known to the members of this Council. Israel is an important and valued ally. The warmth of the human relationship between our peoples is understood. Nothing has happened that in any way alters the strength of our commitment or the warmth of our feelings. We in the Reagan administration are proud to call Israel a friend and ally.

Nonetheless we believe the means Israel chose to quiet its fears about the purposes of Iraq's nuclear program have hurt, not helped, the peace and security of the area. In my government's view, diplomatic means available to Israel had not been exhausted, and the Israeli action has damaged the regional confidence that is essential for the peace process to go forward. All of us with an interest in peace, freedom, and national independence have a high stake in that process. Israel's stake is highest of all.

My government is committed to working with the Security Council to remove obstacles to peace. We made clear from the outset that the United States will support reasonable actions by this body which might be likely to contribute to the pacification of the region. We also made clear that my government would approve no decision that harmed Israel's basic interests, was unfairly punitive, or created new obstacles to a just and lasting peace.

The United States has long been deeply concerned about the dangers of nuclear proliferation. We believe all nations should adhere to the Non-Proliferation Treaty. It is well-known that we support the International Atomic Energy Agency and will cooperate in any reasonable effort to strengthen it.

We desire to emphasize, however, that security from nuclear attack and annihilation will depend less on treaties signed than on the construction of stable regional order. Yes, Israel should be condemned; yes, the IAEA should be strengthened and respected by all nations. And yes, too, Israel's neighbors should recognize her right to exist and enter into negotiations with her to resolve their differences.

The challenge before this Council was to exercise at least the same degree of restraint and wisdom that we demand of the parties directly involved in the Middle East tensions. Inflammatory charges, such as the Soviet statement that the United States somehow encouraged the raid, or that we knew of the raid beforehand, are false and malicious. One can speculate about whose interests are served by such innuendo. Certainly the spirit of truth, restraint or peace are not served by such innuendo. Certainly the process of peace is not forwarded.

Throughout the negotiations of the last days, my government has sought only to move us closer to the day when genuine peace between Israel and itsjuArab neighbors will become a reality. We have searched for a reasonable outcome of the negotiations in the Security Council, one which would protect vital interests of all parties, and damage the vital interests of none, and which would ameliorate rather than exacerbate the dangerous passions and divisions of the area. In that search we were aided by the cooperative spirit, restrained positions and good faith of the Iraqi Foreign Minister Sa'dun Hammadi. We sincerely believe the results will move that turbulent area a bit closer to the time when all the states in the region have the opportunity to turn their energies and resources from war to peace, from armaments to development, from anxiety and fear to confidence and well-being.

CONDEMNING ISRAEL II

Like other members of this Council, the United States does not regard this as a perfect resolution. With respect to the resolution, I must point out that my country voted against the resolution in the International Atomic Energy Agency which is referred to in the present resolution. We continue to oppose it. In addition, our judgment that Israeli actions violated the UN Charter is based solely on the conviction that Israel failed to exhaust peaceful means for the resolution of this dispute. Finally, we also believe that the question of appropriate redress must be understood in the full legal context of the relationships that exist in the region.

Mr. President, nothing in this resolution will affect my government's commitment to Israel's security and nothing in these reservations affect my government's determination to work with all governments of the region willing to use appropriate means to enhance the peace and security of the region.

Address before the Security Council, June 19, 1981.

A CONSTANT FRIENDSHIP

Mr. President, as the General Assembly is aware, this subject was debated at length last June in the Security Council, where matters alleged to be a threat to peace and security are properly brought. The Security Council at that time was able to arrive at the satisfactory conclusion of a unanimous vote which took into account all the relevant aspects of the attack on Tammuz.

My government believes that no useful purpose is served by continuing this debate here today. The matter has already been dealt with in a constructive fashion in the Security Council. All members of the Security Council supported that procedure for dealing with this subject. In our view, action by the General Assembly on this topic, coming as it does on the heels of Israel's condemnation yesterday, does not contribute to the cause of peace in the Middle East. On the contrary, the contentious, unbalanced resolution before this body can only complicate the search for peace in the Middle East.

The present resolution departs in important ways from Resolution 487 adopted unanimously in the Security Council. The present draft speaks unwarrantedly of Israel's "aggression," a legal term scrupulously avoided by the Security Council. Such a characterization raises troublesome legal questions and prejudges thoughtful deliberations and a judicious outcome. The United States government objects strenuously to the use of that term, and insists that such actions must be viewed in their total context, which includes Iraq's refusal to accept the international consensus formulated in Security Council Resolutions 242 and 338 and its refusal to make peace with Israel.

Mr. President, this debate, which has been engendered by the introduction of this provocatively worded item, diverts our attention from what should be the focus of United Nations efforts, namely, the pursuit of peace and security in the Middle East. Two states in the region, with encouragement and appropriate participation of my country, have worked for the last several years in a practical way toward a comprehensive settlement of disputes which have plagued the area for decades. Critics feel that the Camp David process is painfully slow and doomed ultimately to failure. They seek instead an instant solution in one huge leap, willfully disregarding the obstacles and pitfalls which have undermined previous peace efforts. To them I would point out the enormous progress that has been made to date between Israel and Egypt, progress that has met the legitimate

Address before the 36th General Assembly, November 12, 1981.

security needs of each country, has opened the way toward normal commercial and diplomatic relations, and constitutes the only realistic prospect of achieving a lasting peace and a just resolution of the Palestinian problem.

We are now being asked to consider questions that are both irrelevant to this debate and a hindrance to the stated goal of regional peace. The United States, for instance, is asked to cease our arms and other relationships with Israel. Mr. President, the United States' friendship with Israel is a constant and an enduring fact of our foreign policy. It springs from traditions and values shared by the citizens of both countries. It will not be altered by occasional differences over actions taken by one nation or another. Mr. President, various countries in this body provide nuclear technology and large quantities of arms to states in the region. Yet this resolution asks no one to cease supplying arms and other military assistance to Israel's neighbors. The United States, therefore, strenuously objects to the entirely unwarranted and inappropriate language concerning this country's relationship with Israel. We consider this language unbalanced and unfair.

A similar attempt at distraction from the goal of regional peace is the call for the Security Council to investigate Israel's nuclear activities. We oppose any such effort to engage the Security Council in an unbalanced politically motivated activity. In this connection, however, I would like to point out that my delegation has supported resolutions adopted by the General Assembly proposing a nuclear weapons free zone in the Middle East. We support this goal as a way of addressing the issue of nuclear arms in that region.

Finally, Mr. President, I must also object strenuously, and as a matter of principle, to the call for enforcement action in paragraph five of the draft resolution. This would only aggravate tensions at a time when the United Nations should be doing its utmost to reduce tensions and defuse potential causes of conflict. It is for the above reasons, therefore, that my delegation will vote against the proposed resolution.

PERPETUATING THE
ARAB-ISRAELI CONFLICT

Recently, in the United States statement on the "Question of Palestine," we said that, "The United Nations is more than a weapon in one side's political armory. It must not align itself with forces working against a final settlement between Israel and its Arab neighbors by repudiating the sole existing framework provided for in the Camp David accords for the just resolution of the Palestinian problem in all its aspects. Rather than continue to repeat the errors of the past, it is vital that the United Nations not be exploited for partisan purposes and that it strive to preserve the principles of balance and equity on which it was founded."

The General Assembly, unfortunately, chose a different course. It adopted a number of resolutions which depart substantially from Security Council Resolutions 242 and 338, criticize the Camp David accords, and seek to enhance the international status of the PLO, an organization that refuses to accept the basis for any negotiations—Resolutions 242 and 338—and Israel's right to exist.

The adoption of these resolutions by the General Assembly diminishes the ability of the United Nations to further the cause of peace in the Middle East.

Today, the Assembly addresses a new item: "The Situation in the Middle East." One might assume that under this rubric, the General Assembly would want to address the grave issues that now threaten the region. Surely there are enough of them. Iran and Iraq are enmeshed in a seemingly endless war. Iran is plagued with serious internal disorder. Lebanon is struggling bravely against destabilizing forces. Libya pursues subversion and terror beyond its borders. Throughout the region, in fact, the forces of moderation must contend with elements which promote violence, extremism, and instability. And of course the threat of Soviet expansion hangs over the entire region. The Soviet occupation of Afghanistan, as well as the presence of Soviet-bloc military personnel elsewhere in the region, threatens the independence of all nations in the Middle East.

All of these issues should be of vital concern to this Assembly. All ought to be addressed under the item before us today. Yet neither the report of the Secretary-General, nor the speeches of most participants in this debate, have addressed these issues. Instead, the focus of this debate has again been

Address before the 36th General Assembly, December 14, 1981.

on one item, and one item alone: the Arab-Israeli conflict. Once again, the same arguments are repeated, and the attacks on the only successful peace negotiations in the entire history of the Arab-Israeli dispute—the Camp David accords and the Egyptian-Israeli peace treaty—are renewed.

What is accomplished by the endless stream of criticism directed at one member state of this organization? What are the people of my country to conclude when they witness year after year these condemnations of Israel, a friend and fellow democracy?

Indeed, we feel constrained to point out—once again—that the words and actions of the United Nations on this question serve only to undermine further the reputation of this body and its ability to help bring about peace between Israel and her Arab neighbors.

The character of the debate is especially regrettable since the United Nations should be devoting its energies, resources and moral authority to a non-partisan effort to achieve a permanent peace in the Middle East.

With respect to the question of a comprehensive peace between Israel and her Arab neighbors, I want both to review events and look ahead. The basis of peace is to be found in Security Council Resolutions 242 and 338. Those resolutions flow directly from the principles of the United Nations Charter, which require the peaceful settlement of disputes and prohibit the threat or use of force against the territorial integrity of any state.

Mr. President, the United States is fully aware of the complexities of the Arab-Israeli conflict. For this very reason we do not believe that peace can come about by willfully disregarding the obstacles and pitfalls that have undermined previous peace efforts. Certainly it cannot be achieved without recognizing the legitimate rights of the Palestinians and the right of all states, including Israel, "to live in peace, within secure and recognized borders, free from threats or acts of force," as provided in Resolution 242. My government concluded some time ago that the only path toward peace was through negotiations among those who are sincerely committed to peace.

Consider the significance of what has happened on the Israeli-Egyptian border.

These two countries, defying past practice, boldly looking beyond ancient antagonisms toward reconciliation, decided to negotiate with each other and were able to sign a peace treaty in March 1979. Equally important, they began negotiations for the establishment of full autonomy for the Palestinians of the West Bank and Gaza.

Predictably these negotiations have been and will continue to be difficult. But the dedication of my government to their successful completion will not flag, for they remain the only existing realistic approach to achieving a comprehensive settlement.

There are those in the Middle East who appear to have a stake in the perpetuation of the Arab-Israeli conflict and who have done everything possible to subvert the Camp David peace process. We particularly condemn all acts of intimidation and violence whose purpose is to discourage this process. Surely, Mr. President, the time has come to transcend the animosities of the past—animosities that otherwise will continue to be exploited by others outside the region for their own ends.

I want to conclude my remarks, Mr. President, by quoting from the Preamble to the Camp David Framework, which called the historic initiatives leading up to that agreement "an unprecedented opportunity for peace which must not be lost if this generation and future generations are to be spared the tragedies of war."

The government and people of the United States are fully committed to the success of the Camp David peace process. We are resolved to build upon the gains already made.

GOLAN AND POLAND

My country opposes the resolution sponsored by Jordan for reasons which are of importance not only as regards the proper disposition of the current matter before us—that of Israel's Golan Heights legislation—but also out of concern for the future of the United Nations and the ability of the Security Council to perform a positive role in the maintenance of world peace and security.

The resolution with which we are confronted today constitutes, we believe, an aberration, even a perversion of the very purpose which the Security Council is called upon by Chapter VII of the United Nations Charter to perform. Article 39 vests in the Security Council the responsibility to deal with activities that threaten world peace and security. The role the Security Council is called upon to perform is, by definition then, a constructive role: to prevent "an aggravation of the situation." This resolution, we believe, would do the opposite. Far from preventing aggravation, it would become a source of aggravation.

Indeed, it has already succeeded in exacerbating the terribly difficult problems of the Middle East, in dividing people whose cooperation is needed to solve problems, in sowing suspicions and feeding hostilities. A

Address before the Security Council, January 20, 1982.

flood tide of invective has flowed through this hall threatening day after day to overwhelm the spirit of reason and compromise with hatred and cynicism.

The United States has tried hard to demonstrate its determination to be fair and reasonable in confronting the situation in the Golan Heights. We have refused to be drawn into vicious exchanges, or distracted from the search for real solutions that will render more safe and secure the real lives of actual people in the region.

We will not be deterred from our course. We will continue to search for constructive means to achieve peace for Israel and her neighbors.

We believe that a good place to begin is indeed with the implementation of the resolutions of the Security Council of the United Nations. We believe that Security Council Resolutions 242, 338 and 497 can serve as the basis of that constructive search. We urge the implementation of all three.

Mr. President, on this occasion, and in this place where there has been so much talk of aggression, repression and the desire of peoples to live in peace, I cannot forebear to mention the problems of another people in the world who are now being denied peace and self-government. What an extraordinary institution this is that, in the more than a month since the massive, brutal repression of the people of Poland got under way, there has been no mention here of the violations of their human rights, of the violations of the United Nations Charter, the Helsinki Final Act, the Universal Declaration of Human Rights that have occurred there. We should like on this occasion to express our solidarity with the people of Poland as well as with those of the Golan and to affirm the commitment of my government to work for the rights of all peoples currently denied freedom, self-determination and self-government.

Mr. President, we do not approve Israel's annexation of the Golan Heights. Indeed, we do not even believe such annexation has occurred. We believe we should get on with negotiations which will demonstrate that fact.

THIS MISERABLE RESOLUTION

The resolution before this emergency special session of the General Assembly is profoundly objectionable to the United States. We oppose it because it does not contribute to peace in the Middle East: it will make peace harder to achieve.

We oppose the end it seeks—which is revenge and retribution, not conciliation and compromise.

We oppose the means it recommends: which are unreasonably punitive and ill-suited to accomplishing any constructive purpose.

We oppose the use of the United Nations involved here because this body was and is meant to be devoted to building peace and security, and this resolution seeks neither. Instead, it uses this body as an instrument to deepen divisions and exacerbate conflicts.

We oppose this resolution because, like any other cynical use of power, it will leave this body weaker than it already is, less fit to achieve its noble purposes.

By damaging the prospects for peace, this resolution undermines the integrity—indeed, the very raison d'etre—of the United Nations.

Last month in the Security Council the United States voted against a resolution on Israel's Golan Heights legislation because, as we stated at the time, the resolution constituted "a perversion of the very purpose which the Security Council is called upon by Chapter VII of the United Nations Charter to perform." That purpose is to prevent "an aggravation of the situation." The resolution before us today, like the previous resolution, does not prevent an aggravation of the situation: it is itself a source of aggravation. It is also procedurally flawed in that it seeks to assign to the General Assembly responsibilities that Chapter VII of the Charter properly and solely invests in the Security Council.

The United Nations has discussed the Golan Heights legislation now for nearly two months. As my delegation made clear at the outset, we opposed this legislation because it purported or appeared to alter unilaterally the international status of the Golan Heights. Therefore, on December 17th the United States joined other members of the Security Council in passing Resolution 497, thereby making clear our disapproval of the Israeli government's action in extending its civil law over the Golan Heights. We communicated the same message in our bilateral relations.

As we have stated often, the future of the Golan Heights, like that of all the occupied territories, can be resolved only through negotiations pur-

Emergency Special Session of the 36th General Assembly, February 5, 1982.

suant to Security Council Resolutions 242 and 338. Accordingly, we have called upon Israel to rescind its legislation and—most importantly—to reaffirm its commitment to a negotiated solution. In its letter of December 29th to the Secretary-General, Israel did, in fact, reaffirm its readiness to enter into unconditional negotiations with the Syrians over the international legal status of the Golan Heights.

At that point, the only constructive role for the United Nations was to facilitate such negotiations, in accordance with Resolutions 242 and 338. But the resolution before the Security Council did not even mention these resolutions and, needless to say, the current draft resolution doesn't either.

Mr. President, we must go back to basics. Israel is accused of threatening peace. Yet peace is not the situation that prevailed between Israel and Syria before Israel's Golan Heights legislation was adopted. Security Council Resolution 338, which was the basis for the 1973 ceasefire, called upon the parties to "start immediately" to negotiate the implementation of Resolution 242 so that Israeli withdrawal could be effected in exchange for recognition of Israel's existence within "secure and recognized" borders. But no such negotiations took place.

There is no one in this chamber who does not know which party has refused to negotiate peace or even to accept Resolution 242. Yet the resolution before us today and the speeches we have heard take no account of this reality.

Mr. President, the United States greatly desires to have cordial, cooperative, good relations with all the states in the region. My country has devoted enormous effort, in this administration and under previous administrations, to finding a basis for peace and reconciliation. We also want very much a strong United Nations acting in fidelity to the principles of its Charter. For these very reasons we are appalled by this resolution which distorts reality, denies history and inflames passions.

The draft resolution before us calls the Israeli legislation an act of aggression. But no shots were fired, no soldiers were brought into place. And the future of the Golan Heights is no less negotiable than before.

It describes the Israeli legislation as an annexation. It is not. The United States has not recognized it as such. The Security Council in Resolution 497 did not recognize it as such. To now call it annexation only creates an artificial obstacle to negotiations.

This resolution calls for comprehensive sanctions against Israel and for Israel's total isolation from the rest of the world. But can anyone truly believe that such proposals, advanced in a spirit of vindictiveness, will make a constructive contribution to peace?

Mr. President, the United States objects to this resolution because it makes the search for peace more difficult, and because it weakens this body.

We also object to it for less disinterested reasons—we object to the barely veiled attack on the United States present here in the paragraph that "strongly deplores the negative vote by a permanent member. . . ."

The right to cast a veto is vested by the Charter in the five permanent members of the Security Council. The sole purpose of this provision is to permit one of the permanent members to block a proposed action of the Council if for any reason this action is deemed seriously flawed. The United States used the veto for the purpose for which it was intended—to block action which we deemed ill-conceived and imprudent and, moreover, one incompatible with the pursuit of international peace and security to which this body is dedicated. It is not at all appropriate that an action taken in conformity with the spirit and the letter of the Charter should be deplored.

Furthermore, as everyone present understands, this resolution raises basic questions which go to the heart of the relationship of a member state to the United Nations. This is a profoundly serious matter, filled with ominous portent. Questions of membership in this body and its associated agencies should not, indeed cannot be settled by majority passions. The United Nations or any similar organization can only exist if the principle of majority rule is balanced by respect for minority rights. This resolution strikes twice at the principle that minorities also have rights: first when it deplores our use of the veto, and second when it attempts to submit questions of membership to the General Assembly. Respect for the United Nations means respect for its Charter.

We hope that the authors and supporters of the resolution will think deeply about this aspect of their approach, for the health, even the survival of the United Nations depends on respect for both majority rule and minority rights. Nothing is more clear than this.

Mr. President, suppose this resolution passes, as regrettably I suppose it will, what will this exercise have achieved?

An Israeli withdrawal from the Golan? Of course not.
An embargo of economic, technological, military goods destined for Israel? Of course not.
A restoration of the occupied territories? Of course not.
A resolution of the problems of Palestinians? Of course not.
Peace in the Middle East? Of course not.
Will it intimidate the United States, causing it to abandon its Middle East policy, its friendship with Israel, its search for peace in the region? Of course not.

What then, will this resolution accomplish?

What has already been achieved by these weeks of harsh, seemingly endless attacks on Israel, on the United States, on the spirit of reason, moderation, on peace itself? To raise the question is to answer it.

There is, in my country, a child's rhyme, sticks and stones may break our bones but words will never hurt us. The rhyme is profoundly mistaken. Words have consequences.

Words express the ideas, the values and the truths we live by. They are the principal means available for reason to explain purposes and dispel misunderstandings. The United Nations was conceived as a palace of reason, a place where reason would replace violence as the tool for settling disputes.

This miserable resolution before us today demonstrates the sad truth that any instrument can be made to serve purposes remote from its raison d'etre: words can be used as weapons; ploughshares can be turned into swords, and the United Nations itself can be used to polarize nations, spread hostility, and exacerbate conflict.

The use made of the United Nations in this resolution and in the weeks preceding it is indeed worth "strongly deploring" and my government strongly deplores it.

Naturally we shall vote no.

EXACERBATING PROBLEMS

The United States profoundly regrets and strongly condemns the senseless act of violence that occurred on April 11, 1982 at one of Islam's most sacred mosques—the Dome of the Rock. We extend our condolences to all those who have suffered physically and spiritually from this act.

Last Friday, April 16th, President Reagan met with six ambassadors delegated by the Islamic countries represented in Washington. I should like to read the official report of that meeting. President Reagan, it said:

> Expressed his deep personal sorrow and that of all Americans over last Sunday's violence at the hands of a deranged individual in an area sacred to three of the world's great religions.

> The President expressed his sympathy with the concern of the Islamic world over the disruption of the tranquility of one of its most holy shrines. This concern is shared by the members of all faiths. He reiterated his conviction that the peace of the holy places of Jerusalem must be maintained and

Address before the Security Council, April 20, 1982.

confirmed the dedication of the United States to encouraging the conditions necessary for the wellbeing of all those who draw their spiritual inspiration from that city.

The President called upon all the governments and peoples of the Middle East to work to decrease tensions in the area and prevent further acts of violence and loss of life.

We understand that this goal—to decrease tensions in the area and prevent further acts of violence and loss of life—is also the chief objective of the Security Council.

We have considered the matter carefully in our government; regrettably, we do not believe that the resolution before us helps to achieve our shared objective. For these reasons we think it serves no constructive purposes but will further embitter the peoples of the region and deepen the divisions that could lead to conflict. Thus, as much as we condemn the act of violence that occasioned this debate of the Security Council, we must oppose this resolution which, in our view, would make new acts of violence more—not less—likely to take place in the future.

We voted against the resolution because it contains language in the preambular and the operative paragraphs which implies that the responsibility for this terrible event lies not with the individual who was responsible for the incident but with the Israel authorities who have unequivocally denounced the act. The text also implies that Israel has hindered the efforts of the Higher Islamic Council to perform its responsibilities for the administration of the holy places whereas the evidence is that Israel has, in the main, carefully respected the Council's role. To eliminate any misunderstanding, Mr. President, I may add that our vote does not affect our longstanding position on the status of Jerusalem. As President Reagan explained to the Moslem ambassadors last Friday, the United States' position remains as previously stated, that is, that the final status of Jerusalem can only be determined through negotiations among all concerned parties.

PEACEKEEPING IN LEBANON

For the past week the government of the United States has worked alongside other governments in this body and alongside you to negotiate a text that would have the support of the government of Lebanon, the troop

Address before the Security Council, February 25, 1982.

contributors and others who support this important peacekeeping operation. We have also sought a text that would be acceptable to Lebanon's neighbors and respect the vital national interests of all concerned. We believe that the Council has succeeded in negotiating such a resolution. An observer of the Council's activities might wonder why, in fact, it has been so difficult to find consensus on a question about which there was so little disagreement, the question of whether the Council should or should not support General Callaghan's request that 1000 troops be added to the UNIFIL contingent. And we do regret that the Council could not take the simple, straightforward step of enlarging the UNIFIL forces without adding to the resolution some elements that seemed to us extraneous to the basic purpose of the resolution. We regret that it is so difficult here to take constructive action without obstructive, ad hominem attacks on one another.

Mr. President, the government of the United States is nonetheless pleased to support this resolution which provides General Callaghan the additional 1000 troops for the UNIFIL forces which he has said he needed to accomplish his task, to provide the soldiers under his command with the reinforcement and the leisure that they require. My government is committed to the task of extending and reinforcing the sovereignty and troubled area. We are committed also to restoring the sovereignty and the territorial integrity of the government of Lebanon. We believe that the cycle of violence that afflicts the area is profoundly dangerous to the security, peace and well-being of the region and should be addressed in all its aspects and complexities. We expect that the reinforced troops of UNIFIL will be able more effectively to deal with the incursions and violations of all kinds and from all sources. To help achieve these goals, the government of the United States offers its moral, political, financial, and diplomatic support. We also work through our bilateral and regional diplomacy to achieve these goals. We desire to express our gratitude and admiration of the efforts of the distinguished representative of the United Nations Secretariat for his hard work on behalf of peace in this troubled region. Finally, we offer our best, warm wishes to General Callaghan and the UNIFIL troops as they continue their terribly important task.

WAR BY OTHER MEANS

In a letter to President Kittani, which has been circulated at my request as a document of the General Assembly, I stated the reservations of my government with regard to the "resumption" of the Seventh Emergency Special Session on "The Question of Palestine." I desire to repeat these reservations here.

The Seventh Emergency Special Session adjourned "temporarily" on July 19, 1980, having adopted a resolution which authorized "the President of the latest regular session of the General Assembly to resume its meetings upon request from member states." It seems plain that the purpose of this "temporary" adjournment was to allow for a resumption in the same time frame should events warrant. Almost two years have passed. During those intervening twenty-one months, two regular sessions of the General Assembly, two different emergency sessions, and one special session have been held. Yet now, at the request of a group of members and notwithstanding the passage of a substantial period of time, the Seventh Emergency Special Session has been reconvened without regard to the views of other members, or the developments that have taken place in the interim. Clearly, this dubious procedure of a "resumption" has the effect of undermining the provisions of the rules of procedure for convening an emergency special session.

This procedural irregularity provides a fitting framework for the work of this session, which is already on its way to creating new, further obstacles to peace between Israel and her Arab neighbors.

Let me be clear. My government shares the concern of those who are alarmed at the escalation of violence in the Middle East. We are profoundly distressed at the increase of tensions and conflict, the spreading of fear and suspicion, the deepening sense of hopelessness with respect to resolving "The Question of Palestine" and achieving peace and stability in this region rent by violence and hate.

But who among us sincerely believes that the exercise in which we are now engaged—this "resumed" emergency special session—will take us closer toward the goal?

Who among us believes that the cause of peace is served by still another round of bitter denunciation of Israel?

Who among us—I wonder—believes that peace is even the *goal* of this Assembly?

This Assembly can repeat its familiar and unbalanced charges, it can

Emergency Special Session of the 36th General Assembly, April 23, 1982.

issue flamboyant ultimata, and adopt ever harsher resolutions, all with the usual predictable effect. That effect will be to increase—not reduce—tensions; to inflame—not to calm—passions; to widen—not to narrow—divisions; and to make war more, not less, likely to take place.

The fact that this institution, conceived to resolve conflicts, is thus used to exacerbate and embitter divisions among nations is the cruelest of ironies.

But that is not the end of the irony. It is even worse that the United Nations, by its own actions, is being driven further and further away from the very framework of peace which *it* established fifteen years ago. I refer, of course, to Security Council Resolution 242. That resolution remains the only realistic framework for a just and lasting peace in the Middle East. But it is not reaffirmed, it is not even recalled in the current United Nations resolutions, which—to the contrary—violate the spirit of Resolution 242 and undermine its balanced approach to peace.

Security Council Resolution 242, along with Resolution 338 which was adopted in 1973 and which calls for immediate negotiations to implement 242, is built around four main principles:

First, it links Israeli withdrawal from territories occupied in 1967 to the establishment of peace with the Arab parties to the conflict.

Second, it stipulates that Israel should then withdraw to secure and recognize boundaries established in the agreements of peace.

Third, it affirms that agreements of peace should also provide for security arrangements, including demilitarized zones, and guarantees of maritime rights through all the international waterways of the area.

Fourth, it affirms that the goal is true peace, as distinct from "declarations of non-belligerency" or their equivalent.

It was precisely according to this resolution of the United Nations Security Council, and the principles set forth therein, that peace has been achieved between Israel and Egypt, leading to the return of the entire Sinai to Egyptian sovereignty—a process that is due to be completed this very Sunday. That process, which is based on mutual respect and reasoned argument, stands in stark contrast to a different approach which insists on Israeli withdrawal in the absence of peace. The second approach cannot possibly achieve its putative goal, which is a negotiated peace; but, by ensuring confrontations, it can produce spurious "evidence" that peaceful settlement of disputes with Israel is impossible.

My government believes that peace can only be achieved through respect, reason, and compromise. We recognize that while the Camp David process looks toward a comprehensive peace, it has not yet achieved that goal. It constitutes the greatest concrete step toward peace, however, in the history of the Arab-Israeli conflict. And, yet, it is but a step. There remains a great distance still to be travelled. But we believe peace is possible—real peace, peace in accordance with Security Council Resolutions 242 and 338.

We certainly do not underestimate the obstacles to peace settlement in the West Bank and Gaza. Yet we believe that Camp David offers the only viable basis for a settlement that will determine the final status of these territories. Camp David actually goes beyond Resolutions 242 and 338, which call for an agreement among states, by affording the indigenous populations of the West Bank and Gaza the opportunity to participate in the negotiations toward a settlement. Such a settlement can only be achieved through negotiations between the parties concerned—in this instance Egypt and Israel, as well as Jordan and the representative of the Palestinian people. These negotiations still await the establishment of a self-governing authority in the West Bank and Gaza and the agreement of Jordan to enter the talks.

This painstaking and protracted process will require hard bargaining, compromise, and arrangements that establish trust and new patterns of interstate and human relationships. But that is the only way that a just and lasting peace can be achieved. Only such an approach can hope to satisfy to the greatest degree possible the rights of all the parties concerned. Only such an approach can work.

We are now reaching a point when new efforts will be devoted to the completion of the Camp David process. It would be a great tragedy if this process must go forward in the face of opposition from the United Nations. The peace process might suffer, and more certainly the United Nations itself would suffer.

Mr. President, there are, as everyone knows, members of this body who desire to deny membership and/or participation to another member state. There will be, we understand, an effort to pass, in this special session, a resolution that prepares the way for questioning Israel's credentials and the right to participate in the various bodies of the United Nations. To this end, one draft resolution circulating in the corridors now asserts that Israel is not a peaceloving member state, and has repeatedly violated the provisions of the Charter.

But Mr. President, neither this special session nor the draft resolution now circulating in the corridors is consistent with the purposes of the United Nations Charter. Neither seeks (in accordance with Chapter II) to maintain "international peace and security," nor "to develop friendly relations among nations," nor "to achieve international cooperation in solving international problems . . ."; lest of all do they make this institution "a center for harmonizing the actions of nations in the attainment of . . . common ends." This special session is one more event in an ongoing process whose goals are to delegitimize a member state—Israel, to deny it the right to self defense, to secure borders, to survival.

This special session and its accompanying draft resolutions are one more clear example of a strategy whose goals and tactics are clear: use a United Nations body to make "official" demands incompatible with Israel's security and survival, so as then to be able to complain that non-compliance with these impossible demands "proves" Israel an international law-breaker—unworthy of membership in the international community of peaceloving states.

Mr. President, if this organization established to seek, maintain and strengthen peace is used to make war by other means; if its avenues, established to provide a rational basis for discussion and settlement of international disputes, are used as battlefields in a holy war; if its procedures, designed to ensure fairness, are twisted to ensure desired political outcomes—then the purposes and structures to this organization are transformed. And the United Nations itself is transformed. It becomes, quite literally, a different organization, inspired by different purposes, dedicated to different goals, characterized by different modes of behavior; for an institution is, finally, nothing more or less than the regular interactions of its members. When the goals and behavior of the members change, the institution has changed as well.

Mr. President, how much falsification can an institution stand without destroying itself entirely? This world body cannot endure as a moral and political force if its energies are devoted to increasing conflict and conducting vendettas against targeted countries. If the United Nations prefers to make political war rather than peace, it must suffer the consequences in terms of its credibility and reputation. And if, in violation of its own rules, it should decide to exclude the democratic state of Israel from participation, it will inevitably reap the whirlwind.

It is not too late, Mr. President, for a majority of member states to reverse the trend toward irresponsibility and destruction. The time to begin is now, before this trend gathers an irreversible momentum.

THE CYCLE OF VIOLENCE IN LEBANON

I desire to offer an explanation of vote on behalf of my government. Mr. President, the objective of my government is to end the bloodshed and the cycle of violence in Lebanon and to restore full respect for the sovereignty, territorial integrity and independence of that troubled land.

Two previous resolutions of this Council, Resolutions 508 and 509, contained balancing language that took account of the fact that the conflict in Lebanon and across the Lebanese-Israeli border is complex in its origins and that its resolution will require compliance in deed as well as in word with the resolutions of the Security Council.

Unfortunately, the resolution now before us is not sufficiently balanced to accomplish the objectives of ending the cycle of violence and establishing the conditions for a just and lasting peace in Lebanon. For that reason, Mr. President, the United States voted against this resolution.

My government, Mr. President, is now currently engaged in every possible effort to bring the violence to an end. We shall continue those efforts.

LEBANON: A ONE-SIDED APPEAL, A TWO-SIDED CONFLICT

The United States is never indifferent to the sufferings, insecurity or deprivations of human beings caught in war, occupation or natural disasters. Certainly, we have been deeply concerned with the hardships visited on the people of Lebanon during the current conflict. The Lebanese people, we know, have too long suffered violence at the hands of unwanted intruders, unwelcome invaders and occupiers. The concern of my government for the people of Lebanon has been and is being actively expressed in the large contributions for emergency humanitarian aid made by my government, by the appointment of a special administrator for aid and by implementation of extensive, humanitarian aid programs in the region. President Reagan has asked the Congress to provide a total of some $65 million in humanitarian emergency aid for the people of Lebanon. The

Address before the Security Council, June 8, 1982.
Address before the Security Council, July 29, 1982.

President's special envoy, Ambassador Phillip Habib, has worked indefatigably in his efforts to restore peace to Lebanon and a degree of territorial integrity and sovereignty that the government has not enjoyed for
too many years.

Mr. President, there is no room for doubt among reasonable men and
women, I believe, about the commitment of the United States government
to the peace, independence and sovereignty of Lebanon; indeed, for our
commitment to peace, national independence and sovereignty of all nations. Yet, we see serious problems with the resolution proposed by my
friend and distinguished colleague, the representative of the government of
Spain, for the following reasons: First, because of inadequate time either to
gather or confirm the facts about the situation in Beirut and the problems
of access; Second, because of an inadequate opportunity to consult with
our government; and third, because this resolution, we believe, is lacking in
a certain, serious balance which would give it greater weight. It is, surely, in
the first instance, the Palestine Liberation Organization that imposes itself
on the civilian population of Beirut. But, the resolution proposed by my
distinguished colleague from Spain does not ask that that armed force
abandon its occupation of Beirut or desist in its military activities. It calls
only on Israel. Yet everyone understands that Israel seeks to affect supplies
to the PLO forces, not to the civilian population of Beirut.

Mr. President, the United States welcomes the concern of the Security
Council and of the humanitarian agencies of the United Nations for the
suffering in Lebanon, as we welcome the concern of this body for an end to
human suffering everywhere. But, Mr. President, we feel that a one-sided
appeal in a two-sided conflict suggests purposes that are political as well as
humanitarian, and we cannot support these. Certainly, we cannot support
them on the basis of inadequate notice and inadequate information. We
call, therefore, upon the Council to take the time necessary for more careful, balanced consideration of this most serious, wrenching problem. I ask
the suspension of this session to permit consideration and consultation
with our governments.

Mr. President, I should like to say that the United States finds it impossible to participate in such a procedure, strongly objects to the procedure
employed here today, and suggests that it will be impossible for this Council
to function if members are not to be provided an opportunity for consultation with their governments.

In Support of UN Peacekeeping

The Lebanese people are once again enduring the agony which has been too often, too consistently their lot in the last troubled years. Today as we meet during the agony of Lebanon, the purpose and the commitment of the United States government remains the same as it has been during these past painful months—to support the legitimate government and people of Lebanon and the restoration and preservation of their independence, sovereignty, territorial integrity throughout the land and to their internationally recognized borders.

The United States shares the view expressed by the government of France that the international community should assume greater responsibility for assisting the people of Lebanon. We welcome all constructive contributions to bring peace to Lebanon, this time a peace which can perhaps endure. We welcome, therefore, the suggestions of our colleague from the United Kingdom as well.

The people of Lebanon have suffered too long, endured too many months, the torments of violence, death, occupation. They have lived too long in the midst of uninvited participants in their destiny. They deserve a much better fate. They deserve more help from the international community.

The United States position, with regard to a United Nations peace-keeping role in Lebanon, is clear and consistent. Although efforts are made from time to time to cast doubt on our support for a UN peace-keeping role in Lebanon, we have supported a UN peace-keeping role in Lebanon with our votes, our diplomacy and our financial contributions. We have also actively supported a maximum role for UN observers in Lebanon. Repeatedly during the last year, we have sought to enlarge the number and to extend the deployment of these observers in order to reinforce the fragile cease-fires which have from time to time been agreed to, only then, tragically, to be broken.

We have made repeated efforts, formal and informal, alone and conjointly with others on the Security Council and in the United Nations body to enhance the role and participation of UN forces in the tasks of peacekeeping. We worked, for example, arduously at the time when a fragile cease-fire was achieved at the end of September 1983. We had worked in the months prior to that and we will continue our efforts to this end.

Parties to the complex, multi-sided Lebanese conflict have changed. United States government support for a United Nations peace-keeping role

Address before the Security Council, February 16, 1984.

that can perform constructive tasks in an effective manner to bring peace to this country has remained constant. There should be no doubt in anyone's mind about our commitment. Today, as in the past, the United States supports authentic, international peace-keeping efforts in Lebanon. We will support any reasonable proposal concerning real, effective UN participation in helping, constructively, to solve the tragic problems of the region. Yesterday, Secretary Schultz, in Washington, made this clear when he said that "it would be useful to state once again that a UN presence would be useful throughout Lebanon, particularly for such purposes such as protecting Palestinian refugee camps" and reinforcing cease-fires.

He noted, the UN role presumes a return to stability, a balance of forces and some measure of political accord. All of those are, of course, goals we have been pursuing for quite some time. Mr. President, Secretary Schultz' words were reinforced and reiterated by the President in his conversations with the press yesterday and will be reiterated again today, as I understand it.

We have noted that too often our efforts in this Council, in this body have been hampered and marred by the efforts of certain parties to gain short-range political advantage. And too often those efforts to gain short-range political advantage have taken priority over the search for peace. The efforts of some members of the Council to utilize to the fullest existing facilities and authority for UN participation in peace-keeping in Lebanon have been hampered by the pursuit of short-range political goals on the part of some parties.

The United States does not and has not pursued short-range, national political goals in Lebanon. That is also not the purpose of our participation in the Multi-National Force. It never has been. We believe that the United Nations has available today actual or potential instruments in Lebanon which might be useful: a fifty-man observer group (UNTSO), which could be doubled, we understand, on short notice; a nearly 6,000-man peace-keeping force (UNIFIL) in southern Lebanon, much of which is deployed in areas where violence is no longer a major threat.

The United States has consistently supported a UN peace-keeping role. We have been ready to consult with our colleagues on this Council the composition and deployment of such a force. We remain ready at this time to enter serious discussions with our colleagues on the Council and in the Secretariat concerning the composition and deployment of UN forces, preferably throughout Lebanon, to achieve these goals. The United States proposes no pre-conditions. We are ready to participate when our colleagues are ready in the achievement of these goals which may finally bring relief to the suffering people of Lebanon.

REGRETTING SOVIET TACTICS IN LEBANON

The United States seeks to affirm in this public place our high regard for the careful manner in which you have conducted the affairs of the Council during this month of your presidency, and also our respect for the manner in which the French permanent representative has pursued with both patience and skill the effort to achieve a resolution today—a resolution which might provide a new element of peace in the tragic Lebanese situation.

The United States will vote in favor of this resolution and will do so as part of a long-standing and continuing effort to help to re-establish and reinforce the peace necessary for the restoration of the territorial integrity, unity, sovereignty and independence of Lebanon. We will vote in favor of the resolution because we hoped that this resolution would contribute to an end of the violence that maims and kills, without regard to age, role, religion or social condition, its Lebanese targets. The United States will vote for the resolution because we hoped and expected that it might contribute to the protection of Lebanon's civilian population—Palestinians, Druze, Shiites, Sunni Moslems, Christians of all varieties, that is, of all Lebanese people. These have been the goals of United States policy and they remain the goals of United States policy.

We have understood from the beginning of the whole tragic series of problems in Lebanon that international cooperation would be necessary to the restoration of peace and sovereignty in that country. To these ends, the United States has encouraged and participated in international efforts to reinforce peace and self-government in Lebanon. We have worked for many months in the United Nations and outside it, joining in successive resolutions, supporting existing deployments and advocating much broader deployments of UN observers, seeking an enhanced United Nations role. We have worked outside the United Nations, alone and with others, to assist the government of Lebanon to reinforce its peace and consolidate its authority to exercise its sovereign control over its own territory. To these ends we have participated in the Multi-National Force, which force was created because of the unavailability at the time of a United Nations force for that purpose.

The United States has payed a high price for its efforts on behalf of Lebanon. Our embassy has been bombed. Many Americans and others were killed in that bombing. Nearly 300 young American marines, in

Address before the Security Council, February 29, 1984.

Lebanon precisely for purposes of peace-keeping, were murdered as they slept.

Major obstacles have been placed in the way of Lebanon's unity, sovereignty and peace. It is unfortunate to learn today that more obstacles will still be placed in the way of serious efforts to reinforce, achieve and enhance Lebanon's unity, sovereignty and peace. There has been less clarity than desired in much of the public discussion about these obstacles.

Again and again one reads and hears that the terrible violence in Lebanon of the past weeks is the nearly inevitable consequence of Lebanon's tribal and confessional heterogeneity, of the traditional rivalry and hostility among Lebanon's traditionally warring groups. We have heard and read a great deal more today about the internecine tribal, confessional conflicts, and about the presence of Israeli troops in the south, than we have heard about the more than 50,000 Syrian troops and Palestinian and Iranian and other associates in Lebanon. We have heard much less about the systematic use of violence—violence systematically encouraged from outside Lebanon for the purpose, precisely, of preventing unity, sovereignty and peace in Lebanon.

Turning now to the resolution, the United States would like to comment that the establishment of the peace-keeping force of the sort foreseen in the resolution would, if it were to be constituted, stand in a long and distinguished record of UN peace-keeping efforts.

Beginning in 1947 with the United Nations Truce Supervision Organization in Palestine, the United Nations military observers in Kashmir, the United Nations Observer Group in Lebanon in 1958, the United Nations Emergency Force in the Middle East and the Congo, United Nations peace-keeping forces have proven to be an important adjunct to carrying out the primary purposes of the United Nations Charter.

It is never untimely to remind ourselves of those primary purposes of the Charter. They are of course:

1. the maintenance of international peace and security,
2. the maintenance of national sovereignty and independence,
3. the maintenance of territorial integrity of member states, and
4. the alleviation of massive suffering and the protection of fundamental human rights of civilian populations.

Those are noble purposes. The organization was created to serve them. It has served them well with its peace-keeping efforts.

Those peace-keeping efforts have not proved inconsistent ever with the protection of the inherent rights of nations to individual or collective self-defense, which rights also exist under the Charter. The United Nations peace-keeping efforts, indeed, have not proved themselves inconsistent with the rights of any nations or any peoples. It therefore becomes particularly unfortunate that no new peace-keeping effort is to be permitted by this body this day.

If the United Nations were to be permitted to undertake an enhanced peace-keeping role today in Lebanon, we would have on behalf of the United States further and more detailed commentary of the precise terms of the resolution. Since, unfortunately, our Soviet colleague has told us of his intention to veto, I see no useful point to be served by any more explicit commentary on the text of the resolution. I would simply say in commenting on this unfortunate situation and its unfortunate outcome that the Soviet representative has spoken today sowing hate, watering it with lies, and harvesting violence, refusing to cooperate while attacking others precisely for refusing cooperation.

The United States is sick of these calumnies addressed against us. We are sick of the habit of accusing others—and us quite particularly—precisely for actions and policies which are not ours but theirs. The United States regrets these tactics on behalf of our Soviet colleagues. We hope they will abandon these tactics. We hope they will even reconsider their opposition to a new and constructive peace-keeping role for the United Nations in Lebanon for the purpose of enhancing the peace and sovereignty and security of those people who have suffered so long.

Restoring Peace in Lebanon

The United States strenuously objects to the false charges and unfair attack of the representative of the Ukraine. We object strenuously because those attacks absolutely distort and misrepresent our purposes and our policies in Lebanon.

By voting for this resolution, which it believes to be a very imperfect resolution, in many ways an unsatisfactory resolution, the United States government was expressing, in as clear a fashion as possible, its strongly held commitment to the view that all foreign forces should be withdrawn from Lebanon, that the Lebanese population—Christian, Moslem, whatever—should be left, without outside interference from any quarter, to seek

Address before the Security Council, February 29, 1984.

a civilized agreement that would respect the rights and preserve the freedom of all.

Lebanon, we believe, has been and can be an independent, democratic state. As an independent, democratic state, Lebanon exercised its right, under Article 51 of the Charter, to self-defense and to request others to assist in that self-defense for the purpose of reinforcing and maintaining its sovereignty and independence. The United States responded, as did others in the Multi-National Force, to the request of the legitimate government of Lebanon. We have had no purpose there except to assist in the restoration of peace, sovereignty and independence of Lebanon and any suggestion to the contrary is at best profoundly misinformed.

THE QUESTION OF PALESTINE

The United States voted against the resolutions before this body this afternoon because we found those resolutions to be unbalanced, unfair and unpromising. They will not achieve their stated goals. Mr. President, the United States has great sympathy for the people of Palestine, which sympathy we express through large and continuing humanitarian support and social service supports of many kinds through many years. We see these human victims of political warfare as we see refugees everywhere: as tragic residues of the violent politics of our times.

Mr. President, the United States regards these resolutions as an unwarranted and outrageous interference in the internal affairs of the United States. The Charter does not give the General Assembly jurisdiction over the foreign policy of member states, except in those rare instances where those foreign policies are a clear threat to peace and international security as determined by the Security Council to be so. In considering the call for a Middle East Conference in Resolution A/39/L.40, the United States believes that it is also necessary to take into account Resolution A/39/L.20. These two items must be linked in our consideration because they are linked inevitably in their subject matter. Resolution A/39/L.20 charges Israel with not being a peace-loving state. Yet that charge will be linked by our actions this afternoon to the call for an international conference on the Palestinian resolution. Obviously, Mr. President, it is at best inconsistent to apply sanctions against a country and at the same time invite it to a

Address before the 39th General Assembly, December 11, 1984.

conference. It is the justice of Alice in Wonderland: judge first, investigate later. Such an attitude could not possibly lead to good faith negotiations. Good faith negotiations include the subjective concept of honest intent and purpose and also include the objective test of how the matter would appear to a reasonable person in the same circumstances.

This resolution, by its very nature, violates both these concepts of subjective honest intent, of objective fairness. It evidences neither intent and purpose aimed at negotiated solutions, nor is it likely by any subjective test to induce all concerned parties to join in a negotiated solution. Yet the Vienna Convention on Treaties imposes on us all an obligation to negotiate in good faith. This means that each side is to propose and counterpropose, to listen to the other side and speak with the intent of actually arriving at an agreement with which the two sides can live. The process is very important. There is to be give and take, constantly narrowing the original differences until an agreement is finally reached. Good faith requires that such a process be gone through. Unfortunately, the resolution before us subverts the very idea of process.

It precludes a negotiating process. It declares at the outset what the aim of those negotiations are—they are to confirm what the General Assembly declares to be the truth, that totally untenable, unfair assertion that the state of Israel, of all states in this body, is a non-peace loving state. Mr. President, there are many reasons that the idea of an international conference is fatally flawed. One wonders how many nations in this body would support an international conference to resolve the border disputes in which they find themselves. Would Peru and Ecuador submit their border dispute to an international conference of this sort called for here? Would Venezuela and Guyana submit their border dispute to such determination? Indeed, would the United Kingdom and Argentina submit their border dispute to this outcome?

Mr. President, we all know that the conference called for here, whose outcome is already provided, would be an exercise in ideology and in wary by other means against the state of Israel—a propaganda exercise. By calling for a conference under these prejudicial conditions, the fairness of the body is put in question. Mr. President, the United Nations, we believe, should not put its fairness in question. We believe that the United States has the right to have its sovereignty respected, that the state of Israel has the right to expect fair play from this body, and indeed that the peoples of the world have the right to expect that our efforts toward peace and the resolution of conflicts will be good faith efforts toward peace and the resolution of conflict.

Mr. President, I find that one of the resolutions, Resolution A/39/L.39, provides as good evidence as any of the caricature of fairness present in these resolutions. I refer to point D, which calls upon the Department of Public Information in full coordination with the Committee on the Exercise of the Inalienable Rights of the Palestinian People to, and I quote, "publish newsletters and articles in its respective publications on Israeli violations of the human rights of the Arab inhabitants of the Occupied Territories."

Mr. President, I ask where is the dispassion in that requirement? Where is the concern for the human rights of all the inhabitants of that region? Where is the judicious spirit which all members and all peoples have the right to expect from this General Assembly?

A PEACE-LOVING STATE

Three days ago, I had occasion to explain the United States votes against a set of four resolutions submitted under the item: "The Question of Palestine." I wish today to state that the United States also opposes and will vote against Resolutions A/39/L.19 and A/39/L.20 because they are, if possible, more unfair, more unbalanced, more prejudicial and more dysfunctional than the four resolutions which this body considered on Tuesday and against which we spoke then.

At that time, Mr. President, we stated how utterly inconsistent and unproductive it was to accuse a state of being a "non-peace loving state" and then, virtually in the same breath, urge that state to attend an international conference—a conference devoted, mind you, to a search for "peace," as though that country, already branded a "non-peace loving state," might expect fair play from such a conference. We also stated that this prejudicial preparation for a conference, this prior judgment, could not possibly lead to good faith negotiations. We suggested that negotiations lacking good faith were not negotiations at all in any meaningful sense of that term. Such so-called negotiations would instead simply serve as a propaganda forum, a propaganda exercise, which would certainly make the attainment of peace more difficult rather than contribute to the achievement of that desirable goal. The United States opposes such a Middle Eastern conference, but we so note that any positive possibility such a conference might conceivably have are undermined by these types of resolutions.

The United States also objected strenuously to the unfair treatment and

Address before the 39th General Assembly, December 14, 1984.

disrespect shown in those resolutions on "The Question of Palestine" for the sovereignty of a member state of this organization. One of those resolutions, A/39/L.40, regretted the "negative response" of two governments toward such a conference. I mention this reference because one of the resolutions before us today, A/39/L.19, makes an equally inappropriate and unacceptable reference to the United States and to the way my country conducts its foreign policy. Once again, there is an unwarranted and unjustified interference in the internal affairs and decision-making of the United States. Once again, I should remind the General Assembly that its Charter does not give it jurisdiction over the foreign policy of the United States. Operative paragraph 10 of L.19 "considers" that the cooperative agreement between the United States and Israel "would encourage Israel to pursue its aggressive and expansionist policies. . . ." Mr. President, the United States considers this a false and offensive statement. We consider it, as well, misleading as to the likely consequences of our policies.

Mr. President, last night this body took note of an abusive practice which the United Nations has been guilty of for some time; it took note of the practice of singling out particular countries for special criticism. More importantly, last night we all took a step in the direction of correcting this abuse. As this body is aware, such selective name-calling is almost entirely reserved for the United States and Israel. It is very selective indeed. The Soviet Union goes unnamed in the resolution on Afghanistan; Vietnam goes unnamed in the resolution on Kampuchea—in both of these cases, aggressive, expansionist invasions and occupations took place. Yet no names are named. In the current resolution, there is fear that some policy might lead to an aggressive, expansionist policy. Yet names are named.

Last night, however, the General Assembly took the wise and courageous step of removing four derogatory references to the United States. This was done in the interest of fairness and justice, and in the interest of the United Nations' ability to play a constructive role in the future. We hope the General Assembly will do no less today. That is why my delegation has asked for a separate, recorded vote on paragraph 10 of L.19. We would hope, Mr. President, that this needed corrective action would continue, but we are faced today with another resolution which, although through its slightly veiled reference in L.20 to a permanent member of the Security Council which prevented the Council from adopting sanctions against Israel, would continue this obnoxious practice of selective name-calling.

These then, Mr. President, are my country's strong objections to the singularly offensive treatment of my country in these resolutions and, indeed, too often in this debate. They alone constitute ample reason for voting against the two resolutions. But there is more, and this goes to the thrust and overall purpose of the resolutions. These resolutions speak repeatedly of aggression, of threats to international peace and security, of the maintenance of international peace, of Israel as "not a peace-loving member state," and of wide-ranging sanctions in the military, diplomatic, economic, technological and cultural fields. They condemn, strongly condemn, reject, deplore, strongly deplore, etc.

Mr. President, the people of the Middle East, all the people of the Middle East—Arabs, Israelis and all other people in that region—desire peace. They need peace. They deserve better from this Assembly than the negative finger-pointing which these resolutions contain. They deserve a positive approach, hopeful ideas and a constructive spirit to come out of our debates. They deserve good faith.

The United States, for its part, will not be distracted nor will we lag in our efforts to work for peace between Israel and its neighbors. We believe that the basis for such a goal already exists in Security Council Resolutions 242 and 338, which call for direct negotiations and securable borders for all states in the region. A focus in our debates on practical means to implement these two resolutions could go far in bringing an equitable and comprehensive solution to at least one major dispute in the Middle East.

Terrorism in the Security Council

Today, we in the Security Council are asked to address the realities of the situation in Lebanon and the problems posed by the violence and counter-violence of the continuing conflict inside that country: that conflict takes place among the various groups of Lebanese citizens and is associated with the withdrawal of Israeli forces and the continuing presence of other foreign forces. These are matters of great concern to all of us. But, Mr. President, as the representative of the United States, I must call the attention of the Council to a matter of very special concern to my country.

My government has been subjected in the past week to direct threats against its nationals in Lebanon; nationals serving in peacekeeping task forces of the United Nations. Those threats have been specifically linked to our actions in the Security Council in a vile attempt to influence the participation and vote of the United States in this body.

The United States, of course, welcomes the assurances of the government of Lebanon that it does not encourage reckless behavior of this kind,

Address before the Security Council, March 7, 1985.

but seeks rather to discourage it. But none of us in this Council, and no one who values the work of the Council, can ignore the realities posed by these threats. Prior threats to the United States concerning a prior Security Council meeting in a not dissimilar context resulted in the grievous loss of American and Lebanese lives. I should like to remind the Council briefly of these facts.

A telephone message was received by the Agence France Presse office in Beirut on September 8, 1984. The caller, claiming to be a representative of the so-called Islamic Jihad organization, said the organization would strike very shortly at a "key American interest in the Middle East." The caller said his organization's members were prepared to sacrifice their lives to destroy American or Zionist institutions of even secondary importance. The caller also said that President Reagan's administration had demonstrated its "contempt" for Moslems when it vetoed, on September 6, the Security Council resolution, which had been submitted by Lebanon.

On September the 20th, at 11:30 AM Beirut time, a van approached the northern entrance access to the American Embassy Annex in the suburb of Awkar, northeast of Beirut. The Annex is located on a residential street, blocked at both ends by barricades. The driver of the van opened fire on guards at the barricades, disabling some of them. Under fire from other guards, the vehicle maneuvered through the barricades and proceeded toward the Embassy building. It was stopped by firing 20 feet short of the northern end of the building, still outside the compound proper, and at that point it detonated. The building was severely damaged, two American employees of the Embassy and ten Lebanese employees were killed in the explosion. Some 59 employees and visitors were injured, eighteen of them seriously enough to require hospitalization.

This time, in this not dissimilar context, as the Council considers once again a complaint of the government of Lebanon against Israel, the United States has received three specific threats which I should like to review with the Council.

On February 28, 1985, Observer Group Lebanon (OGL) headquarters received a report from a senior United States UN military observer of a threat against U.S. officers serving with UNTSO in south Lebanon if the U.S. vetoed the Lebanese resolution.

On March 1, 1985, a U.S. officer serving with OGL informed OGL headquarters of a second threat to American officers serving with the UN in south Lebanon. This threat was passed to American members of the team Tyre by a regular contact whose reporting was considered generally reliable. We have no evidence that this and the previous threat were connected.

On March 5, 1985, UN officials in Lebanon received a threat from "an important Amal representative" against Security Council members who used their veto on the Lebanese Security Council resolution. Specifically, a UN military official in Lebanon was told "countries which use their right of veto in the Security Council will face strong problems." The United States and the United Kingdom were specifically mentioned. Other less specific threats have also been received in the period of the past week.

Mr. President, the bitter legacy of the previous experience with violence in Lebanon, linked explicitly by threatening callers to Security Council action, lingers—presumably for all members of the Security Council and for all persons concerned with world order.

It is important that the Council take a moment to consider the ingredients of minimal world order. The United Nations Charter tells us that its central tenet must be freedom from fear—freedom from violent threats against the territorial integrity or political independence of the state—freedom from violent threats against any member of the United Nations, certainly against any member of the Security Council. This, one would have thought, is axiomatic, since the peril that arises from violations of this basic rule are readily apparent. Obviously, the Security Council cannot function effectively to maintain international peace and security, or even to *seek* to maintain international peace and security if its members are subjected to the use and threat of violence.

Mr. President, it has been suggested informally in the last days by certain persons in this body, that such threats are of little consequence and should not stand in the way of the pressing business of the Council. *But I should like to suggest that the Council has no more pressing business than maintaining its own processes free from intimidation and violence.*

I should like, too, to be clear—the United States does not seek a pretext to raise the issue of terrorist threats. The United States does not seek to avoid discussion of the situation in Lebanon. Quite the contrary. The United States stands ready to discuss and to join in constructive action on Lebanon's problems. For this reason we urged, at the last meeting of the Security Council, a resumption of direct talks between military representatives of Israel and Lebanon in Naqura in order to facilitate a more peaceful Israeli withdrawal. For this reason we have strongly supported the Secretary-General's recommendations concerning the restoration of peace in this area.

Mr. President, on instructions from my government, I brought our concerns about threats to American personnel to the attention of the Secretary-General. The United Nations headquarters saw fit, on the basis of its own review of the situation, to call for the withdrawal of United States personnel from United Nations peacekeeping forces in Lebanon. I should like to emphasize that the United States has been and continues to be a warm and active supporter of United Nations peacekeeping functions in Lebanon and outside it. We have consistently sought in the past two years to enlarge the role of United Nations observers and United Nations peace-keeping forces in Lebanon.

Mr. President, we cannot imagine a greater chilling effect on the peace-keeping functions of the United Nations or on the free exchange of ideas than threats and use of violence. No process of discussion, debate, compro-mise, or rational decision-making can possibly take place under the threat of violence. *This body is, therefore, directly threatened by threats against any member of this Council in relation to any process of this Council.*

Mr. President, the United States remains committed to rational discus-sion, debate and decision-making by this Council, and we remain com-mitted to the work of the Council in seeking a solution to Lebanon's continuing agony. Our own goals with regard to Lebanon are clear. They are: the withdrawal of all foreign forces for which we have voted repeatedly and which we have repeatedly urged; a stable and secure Lebanese-Israeli border for which we have worked from the time of Resolutions 242 and 338 down to the present day; and the extension of central government authority over all Lebanese territory, including the south. The United States welcomed the announcement of the second phase of the Israeli withdrawal from Lebanon, which marks a further step in Israel's plan for a full withdrawal. The United States is convinced that the best hope for peace and security for the people of southern Lebanon will be a rapid and coordi-nated Israeli withdrawal resulting in the restoration of Lebanese govern-ment sovereignty and control over the region and the withdrawal, indeed, of all foreign forces from Lebanon and the restoration of full sovereignty of the government of Lebanon in all its territory.

In this regard, the United States has repeatedly called on all parties to exercise restraint and to seek to break the violent cycle of action and reaction which has resulted in the loss of life and destruction of property: an end to this human tragedy that has wracked Lebanon in these recent years. We have especially urged the parties to take advantage of the Naqura process as the best means of arranging these desirable ends.

Mr. President, there *is* a cycle of violence in Lebanon. That cycle of violence is fed by unbalanced, unfair resolutions, as well as by terrorism, aggression, retribution and hate.

The most pressing question before the Council today is whether the cycle of violence that has wracked Lebanon will be permitted to spread to this body, itself, endangering this last enclave in which the parties to a conflict may come and seek a hearing from the nations of the world.

The Security Council can function only if the parties to conflict respect the right of all members to speak and vote according to their best interests and their best judgment. No member of the Council, of the General Assembly or, indeed, of any United Nations body is safe if intimidation, coercion, violence are admitted into the deliberations of our institutions. The United States, therefore, calls on members of the Security Council to repudiate the threats against the deliberative process of the Council itself.

THE AGONY OF LEBANON

On behalf of the United States delegation and of the United States in its role as host government of the United Nations, I should like to convey to the Soviet delegation the sincere condolences of my government on the occasion of the death of the Chairman of the Presidium of the Supreme Soviet of the Union of Soviet Socialist Republics, Konstantin Ustinovich Chernenko. We should also like our condolences to be extended to his family.

At a time when representatives of our two governments are about to begin discussions in Geneva on ways to reduce and finally eliminate the danger of nuclear war, this solemn occasion reminds us of the grave responsibilities which we bear for the maintenance and strengthening of world peace. The decision of the Soviet and American delegations in Geneva to begin their discussions on schedule, despite the passing of Chairman Chernenko, demonstrates both our commitments to this process.

Mr. President, I should also like to extend the condolences of the American delegation and of the United States in our role as host country to the family and government of Prime Minister Tom Adams of Barbados, who died yesterday. Prime Minister Adams gave distinguished, courageous and democratic leadership to the Barbadians, and we greatly regret this loss.

Mr. President, the United States regrets that it is confronted here in this Council with a resolution which it cannot support. My country is, in fact, deeply committed to peace for the people of Lebanon and sovereignty for the government of Lebanon. The United States would greatly prefer to join in a consensus resolution which commits this body to a sincere effort to deal with the problems of Lebanon, while respecting the rights of all member states of the United Nations. We would have been happy to join in negotiations to the end of achieving such a consensus resolution and, in a

Address before the Security Council, March 12, 1985.

spirit of good faith and good will, to have worked to find a formulation that addresses the needs of Lebanon and the possibilities for peace.

Indeed, Mr. President, the United States is *still* ready to join in a statement that reflects the dismay of the Council concerning the escalation of violence in Lebanon, expresses our deepest sympathy to victims of that violence, urges restraint on all parties, calls on all parties to implement recommendations contained in the Secretary-General's report, affirms the application of the Fourth Geneva Convention to the occupied areas of Lebanon, reaffirms our commitment and that of all members to the full restoration of Lebanon's sovereignty, independence, territorial integrity and unity. We also would be happy to join in any action by the Council which took account of the threats of violence aimed at these deliberative processes.

Unfortunately, Mr. President, the government of Lebanon was uninterested in an approach which would have had the support of all members of this Council and, instead, came to the Council with a resolution it declined to modify in any way. We regret that the government of Lebanon declined to discuss the text. We regret that the government of Lebanon presented an unbalanced resolution in the first place.

The United States government has worked long, hard and very sincerely to assist in securing the withdrawal of all foreign forces from Lebanon. We support the Secretary-General's report. We support the Naqura talks for an orderly withdrawal of Israeli forces. The United States government worked hard and in good faith to create conditions that will restore full sovereignty to the government of Lebanon and the control of all of Lebanon's territory to the people of Lebanon.

Our efforts, alas, have met no success, so far. The tragic cycle of violence in Lebanon continues. Peace has not been brought to Lebanon because too many parties in and around Lebanon have preferred conquest to peace. Foreign troops and foreign groups in Lebanon join warring, indigenous factions in drenching that tragic land in blood. There is a cycle of violence in Lebanon, and that fact in the world is not altered by its denial in this Council.

Mr. President, the United States believes that this resolution does not accord Israel fair treatment. We believe this debate has not accorded Israel fair treatment. We believe it has not respected the realities of Lebanon. We are disturbed that the lack of fairness apparently does not embarrass many members of this Council. The fact is that members of the United Nations have a habit in this body of accusing Israel of the most extraordinary crimes.

It has not been very long since a long list of speakers accused the government of Israel of poisoning thousands of Arab schoolgirls. But investigation by international health authorities found no evidence of that poisoning. On another occasion the government of Israel was accused of the wanton murder of refugees in Ein-el-Hilweh. But objective investigation established that no murder had taken place. I cite these examples not to exculpate Israel of any wrongdoing, but to point to the profound and persistent hostility to Israel which is repeatedly manifested in this body. That hostility, which singles out the state of Israel, is manifest even when this body confronts violence done to Israel. That hostility unfortunately leads, I believe, to unbalanced decisions, unbalanced resolutions.

The resolution we have considered today is such an unbalanced resolution. We believe that it applies double standards; indeed, we believe that double standards have dominated the deliberations, as we believe that doublespeak was the *lingua franca* of much of this debate.

We note that the representative of Vietnam, whose 200,000 troops wreak war on the people of Cambodia, is concerned about the presence of foreign troops in Lebanon. We note that Cuba, who has foreign troops stationed in a dozen countries in the world, is concerned about the violation of the sovereignty of Lebanon. We note that the PLO condemns violence here— Israeli violence, of course. We note that it was Syria who assured us of how happy Lebanon is to have Syrian troops in Lebanon.

Mr. President, the United States ardently supports the withdrawal of all Israeli troops from Lebanon. We have worked to that end, we will do so in the future. The United States sincerely supported Resolutions 508 and 509, and we sincerely supported, then and now, the withdrawal of all foreign troops from Lebanon and the enjoyment of full sovereignty by Lebanon. The United States opposed Israel's entering Lebanon in the beginning. We fully support the applicability to Lebanon's occupied territories of the Fourth Geneva Convention. But, Mr. President, we cannot acquiesce in this resolution because we do not believe an unbalanced resolution will end the agony of Lebanon.

The United States believes it is not too late for the Security Council to reaffirm its commitments to peace in Lebanon. We believe it is not too late for the Security Council to engage in a serious search for constructive means to that end. In the meanwhile, the United States will vote against the resolution.

Part II
THE UNITED STATES
IN THE WORLD

3
The Americas

BOLIVAR, WHO LOVED LIBERTY*

With Louis Aguilar

It is a very great pleasure to be here today to participate in the celebration of one of the most distinguished men of the modern age, Simon Bolivar. I believe we are gathered today, not to engage in polemics, in attacks or counter-attacks, but to celebrate this great man whose life and work have so profoundly shaped Latin America, the Americas, the Western world, and, indeed, the modern world. It is a very great privilege for me to be able to address this group on this occasion.

One hunded years ago representatives of a group of Latin American states gathered in Caracas to honor Simon Bolivar's memory on the centennial of his birth. The delegates to that conference of 1883 met to discuss issues of Latin American solidarity and sovereignty, and to seek practical means to improve understanding between the Spanish-speaking nations on the continent. That conference, which was inspired by one convened in Panama in 1826 by Bolivar himself, was, in turn, the starting point for other meetings of the nations of the Americas. Today, one hundred years later, we in this world body could well repeat the opening words of the resolutions adopted by that first centennial conference: "The greatest and most solemn tribute that can be paid to the Liberator's memory by . . . the republics attending the centennial celebration is to bring new life to the ideas and goals that Bolivar formulated and pursued during his brilliant public career."

Without doubt, that constituted the maximum tribute one hundred

Address before the UN General Assembly, July 22, 1983.

years ago. Without doubt, it continues to be so in our day. To give sub-stance to the tribute, however, we must first identify key aspects of Simon Bolivar's "ideas" and "goals"—and explore their very essence.

Their common source was, we know, the oath that Bolivar took when he scaled Monte Sacro, outside Rome—the Aventine Hill in the outskirts of the city where the plebians once met to voice their protests against the abuses by Roman patricians and aristocracy. The young Bolivar had gone to the historic site with his mentor, Simon Rodriguez. He had observed Europe and the progress that it was making, but for Bolivar the solution to what he called "the great problem of man living in freedom" lay in Amer-ica, in his own continent. At Monte Sacro, near the Tiber, he pledged his efforts to achieving liberty for his homeland and to finding ways to provide security for free men.

Bolivar's whole life was guided by his view of freedom as a goal, and his aim throughout was to forge the best possible government, which, for him, was the government that would guarantee liberty. By virtue of his thought and actions, as statesman and as soldier, Simon Bolivar is the great apostle of freedom. That is why the title bestowed on him by the municipality of Caracas in 1813 was so appropriate; they named him "the Liberator," and he accepted the title, saying it was "more glorious and gratifying . . . than the sceptre of all the empires on earth." Years later Simon Bolivar con-fessed: "My overriding passion . . . and my greatest weakness is my love of liberty . . . My impetuous passion, my greatest longing is to win the name of lover of liberty." That passion places Bolivar at inevitable odds with every form of servitude; his views are irreconcilably opposed to all systems that would seek to limit man's freedom to serve any dogma or any State.

Bolivar's writings are full of his concern to define suitable forms of government for Latin America once independence had been won and nor-malcy could be restored. Contrasting the needs of war and peace, he said in his address to the Constitutional Congress of Peru: "Now that the nation has achieved domestic tranquility and political freedom, it must not per-mit any rule but the rule of law."

Bolivar believed that freedom is the natural state of men in society. He believed that the rights of individuals should be limited only minimally in the interests of society as a whole, and that the state's true function is to protect those rights. He always held that "popular sovereignty is the only source of legitimate authority of states." For him "public opinion" was "the chief strength" that a government could have, and governments were obliged to respect it.

In 1828 Colombia was torn by civil strife, and Bolivar was granted lim-itless authority to govern. But even then he declined to use that limitless authority until a majority of the people of the republic had ratified the grant. And then he issued a decree ordering strict compliance by his government with the rule of law. He not only believed in freedom, he fashioned institutions through which freedom could be expressed and protected. He established a Council of State to act as a "buffer" on his powers during the state of emergency that had been declared. Even under those extraordinary circumstances he said, "I shall always be a defender of public freedom, and true sovereignty will remain an expression of the nation will . . . The people is the source of all legitimacy, and they know best what is right and just."

In his concern to protect freedom, Bolivar emphasized the importance of civilian rule. He declared, "I prefer the title of 'Citizen' to that of 'Liberator,' because the latter has its origins in war, but the former has its origins in law."

Freedom of thought and expression occupies a central place in Bolivar's writings on government. Evoking the lack of that freedom during colonial times, he declared before the Congress of Angostura, "We have been ruled more by deceit than by force . . . Slavery is the daughter of darkness; an ignorant people is the blind instrument of its own destruction. Ambition and intrigue abuse the credulity and lack of experience of men without political, economic and civic knowledge. These men accept pure illusion as reality; they take license for liberty, treachery for patriotism, and vengeance for justice." I must say Bolivar sounds a great deal like Plato in those sentiments, but he was always original as well.

The Liberator believed that once independence had been won, the only way to govern legitimately would be by listening to the will of the governed through a free press. "A ruler," wrote Bolivar to General Paez, "must listen to even the harshest truths, and once they have been heard, he must profit from them by correcting the evils that error causes." As he said to the president of the Council of Government of Peru, "Our abuses and ineptitude should be strongly denounced . . . [The press] should draw vivid pictures [of these things] to capture the minds of the citizens." To underscore the importance of public opinion, Bolivar pointed out that in monarchies, moralists and philosophers advised princes to consult with their vassals and heed their advice. He concluded that it was all the more "necessary to do so under a democratic government, where the will of the people, places the rulers in command so that they may do the greatest possible good, and not the least evil."

Bolivar was fully versed in the "Declaration of the Rights of Man" and the Bill of Rights, and he was the most enthusiastic of supporters of the guarantees of individual rights in the constitutions and laws of France, England and the United States. In the constitutional texts that he helped to draft, high priority was given to freedom of speech. The constitution of the republic of Venezuela of 1819 provides: "The right to express thought and opinion orally, in writing, or in any other form is the first and most precious gift of nature." And the draft constitution of Bolivia contained a similar formulation: "Everyone shall be entitled to express his thoughts orally or in writing and to publish them in the press free of prior censorship."

Bolivar's love of liberty, his defense of individual rights and his rejection of tyranny have made him from time to time the target of sharp criticism from proponents of theories that subordinate the human person to the state. They have maligned him to discredit his ideas and goals, but those ideas and goals have prevailed nevertheless, to the point where Bolivar's detractors have been forced to recant or alter their views—or at least to restate them as if they had—so as not to alienate freedom-loving peoples in the world, who see in Bolivar a hero and an example, as well as a source of encouragement in their own struggles to preserve freedom.

It would be wrong to conclude these brief remarks without speaking about one last subject of major concern to Bolivar, particularly because the subject is of the greatest relevance to this body, namely, his desire for international solidarity.

On the bicentennial of the Liberator's birth, we should honor his memory by dedicating ourselves to the defense of his dreams of justice and freedom in the continent, in the hemisphere, in the world. We should dedicate ourselves to moving nations living without full freedom towards the benefits of freedom and democracy; to persuading governments of the urgent need to create conditions necessary for democratic government through respect for human rights. Let us do these things as Bolivar suggested in speaking of the future that he sought for the American continent: "Let us see to it that love, with its universal bond, unites the children of the hemisphere of Columbus, and that hatred, vengeance and war are chased from our hearts, to be used only . . . on those against whom they may justly be used: against tyrants."

The United States is honored to participate in this celebration of the life, the dreams and the legacy of Simon Bolivar.

NICARAGUA'S EXTRAVAGANT, BASELESS CHARGES

In his letter requesting this meeting, the coordinator of the Nicaraguan government, Mr. Daniel Ortega Saavedra, made some extraordinary charges against the government of the United States. We naturally desire to respond to the grave charges that Mr. Ortega has leveled against our policies and our intentions.

The essence of Mr. Ortega's complaint is that the United States is about to launch a "large-scale military intervention" against his country. Thus he wrote, in the letter in which he requested the meeting, of "an ever increasing danger of a large scale military intervention by the armed forces of the United States [which] constitutes a grave threat to the independence and sovereignty of the Central American countries and to international peace and security." He spoke of the "interventionist strategy of the government of the United States" and of statements and "concrete actions that clearly evidence an intention to attack Nicaragua and intervene directly in El Salvador." To support his arguments, Mr. Ortega charges us with the "systematic repetition of . . . aggressive satements [which] seriously affects the normal conduct of international relations . . . with bellicose statements." The United States' actions, Mr. Ortega asserts, violate the Charter of the United Nations, the "principles and goals" of the United Nations, and constitute a "grave threat to the independence and sovereignty of the Central American countries and to international peace and security."

The attack made by Nicaragua is not haphazard; its charges are not random: The government of Nicaragua has accused the United States of the kinds of political behavior of which *it* is guilty—largescale interventions in the internal affairs of neighbors, persistent efforts to subvert and overthrow by force and violence the governments of neighboring states, aggressive actions which disrupt the "normal conduct of international relations" in the region—acts and intentions inconsistent with the Charter of the United Nations. These charges—as extravagant as they are baseless—are an interesting example of projection, a psychological operation in which one's own feelings and intentions are simultaneously denied and attributed—that is, projected—to someone else.

Hostility is the dominant emotion and projection the key mechanism of the paranoid style of politics which, much to our regret, has characterized the political behavior of the Sandinista leadership. The principal object of

Address before the Security Council, March 25, 1982.

Sandinista hostility, I further regret to say, is the government and people of the United States.

Nicaragua's new political elite—which calls itself Sandinista—has constructed a historical myth to justify its demand for full power. According to this myth, the United States is responsible for all problems and disasters—natural and social—that Nicaragua has ever suffered; the Sandinista anthem describes us as the enemy of mankind; and Sandinista ideology defines us as implacably opposed to national independence, economic development, and peace. Since the moment of their arrival in power the Sandinistas have predicted that the United States was about to overrun them. The Yankees are coming, they have reiterated. The counterrevolutionaries will get us if we don't silence criticism, mobilize the population, and destroy freedom.

The familiar totalitarian assertion that they are surrounded by enemies internal and external has been heard again and again to justify the elimination of opponents and the concentration of power in a tiny, one-party elite.

In the past two and one-half years, Nicaragua's hopes for greater freedom, democracy and security from government tyranny have very nearly died as the new rulers moved expertly first to establish and then, progressively, to exercise control over the various sectors and institutions of Nicaraguan society. The extension and consolidation of power has followed the pattern of "coup d'etat by installments" (Konrad Heiden's description of the Nazi seizure of near total power of German society).

One step at a time the Sandinista directorate moved against the faint-hearted "bourgeois" democrats in their ranks. One sector at a time they have moved against Nicaraguan society—now seizing radio, television stations, newspapers, now nationalizing new industries, now tightening control of the economy, now moving against the independent trade unions, now banning a bishop from access to television, now organizing and reinforcing the Sandinista defense committees that bring the revolution, with rewards, demands, and surveillance, into every neighborhood.

Alongside it all came a dramatic, extraordinary expansion of Nicaragua's army, militia and international role. Today's national guard is many times the size and strength of the one that reinforced Somoza's regime. It reinforces a political machine many times more sophisticated than Somoza's.

A political scientist describing the Nazis' consolidation of power in a single German town noted, concerning that process of destruction of society and politicization of human relations:

> Hardly anyone in Thalburg in those days grasped what was happening. There was no real comprehension of what the town would experience if Hitler came to power, no real understanding of what Naziism was.

It is no easier to understand what is happening to Nicaragua. And at each stage the government's demand for power has been accompanied by new charges concerning enemies without and within.

We are confronted in Nicaragua with the familiar patterns of doublespeak with which would-be totalitarian rulers of our times assault reality in the attempt to persuade us, and doubtless themselves, that making war is seeking peace; that repression is liberation; that a free press is a carefully controlled one. Thus on February 19, 1982, Daniel Ortega solemnly assured the opening session of an international conference (COPPAL) that the forced, violent transfer of Miskito Indians was naturally carried out only to protect their human rights.

In their statement of February 18, 1982, Nicaragua's Bishops described these forced relocations as involving grave violations of the human rights of individuals, families, and entire populations of peoples. These include:

- relocations of individuals by military operations without warning and without conscientious dialogue;
- forced marches, carried out without sufficient consideration for the weak, aged, women and children;
- charges or accusations of collaboration with the counterrevolution against all residents of certain towns;
- the destruction of houses, belongings and domestic animals; and
- the deaths of individuals in circumstances that, to our great sorrow, remind us of the drama of other peoples of our region.

Given this pattern, it is no surprise that last week, as Commander Ortega leveled new charges against the United States, the Nicaraguan government suspended its constitution and promulgated a new Law of National Emergency that threatens to eliminate the limited liberty and pluralism that remains.

- All discussions in the Sandinista-controlled Council of State of the proposed media and political parties laws have been suspended.
- The Ministry of Interior has made an unspecified number of "preventive arrests" of people who are *suspected* of having ties with counter-revolutionaries.
- Radio Catolica has been closed down indefinitely and all radio news programs, except official statements, are prohibited.
- *La Prensa* and all other media are required to submit news stories for prior censorship. Yesterday it was unable to publish since 50 percent of the paper was found objectionable.
- Opposition political leaders have been informed that they cannot leave the country; the passport of one politician was seized when he attempted to make a routine trip abroad.

- A new "patriotic tax" is to be imposed on businesses to help finance its latest mobilization campaign.

Thus the dialectic of revolution unfolds; liberation has already produced its antithesis in Sandinista Nicaragua. Old familiar arguments are invoked to justify new, more effective repressions.

It did not need to be thus. Nicaragua's new government could have satisfied the longing of its people for peace instead of making war on the people. They could have accepted the United States' offer of friendship. The United States government did not oppose the Sandinista rise to power. It has not attempted to prevent its consolidation. With our help, the government of Nicaragua received more loans in two years from the International Development Bank than the Somoza government had received in any *decade*. The fact that the United States government gave the Sandinistas moral and political support in the crucial phases of the civil war; cut off their opponents' supply of arms, ammunition and gasoline, and negotiated the resignations of Somoza and Urcuyo, did not affect the Sandinista leadership's view of the United States' attitudes—neither did the 75 million dollar supplemental aid bill rushed through Congress to assist in the job of reconstruction nor our active support for Nicaragua's credit applications in multilateral lending institutions. The United States provided more aid than any other government to the Sandinista regime during its first 18 months in power.

Did this support from the United States alter the Sandinista leadership's hostility? Alas, it had no such effect.

By its words and deeds, the United States government—the Congress and the executive branch—demonstrated not only its respect for the sovereignty of the Nicaraguan political process, the right of Nicaraguans to determine their own government, but also our desire to give a boost to Nicaragua's new government, to help it overcome the devastation of civil war. But Sandinista ideology overcame the reality of United States assistance. The fact of United States support for economic reconstruction and national independence in Nicaragua proved less powerful than the stereotype—we remained the Yankee enemy of mankind.

Like others in this century who have seized power by force, the Sandinista leaders are haunted by the expectation that they will fall victim to the violent intrigues by which they won power and exercise it.

It is, of course, *they* who systematically seek to subvert and overthrow neighboring governments. El Salvador has the misfortune to be the principal target.

A clandestine support system established in 1978 at the time of the Nicaraguan civil war continued to operate after the fall of Somoza in July

1979 with a new final destination—El Salvador. The existence of this support system has been repeatedly and vigorously denied by Nicaraguan and Cuban spokesmen. Yet a considerable quantity of solid information shows that those denials are false.

Nicaragua offers a support system with three major components: external arms supplies, training, and command and control.

Within weeks after the fall of Somoza in July 1979, the Sandinistas began to cooperate in support of the Salvadoran insurgents by establishing training camps and the beginning of arms supply networks. This clandestine assistance initially involved local black markets and relatively limited resources. In 1980, after meetings in Havana had unified Salvadoran Marxists into a single military command structure, the Sandinista leadership agreed to serve as a conduit for an arms trafficking system of unprecedented proportions, originating outside the hemisphere. That structure remains in force today.

Arms and ammunition for the Salvadoran insurgents reach Nicaragua by ship and occasionally by direct flights from Havana to Nicaragua. Three Nicaraguan ships, the Monimbo, the Aracely and the Nicarao, frequently transport arms and ammunition to Nicaragua from Cuba in their cargo. Salvadoran guerrilla headquarters near Managua arranges for their shipment into El Salvador. The timing of the resupply operations appears to be coordinated with the planned level of fighting, since before each surge in the fighting we have detected large deliveries.

When a clandestine shipment of arms is captured or a safehouse is found containing arms and terrorist supplies, it is often impossible to know with certainty whether the ultimate recipients are Guatemalan, Honduran, Costa Rican or Salvadoran terrorists, since the arms supply networks established by Cuba and Nicaragua are funneling lethal military supplies to terrorists and guerrillas in all four countries.

A few examples, chosen from among dozens, will illustrate the pattern of arms flow.

> The Papalonal airfield provides a clear case of the direct airlift of weapons from Nicaragua to guerrillas in El Salvador. Papalonal is a commercially undeveloped area 23 nautical miles northwest of Managua, accessible only by dirt roads. In late July 1980, the airfield was an agricultural dirt airstrip approximately 800 meters long, but by early 1981 the strip was lengthened by 50 percent to approximately 1,200 meters. A turnaround was added to each end. A dispersal parking area with three hardstands—a feature typical of a military airfield—had been constructed at the west end of the runway. Three parking aprons were cleared, and six hangar/storage buildings were constructed on the aprons; the hangars were used to stockpile arms for the Salvadoran guerrillas. C-47 flights from the airbase corresponded with sightings in El Salvador, and several pilots were identified in Nicaragua who reg-

ularly flew the route into El Salvador. This particular route was closed in March 1981, but some air infiltration continues to this day, despite difficulties in pilot recruitment.

Weapons delivery by overland routes from Nicaragua passes through Honduras. Several examples of this arms traffic can be identified. Honduran authorities have intercepted various shipments of arms en route from Nicaragua and in concealed caches in Honduras. In early January 1981, for example, Honduran police caught six individuals unloading weapons from a truck enroute from Nicaragua. The six identified themselves as Salvadorans and as members of the International Support Commission of the Salvadoran Popular Liberation Forces (FPL). They had in their possession a large number of altered and forged Honduran, Costa Rican, and Salvadoran passports and other identity documents. This one truck contained over 100 M-16/Ar-15 automatic rifles, fifty 81-MM mortar rounds, approximately 100,000 rounds of 5.56-MM ammunition, machine gun belts, field packs, and first-aid kits.

In April 1981, Honduran authorities intercepted a tractor-trailer truck which had entered Honduras at the Guasule crossing from Nicaragua. This truck was apparently heading for Guatemala. Ammunition and propaganda materials were hidden in the side walls of the trailer. The same arms traffickers operated a storehouse in Tegucigalpa, Honduras, with a false floor and a special basement for storing weapons.

A special legislative commission established in June 1980 by the Costa Rican legislature confirmed in its May 1981 report that a clandestine arms-supply link between Costa Rica and Nicaragua was established during the Nicaraguan civil war, and that the link continued to function between Costa Rica and El Salvador once the Sandinistas had come to power in Nicaragua.

In April and July 1981, Guatemalan security forces captured large caches of guerrilla weapons at safehouses in Guatemala City. Several of the vehicles captured at the Guatemala City safehouses bore recent customs markings from Nicaragua, thus suggesting that the operation was part of the well-established pattern.

Within the past three months, shipments of arms into El Salvador reached unprecedented peaks, averaging out to the highest overall volume since the "final offensive" last year. The recent Nicaraguan-Cuban arms flow into El Salvador has emphasized both sea and—once again—overland routes through Honduras.

Last month, a Salvadoran guerrilla group picked up a large shipment of arms on the Usulutan coast after the shipment arrived by sea from Nicaragua.

On March 15, 1982, the Costa Rican judicial police announced the discovery of a house in San Jose with a sizeable cache of arms, explosives, uniforms, passports, documents, false immigration stamps from more than thirty countries, and vehicles with hidden compartments—all connected with an ongoing arms traffic through Costa Rican territory to Salvadoran guerrillas. Nine people were arrested: Salvadorans, Nicaraguans, an Argentine, a Chilean and a Costa Rican. Costa Rican police so far have seized 13 vehicles designed for arms smuggling. Police confiscated some 150 to 175 weapons from mausers to machine guns, TNT, fragmentation grenades, a grenade launcher, ammunition, and 500 combat uniforms. One of the captured terrorists told police that the arms and other goods were to have been delivered to the Salvadoran guerrillas before March 20, "for the elections."

Nicaragua's fraternal assistance to its neighbors is not limited to arms. Training is also provided. This coordinated Nicaraguan and Cuban political and military training creates the framework for the use of the arms by guerrillas operating within El Salvador and elsewhere in Central America. Since at least mid-1980, Salvadoran guerrillas have been trained in Nicaragua in military tactics, weapons, communications, and explosives at temporary training schools scattered around the country and on Sandinista military bases. At several military sites in Nicaragua, Salvadorans receive training under guidance from Cuban and other foreign advisors. For more specialized training, guerrillas transit Nicaragua for Cuba. They are provided false identity documents to help them transit third countries. Guerrillas trained in Cuba are reinfiltrated through Nicaragua back into El Salvador. The attacks on Ilopango airport in January 1982 and on the El Oro bridge in October 1981 were clearly performed by saboteurs who had employed the benefits of such sophisticated training.

Honduran police raided a safehouse for the Moranzanist Front for the Liberation of Honduras (FMLH) on November 27, 1981, in Tegucigalpa. And while the Honduran police were attempting to search the house, a firefight broke out. The police ultimately captured several members of this group. This cell of the FMLH included a Honduran, a Uruguayan, and several Nicaraguans. The captured terrorists told Honduran authorities that the Nicaraguan government had provided them with funds for travel expenses, as well as explosives. Captured documents and statements by detained guerrillas further indicated that:

- the group was formed in Nicaragua at the instigation of high-level Sandinista leaders;
- the group's chief of operations resided in Managua; and
- members of the group received military training in Nicaragua and Cuba.

Guerrillas at one safehouse were responsible for transporting arms and munitions into Honduras from Esteli, Nicaragua.

Command and control services are also provided by Nicaragua. Planning and operations are guided from this headquarters where Nicaraguan officers are involved in command and control. The headquarters coordinates logistical support for the insurgents to include food, medicines, clothing, money—and most importantly—weapons and ammunition. The headquarters in Nicaragua decides on locations to be attacked and coordinates supply deliveries. The guidance flows to guerrilla units widely spread throughout El Salvador.

The pattern is clear. It continues to this day. We very much wish the government of Nicaragua would cease its efforts to repress its people and overthrow neighboring governments. We thought perhaps progress to this end was in sight. Frankly we are surprised by the Nicaraguan government's decision to expand and embitter regional conflict at this moment.

Mr. Ortega says it is because Nicaragua fears that the United States government is about to invade. But, of course, that is ridiculous. The United States government is not about to invade anyone. And we have so stated on many occasions.

It is true that once it became aware of Nicaragua's own intentions and actions, the United States government undertook overflights to safeguard our own security and that of other states who are threatened by the Sandinista government. These overflights, conducted by unarmed high-flying planes, and for the express and sole purpose of verifying reports of Nicaraguan intervention, are surely no threat to regional peace and stability. No, the threat to regional and world peace lies in the activities these photographs expose. One can understand the government of Nicaragua's preference that no such photographs exist.

The United States is frankly surprised and puzzled by Nicaragua's appeal to this Council. As most members of the Security Council understand, Mr. Ortega's contentious charges come at a time when we and others are looking for a basis on which to settle peacefully the differences of the parties involved. The government of Nicaragua has attempted to broaden and deepen the conflict. Only last week the government of Nicaragua stated a desire to negotiate but then, after two high government officials visited Cuba, called for this meeting to air baseless charges in this most public and important forum.

The United States seeks peace in Central America. We have repeatedly attempted to explore ways with the Nicaraguans in which our governments could cooperate in alleviating the tensions in the area. We have submitted proposals to the Nicaraguan government, and we have received no response. Instead, the Nicaraguan government replied—in October—as it has today—by sending Daniel Ortega to the United Nations to deliver an attack on the United States.

Assistant Secretary of State Thomas Enders went to Managua last August, to try to communicate with the leaders of the government of Nicaragua, to offer a way out of confrontation if they would restrain their military buildup and cease their support for insurgencies in neighboring countries. At that time we offered a specific agenda for discussions; we offered to consider their concerns if they would consider ours. We also agreed to restrain public rhetoric while this proposal was considered.

The response was not long in coming. On September 15, Humberto Ortega made a major speech in Managua during which he vilified the United States, and on October 5, Nicaraguan Junta Coordinator Daniel Ortega addressed the United Nations General Assembly, attacked the United States for past intervention in Central America, accused the United States of causing the world's economic problems, and attacked us laughing.

In recent weeks our secretary of state has met with the foreign minister of Mexico in yet another attempt to engage the Nicaraguans in a meaningful dialogue. And how has the Nicaraguan government again responded? By again sending Mr. Ortega to the United Nations, apparently in search of a propaganda victory—and an exacerbation of conflict.

The Nicaraguan government has said it wants peace; it has stated that it wishes better relations with the United States. But, unfortunately, its actions do not match its pretentions. If the Nicaraguan government was genuinely interested in alleviating tensions, would it continue to act as a conduit for war material aimed at subverting the government of El Salvador? Would it have undertaken a campaign of systematic violence against the Indian communities on the east coast, displacing 25,000 Indians from their ancestral homes on the pretext of a security threat from a peaceful, democratic neighbor? Would it have doubled the number of Cuban military and security advisors in the past year? Would it have continued seeking to augment its military forces and arsenal? Would it have declared a state of siege effectively neutralizing the opposition? And, most importantly, would it have continued incessantly to pour arms into El Salvador, even increasing the flow of arms, bullets, and now propaganda just when the people of El Salvador have been given an unprecedented opportunity to express their views?

Given this history we are understandably skeptical when the government of Nicaragua declares it wants peace, or that it wishes better relations with the United States. How, we ask, is this professed interest in peace reconciled with Comandante Humberto Ortega, when he states that the opposition will be "hanged from the lampposts?" Or with Comandante Bayardo Arce when he tells us that the Nicaraguan government will continue to pour arms into El Salvador, no matter what we do or say?

In spite of this harsh response on the part of the government of Nicaragua, our offer to engage in a dialogue was repeated by Secretary of State Haig at the OAS General Assembly meeting in December, 1981. Secretary

Haig said "the United States has made proposals to Nicaragua to normalize relations. If Nicaragua addresses our concerns about intervention and militarization, we are prepared to address their concerns. We do not close the door to the search for proper relations." Again, the Nicaraguan government has not responded to our offer.

On February 24, 1982, President Reagan said "we seek to exclude no one (from the benefits of our Caribbean Basin Initiative). Some, however, have turned from their American neighbors and their heritage. Let them return to the traditions and common values of this hemisphere and we would welcome them. The choice is theirs."

Finally, just a few weeks ago, the president of Mexico offered his good offices in the effort to reduce tensions between Nicaragua and the United States. We welcomed that initiative. In a press conference in New York on March 15, Secretary Haig reiterated the five points which we believe can serve as the basis for an improvement of relations between the governments of the United States and Nicaragua and which were conveyed earlier to the Nicaraguans.

- A commitment to mutual non-aggression through mutual high-level reassertion of our Rio Treaty engagements.
- A United States political commitment on the activities of Nicaraguan exiles in this country.
- A regional undertaking by Nicaragua not to import heavy offensive weapons and to reduce the number of foreign military and security advisers to a reasonable, low level.
- A proposal to the United States Congress for renewed United States aid to Nicaragua.
- Action by the Nicaraguans to get out of El Salvador—to wind up the command and control, the logistics operations, including delivery of weapons and ammunition, and operation of training camps.

And now, even as representatives of the Mexican and United States governments are consulting on this initiative, the government of Nicaragua, fully aware of what is going on, has once again made a move that can only increase tensions, not reduce them.

Although we find its actions puzzling, we have not interposed any objections to the request of Nicaragua that an opportunity be granted for their head of state to present an exposition to the Council, even though the government of Nicaragua, for whatever reasons, chose to ignore procedures well-established in both the Charter of the United Nations and the Charter of the Organization of American States. As members of this Council know, Article 52 of the United Nations Charter encourages efforts to achieve the peaceful settlement of disputes through regional arrangements and gives priority to them. Article 23 of the OAS Charter specifically singles out the role of the OAS in settling regional disputes before such disputes are referred to the Security Council.

The government of Nicaragua should be among the first to recall the existence under the OAS of the 17th meeting of foreign ministers which dealt in 1978 and 1979 with events in Central America threatening to the peace of the region. Indeed, in 1979, the Nicaraguan Government of National Reconstruction termed the resolution the 17th meeting of foreign ministers as "historic in every respect." That meeting was never terminated. The question of Central America remains before the OAS. Just yesterday, in the Permanent Council of the OAS, the foreign minister of Honduras made serious proposals for efforts to bring peace to Central America.

The Organization of American States, thus, not only has jurisdiction of this matter in accordance with the provisions of the United Nations and OAS Charters, it is also formally seized of the matter. It is clear that the OAS is the appropriate and primary forum for consideration of the matters addressed by Nicaragua.

We appeal once again to the government of Nicaragua to join with us and other neighboring governments in resolving differences, ending interventions, living in peace in this hemisphere.

RESPECTING INDEPENDENCE AND SOVEREIGNTY

By way of reply, I should like to begin by thanking the various members of the United Nations who have spoken today in support of the principles of national self-determination, national independence, strict respect for territorial integrity, and the principles of non-intervention in the affairs of other states. Those are principles which are very dear to my country and which the United States in its foreign affairs does its very best to honor in a serious and consistent fashion.

I should like also to express the United States' sincere agreement with the principles of international law which were cited by the distinguished representative of Guyana and various other speakers today, particularly with reference to the use of force and threats of force in the affairs of nations.

Address before the Security Council, March 26, 1982.

The United States is very profoundly committed to the principles of non-use of force in international affairs and committed also to following and abiding by the principles of the Charter of the United Nations concerning the use and non-use of force.

I should also like to express the solidarity of the United States with all those people who hope for change, for democracy and development in Central America.

I cannot forbear noting that there have been some rather odd disjunctions between some aspects of political reality and political symbolism today. I find it interesting, as an observer of political affairs as well as a representative of my country, to hear the government of Vietnam speaking with such conviction about the principle of respect for national independence. I trust that members of the United Nations would all agree that respect for the principle of national independence should apply in Kampuchea as well as in the rest of our countries. Similarly I found it interesting yesterday to listen to the representative of Angola pay homage to the principle of respect for national independence since Angola is a nation, of course, whose national independence is in some sense subject to the will of 30,000, 25,000, 20,000, however many thousand foreign troops who occupy that land with the consent of that government which is here invoking the principle of national independence.

I find it, I suppose, particularly interesting to listen to the representative of the government of Cuba commenting on peaceful affairs in this hemisphere and respect for the principles of national independence and non-intervention. Cuba is a very strange nation which today, as members of this Council know, maintains some 40,000 soldiers in Africa alone where those troops dominate two countries, doing for the Soviet Union there what the Ghurka mercenaries did for nineteenth century England. In Central America, Cuba is attempting to export aggression, subvert established governments and intervene in a most persistant and massive fashion in the internal affairs of more than one nation in that region. In Nicaragua alone it maintains no less than 1,800 to 2,000 security and military personnel. In other words, as Assistant Secretary Thomas Enders noted yesterday in his testimony before the Congress of the United States, "Cuba is a would-be foreign policy giant superimposed on an economic pigmy whose peoples have had to sacrifice all hope for a rising standard of living in order to gain advantages in foreign affairs." Those advantages are largely purchased for it by some three billion dollars annual economic aid from the Soviet Union and a great deal more military aid of course. My country naturally welcomes any move of the government of Cuba toward greater concern for economic development and well-being of its people.

Finally, commenting on the use of language and the realities of politics, it occurred to me that members of the Council might be interested in a recent article concerning Sandino and Sandinismo in Nicaragua, since we are discussing here the letter of the coordinator of the Nicaraguan junta. A prestigious writer, Pablo Joajuin Chomorro y Cardinale, was assassinated in the final days of the Somoza regime, as you perhaps know. His death was a precipitating factor in the successful revolt against the Somoza regime leading eventually to the installation of the current junta in Nicaragua. Pablo Joaquin Chomorro was a very highly respected writer whose name is from time to time invoked by the leaders of the revolution but not as often as that of Sandino. And he was, of course, the editor and publisher of *La Prensa*, the last remaining independent newspaper in Nicaragua—which may or may not have been permitted to publish today. Chomorro wrote:

> Sandino should be exalted precisely as a contrast to the communists who obey signals from Russia and China. Sandino fought against the United States Marines but he did not bring Russian Cossacks to Nicaragua as Fidel Castro did in Cuba. There is a great difference between the communist Fidel Castro who in his false battle for the independence of his country has filled it with Russian rockets, soldiers, planes and even canned goods, and a Sandino who defended the sovereignty of his ground with homemade bombs but without accepting the patronage of another power. For this reason, Sandino was great because he was not handed over to communist treason as Castro but fought within an Indo-Hispanic limit. Naturally the communists who attacked and slandered Sandino when he was in the mountains now try to use him because they have no moral scruple to restrain them. Sandino was a pure product of our land, very different from the products exported by Russia or China and as such we must exalt and preserve his memory. The value of his exploits is a Nicaraguan value, not Soviet, and his nationalism is indigenous not Russian. Sandino is a monument to the dignity of our country and we must not permit the communists with whom he never communed to besmirch his memory in order to use his prestige and to succeed, someday, on the pretext that they are fighting imperialism in delivering over our land to Russia as Castro did with Cuba.

I would finally like simply to mention that there has been a good deal of talk of change in Central America today and there has been a good deal of invocation of hope for change for the people of Central America. The government of the United States hopes very much for change in Central America; we hope it will be as peaceable as possible and bought at as low a price to the people of Central America as possible. An example of peaceable change may be observed this very weekend in El Salvador where free elections with a free press, free assembly, with competition among parties and candidates will take place. The risks of free election are, as every office holder knows, very great. When a government risks a free election it risks being defeated. It takes a very brave government who is more committed to freedom and democracy than to retaining power to run such a risk. My government congratulates the government of El Salvador for being willing to risk its power for the sake of freedom.

WHY ORTEGA OPPOSES FREE ELECTIONS

As this discussion of Commander Ortega's letter to the Security Council draws to a close, I should like to make several observations concerning his complaint against the United States, and also concerning the debate that has taken place in this chamber in the past days.

First, I desire to reiterate that the great fear cited by Commander Ortega that the United States is about to invade Nicaragua is groundless. The United States has no intention of invading Nicaragua or anyone else. I have already emphasized the Sandinista leadership's past misunderstanding of the attitudes of the U.S. government. I desire to reiterate once again that the U.S. government did not attempt to prevent the Sandinistas' accession to power. It helped them. The United States did not attempt to prevent their consolidation of power; we helped them. The United States did not oppose their efforts to reconstruct Nicaragua's economy; we helped them. The record concerning U.S. economic assistance—direct and indirect—to the government of Nicaragua is clear. There is no need to labor it. I shall not do so.

Second, I have also reiterated the attachment of my government to the principles of nonintervention in the internal affairs of other states; our respect for territorial integrity and national independence; the peaceful settlement of disputes and to those principles of the UN Charter that govern the use and non-use of force. Obviously, none of this means that the United States renounces the right to defend itself, nor that we will not assist others in defending themselves under circumstances consistent with our legal and political obligations and with the Charter of the United Nations.

Unfortunately, not all governments which have participated in this debate are equally attached to principles of non-use of force, respect for territorial integrity or national independence. There is an interesting correlation between the nations who have *supported* Nicaragua's complaint against the United States and those who *opposed* the resolution calling for withdrawal of Soviet troops from Afghanistan.

Address before the Security Council, April 2, 1982.

The principles of nonintervention and respect for national independence cited in this debate did not lead Angola, Cuba, the German Democratic Republic, Grenada, the Lao People's Democratic Republic, Libya, Madagascar, Mozambique, Seychelles, the Syrian Arab Republic, the Soviet Union, or Vietnam to join 116 other nations in calling for an end to the occupation of Afghanistan. All those nations opposed the Afghanistan resolution.

Zeal for national independence and noninterference did not move the governments of Algeria, Benin, the Congo, India or Uganda to seek an end to the occupation of Afghanistan. All abstained.

It is not, moreover, only the national independence of Afghanistan which inspires so little response from among those who have expressed solidarity with these principles in the last few days: Neither Angola nor the Congo, nor Cuba, nor the German Democratic Republic, nor Grenada, nor the Lao People's Democratic Republic, nor Libya, nor Mozambique, nor Seychelles, nor the Soviet Union, nor Vietnam, Algeria, Benin, India, Madagascar, Mexico, Panama, Uganda, Tanzania nor Zimbabwe was moved by these principles to support the call for an end to the continuing military occupation of Kampuchea.

Will members of this Council be surprised to be reminded that the government of Nicaragua was itself not prepared to extend to the people of Afghanistan and Kampuchea the rights to peace, national independence and territorial integrity it seeks for itself now? Nicaragua supported *neither* the resolution calling for an end to the occupation of Afghanistan *nor* Kampuchea.

This sort of selective invocation and application of universal principles does not strengthen either the principles or the organizations dedicated to their realization and implementation. It breeds cynicism. It harms the United Nations. It mocks the search for peace.

Third, I desire to clarify the position of my government with regard to the jurisdiction and role of the United Nations and regional organizations. Despite efforts by the government of Nicaragua to indicate otherwise, it should be clear that the United States government believes that any member state has the right under the Charter to bring an issue before the Security Council which seriously threatens international peace and security. As members of the Council know, the United States did not oppose Commander Ortega's request to present an exposition to this Council, even though we were objects of that complaint. But while the Charter grants that right to all members, it is equally clear that the Charter encourages the resolution of disputes through regional arrangements.

The Charter of the United Nations contains a chapter relating expressly to regional organizations. Paragraphs 2 and 3 of Article 52 of the Charter contain the explicit provisions designed to encourage resolution of regional disputes in the relevant regional organization. These paragraphs read, respectively, as follows:

> The members of the United Nations entering into such arrangements or constituting such agencies shall make every effort to achieve pacific settlement of local disputes through such regional arrangements or by such regional agencies before referring them to the Security Council.
>
> The Security Council shall encourage the development of pacific settlement of local disputes through such regional agencies either on the initiative of the states concerned or by reference from the Security Council.

Those who attempt, as the government of Nicaragua has attempted, to describe the legal obligations of members of the regional organizations without reference to these provisions ignore *inter alia* fundamental provisions of the Charter. It is an elementary rule of interpretation of treaties that effect must be given to all provisions of the Charter—*ut res magis valeat quam pereat*. In this context it is worth recalling Article 2, paragraph 2 of the Charter which requires good-faith fulfillment of the obligation assumed by each and every member. Ignoring the existence of undeniably relevant provisions of the Charter would appear to raise serious questions.

Nicaragua's studied avoidance of those provisions in a long communication ostensibly devoted to an analysis of the subject demonstrates not only that its concern is less with law than with politics, but that it is prepared to seek political advantages even at the price of serious legal distortions.

Unfortunately, there have been other evidences, inside the chamber and outside it as well, that the government of Nicaragua is less concerned with rights than with advantages.

Its failure to support the national independence of the peoples of Afghanistan and Kampuchea; its continuing efforts to undermine and overthrow neighboring governments, especially El Salvador; its importation of heavy offensive arms; its militarization of Nicaraguan society—all establish that we are dealing here with a government that seeks for itself rights it is not willing to grant others.

Nicaragua invokes the principle of nonintervention but claims the right to intervene in the internal affairs of neighboring states.

Nicaragua demands that others respect its national independence but does not respect the sovereignty or right to national self-determination of its neighbors.

Nicaragua claims the right to seek advisers and arms wherever it chooses—as an exercise of its sovereignty—but would deny its neighbors the same right.

Nicaragua claims the right to live in peace while fomenting internal war in neighboring countries.

The facts, as I stated last week, are that the government of Nicaragua is an active party to a massive intervention in the affairs of her neighbors. The government of Nicaragua is engaged in training guerrillas and in directing command-and-control centers. It is involved in infiltrating arms and guerrillas, destroying electric power stations, blowing up bridges, and terrorizing civilians. Her leaders come before the Security Council of the United Nations seeking international protection for these activities.

The government of Nicaragua espouses and practices a very particular conception of nonintervention, a very particular conception of non-alignment; the kind that, in the end, saps the meaning and power of both.

The letter of Mr. Daniel Ortega Saavedra, and the Security Council debate that it has prompted, remind me of a statement by the late French philosopher George Bernanos, who once said that "the worst, the most corrupting, of lies are problems poorly stated." Mr. Ortega states "the problem" as having to do with the danger posed by the United States to the independence and sovereignty of the countries of Central America. This definition of the problem merely obfuscates the real issue that is at stake in Central America, which is a conflict between two concepts of organizing society, two ideologies—if you will—one democratic and the other totalitarian.

The elections held Sunday in El Salvador symbolize one of these approaches—the democratic one—while the Nicaraguan regime's systematic refusal to hold elections symbolizes the other—totalitarian—approach.

That election, with its enormous turnout of voters, was a tribute to the Salvadoran people and to the vitality of the democratic idea.

What a stolid, courageous, unflinching people these Salvadorans are! Despite the possibility of massive violence at the polling places and threats of retaliation by guerrilla forces against voters the Salvadorans still voted in huge, unprecedented numbers. Why did they do so?

In Monday's *Wall Street Journal*, there was an interview with one of these voters, Ana Maria de Martinez, who "was typical of some voters who thought they would beat the crowds by showing up early at the polling stations. This mother of two children got to the National Technical Institute, a polling place, around 5 a.m. But so did a lot of other people, and by 9 a.m. she was still two blocks from the gate entrance. 'I'll wait here all day if I have to,' she said, fanning her face with her wallet. 'The rest of the world seems to have made decisions about El Salvador. Now it's my turn.'"

Some people said that free and fair elections could not be held in El Salvador. They were wrong.

But there were others who have been against elections in principle, regarding them as a tool of the bourgeoisie and a misrepresentation of the popular will which could best be expressed through armed struggle. In Salvador this view, preferring the bullet to the ballot, is held by the various guerrilla factions whose coordinating front is appropriately named after Farabundo Marti, the Salvadoran communist. One of these guerrilas, Commandante Ana Guadalupe Martinez, is quoted in this week's issue of the *Economist* of London as saying that "Elections are there to ratify a popular government. . . . If laws exist which represent the people, elections are not very important."

The idea that the will of the people can be better expressed through a revolutionary elite than through free elections is, of course, a fundamental tenet of Leninism. It is, I need hardly point out in this forum, fundamentally at variance with Article 21 of the "Universal Declaration of Human Rights" which states:

> The will of the people shall be the basis of the authority of government; *this will shall be expressed in periodic and genuine elections which shall be by universal and equal suffrage and shall be held by secret vote or by equivalent free voting procedures.*

The FMLN is not the only element in Central American politics that opposes free elections as defined in Article 21 of the "Universal Declaration of Human Rights." The Sandinista leadership also opposes such elections. Indeed, they have called the Salvadoran election "an absolute denial of democracy and civilization." They did not always speak thus. One month before achieving power, in June 1979, when they were still seeking supporters, the Sandinistas promised the Organization of American States that they would hold free elections when they assumed power. Once in power, however, they quickly reneged on that promise.

In the spring of 1980, the Sandinistas consolidated their control over the Council of State, enlarging it and packing it with their own supporters to ensure a permanent majority. In July 1980, Sandinista Defense Minister Humberto Ortega announced that there would be no need for elections since the people had already "voted" during the revolution. Elections could not be held, it was said, until the people had been "re-educated."

The following month, in August 1980, Humberto Ortega announced that elections would be put off until 1985. Even then, it was stated that these would not be "bourgeois" elections—the kind of elections, that is to say, called for in the Universal Declaration, but rather "people's elections" in which, in the words of Interior Minister Tomas Borge, power "will not be raffled off." Meanwhile, no "proselytizing activities" on behalf of any candidate, no discussion of candidacies would be permitted before candidates were officially designated by an electoral agency which itself would not be created until 1984. Violations would be punished by terms of three months to three years in jail.

Meanwhile, vigilante mobs have been encouraged to intimidate the opposition. The MDN and the Social Democrats, two of Nicaragua's principal opposition parties, have repeatedly been the victims of semi-official mob violence. In a speech delivered last fall, Humberto Ortega stated that the Sandinista regime is "guided by scientific doctrine, by Marxism-Leninism" and threatened to hang dissenters against the regime's policies "along the streets and highways of the country." Shortly thereafter, four Nicaraguan business leaders who signed a letter protesting against this speech were arrested and sentenced to seven months in prison.

The Sandinistas' description concerning elections is part of a larger policy of revolution by obfuscation. They have pretended to be democrats. For a long time they pretended not to be Marxist-Leninists, and today they pretend there is no contradiction between Sandinism and Marxism-Leninism.

As those familiar with the history of Augusto Cesar Sandino know, his nationalism provoked suspicion and criticism from those who supported submission to Moscow's so-called internationalism. His desire for "absolute sovereignty," for a "free country" and for leaving the solution of economic and social problems to democratic decision was naturally rejected by communists as bourgeois and counter-revolutionary. The communist attacks against Sandino, therefore, began when he was in Mexico. Because he refused to adjust his fight for "Country and Liberty" to the plans of the Mexican communists, the secretary-general of the Mexican Communist party called him a traitor and denounced him upon his death.

It is particularly instructive, in light of the different attitudes toward free elections today in El Salvador and Nicaragua, to contrast Sandino's views with those of Jose Agustin Farabundo Marti, the leader of the Salvadoran Communist party who joined Sandino's struggle for a time but was eventually sent home because of his communist ideology. "My break with Sandino," he said, came about "because he did not wish to embrace the communist program which I supported. His banner was only for independence, a banner of emancipation, and he did not pursue the ends of social rebellion." Years later, this account was confirmed by Sandino himself who said that "On various occasions attempts were made to distort this movement of national defense, converting it rather into a battle of a social character. I opposed this with all my strength."

In its effort to consolidate totalitarian power at home and mortgage the national independence of Nicaragua to Moscow and Havana, the Nicaraguan regime stands squarely in the tradition of Farabundo Marti whose descendants, acting in that tradition, tried unsuccessfully to sabotage through violence the free elections in El Salvador and who, if they came to power, would adopt the same contemptuous attitude toward free elections that those who call themselves Sandinistas have adopted in Nicaragua.

It is hardly a coincidence that many of the countries who have supported Commandante Ortega's letter in the course of this debate share his regime's principled opposition to free elections. These countries include Cuba, Vietnam, Angola, the Soviet Union, Laos, Mozambique, Grenada, Iran, the German Democratic Republic, and Poland. In none of these regimes, which call themselves "people's democracies," are governments chosen by or accountable to the people. All of them oppose—because they fear—the free expression of the will of the people through free elections as called for in Article 21 of the "Universal Declaration of Human Rights."

I have already expressed to the Council my government's surprise at Nicaragua's decision to bring its complaint to the Security Council at precisely the moment when there seemed to be progress toward direct negotiations among the nations most directly involved. We have noted as well that this is not the first time that U.S. initiatives aimed at resolving disputes have been met by deliberate escalations.

Why did the Nicaraguans come, at this time, to this forum, with their harsh rhetoric and wild charges? To distract attention from El Salvador's elections? If that was their purpose then they have failed.

To distract attention from the intensified repression going on in Nicaragua since the government declared an "emergency"? If this was their purpose they have largely succeeded. Not much note has been taken here of the new repressive measures aimed above all at the press. Yet strict prior censorship has prevented the appearance of *La Prensa*, which is not only prohibited from printing news on a great many subjects, but has also been forbidden to print blank spaces. Even the pro-Sandinista *El Nuevo Diario* ran afoul of the censors' vague standards and strict enforcement. A twenty-four hour suspension was imposed after it announced the government had declared a state of siege.

It has been suggested, too, that Nicaragua's complaint here merely reflects a (not unwholesome) desire to let off steam and express its frustrations at having a superpower for a neighbor. But this is a serious international forum, not a Turkish bath. It has also been suggested that being the object of such a complaint is a kind of occupational hazard of superpowers; that this complaint is analogous to that made against the Soviet Union on Afghanistan. An analogy would exist, we are quick to note, only if the United States had forcibly eliminated the government of Nicaragua, shot its chief of state and moved in 100,000 combat troops to subdue and occupy the country. But, of course, my government has no intention of doing any such thing.

We desire to live at peace with all our neighbors. We shall continue our efforts to develop a constructive relationship with the government of Nicaragua. Secretary of State Alexander Haig has made clear that we are prepared to work on the basis of mutual respect to that end.

Various proposals have been offered for conciliation among the nations of the region and the hemisphere. The United States, interested in the constructive resolution of tension and conflict, remains ready to do its part to ensure peace in the region and to enhance the prospects for democracy and development for all our people.

THE RIGHT OF REPRESSION

We are living through an extraordinary period. One of the characteristics of this extraordinary period in which we now find ourselves is the regular proliferation of rights. New rights, unprecedented in human history, are invented and claimed and, as with all rights, outrage is expressed when these presumed rights are violated. Twice this month we have heard new rights invoked. We have heard one country invoke the right to aggression, and express outrage when its right to overthrow a neighboring government was violated. The same government was outraged again when its right to occupy a neighboring territory was violated.

Now comes the government of Nicaragua claiming as yet a new right—the right of repression of its own people—the right of repression of its own people with impunity and with immunity from any consequences thereof. The government of Nicaragua today has suggested that someone is violating its right to repress its people and even its right to direct attempts to overthrow neighboring governments. And it has come to this international forum, appealing that we protect it against the frustration and bitterness of its own people while it builds a harsh new military dictatorship with which to repress those people whom it promised democracy. That is precisely the appeal of the Nicaraguan government to this Council today—an appeal to protect Nicaragua in the free exercise of its right to repression, repression at home, aggression abroad.

Address before the Security Council, March 23, 1983.

This is a new right which we have not heard invoked before; but the myths by which it is accompanied are unfortunately already familiar. Those myths are as follows:

- That Nicaragua is in the grips of a democratic revolution whose purpose is to liberate the Nicaraguan people from the yoke of dictatorship;
- That Nicaragua wants to live in peace with her neighbors; and
- That Nicaragua is about to be invaded by the United States, or Honduras, or someone.

I think these three myths deserve a bit of examination by this Council as we consider the proposals before us today.

The first is the myth that the Sandinista military dictatorship is a democratic revolution. God knows the people of Nicaragua have longed for a democratic revolution. They joined almost unanimously in a fight against the heavy-handed dictatorship of Anastasio Somoza. They joined in the struggle because they were promised democracy. The promises that the so-called Sandinista junta made to the people of Nicaragua and to the Organization of American States are very clear. I think those promises are interesting and important and relevant so we should examine them. They are expressed with special clarity in a letter addressed by the FSLN to the Organization of American States dated July 7, 1979—that is the same month that the FSLN became the government of Nicaragua. On the basis of those solemn promises voluntarily offered to the Organization of American States many nations offered their support to the FSLN in its efforts to become the government of Nicaragua. I should like to read that letter. It says,

> Mr. Secretary-General [the Secretary-General of the Organization of American States] we are pleased to make available to you and to the ministers of foreign affairs of the member states of the Organization a document containing our plan to secure peace in our heroic, long suffering country at the moment when the people of Nicaragua are consolidating its political and military victory over the dictatorship.
>
> First, we have developed this plan on the basis of the resolution of the seventeenth meeting of consultations of June 23, 1979, a resolution that was historic in every sense of the word. It demands the immediate replacement of the genocidal Somoza dictatorship which is now nearing its end and backs the installation of a broadly representative democratic government in our country such as the one we have formed. While saying that the solution to this problem is exclusively within the jurisdiction of the people of Nicaragua, it appeals to a hemispheric solidarity to preserve our peoples' rights to self determination. We are presenting to the community of nations of the hemisphere in connection with our plan to secure peace, the goals that here in-

spired our government ever since it was formed. They have been set forth in our documents and political declarations and we wish to ratify some of them here.

1 Our firm intention to establish full observance of human rights in our country in accordance with the United Nations' "Universal Declaration of the Rights of Man" and the Charter of Human Rights of the OAS. Our observance of human rights has already been made plain by the way the Sandinista National Liberation Front has treated hundreds of prisoners of war. Our government thus invites the Inter-American Commission on Human Rights to visit our country as soon as we are installed in our national territory.
2 Our wish that our installation in Nicaragua come about through a peaceful and orderly transition. The government of national reconstruction would take it as a gesture of solidarity if the foreign ministers of the hemisphere were to visit our country and we hereby extend to them a fraternal invitation to do so.
3 Our decision to embrace civil justice in our country and to try those incriminated of crimes against the people. According to the regular law by the heroic struggle, the people have won themselves the right to let justice prevail for the first time in half a century and will do so within the framework of the law without a spirit of vengence and without indiscriminate reprisals.
4 Those collaborators with the regime that may wish to leave the country and that are not responsible for the genocide we have suffered or for other serious crimes that demand trial by civil courts may do so with all necessary guarantees which the government of national reconstruction authorizes as of now. The departure of these persons may be supervised by the Inter-American Commission on Human rights and by the International Red Cross.
5 The plan to call the first free elections our country has known in this century so that Nicaraguans can elect their representatives to the city councils, and to a constituent assembly, and later elect the country's highest authorities.

Mr. Secretary-General, it is now up to the governments of the hemisphere to speak so that the solidarity with the struggle our people has carried forward to make democracy and justice possible in Nicaragua can become fully effective. We ask that you transmit the text of this letter to the foreign ministers of the OAS.

Yours most respectfully, Junta of the Government of National Reconstruction, Violeta de Chamorro, Sergio Ramirez Mercado, Alfonso Robelo-Callejas, Daniel Ortega-Saavedra.

It is an interesting letter. Those were presumably serious commitments, seriously entered into, commitments with respect to human rights, with respect to the freedom of all Nicaraguans, including minorities, commitment to free elections, commitments to a government of civil law, a rule of law. We cannot be indifferent to what happened to these commitments.

First, let us look at the commitment to respect for human rights including, of course, that most basic human right, democratic right, the right to opposition, the right to autonomous activity, which is the very basis of a pluralist society. It is particularly sad to see what happened to those persons who joined the FSLN in establishing this government and making those commitments. Take, for example, the private sector. In November 1980, Sandinista security forces murdered the private sector leader, Jorge Salazar, who was unarmed in what everyone in the world understood to be a transparent set-up. The private sector organization, COSEP, and the independent political parties at that stage withdrew from the Council of State in protest. In October 1981, the leaders of COSEP, the umbrella, private sector organization established to cooperate with the Sandinista revolution, were arrested and jailed for four months because they issued a statement criticizing official policy. Sandinista expropriation of private enterprise raised the government share of the economy progressively, but the offense of the leaders of COSEP was not to resist that progressive incorporation of the economy into the government except by expressing, presumably, criticisms of it—exercising their right of free speech.

But it was not only the private sector that suffered very quickly the repressive policies of the Sandinista government. Labor unions were harnessed and harassed when they tried to resist being incorporated into the state. Their leaders were beaten and arrested. Highly-controlled government labor and peasant organizations were established and promptly lost a good many of their members. The independent press, whose rights were promised by the FSLN on assuming office, was quickly repressed. The electronic media were submitted to a tight vise of government control, and all organs of the newspapers, except for a single independent voice, *La Prensa*, which for years was the opposition to the Somoza government, were "coordinated," that is controlled, by the government. Since then, *La Prensa* has been repeatedly shut down and is heavily censored. Government controlled newspapers and media publish only news stipulated by the ministry of the interior. *La Prensa* is subject to prior censorship: frequently it is forbidden to publish interviews, news; virtually always it is forbidden to publish criticism. It is also forbidden to publish information concerning what it is forbidden to publish.

Churches of Nicaragua have been progressively repressed. Archbishop Obando y Bravo, who had been, like the COSEP leaders, a supporter of the revolution and a strong opponent of the Somoza regime, was banned from performing mass on television. The Catholic church's radio was closed several times and eventually incorporated into a system of government control. Clergy have been repeatedly subjected to humiliating attacks. A Sandinista attempt to establish a parallel "peoples' church" followed unsuccessful efforts to intimidate the hierarchy of the Roman Catholic Church of Nicaragua. A variety of Protestant sects, including Evangelicals, Mormons, Adventists, Jehovah's Witnesses, and Moravians have been attacked, their centers taken over by Sandinista defense committees, their pastors harassed. At least fifty-five Moravian churches on the Atlantic coast have been burned.

In addition to this systematic persecution of opposition forces, the government of Nicaragua has violated its commitment to elections and to freedom of opposition. It has grown progressively intolerant, disillusioning a very large number of its original leadership.

It is very important to know that among the thousands of Nicaraguans today living in exile in Honduras and Costa Rica, Panama, the United States, Venezuela and all sorts of countries, a large number supported, assisted and joined the Sandinistas in their opposition to the Somoza government. Among these dissidents is one signatory of the letter I read, Alfonso Robelo, and the Sandinistas' first two ambassadors to Washington. Violeta Chamorro, another signatory of the OAS pledge, quickly resigned from the government and continues in the struggle to maintain some sort of voice of freedom inside Nicaragua. In April 1982, after nine months underground, former FSLN commander, Eden Pastora, the famous Commander Zero, denounced the Sandinista regime's ties to Cuba and the Soviet Union and announced that his own exile organization would challenge the FSLN control of Nicaragua. These are the people whom we hear today described as Somozistas. These so-called Somozistas, who lead the struggle against the Sandinista dictatorship, are for the most part democrats long determined to free Nicaragua from dictatorial control and to establish democratic government. They naturally were dismayed as their goals receded even further into the future as Nicaragua's government became a progressively more repressive military dictatorship headed by some nine military commanders who govern the country today by decree and by force. The spirit of intolerance which characterizes Nicaragua's government was clearly expressed in the threat of Commandante Umberto Ortego to hang the opposition from lamp posts outside of Managua.

The promise for elections has receded even further. Finally it was announced that elections would be held in 1985 or not before 1985, that the discussion of candidates for those elections would be banned until some time in 1984 and punishable by imprisonment not under civil law at all, but under a state of siege.

The repression against the Catholic church continued apace and was, I think, most clearly expressed in Nicaragua's response to the visit of the Pope. Pope John Paul II had expressed his utter opposition to efforts of the Nicaraguan government to establish a kind of puppet popular church. In preparation for the Pope's visit, the architects of the "people's church" made efforts to delay papal communications and finally to diminish the crowds permitted to hear the papal message. The British magazine, *The Economist*, noted that the Sandinistas, and I am quoting now,

> ... packed a papal mass in Managua with their supporters who heckled the visitor. He was spirited out of Managua to the provinces in order to keep him from appearing too often alongside Managua's anti-Sandinista Archbishop Obando y Bravo. The Pope showed his own brand of passive resistance. The picture showing him with arms folded and head bowed in disapproval as Commander Ortega delivered his tirade could not be kept from the front pages. However, most ordinary Nicaraguans were kept from contact with the Pope.

The clearest expression of the attitude of the official Sandinista government to the Pope's visit is perhaps expressed in a broadcast on a government radio station, where one of the reporters said, and I quote, "Despite the fame ascribed to Vatican diplomacy, the Pope engaged in political aggression delivering a speech that was really political aggression ... against the people. This is why the people responded as they did."

The Nicaraguan government has repressed so many sectors of its own population that it hardly seems fair to single out a single sector, yet the harshness with which they have treated the indigenous peoples of the Atlantic coast, the Miskito and Sumo and Rama Indians, deserves special note by any group with a serious concern about the nature of the government of Nicaragua. The Miskito Indians were forceably driven from their ancestral homes, their churches burned, their villages burned, their children forceably separated from them in many cases. Thousands fled to Honduras where they today live in refugee camps, deep inside Honduras, by the way, and not on the border. Those who did not flee have been herded by the Nicaraguan government into camps, internment camps, where they are overcrowded and underoccupied and disease is rampant. Actually, the foreign minister of Nicaragua himself said that it may be that it is just to level some criticism against the first phase of the resettlement of the Miskito Indians in the north of the country. "The resettlement was not carried out with as much force as has been sometimes claimed," said the Nicaraguan foreign minister, "but, nonetheless, the mistake was that it happened too quickly. Greater attention should have been paid to explaining the necessity of resettlement to the Miskitos." No consent was sought of the Miskitos. No explanations were offered. The Miskitos were simply forced to abandon their homes and way of life.

The charges that Nicaragua has made against the United States are no more persuasive than the commitments it made to the Organization of

American States. The government of Nicaragua has repeatedly asserted the hostility of the government of the United States to it. Indeed, we might say that it suffers from an obsession concerning the hostility of the United States. That obsession, as has been frequently noted, is expressed in its national anthem in which it refers to us as nothing more or less than the enemies of mankind.

The Nicaraguan government has charged repeatedly that the United States supported the government of Anastasio Somoza and offered implacable opposition to its rise. The facts are otherwise. The United States government, which provided no economic or military aid to the Somoza regime during its struggle for survival, acted immediately to assist the Nicaraguan revolutionary government on its accession to power. From July 19, 1979, when the FSLN triumphed, to September 30, 1979, the United States provided a total of $24.6 million in emergency relief and recovery assistance. This emergency assistance consisted of emergency food and medical supplies often shipped by air, assistance in housing reconstruction and a special grant of grain. From July 1979 through January 1981 approximately $118 million in direct U.S. assistance was provided to the new government of Nicaragua.

In addition to bilateral aid, the United States actively supported all loans to Nicaragua in multilateral lending institutions, helping them to receive from the Inter-American Development Bank $262 million in loans from mid-1979 to the end of 1980, an amount almost double what the Somoza government had received in the preceding twenty years. *During the first year and a half of its life the Sandinista government of Nicaragua received more economic aid from the United States than from any other country.* It is absolutely false to suggest that the government of the United States attempted to oppose the government of Nicaragua in its effort to liberate Nicaragua from the dictatorship of the Somoza regime.

It is almost absolutely false to suggest that it was the Reagan administration which made the decision to terminate aid to Nicaragua. It was, in fact, in the last months of the Carter administration that the decision to cease U.S. aid to Nicaragua was made. And it was made because the government of Nicaragua was repeatedly and systematically found to be violating its agreement not to cooperate with or support terrorism or violence in other countries or to intervene in the internal affairs of other countries. It was made also because Nicaragua was violating its commitment to establish democracy and freedom for its own peoples.

The government of Nicaragua claims that she is a peace-loving state surrounded by threatening neighbors. The facts, again, are very different. The facts are that Sandinista Nicaragua has, since its accession to power, concentrated on building a military machine that is unequalled now or ever in Central America. A rapid arms buildup was undertaken immediately after the Sandinistas came to power, and such a buildup threatens the security of her neighbors. With a population of 2.7 million people, Nicaragua now has active duty forces which number approximately 25,000—at least twice the size of Somoza's national guard—with another 50,000 reservists and militia. To accommodate and train this force, large numbers of military garrisons have been built and enormous quantities of arms have been imported from the Soviet bloc.

More than 2,000 Cuban military and internal security advisors are in Nicaragua. Several hundred Nicaraguans are training or have completed training in Cuba and other Eastern European countries. Sophisticated weapons, including Soviet-made T-55 tanks, amphibious ferries, helicopters, and transport aircraft, have been added to Nicaragua's arsenal, giving Nicaragua a military establishment which far exceeds her own defense needs, obviously, and far exceeds any military force ever seen in Central America. In contrast, Costa Rica has no standing army. Honduras, which has one million more people than Nicaragua, has total forces of about 17,500.

Nicaragua charges that the United States, aided by Honduras, is now intervening in her internal affairs and threatening the peace of the region. This assertion has been heard here, of course, before. It was, indeed, about a year ago, March 25th, that we heard the complaint of Mr. Daniel Ortega that the United States was about to launch, and I quote, "an imminent, large-scale military intervention." He wrote in a letter, in which he requested a meeting of the Security Council, of "an ever increasing danger of a large-scale military intervention by the armed forces of the United States which," he said, "constitutes a grave threat to the independence and sovereignty of the Central American countries and to the international peace and security." He spoke of the interventionist strategy of the government of the United States and asserted that his government had clear evidence of the U.S. intention to attack Nicaragua directly and also intervene directly in El Salvador.

We assured the government at that time that we had absolutely no intention of engaging in a large-scale military invasion of their country. The facts are, of course, as we pointed out then: *that Nicaragua herself is the country in Central America which is involved in a major effort to destabilize other governments.* The efforts of the government of Nicaragua to destabilize the government of El Salvador are so clear that they cannot be any longer denied even by the government of Nicaragua who, for many months in the face of even greater evidence, steadfastly denied the truth of this assertion.

The government of Nicaragua has sought to destabilize the government of El Salvador by sending large and continuous shipments of arms into that country (over 200 tons in 1981); by providing training and support to El Salvador's guerrillas; by directing guerrilla military actions in El Salvador from command and control centers inside Nicaragua.

Nicaragua has so repeatedly violated Honduras' sovereignty and territory with covert shipments of arms over her borders that it is literally the case that one loses count of the instances. Nicaragua has also engaged in the effort to foment guerrilla forces inside Honduras and stocked arms inside Honduras. Some ten tons of explosives and small arms and thousands of rounds of ammunition, sophisticated communications equipment, uniforms, propaganda, trucks and cars for transporting arms were uncovered in safe houses in Honduras by the end of 1982.

Nicaragua has also systematically violated the rights of Costa Rica by attempts to deny Costa Rica the use of the San Juan River. It has violated Costa Rica's border and made arrogant threats that attempt to deny Costa Rica the right to the development of its own territory.

Nicaragua has not been interested in confirming the facts about the activities or intentions of its neighbors. The Nicaraguan government, for example, rejected an invitation from the United States and Honduras to observe joint military exercises held in the region. On February 18, 1983, the Honduran government invited the Sandinista foreign minister to inspect exile camps allegedly located in southern Honduras and on February 23, the Sandinista regime rejected the offer. The Nicaraguan government has recently become quite open about its own approach to its neighbors. Radio Venceremos, broadcasting from Managua, has said recently "our war is and will continue to be national, but we view our plans in the framework of a regional conflict to which there are interests of the people of Central America, the Caribbean and Latin America." They asserted in that same program that "the rebels throughout the area have imported arms through all the routes we could find," and that "we have used all of Central America and other countries for those purposes." The *Washington Post* commented that the broadcast appeared to support charges brought by the Reagan administration that the insurgency found in other Central American countries was encouraged and armed and participated in by the government of Nicaragua.

The government of Nicaragua has repeatedly declined to participate in efforts of its neighbors to find peaceful solutions to the conflicts which plague the areas. On October 4, 1982, in San Jose, there was articulated the so-called final act in which the democratic states of the region for the first time set forth conditions they regarded as essential to achieve peace in Central America.

Those conditions, endorsed by the democratic states of the region and endorsed, I may say, by the United States as well, provide, we believe, a standing invitation as well as a solution, a plan for the resolution of the problems and insecurities that afflict the region. They provide in summary:

- That all countries forego violent or subversive activities inside any other country;
- That all arms trafficking from outside the area would cease;
- They provide for a ban, which would apply to all governments, on the importation of heavy weapons and limitations on all armaments and forces to those required for defense;
- They provide for withdrawal of all foreign military and security advisors and troops under fully verifiable and reciprocal conditions;
- They provide absolute respect for the principle of non-intervention and the peaceful solution of disputes;
- They provide respect for human rights, including fundamental freedoms such as freedom of speech, assembly, religion and the right to organize political parties, labor unions and other organizations;
- They provide for the establishment of democratic, representative and participatory institutions through regular elections in an atmosphere of political reconciliation within each state.

One of the most striking facts about the San Jose Declaration and the principles set forth there as the basis for peaceful resolution of the problems of the region is their resemblance to commitments made by the FSLN at the moment of its accession to power—the commitments made in its letter to the OAS.

In proposing to the government of Nicaragua that it join with other countries in the region in the affirmation of those principles, one proposes only the re-affirmation of the principles with which it announced its own arrival in power.

That distinguished English philosopher, John Stuart Mill, believed that a people's quest for liberty is an irrepressible drive. It may be put down once, twice, repeatedly, but never permanently. The recent political history of Nicaragua clearly illustrates the truth in John Stuart Mill's vision. Having valiantly fought to overthrow a despotic military dictatorship, the Nicaraguans momentarily breathed the exhilarating air of freedom.

This triumph of freedom over tyranny, of the people over their oppressors, was tragically short in the case of Nicaragua. The long-suffering Nicaraguan people saw their hopes for freedom and human rights gradually suffocated by yet another form of tyranny. To a people well versed in forms of despotism, the new developments after the triumph of Sandinism were ominously familiar. The emerging pattern was easily recognizable. A few self-appointed individuals, lacking popular support, resorted to armed violence to maintain themselves in power. Instead of popular support, the new government increasingly relied on military means. Instead of consultations, it relied on coercion. Instead of respecting human rights, it chose to trample them. Instead of allowing for the free play of political forces of society, it systematically sought to destroy them.

Is it any wonder then that the Nicaraguan people, versed as they are in recognizing tyrants, would increasingly turn against those whom they originally believed to be their liberators? Is there any surprise in the fact that the Nicaraguans, thirsty for real freedom, are now once more ready to fight for it as they did in the past? I believe not.

Somozismo and Sandinismo turn out not to be unlike each other. They are both military dictatorships denying the Nicaraguan people their human rights and their human freedoms, their political rights and their political freedoms.

The fact is that the right to repression cannot be granted by anybody. The right to repression is not a human right or a political right. The right to violate others' territorial integrity and sovereignty, the right to intervene in the internal affairs of others cannot be granted by this body to the government of Nicaragua or any other government. It violates the Charter of the United Nations. It violates the commitments of this body to all its members. It violates civilized conduct.

There were references by the distinguished representative of Nicaragua to the political will of the American government. There were references also to the will of the Nicaraguan people to be free and independent. I should like to say that the political will of the present United States government is no different than the political will of the people of Nicaragua—to be free and independent. We fully support them in that determination.

An appeal was made by the government of Nicaragua's representative that the United States put an end to its support for disturbances inside Nicaragua. I should like to make an appeal to the government of Nicaragua to put an end to its repression of its own people, to put an end to its destabilization of its neighbors. I should like to appeal to the government of Nicaragua to affirm its political will to fulfill its promises to the people of Nicaragua, and to its fellow members of the Organization of American States. We appeal to the government of Nicaragua to be true to its own promises, to provide its people those human rights and freedoms, that democracy, that opportunity for peace and prosperity which it promised to them.

I should like in closing to affirm the political will of the government of the United States either to join with other countries of this hemisphere, or to stand aside while other members of this hemisphere work out solutions which provide for exactly the political goods promised by the Sandinista government to its people: respect for human rights, respect for good neigh-borliness, respect for the right of people to choose their own governments through competitive and free elections, and to make their own law.

Consolidating Totalitarian Control

We do not live or act, Jacob Burkhardt observed, for ourselves alone, but for the past and future as well. What happens here in the Security Council reflects the expectations and hopes of those who framed the institution and defines the hopes and expectations that may be reasonably attached to it for the future.

It is, at best, ironic that the interactions of the past days should have coincided with our ongoing discussion of the Secretary-General's report.

We have witnessed in the so-called consideration of the Nicaraguan com-plaint the kind of cynical debasement of the process of conflict resolution which underlies and largely explains the various specific failures which are outlined in the Secretary-General's report.

Nicaragua's new dictators—who share their mentor's preference for wearing military uniforms, carrying weapons and calling each other by military titles—have come to this Council seeking international support for their policy of internal repression and external aggression.

They appeal to this Council to guarantee their right to continue these policies without fear of opposition from other Nicaraguans who, finding all means of peaceful political competition closed to them, seek to open their political system and reclaim their society from the strangulation of total-itarian controls and foreign exploitation.

For let us be clear that Nicaragua *has* closed its political system and Nicaragua *does* engage ever more openly in aggression against her neigh-bors.

I spoke earlier about the systematic effort of Nicaragua to consolidate totalitarian control of Nicaraguan society, about the silencing of criticism, the destruction of indigenous societies filled with people who ask only to be left alone, about the use of "divine mobs" to intimidate oposition, about the crude attacks on the Catholic and other churches extending even to the Pope himself. I did not mention yesterday that this repression is carried out by a new secret police apparatus—the Sandinista State Security, whose

Address before the Security Council, March 25, 1983.

thousands of recruits have been trained by Cuban professionals in the suppression of internal dissent.

Thus do fraternal "socialist" societies of the totalitarian variant assist one another. Nicaragua's new dictators not only receive help, they also offer fraternal assistance to armed guerrillas seeking to overthrow the governments of neighboring states.

Indeed, the representatives of Nicaragua no longer even bother to deny that *they* train and export guerrillas and arms to and through neighboring countries, though it has not been long since they answered with wide-eyed lies evidence of their many activities aimed at the destruction of the economies and overthrow of the governments of El Salvador, Guatemala, Honduras and other neighboring states.

Between them, Cuba and Nicaragua have managed enough fraternal help to the guerrillas or the region to bring to a halt the economic development that was steadily improving life and prospects in the area; to sow death and destruction in El Salvador and reap insecurity in Honduras, Costa Rica and elsewhere in the region.

Examples abound of the systematic creation and support by Cuba and Nicaragua of war against the other Central American states:

In December, 1981, after meetings in Havana with Salvadoran guerrilla leaders, Fidel Castro directed that external supplies of arms sold to FMLN units be stepped up to make possible an offensive to disrupt any chance for a peaceful vote in the March, 1982 elections.

In addition to vitally needed ammunition, these supply operations included greater quantities of more sophisticated heavier weapons. In 1982 deliveries included M-60 machine guns, M-79 grenade launchers, and M-72 antitank weapons, thus significantly increasing guerrilla firepower. Individual units also regularly received tens of thousands of dollars for routine purchases of non-lethal supplies on commercial markets and payments (including bribes) to enable the clandestine munitions pipeline to function.

Following the setback caused by their overwhelming repudiation in Salvador's March, 1982 elections, the FMLN leaders repeated the pattern following their 1981 failed "final offensive." This time with still more help.

After two years of combat, the FMLN headquarters in Nicaragua has evolved into an extremely sophisticated command and control center. Guerrilla planning and operations in El Salvador are guided from this headquarters in Nicaragua by Cuban and Nicaraguan officers. FMLN headquarters coordinates logistical support for guerrilla units widely spread throughout El Salvador, including food, medicines, clothing, money and—most importantly—weapons and ammunition.

On March 14, 1982, the FMLN clandestine Radio Venceremos (then located in El Salvador) broadcast a message to guerrillas in El Salvador urging them "to maintain their fighting spirit 24 hours a day to carry out *the missions ordered by the FMLN general command.*" (emphasis added)

Thus, the Nicaraguans provide the arms and weapons to destroy their neighbor's economy and direct the effort from their territory. But their activities are not restricted to El Salvador. They also seek to subvert their democratic neighbors, Honduras and Costa Rica, while using their territories as intermediary points to channel and disguise outside support for the Salvadoran guerrillas. In Honduras, Nicaraguan agents and Salvadoran extreme left groups have:

> Maintained links with almost all the Honduran terrorist groups to assist them in subversive planning, training and operations.
>
> Played a role in the increased terrorism in Honduras. Discussions were held in mid-1982 among the Cubans, Sandinistas, and Salvadoran insurgents about steps to take against the Honduran government.
>
> Captured Salvadoran and Honduran terrorists have admitted that explosives used in bombing attacks in the Honduran capital were obtained in Nicaragua. Other information indicates the Cubans had a hand in planning the seizure of 108 hostages in San Pedro Sula in September, 1982.

The Morazanist Front for the Liberation of Honduras (FMLH) was described in the pro-government Nicaraguan newspaper, *El Nuevo Diario*, by "Octavio," one of its founders, as a political-military organization formed as part of the "increasing regionalization of the Central American conflict." As a result of a raid on November 27, 1981, the Honduran police ultimately captured several members of this group. The captured terrorists told Honduran authorities that the Nicaraguan government had provided them with funds for travel expenses, as well as explosives. Captured documents and statements by detained guerrillas further indicated that the group was formed in Nicaragua at the instigation of high-level Sandinista leaders. The group's chief of operations resided in Managua and members of the group received military training in Nicaragua and Cuba. Other captured documents revealed that guerrillas at one safehouse were responsible for transporting arms and munitions into Honduras from Esteli, Nicaragua.

In Costa Rica, where the government has attempted to stop the continued use of its territory for supplying weapons to the region's Marxist-Leninist guerrillas, Cuba and Nicaragua targeted the government's efforts. During 1982, for example:

> The Cubans and Sandinistas provided weapons and training for Costa Rican leftist terrorists.

Nicaragua has instigated terrorist actions in Costa Rica, leading to increased tensions between the two countries. Although the Sandinistas denied complicity, the July 3, 1982 bombing of the Honduran Airlines office in San Jose took place at Nicaragua's direction, according to German Pinzon, a Colombia M-19 member who was arrested by Costa Rican authorities on July 14, 1982. Pinzon, who confessed to placing the bomb, said that Nicaraguan diplomats in Costa Rica had recruited and trained him for the bombing operation. With the help of Pinzon, the Costa Rican government caught the Nicaraguan diplomats *in flagrante*. They were declared *persona non grata* and expelled from Costa Rica on July 17, 1982.

Since the beginning of 1982, several guerrilla arms caches and safehouses have been uncovered in Costa Rica. Some arms may be for use by radical groups inside Costa Rica, as well as for shipment to guerrilla movements in El Salvador.

Mr. President, the evidence of systematic, continuing aggression by Nicaragua against her Central American neighbors is as clear as is the evidence of Nicaragua's repression of her own people and the betrayal of the solemn promises made by her military rulers to the Nicaraguan people, the Organization of American States and the world.

Of course, massive intervention in the internal affairs of her neighbors is not the only evidence of the junta's contempt for the principles of non-intervention, respect for territorial integrity and sovereignty, self-determination and the non-use of force.

Nicaragua demonstrates contempt for all these principles of the Charter when she supports the Soviet Union's continued brutal occupation of Afghanistan and the Vietnamese invasion and brutal occupation of Cambodia. When her so-called Sandinista governors support the invasion and occupation of these countries and the use of chemical weapons against those peoples, they demonstrate how little they deserve the name Sandinista, how utterly they have betrayed the principles and legacy of Sandino. Pablo Chamorro, editor and publisher of *La Prensa* before his assassination and a writer whose name is from time to time invoked by the leaders of the Nicaraguan revolution, wrote of Sandino, a passage which I quoted a year ago and which is just as relevant today:

Sandino should be exalted precisely as a contrast to the communists who obey signals from Russia and China. Sandino fought against the United States Marines but he did not bring Russian Cossacks to Nicaragua as Fidel Castro did in Cuba. There is a great difference in the communist Fidel Castro who in his false battle for the independence of his country has filled it with Russian rockets, soldiers, planes and even canned goods and a Sandino who defended the sovereignty of his ground with homemade bombs but without accepting the patronage of another power. For this reason, Sandino was great because he was not handed over to communist treason as Castro but fought within an Indo-Hispanic limit. Naturally the communists who attacked and slandered Sandino when he was in the mountains now try to use him because they have no moral scruple to restrain them. Sandino was a pure product of our land, very different from the products exported by Russia or China and, as such, we must exalt and preserve his memory. The value of his exploits is a Nicaraguan value not Soviet, and his nationalism is indigenous not Russian. Sandino is a monument to the dignity of our country and we must not permit the communists with whom he never communed to besmirch his memory in order to use his prestige and to succeed, someday, on the pretext that they are fighting imperialism in delivering over our land to Russia as Castro did with Cuba.

We should not deny, however, that Nicaragua's dictators derive as many benefits from her incorporation into the Soviet bloc as her people derive sorrows.

In this Security Council in the last days we have observed the fraternal support Soviet puppet states provide one another in this arena. We have also observed how they mock the values and the procedures of the Security Council.

When such basic values of international order as respect for territorial integrity, national independence or human rights are invoked by states such as Grenada, Vietnam and Cuba, who have already made clear their support for the occupation of Afghanistan and Cambodia and their indifference to the gassing of those peoples, and when we hear the representative of the Soviet Union speak of intervention, of mercenaries, of invasions, of subservience, we know we are in the presence of an attempt to sow confusion not understanding, an exercise in intellectual terrorism which mocks the values of the Charter and, above all, the process of reason on which this body must rely.

This Council cannot be taken seriously as a forum for the resolution of disputes if it permits itself to be transformed into a weapon in an ongoing conflict.

We are aware, Mr. President, of the theory articulated by Frederick Engels, among others, that there are no neutral processes; that all notions of truth, law, and fairness merely reflect economically based power relations. We know that according to this doctrine truth is what the most powerful say it is and fairness is whatever the most powerful defines it be to. *We believe that we are witnessing here an effort to transform the United Nations into an arena where power—as measured by numbers and volume—defines what is good, what is true, what is fair, what is peace.*

What is true is what the so-called progressive nations say it is.

What is fair is what serves their interests.

What is legitimate is what expands their power.

Thus, it is legitimate for communist governments to train and arm guerrillas and make war on their non-communist neighbors.

It is illegitimate for non-communists to attempt to defend themselves or for others to help them to do so.

According to this logic, movements which expand communist power are, by definition, national liberation movements; everything is permitted to achieve their ends. Nothing is permitted beyond their targets, not even the right of self-defense.

We have seen in the past days discouraging indications that the confusion and intimidation have already had insidious effects.

We heard Mexico endorse Nicaragua's right to self-determination and freedom from foreign interference. And in the same speech we heard the same representative of Mexico call for an end to all military assistance to El Salvador, which presumably has no right to self-determination or freedom from foreign intervention.

We heard the representative of Zimbabwe identify his country and people and their problems with those of the Sandinistas and allude darkly to their common experience with powerful, unscrupulous neighboring nations. We listened to his concern for Nicaragua's independence and territorial integrity and his indifference to the same rights for Nicaragua's neighbors.

We heard the representative of Tanzania give his distorted account of who is infiltrating terrorists and arms into whose territory, and who is seeking peace. We heard him invoke Nicaragua's right to live in peace and choose her own political, social, and economic system, without any indication that those rights extended also to her neighbors.

We heard the representative of China express his admiration for the "Nicaraguan struggle" and call for an end to the intervention in the region of "a super-power" as though it were only "a super-power" that posed obstacles to the people of the region to solve their own problems.

We listened while the representative of Panama discussed the problems of Nicaragua without ever mentioning Nicaragua's massive, continuing efforts at destabilization of her neighbors.

We heard the representative of Pakistan express confidence in the Nicaraguan government's will to peace and non-intervention, their desire to live in peace with their neighbors.

In sum, Mr. President, we have heard in the past days repeated indications of the corrosive effects of systematic bias, systematic lies, systematic redefinition of key political values and distortion of the key political processes of this body designed to support international peace.

In his Nobel lecture, Alexander Solzhenitsyn confronted again the relationship between tyranny and the systematic distortion of reality. He commented:

> Whoever has once announced violence as his METHOD must inexorably choose lying as his PRINCIPLE. At birth, violence behaves openly and even proudly. But as soon as it becomes stronger and firmly established, it senses the thinning of the air around it and cannot go on without befogging itself in lies, coating itself with lying's sugary oratory. It does not always or necessarily go straight for the gullet; usually it demands of its victims only allegiance to the lie, only complicity in the lie.

Mr. President, whoever in this arena supports Nicaragua's right to commit repression at home and aggression against her neighbors, whoever is ready to respect Nicaragua's right to self-determination, self-government, non-intervention and peace, and takes no account of the rights of her neighbors to the same protections *against* Nicaragua, has become an accomplice in the betrayal of these values and this process.

This betrayal is inconsistent with the search for peace. It must be repudiated before this body will be able to participate in the process of conflict resolution. It is not too late for the nations of Central America to forego violence, to enter on the pathway of negotiations, internal reconciliation, democracy, and development. Let us make certain that what happens in this body facilitates that process. Thank you.

Right of Reply I by Ambassador Kirkpatrick

I would comment, first of all, concerning the Soviet representative's exercise in cliometrics, that it suffered from what such quantitative, historical analyses often do, namely, the effort to add non-additive, that is non-comparable events. Most of the non-comparable events which he attempted to add were drawn from the remote past. Fortunately, however, we are a new nation, and his list was relatively short. The U.S. has long since given up intervening in anyone's affairs.

Now, if we were to attempt to do a comparative analysis of Soviet aggressions against neighboring peoples, the job, I am afraid, would require a computer. The quantities are so great. One would, of course, begin with the peoples of the so-called autonomous Soviet Socialist Republics themselves, the Ukraine, for example, the people of Tashkent, Latvia, Lithuania, Estonia—I'm choosing almost at random—of course, more recently the miserable people of Afghanistan. The truth is that the Soviet record of armed aggression against the peoples of her own empire is so well known that it does not really bear repetition.

May I say that I am very pleased to hear the representative of Zimbabwe affirm their support for the universal application of the principle of non-intervention. That is, in fact, what the Charter of the United Nations requires of all of us, and we hope that all of us are, in fact, prepared to grant.

So far as the representative of China is concerned, I think one can hope that China too will affirm that same universality in application of the principles of non-intervention in the affairs of other states.

Right of Reply II by Ambassador Kirkpatrick

First, I would like to point out to my distinguished colleague from the Soviet Union that the country for whose name he was searching concerning the 1965 action is the Dominican Republic, which has ever since enjoyed independence and democracy.

There is, as one of my colleagues has pointed out to me quite correctly, one very important difference between those countries in which the United States in an earlier time and an earlier mode occasionally intervened and those governments and states and peoples in whose internal affairs the Soviet Union has intervened. That difference is that, like the Dominican Republic, the states which were the objects of U.S. intervention are today independent states, mostly democratic states, who enjoy self-government and self-determination. In contrast, those states like Afghanistan or Latvia, Lithuania, Estonia or any of the nations of Eastern Europe who had the misfortune to be intervened by the Soviet Union have not, until this day, re-established their autonomy.

Right of Reply III by Ambassador Kirkpatrick

I should like to reply unequivocally that the United States government has no aggressive designs against the government of Nicaragua, or against the Nicaraguan people. The United States, indeed, has no intention of invading anyone or of conducting an armed action against anyone or of occupying any other country. The United States government has no interest in any territorial aggrandizement whatsoever. And so far as the people of Nicaragua are concerned, we desire nothing whatsoever for the people of Nicaragua except the fulfillment of precisely those promises which the government of Nicaragua, the Sandinista junta of Nicaragua, made to the people on its accession to power.

THE RIGHT TO DESTABILIZE NEIGHBORS

I should like to begin my remarks by congratulating you on your accession to the presidency of the Security Council, and express our confidence in your sense of fairness and your skill in the conduct of the affairs of this Council.

Mr. President, it is an extraordinary experience to hear the representative of Nicaragua's harsh dictatorship invoke the principle of non-intervention in internal affairs, the Charter of the United Nations and other international laws, and accuse the United States of invasion. It is an extraordinary experience to hear the representative of Nicaragua's harsh dictatorship speak of the rule of law, talk about American public opinion polls, quote American media and even American elected officials. I am especially struck by the invocation of the principle of non-intervention by Nicaragua's dictators. Since they have come to power they have been busy fomenting war in the region, destroying the peace and the possibility of progress in El Salvador and Honduras and other neighboring states, and forcing militarization on the region.

Mr. President, the United States does not invade small countries on its borders. We do not have 100,000 occupation troops in any country in the world, least of all on our borders. Our neighbors need have no such concerns. I thought, however, since the representative of Nicaragua has relied so heavily on American media this morning in his presentation to the Council, the record ought to be set straight. I thought I might have recourse as well to some American media concerning events in Central America and the respect which the government of Nicaragua habitually shows to the principle of non-intervention in the affairs of its neighbors.

The current *Time* magazine, for example, has a very interesting article, which I recommend to the members of the Council. It is entitled, "How the Salvadoran Rebels Order Outside Help for Their Revolution." It begins by saying, "the building of a Nicaraguan arms link to El Salvador began almost as soon as the victorious revolutionaries took power in the Nicaraguan capital of Managua in July, 1979." It has maps with arrows which describe supply routes—they're not quite as good as our government maps, but they're not bad. They are good enough so that the members of the Council can get a general impression about the regular flow of arms from Nicaragua through Honduras into El Salvador.

The article itself describes various arms infiltration routes. One, for example, it says "hugged the Honduran Pacific coast between Nicaragua and

Address before the Security Council, May 9, 1983.

El Salvador, then angled into the remote areas of El Salvador where Marxist rebels hold almost undisputed sway. U.S. analysts estimate that 15 to 20 such land routes exist across Honduras." One wonders about Honduras' right to be free of infiltration by its neighbors. The article goes on to say, "other military shipments come in by air and sea. Sandinista smugglers have been known to move supplies directly across the 20-mile-wide gulf of Fonseca. When the going is safe the Nicaraguans make nighttime forays from the Pacific gulf port of Potosi aboard small fishing boats equipped with false bottoms, or 50-foot frame canoes. That practice has now been curtailed because of the patrols of U.S. electronic surveillance ships in the area and the greater vigilance of the Salvadoran and Honduran navies." One can readily understand why neighbors engaging in such practices would not want any electronic surveillance in their region.

The article continues: "At night the Jiquilisco region is also known as a favorite destination of arms-laden helicopters (from Nicaragua)) and light fixed-wing aircraft. . . . An important alternative air route for the smugglers (from Nicaragua) is from the former British colony of Belize into Guatemala. After that, the rebels and their supplies filter south into Salvadoran rebel strongholds." Apparently the government of Nicaragua has a bit of a problem respecting the right of the government of Guatemala to be free of infiltration across *its* borders as well.

The article is very detailed. It sums up its point about the extent and detail of the supply route between Nicaragua and El Salvador with a line which it also uses for its title: "Like a Sears, Roebuck Catalogue." It says that rebels in El Salvador can order from Nicaragua whatever they need. One unit may say I need candles, boots, batteries, diarrhea medicine, bullets and mortar rounds. If they don't get what they want, they complain. The fact that they complain shows they have a pipeline they think they can depend on.

The consequence, of course, of this gross violation of the principle of non-intervention in the life of neighboring states by the government of Nicaragua is the destruction of peace in the region. It is especially tragic for the society of El Salvador, where the economy has been deliberately targeted and deliberately destroyed. I pointed out not long ago in a discussion of this same issue that some 34 bridges and 145 electrical transmission towers had been destroyed in El Salvador last year, that some 18,000 Salvadorans had been put out of work by this destruction. The president of the United States spoke two weeks ago to the Congress and pointed out in his speech, and I quote: "Tonight in El Salvador because of the ruthless guerrilla attacks much of the fertile land cannot be cultivated. Less than half the rolling stock of the railways remains operational. Bridges, water facilities, telephone and electric systems have been destroyed and damaged. In one 22-month period there were 5,000 interruptions of electrical power, one region was without electricity for one-third of a year." Thus the consequences for one of Nicaragua's neighbors of Nicaragua's respect for the principle of non-intervention.

The distinguished representative of the government of Nicaragua has referred repeatedly to the debate now underway in the United States, among Americans, about what American policy should be with regard to the area. He is quite right, of course. There is a debate. And the debate is on the question of whether the United States should help the people of El Salvador and the people of Nicaragua to defeat the effort to impose upon the totalitarian dictatorships with the assistance and by means of arms filtered to them by a ruthless, terrorist international. There is a debate in the United States about whether the United States should leave small countries powerless, small peoples helpless, without defense against conquest by violent minorities trained and armed by remote dictators. Such a debate is underway in the United States. It is not complete and we will continue that debate in our own way. We will continue it not by the method of lies but by the method of democracy.

The method of democracy relies on discussion. We will make our decision at the end of our debate and we will make that decision by democratic means. We very much wish that the government of Nicaragua would join us in such a democratic decision process. We very much wish that there could be debate in Nicaragua about the public policies of that government. We very much wish that the people of Nicaragua, its journalists, its political leaders were free to make their arguments in public arenas, to discuss the questions before that people, to criticize their government, to rise in legislative arenas and state their criticisms freely. We wish that the people of Nicaragua had the opportunity to be polled by honest and objective public opinion organizations. We wish that the people of Nicaragua had the opportunity to settle *their* discussions and decisions and debates by voting. We in the United States will live by the results of our democratic processes. We can wish nothing better for the people of Nicaragua than that they be given comparable opportunity.

The relationship between the government of Nicaragua and its people is, of course, at the heart of much of the discussion here. What is the nature of this problem? What is the nature of what the Nicaraguan representative calls an "American invasion"? Needless to say, there is no American invasion of Nicaragua. It is a fact that there is fighting in Nicaragua. It is a fact that there is very widespread unhappiness, indeed misery, in Nicaragua. It is a fact that the government of Nicaragua has a problem. The nature of that problem is, of course, not international. The nature of that problem is national. Nicaragua's problem is with Nicaraguans. In Nicaragua today

Nicaraguans fight other Nicaraguans for the control of their country's destiny.

I thought since the representative of Nicaragua had brought to the attention of the Council so many items from the American press, I might impose on the Council a second item from yesterday's *Washington Post* which was referred to by the representative of Nicaragua. (Demonstrating the advantages of free discussion, by the way, you can find a lot of different kinds of evidence in our newspapers.) The item that I would like to bring to the attention of the Council is a column by Jack Anderson, who is a well-known liberal columnist in the United States, not a reliable supporter of the administration that currently governs the United States.

The column is called "A Popular Force," and I would like to read from it briefly.

> While the Congress debates the Reagan administration's clandestine operations in Nicaragua, the American public is beset by conflicting information about exactly what is going on there.... To get some reliable, firsthand answers to these crucial questions, I sent my associate, Jon Lee Anderson to the troubled region. He has just returned from a week-long foray into northern Nicaragua with anti-Sandinista guerrillas. They belong to the Nicaraguan Democratic forces (FDN), the major group of ... insurgents.
>
> He traveled with a well-armed, 50-member guerrilla band led by a commander whose nom de guerre is El Gorrion—The Sparrow. Their base camp was deep in the rugged mountains of Nicaragua's Nueva Segovia province, near the Honduran border.
>
> It quickly became obvious that the guerrillas had the support of the populace. They were fed and protected by local peasants at every step. Traveling on foot and only by night to avoid detection by government troops, the guerrillas spent the days hiding in 'safe houses,' often within shouting distance of government-held towns. If the peasants had wanted to betray them, it would have been a simple matter to tip off the Sandinista militia to their hiding places. The peasants also provided The Sparrow with up-to-the-minute intelligence on the whereabouts, movement and strength of the Sandinista forces.
>
> The anti-Sandinista military prowess is not so clear-cut. My associate discovered this to his dismay when he accompanied The Sparrow's band on a planned pre-dawn ambush of government troop carriers along a country road.
>
> ... The guerrillas were themselves surprised by sniper fire from hilltop positions above them and were forced to pull out. The retreat was carried out skillfully, however, and two nights later the guerrillas avenged their defeat with an attack on the hilltop sniper's nest. The FDN commandos treated the snipers to a half-hour barrage of rockets, grenades and machine-gun fire, before returning satisfied to their base camp.
>
> Most of the FDN guerrillas ... were local peasants, not Somocista exiles. But there were also former National Guardsmen, and they tend to be in com-

mand because of their military experience. Still, the core of the Sparrow's group consisted of locally recruited peasants. In fact, on my associate's last day with the rebel band, he witnessed the arrival of 50 new recruits, all of them peasants from the neighboring province of Madriz. One of the new recruits was a defecting Sandinista army instructor. There were other ex-Sandinistas in the guerrilla troop. One was Dunia, a star graduate of the Sandinista's post-revolution literacy campaign. Dunia did so well she was rewarded with a junket to Cuba. She is now the camp medic for the Sparrow's band.

The rebels and their noncombatant collaborators cited a variety of reasons for their disenchantment with the Sandinistas: enforced food rationing, expropriation of the farmers' markets, enforced organization of peasant co-ops, the Sandinistas' anti-religious policies and harassment of the Catholic Church. The Sandinistas themselves indirectly aided the guerrillas' recruitment of at least a dozen of the new arrivals. They said they had been under increasing pressure to join the militia. Forced to take sides, they chose the 'contras.'

Still, it was not an easy choice for many. They expressed genuine anguish at being forced—one way or another—to fight against fellow Nicaraguans. 'We don't want to fight our Nicaraguan brothers,' they said. The ones they're after are the Sandinista leaders and their Cuban, East German, Bulgarian and other foreign advisors.

That's not the end of the column; there are two paragraphs left for anyone who is interested.

I would like to reiterate to the Council that the United States government has repeatedly throughout the brief history of the Sandinista dictatorship, sought to establish constructive relations with that government and, during the period of its destabilization of the area, sought to work with others in the area to achieve regional peace.

In August, 1981, on a special mission to Managua, Assistant-Secretary of State Thomas Enders presented a five-point peace plan to the Sandinistas to reduce regional tensions. Based on the termination of Nicaraguan support for guerrilla groups, the plan called for a U.S. pledge to enforce strictly laws governing exiles' activities in U.S. territory, re-affirmation of non-intervention and non-interference by all parties, limits on arms and military forces, resumption of U.S. economic assistance to Nicaragua which had been very substantial and a U.S.-Nicaraguan cultural exchange program. The Sandinista government made no substantive response.

On April 19, 1982, U.S. Ambassador Anthony Quainton delivered an eight-point peace proposal to the Sandinistas that called for an end to Nicaraguan support for guerrillas in neighboring countries. It called for limits on arms and foreign military advisors, a joint pledge of non-interference and non-intervention, arms limit verification measures, resumption of U.S. economic assistance, implementation of cultural exchange programs and the reaffirmation of Sandinista commitments to pluralism, free elections and a mixed economy. The Sandinistas made a non-substantive response that did not even address the U.S. plan. They presented only rhetorical counterproposals.

On October 19, 1982, eight regional democracies, including the United States, set forth the essential conditions for peace in Central America, again including verifiable limits on arms and foreign military advisors, national reconciliation through the democratic process, a halt to support for insurgent groups, mutual respect for pledges of non-intervention and respect for basic human rights. The countries asked Costa Rica to discuss these conditions with Nicaragua. That, too, came to nought.

In addition, the Sandinistas have rejected other proposals put forth by their neighbors. As late as 1983 they refused to meet with Costa Ricans, Hondurans, Salvadorans and Guatemalans in multilateral discussions supported by the Contadora Group, but you've already heard about this.

The Sandinista insistence on bilateral rather than multilateral talks underlines its desire to resolve its external problems while avoiding the issue of its export of revolution, war and misery to its neighbors. The record speaks for itself. I should just like to close these remarks by reminding members of the Council that in his speech to the joint session of the U.S. Congress, President Reagan asserted, and I quote,

> To support these diplomatic goals in the region, I offer these assurances, and I should like to offer these assurances again to the Council on behalf of the government of the United States.
>
> The United States will support any agreement among Central American countries for the withdrawal—under fully verifiable and reciprocal conditions—of all foreign military and security advisors and troops.
>
> We want to help opposition groups join the political process in all countries and compete by ballots instead of bullets.
>
> We will support any verifiable, reciprocal agreement among Central American countries on the renunciation of support for insurgencies on neighbors' territory.
>
> And, finally, we desire to help Central America to end its costly arms race and will support any verifiable, reciprocal agreements on the non-importation of offensive weapons.

Finally, I would like to say to members of the Council that every nation in the United Nations, especially small nations, especially nations with powerful neighbors, should ponder carefully this case, should think well about what is being demanded once again of this Council by the government of Nicaragua. The government of Nicaragua has once again come to us demanding of the United Nations international protection while it destabilizes its neighbors. It is claiming that a people repressed by foreign arms of a superpower has no right to help against that repression. That is a principle that I should suppose every member of the United Nations who is, in fact, committed to principles of national independence, self-determination, and non-intervention would do well to think hard about.

WHO SEEKS PEACE IN NICARAGUA?

Mr. President, the hour being late, I will try to be very beief. I would simply note that one hears here a very great deal of falsification of history and of current events.

The first point that I would like to make concerning these most recent falsifications is simply that the United States is neither a champion of Central American cooperation nor an opponent of Central American cooperation. If the countries of the region desire in fact to meet together to try to work out solutions to their problems, the United States poses no obstacles to that. No more do we pose obstacles to the desire of, shall we say, Libya and Chad to try to find solutions to their problems within the framework of the OAU or a great many nations of this United Nations who have come before this body and preferred, in fact, to find regional solutions. The United States neither champions that nor opposes it. We believe, in general, in the right and the practicality of nations most immediately involved in conflicts seeking to work out solutions to their problems.

Second, the United States has not invaded Nicaragua and does not intend to do so. The most that the United States has been reproached for or accused of by serious people is providing arms and advice to Nicaraguans fighting for their right to national self-determination.

Third, concerning one more falsification, the question of *who* has done *what* with regard to *which* meeting at *what* past time. The past is always less important than the present. The principles that are presumably at stake here are relatively clear, I think. The Central American democratic community, to which the Nicaraguan foreign minister objects, issued a declaration—the Declaration of San Jose—which asserted some principles, many

Address before the Security Council, May 16, 1983.

of which have also been identified by the Contadora group as principal concerns in the area. Those include: an end to the importation of all arms from outside the area into the area, with verification of that; an end to the importation of foreign advisors and the end of the use of foreign advisors throughout the area and verification of that.

In addition to that, there has been recent re-affirmation in the most current declaration of the Contadora of some other principles which were affirmed at San Jose. Those include, and I'm reading now from the UN unofficial translation of the Contadora communication: "Self-determination and non-intervention in the affairs of other states; the obligation not to allow the use of territory of one state for acts of aggression against another; the peaceful settlement of disputes; and the prohibition of the use of force to resolve conflict."

Mr. President, to the best of my knowledge, the basic problem which confronts the region is that one state in the region, namely Nicaragua, is precisely unwilling to affirm respect for the territorial integrity of other states, is unwilling to affirm its obligation not to allow its territory to be used for acts of aggression against another. It still claims for itself unique enjoyment of these rights. I believe that the Security Council should see very clearly that the United States, and I suspect all the other states involved in the Contadora process, except perhaps Nicaragua, are willing in very short order to agree to respect for self-determination and non-intervention in the affairs of other states; the obligation not to allow the territory of one state for acts of aggression against another; the peaceful settlement of disputes; and the prohibition of the threat of the use of force to resolve conflicts.

There has been a reference to the dreams of the people of Central America. The people of Nicaragua have dreams, too, and those dreams have been very cruelly betrayed. I believe that if the government of Nicaragua would simply keep the promises it has solemnly made to its own people, which promises we have frequently reviewed here—respect for human rights, for democratic processes—and would be willing to live in peace with its neighbors, if there were a will to do those things and to respect the principles of the Charter, then the precise format in which those questions were discussed and decided would turn out to be quite unimportant.

STUNNING CYNICISM

I would just like to reply to certain of the assertions made by the distinguished representative of the Soviet Union. I should like to note first the stunning cynicism of his remarks. It is indeed stunningly cynical for the representative of the Soviet Union, whose country undertook to flood the region of Central America with arms, heavy weapons which had never been seen in the region, and military advisors of an extraordinary assortment who have in common a particular relationship with his own country—a relationship which is characterized by the hegemony of the Soviet Union vis-a-vis the various client states. Those are the people who have introduced heavy weapons into Central America. Those are the people who have undermined economic progress and development in the region which was in fact proceeding at quite a steady rate before the deliberate efforts at militarization and destabilization of the region.

The suggestion was also made by the distinguished delegate of the Soviet Union that the United States sought to determine the internal life of the government of Nicaragua and should, in fact, be indifferent—should bug off—from any concern about the organization of its politics or economics. I should just like to say that the United States does not attempt to influence in inappropriate ways the organization of any country's economic system. We hope that all countries in the world will organize their economic systems in such a fashion that they will be productive of goods and for the well-being of their people. But that we regard wholly as their decision. We also regard the form of government of other countries as their decision.

We cannot, however, be indifferent to gross violations of human rights by other governments nor does the Charter of the United Nations suggest that we should do so. The Charter of the United Nations, in fact, identifies respect for human freedom and other human rights as central concerns of this organization and of all member states of this organization.

The United States also belongs to some other organizations and takes cognizance of obligations which are contracted vis-a-vis other organizations. We have noted here, for example, that the government of Nicaragua undertook some solemn commitments to the Organization of American States concerning the kind of government it would organize were it, in fact, to become the government of Nicaragua. It undertook commitments to organize democratic institutions, provide its people with democratic institutions in respect of their human rights and rule of law—regular, civil rule of law, quite specifically. We have suggested that those commitments

Address before the Security Council, May 18, 1983.

have not been fulfilled. And since the ruling clique of Nicaragua secured the assistance of the Organization of American States in its rise to power on the basis of those commitments, it raises some question about the bases of their government.

The representative of the Soviet Union also referred to the bloody crimes of the United States, I think was his phrase. The phrase reminded me of an item which I had read yesterday in a European newspaper concerning the death of some 3,000 Afghan civilians last week due to bombing of civilian populations by the nearly 150,000 Soviet occupation troops of that beleaguered country. The article that I read also noticed that neither the United Nations Security Council nor any other body of the United Nations had taken any note of this mass slaughter of Afghans. I would like, while we are talking about bloody crimes, to take formal note of the suffering of the Afghan people.

I would finally just like to say that it has been suggested by the Soviet representative and some others that they support regional efforts to achieve peace, and I would emphasize that that is, of course, precisely what we all support. If they support regional efforts to achieve peace, then there is unanimity because certainly the rest of us support regional efforts to achieve peace. The United States, for its part, stands ready at any time to support any agreements to end the importation of all arms and foreign military advisors into the region—any agreement to do so which is verifiable—and to support any agreement that provides for the mutual respect of borders by all countries in the region, and the non-interference in the affairs of one another and the end to all efforts at destabilization. Thank you very much.

CHOOSING THE ARENA OF DISCUSSION

The United States speaks in its role as a republic of the Americas, concerned about the present and the future of our hemisphere, concerned about the destiny of our neighbors and ourselves. These are, of course, matters of deep, national concern to us as nations and as Americans.

The United States expected that the Contadora process, which has been so widely endorsed by countries all over the world, would indeed be permitted to continue along its pathway in the search for peaceful solutions and negotiated agreements to the difficult problems which afflict Central America. The

Address to the General Committee of the 38th UN General Assembly, October 4, 1983.

United States ordinarily supports the inscription of all subjects of international concern in any United Nations body unless there is a specific, legal, jurisdictional reason that puts a subject beyond the jurisdiction of the United Nations and defines it as a matter of solely internal concern.

We have been impressed by the firm opposition of most of the countries concerned in the Central American conflict. We have been distressed by their suggestion that activities undertaken here may interfere with what most of the nations of the world, certainly including ours, believe is the best hope for peaceful solution and a prevention of the spread of conflict in that troubled area. The United States is deeply committed, however, to processes of full discussion; we are fully committed to all processes which show promise of contributing to peace rather than to war. We believe that that loose assemblage of regional countries called Contadora, though unofficial, though informal, represents the best hope currently available to the world—to the countries of this region. As previous speakers have indicated, that regional process called Contadora has so far been successful, at least, in preventing the spread of this menacing conflict. The countries involved opposed, 4 to 1, the inclusion of this item on the agenda.

From the United States' point of view, there is only one serious question to be confronted here: it is whether the desperately serious conflict confronting the countries of Central America should be left to those most directly concerned or should be submitted to the General Assembly. We have heard talk of gentlemen's agreements. We have already confronted in this organization the dangers of globalizing, ideologizing conflict. Should the countries of the region attempt to discuss, dispute, resolve this difficult conflict for themselves, perhaps, following the model of those most skillful members of the United Nations at conflict resolution, our African brothers? Should they take their conflict to this global body? The United States supports any process which promises to defend the national independence of the countries of our region as well as theirs, which commits itself to respecting the sovereignty of all these nations. We support the demand of nations of our region as well as other regions to the right to solve their problems without the intervention of others. We are prepared to support the solution which the nations of the region prefer.

Listening to this debate today I judge that their decision is clear; they prefer to deal with these regional problems through regional processes—they prefer to continue to attempt to settle their disputes among themselves. The United States supports their right to make this decision in matters which so deeply concern their national interests and ours and we shall support them as they proceed to decisions on this matter. Thank you.

Thank you, Mr. President. I must say, as a representative of the United

States, that we grow rather weary of hearing the endless talk and vacuous accusations of the government of Nicaragua concerning some fictitious war of the United States against Nicaragua. We have heard only today, under the guise of a discussion of an item on the agenda, scurrilous accusations against the good name and reputation of the United States, accusations against our intentions and, if I may say so, against our efficiency. We have heard comments about the United States' "dirty war" against Nicaragua. We have heard suggestions that the United States brings other nations into "its" war against Nicaragua.

Mr. President, I have said this before and I feel moved to say it again: the United States is not at war against Nicaragua. The United States is at peace with Nicaragua. The United States has no intention of invading Nicaragua, as has been suggested for the last two or so years. During those two or so years, the United States has moved repeatedly to try working both alone and with its colleagues in the region, precisely to bring enduring peace to the region and to work out, especially, more amicable relations with Nicaragua—all without success.

Nicaragua is prone to these recurring fantasies that the United States has declared war on it. I should like to say, Mr. President, that if the United States were ever to declare war on Nicaragua, there would be no doubt in anyone's mind that this had occurred. It has not occurred. It is not about to occur. But if such a condition were to exist, it would be unambiguous. The representative of Nicaragua spoke of my colleague Fred Ikle's speech, in which he spoke of the United States' desire for the victory of democratic forces in Nicaragua. He was referring, of course, not to United States but Nicaraguan forces, and I should like to say that the United States does indeed hope for the victory of democracy in Nicaragua. We believe very deeply in government by consent. We believe very deeply that the people of Nicaragua deserve all those benefits which the Sandinistas promised them in July, 1979, and have systematically denied the people of Nicaragua ever since. As a matter of fact, I might add that the United States hopes for the victory of the forces of freedom and democracy everywhere.

Finally, I may say, Mr. President, that the United States, because it does not fear freedom, does not fear open debate of any subject either in this arena or in any other. The difference here today on the question of inscription between Nicaragua and some other countries is not a difference between Nicaragua and the United States; it is a difference between Nicaragua and her neighbors and associates in the Contadora process. I do believe that all those assembled here who support that process should be clear about that. The United States, for its part, is prepared to discuss these issues in any arena that our colleagues decide is desirable. Thank you, Mr. President.

Bourgeois Conceptions of Fairness

I have listened with interest to the extraordinary statement of the representative of Nicaragua which we have just heard. Mr. President, I should like to say that the United States does not accept as accurate—as a description of our role or any conditions in the world—the statements of the government of Nicaragua either in their letter to the President of the Security Council or in their remarks just made.

The United States would have preferred not to speak at all tonight had there not been such an extraordinary distortion of our history and our policies, our practices and also of theirs. We are interested that the government of Nicaragua is so agitated tonight, agitated once again with fantasies of being invaded by the United States. I should like to say that in the realm of psychopathology these concerns are well understood. They are examples of projection. Those who are subject to them are countries who cannot imagine behaving in any other way than the ways they accuse others of behaving. I think it is doubtless true that the government of Nicaragua cannot imagine a government having great strength and not using it against hapless, helpless neighbors. The government of Nicaragua, having small strength, uses it in an uninhibited fashion against its neighbors and imagining that everyone and all countries would behave that way, is obviously concerned about having more powerful neighbors. It is trapped in the fantasies of power hungry dictators, locked in—Thomas Hobbs said it—a restless striving after power that ceases only in death.

The fact is that the United States does not require lectures on constitutional law and the observation of treaties from the government of Nicaragua. We are quite aware of the status of treaties in our own constitutional system. We are a government of laws. We freely and resolutely submit ourselves to our laws and to the disciplines of our laws, our courts, our legislatures and our populations who elect those legislatures to hold us to our own values and our promises. As I have said here before, we could hope nothing better for the people of Nicaragua than that they be permitted as a free electorate to discuss their public issues, to choose their representatives, to elect their governors, to make their decisions. I found it very interesting to hear the representative of the Nicaraguan junta describe the various provisions of the Rio Treaty and the OAS Treaty to which his government is a signatory. The government of Nicaragua will, of course, have an opportunity to discuss these questions tomorrow in the Organiza-

Address before the Security Council, October 26, 1983.

tion of American States where the Association of Eastern Caribbean States will be discussing the issues involved in the tragic events in Grenada.

I found it interesting to hear the representative of the government of Nicaragua describe as unacceptable the decision of the states of the Eastern Caribbean to invoke the treaty which binds them in a pact of mutual assistance as well as mutual respect for sovereignty. He seemed to suggest that their size—the fact that they were small states—somehow rendered it inappropriate that they should link themselves to each other by treaty relationship and even more inappropriate that they should have invoked the treaty which they had written and signed for their mutual protection. It was interesting to hear him refer to the United States having convoked a meeting of the Condeca Group. Once again, of course, the familiar disregard of history was present. The United States did no such thing. It was interesting to hear him reproach the United States for lack of respect for the sovereignty and national independence of neighboring states when, in fact, the United States is meticulous in its respect for the sovereign rights of our neighbors and also for their national independence. We respect even the right of our neighbors to make serious mistakes, as when they choose governments like that of the government of Nicaragua.

We listened with interest as we heard the representative of the government of Nicaragua reproach the United States government today with every act ever committed by any citizen or even any inhabitant of our country since we either were or were not discovered by Columbus some 500 years ago: William Walker, the interventions that presumably prevented Panama's successful rebellion against Colombia—of course he then forgot to mention that the United States had also intervened in a later phase to *help* Panama in a rebellion against Colombia establish itself as an independent state. The relevance of these historic events on our country, some of which are reprehensible, some of which are not reprehensible, all of which constitute an absolutely biased and hysterically distorted history of the Western Hemisphere again testify only to the lack of any capacity for analysis of the past or present.

It never occurred to me in my most condemnatory moments, as I reflected on the policy of the current government of Nicaragua, to reproach it with all of the crimes of its Samosista predecessors. It never occurred to me to reproach the current government of Nicaragua with all of the crimes of the oligarchs who governed that country for centuries and repressed its peasants. It never even occurs to me to reproach our Soviet colleagues for the excesses of some of their czarist predecessors. But the representative of Nicaragua has introduced into these considerations false history with false relevance to contemporary events. It invites us to reflect not on the events in the Eastern Caribbean, not on the organization of the government of

Nicaragua nor of its policies, but on its more recent history in which it made solemn promises to the Organization of American States, which promises it promptly disregarded, and equally solemn promises to its own people, which promises it cast aside and forgot. Frankly, it wouldn't have occurred to me to discuss any of these issues at midnight, nor did I propose to linger over them. I do recommend, however, that if our colleague from Nicaragua is seriously interested in these questions of the application of the amendments and provisions of the Rio Treaty and the Organization of American States founding act, that he pursue them in the appropriate arena, which of course is the OAS.

Finally, I would like to say simply that the United States regrets the fact that we are meeting here tonight in clear violation of the bourgeois conceptions of fairness to discuss this issue. We would have thought it more appropriate, as I said to my colleagues in informal consultations, to have conducted our discussions tomorrow morning, perhaps tomorrow afternoon, to have honored the normal practices of the Security Council and provided the head of state of the presidency of the Organization of East Caribbean States the opportunity to be present at the debate in which they are so deeply involved and by which they are affected. The Security Council in its wisdom decided otherwise, reminding us once again perhaps that bourgeois conceptions of fairness are just that, bourgeois, liberal, democratic conceptions of fairness—respected only by bourgeois governments. But so then, of course, Mr. President, is the conception of the Security Council itself, a residue of a liberal, democratic, bourgeois civilization and dream. A dream of nations meeting together committed to peace, dedicated to the pursuit of fairness, ready to judge each other by the standards to which it is willing to submit. This meeting tonight and most especially the extraordinary statement of our Nicaraguan colleague remind us that these may indeed be outdated notions, but, Mr. President, if these are outdated notions, so is this an outdated institution. Thank you.

NICARAGUA'S FALSE CHARGES

The French writer, Georges Bernanos, once wrote that "the worst, the most corrupting of lies are problems poorly stated." The purpose of those who brought the issue of Central America to the General Assembly today,

Address before the 38th General Assembly, November 8, 1983.

who asked for this debate, is to enlist the United Nations in defining the problem in Central America in a manner that corrupts the truth. Their goal is to cloak their own aggressive and violent policies in a mantle of United Nations rhetoric about non-intervention and the non-use of force. Their goal, quite specifically, is to use the principles of the United Nations Charter to justify actions that, precisely, violate and subvert those principles of the United Nations Charter.

The representative of Nicaragua would like to have the United Nations endorse his own government's perverse definition of the problem in Central America. According to this definition, Nicaragua is a peace-loving state with no designs on its neighbors. It maintains fraternal relations with Cuba, the Soviet Union, East Germany, Bulgaria, Libya and several other similarily inclined "peace-loving" states, simply for the purpose of promoting social justice, internal peace and self-determination. Of course, it also maintains a large military establishment, "four times as big and eight times as strong" as the late dictator Anastasio Somoza's Guardia Nacional, as the present commander of Nicaraguan forces put it last year. But this, of course, is only for the purpose of self-defense, which presumably is required against Nicaragua's neighbors.

The government of Nicaragua is convinced, or so it would like to have us believe, that an invasion of Nicaragua by the United States is imminent. The government of Nicaragua has brought this issue of Central America to the Security Council three times over the past year and a half, always alleging that a massive military invasion by the United States is imminent. Now it has come to the General Assembly with the same charge. This imminent invasion, of course, never takes place; nor does the government of Nicaragua ever produce a scintilla of evidence to demonstrate that it is about to occur. It is reduced to complaining that the United States assists Nicaraguans struggling inside Nicaragua for their right to self-determination and self-government.

What we have in the government of Nicaragua's claims is a combination of bravado and paranoia, induced for the purpose of justifying a tightening of internal repression and the further build-up of military force, with the hope, doubtless, of increased Soviet bloc military aid. The United Nations is then enlisted to give the appearance of international legitimacy to these plans.

The mind-set of the Nicaraguan regime, this combination of bravado and paranoia, was, perhaps, exemplified best in the speech which Interior Minister Tomas Borge gave before members of the National Firefighting System on October 29th of this year. Nicaragua would defeat the U.S. army, said Tomas Borge "even if they reduce our cities to ashes." If the United States had to call on elite forces to defeat Grenada, said Commandante Borge in a reference to the rescue mission by the United States and several eastern Caribbean states in Grenada several days earlier, then, he continued, against Nicaragua it would have to resort to "Batman, Superman and Spiderman."

The substance of Nicaragua's case before this body has about as much relation to reality as do the childish fantasy figures invoked by Mr. Borge. What is the reality? What is an accurate statement of the problem of Central America?

The reality is that the Sandinistas came to power in 1979 through armed struggle and thereafter proceeded to violate all of the promises they made to the Organization of American States and made to the Nicaraguan people regarding internal pluralism and democracy and peaceful relations with their neighbors. The Sandinista revolution, then, has not only betrayed the promises made to the OAS, the promises made to its own people; it has betrayed as well the values and traditions of its own namesake. Augusto Cesar Sandino was not a Marxist-Leninist; as I have repeatedly reminded colleagues in the United Nations, he supported nationalism and not the Soviet Empire. On that basis he would have criticized Cuba's submission to Moscow's so-called internationalism, for he desired sovereignty for his country, and desired a free country. He was very harshly criticized by communists while he was still alive for bourgeois and counterrevolutionary tendencies. The communist attacks against Sandino began when he was in Mexico because he refused to adjust his fight for "country and liberty" to the plans of the Mexican communists. For that reason, the secretary general of the Mexican Communist party called him a traitor and denounced him upon his death.

It is precisely "country and liberty" that the so-called Sandinistas have betrayed in imposing a Marxist-Leninist dictatorship over the Nicaraguan people, in subordinating Nicaragua to Cuba and in a larger sense to the objectives of the Soviet Union and its global empire. Instead of the elections promised to the Nicaraguan people, the so-called Sandinistas provided subjugation and dictatorship. Instead of self-government promised by the so-called Sandinistas, they have provided a rigged council of state. Instead of the pluralism promised the people of Nicaragua, the so-called Sandinistas have purged all democratic opposition. Instead of pluralism and respect for human rights, the so-called Sandinistas have driven the Miskito Indians, that harmless, indigenous people that seeks only the right to live its own life peacefully, from the Atlantic coast. Instead of the freedom of religion pledged by all signatories to the Universal Declaration of Human Rights, the so-called Sandinistas have repressed the church and the Pope on his visit. Instead of respect for the right to organize free trade unions and bargain collectively, the so-called Sandinistas have repressed free trade unions in Nicaragua. Committees in defense of Sandinismo have multiplied alongside the mobs which seek to impose the arbitrary decisions of those committees.

Of course, Nicaragua is only a pawn in a larger game—a game in which one of the larger players is Cuba, which is itself a pawn in a still larger game, a mere proxy for the Soviet Union. It is no secret in this body that the Soviet Union has targeted various nations in Latin American as particularly attractive objects for its expansionist designs. The Soviet Union has quite clearly, quite openly, beginning in the late '60s, begun to identify the armed road as the way to power and influence in this hemisphere. Their theoreticians, writing in Soviet military and strategic journals, have since noted that in Latin America only the armed struggle has so far succeeded as an instrument for the establishment of Marxist-Leninist governments and the spread of revolution.

I am always struck by the frank way in which Soviet theoretical journals and theoreticians discuss their reliance on violence as an instrument for expansion. The Soviet military encyclopedia of 1978, for example, in an article on Latin America, commented: "The change in the correlation of forces in the international arena in favor of socialism has led to the activization of the struggle by the peoples of Latin America which opens the way to socialism in the Western Hemisphere." What is it that has opened the way to socialism in the Western Hemisphere? Not changes in economic conditions, not changes in social conditions, but change in the correlation of forces in the international arena. Or listen again: "National liberation struggle is a form of war waged by peoples of colonial and dependent or formerly colonial territories in which socialist countries become the decisive factor when peoples launch an armed struggle against internal reactionaries." That is, the national liberation struggle is a form of war in which socialist countries like the Soviet Union and Cuba become the decisive factor when the peoples launch an armed struggle against so-called internal reactionaries. This is very straightforward; it gives us a lot of insight into the role of force, quite specifically the role of Soviet force, Soviet military strength, in such areas as, for example, Central America, today. Where people have launched an internal struggle, then Soviet military force directly, or by way of Libya or Cuba, becomes the decisive instrument, or at least it is intended to become that.

The complement to the Soviet use of force is the effort to sell this policy in the United Nations and in influential circles outside this body, to sell the perverse doctrine which grants to national liberation movements, that is, Soviet-backed, Soviet-defined, national liberation movements, a monopoly of the legitimate use of force. According to this doctrine, the use of revolutionary violence, that is, violence committed by those linked to the Soviet

Union and its clients, is defined as a just protest against, by definition, unjust social and political circumstances.

Small bands of violent men have discovered in our times that by the skillful use of violence and propaganda they can win power against overwhelming numbers. They begin with terror, which has been aptly defined as the deliberate, systematic murder, maiming and menacing of the innocent to inspire fear in order to gain political ends. Such deliberate use of terror is relied upon to produce a revolutionary situation. It has become the preferred tactic of contemporary revolutionary conflicts. This now familiar cycle is accompanied today by a chorus of moral outrage from a self-designated constituency of client states linked to the Soviet Union who apply, in bodies like this one, to win symbolic support for the violence used outside. The pattern is by now discouragingly familiar. Choose a weak government, organize a national liberation front, add a terrorist campaign to disrupt order and provoke repression—which serves to weaken an already weak economy—then intensify the violence. The brittle institutions of many, conceivably even most Third World governments, will crumble under such strains. The skillful use of what used to be called Fifth Columns, enables the Soviets to foment coups and civil wars under the guise of indigenous politics.

That is not all. Once a transfer of power has been achieved and a dictatorship friendly to the Soviet Union has been established, the Soviets seek to guarantee its irreversibility by providing thousands and thousands of technicians, advisors, troops, "workers" such as those we saw in Grenada, to prop up and guide the new government. Thus, the extraordinary array of Soviet bloc military and civilian personnel in Nicaragua, Angola, Benin, Ghana, Congo, Mozambique, Guinea-Bissau, Cuba, Democratic Yemen, Syria, Ethiopia, and so forth. In those countries one finds extraordinary international brigades accumulated from East Germany, from Czechoslovakia, from Bulgaria, from Libya—the same governments we hear speaking to the problem here—from Vietnam, from the PLO, from all parts of the Soviet's worldwide empire, brought to bear on the weak institutions and the relatively helpless people who almost invariably desire, above all, to be left alone to solve their problems, enjoy their own national self-determination and seek the development of their countries.

The Soviet government and its allies do not, we should be clear, rely on the laws of history or the appeals of communism to bring about what they call revolution or to insure its irreversibility. They rely instead on the manipulation of values and the technology of violence.

Mr. President, frankly, the United States has grown weary, as I am certain this body has grown weary, of the repetitious appeals of Nicaragua to discuss the same subject here under the same circumstances each time with no more evidence to support its fictitious charges than it had the time before. The United States has grown weary of Nicaragua's repeated efforts to come to this body seeking international approval for its right to engage in repression at home and subversion abroad and to pretend all the while that it is seeking peace. This Assembly knows by now, I should hope, a good deal about Nicaragua's peace-seeking in Central America. There has at least been an opportunity for our colleagues in the United Nations to learn about that. Meanwhile, Nicaragua acts in Central America to subvert its neighbors with terrorist training camps, with arms depots, with arms shipments. On September 21st, for example, there was reported in the United States press the destruction by anti-Sandinista forces of an arms trans-shipment camp used by the Sandinistas to supply Salvadoran guerrillas. Those arms trans-shipment activities were, as the story made amply clear, no secret at all to the people of the region. Last month the Honduran government discovered over 100 guerrillas who had been trained in Cuba and had been infiltrated into Honduras through Nicaragua for the purpose of setting in action in Honduras just such a process as I have described.

Nicaragua purports to support the Contadora process. Yet, I hope that this body has taken note that each time that the Contadora process seems about to make progress, Nicaragua comes to the United Nations seeking, in essence, a change of venue, a new beginning whose purpose presumably is to undo what the hard work of other nations involved in the Contadora process is on the verge of achieving. Now it has happened again. Nicaragua has come so often to this body with charges that the United States is about to undertake a military invasion just as the Contadora process seemed about, in fact, to make progress toward insuring that the states in the region could live in security, each from the other, each comfortable in its own knowledge that no one would arm or subvert anyone, that it has become a pattern.

Mr. President, it has been said here repeatedly in the last days that the United Nations Charter prohibits the use of force, which, of course, it does; and that is a very important provision in the United Nations Charter. But the Soviet Union and Cuba and Nicaragua and their friends claim an exemption from this prohibition in the United Nations Charter for wars of national liberation. That claim of exemption from wars of national liberation is made clearly and repeatedly. It has been made clearly and repeatedly as well by spokesmen for the Nicaraguan government. The use of force by the Soviet Union and states allied to it is described then not as a use of force but as a war of national liberation. But Article 51 of the United Nations Charter, Mr. President, does not require that a nation render itself a sitting duck; that a nation acquiesce in its own terrorization by its neighbors; that a nation acquiesce in being overrun by something defined, not as force, but as a national liberation movement. Either there are no exemptions from the prohibition against the use of force or one exemption paves the way for another.

The United Nations Charter was designed to protect peace and human rights. No constitution designed to protect peace and human rights can be used to destroy those values. If one side in a struggle violates international law, as in the use of violence in behalf of a national liberation movement, than the victim may use force to force the other side to comply with the provisions of international law. This body cannot grant Nicaragua the right to repress its own people and destabilize its neighbors. Nobody has that right, nobody can grant such rights.

What this body can and should do today, and the United States very much hopes will do, is to act resolutely in support of the Contadora process without "ifs," "ands," "buts," without any conditions whatsoever. The Contadora process provides the best hope existing in the world today for the peaceable resolution of the conflict which today renders life dangerous in Central America. The Contadora process provides the best hope for an end to violence and for the foundation and restoration of cooperation among the countries of the isthmus, especially the countries of Central America. The Contadora process has developed a document of objectives which calls attention to the principles of international law governing the actions of states in areas of self-determination. It affirms the sovereign equality of states, the peaceful settlement of disputes and the rejection of the threat or use of force, the export of terrorism and subversion, respect for the promotion of pluralism in its various manifestations, support for democratic institutions, promotion of social justice. The ratifying states declared their intention to achieve these 21 objectives designed to promote the development of democratic institutions, to promote detente, to reduce tensions within the region, to enhance respect for territorial boundaries, to end the arms race, the export of terrorism and subversion, and to promote economic and social development.

Mr. President, we believe that the General Assembly of the United Nations has a solemn obligation to grant unequivocal, unconditional support to the Contadora process. This is what the government of the United States does and we would like to invite and encourage all other governments here today to join us. We think that there is an unusually clear choice before us today, before this body in this debate: Either we can promote peace or, by globalizing and ideologizing and exacerbating differences, we can promote a continuation of insecurity, subversion, arms race and tyranny in Central America. We very much hope that this body will decide to promote peace and to do so by way of unequivocal support for the Contadora process.

TURNING SWORDS AGAINST THE PEOPLE

Once again the Security Council has been called into session to hear a complaint by the government of Nicaragua against the government of the United States. By now the Council must be quite familiar with the thrust of the Nicaraguan complaint, it having been put before this body in one form or another on some six occasions over the past two years. The details change but the substance of the complaint remains essentially the same: that Nicaragua is the peaceable, innocent victim of an aggression that is orchestrated, if not carried out, by the United States.

Previously it had in fact been suggested last year—and the year before—that the United States was just on the verge of a massive military invasion of Nicaragua. That charge is absent this year, but the essence of the complaint has changed little beyond that important specific.

Mr. President, it is probably not surprising that the Nicaraguan complaint comes before this Council in the wake of the elections in neighboring El Salvador. That happened in March, 1982 as well, and that happens virtually every time we have a debate on Central American policy in the United States Congress.

The Marxist-Leninist government in Nicaragua cannot have been happy with the election in El Salvador, and indeed, we have just heard the representative of Nicaragua suggest that the elections in El Salvador only make the situation more difficult and complex. One must ask: difficult for whom? complex for what?

Mr. President, the Nicaraguan government itself promised democracy, national independence and self-determination to the people of Nicaragua before that government came to power. It made those promises in writing. It made those promises in public arenas. It made solemn pledges as it sought help from the Organization of American States, from the United States and from its neighbors. And, indeed, the Sandinistas received help from the Organization of American States, from the United States and from Nicaragua's neighbors in their efforts to overthrow the dictatorship headed by Anastasia Somoza.

It is interesting that the government of Nicaragua, which sought and received help from those regional groups and those neighbors, does not today appeal to those regional groups and those neighbors in the hemisphere to help it with its current problem. Could it be because they are too well informed?

Nicaragua began the process of militarization and the introduction of

Address before the Security Council, March 30, 1984.

foreign advisors in Central America. Nicaragua began the process of de-stabilization of its neighbors. I have no interest today, Mr. President, in laying all the facts on these matters before the Council. The Council is presumably familiar with most of them. I would just point out, concerning the process of militarization of Central America which was begun by the government of Nicaragua, that today Nicaragua continues to increase its army and its stores of weapons. It now has some 107,000 persons under arms, including the army, the reserve and the militia. It continues to receive weapons from diverse places in the Soviet bloc, augmenting an already formidable arsenal of tanks, heavy artillery, armed personnel carriers and multiple-rocket launchers.

I would mention, too, in addition to the process of militarization, that Nicaragua began the process of introducing foreign military personnel into Central America. Today it maintains much the largest contingent of foreign military advisers in the area, some 3,500 or more Cuban and other military security advisers, more than 100 Soviet and other Eastern bloc advisers, Libyan advisers, PLO advisers, some 5,000 to 10,000 civilian and other advisers from Cuban and other blocs countries, an increasing number of whom are young males who have completed military training.

Nicaragua also began the process of destabilizing her neighbors in the hemisphere. Again, I have no desire today to burden the Council with a comprehensive list of Nicaragua's efforts. There may be time for that in the course of this discussion. But I would simply remind the Council that Nicaragua continues to assist guerrillas in other countries, principally but not exclusively the FMLN and FDR in El Salvador, through shipments of arms and other supplies, through training, and through the provision of command and control centers.

Nicaragua comes before this Council once again, as it has six times in the past, seeking to prevent its neighbors from defending themselves against Nicaraguan-based efforts at the subversion and overthrow of neighboring countries' governments.

Mr. President, it cannot be, as we have said before, that one country has the right to destabilize by violence its neighbors and that it has no right to defend itself.

It cannot be, Mr. President, that one country, Nicaragua, has the right to introduce foreign arms and advisers to destabilize its neighbors and that they have no right to defend themselves.

It cannot be, Mr. President, that one country, Nicaragua, has the right to the most advanced technical material and that its neighbors have the right to only primitive weaponry.

Mr. President, the government of Nicaragua continues its efforts at internal repression as well as external destabilization. Again I have no desire today to take the time of the Council with a full description of Nicaragua's internal repression in the year since we last discussed this matter. I would, however, bring to the attention of the Council and others interested the fact that, at this moment as we meet here, more than 1,000 Miskito Indians are fleeing today from the Sandy Bay Norte area of Nicaragua. The area is north of Puerto Cabezas, about which we have heard a good deal. Thus more than 1,000 Miskitos this day fleeing Nicaragua are headed toward Honduras, fleeing from the camps into which they have been forced by the Nicaraguan government in gross violation of their human rights. As they flee, knowing that they will live under hard physical conditions in Honduras, they are being bombed by Sandinista "push-pull" fighter aircraft. They are being harassed, fired upon. Every effort is being made to prevent their exodus from Nicaragua, as every effort was made to prevent their living in freedom and peace in Nicaragua.

Mr. President, Nicaragua has apparently still not learned that those who wield swords against their own people and their neighbors risk having those swords turned against them. Nicaragua comes to this Council to seek protection while it undermines and overthrows neighboring governments and represses its own people. It comes to this Council speaking of "mercenaries" who attack the government of Nicaragua. We have heard in our times from totalitarian governments many examples of the efforts of governments to de-humanize their own people, to declare their own fellow citizens non-people. Totalitarians regularly define those who oppose them as non-people. The counterrevolutionaries, described by the representative of Nicaragua, Mr. President, are Nicaraguans. They are Nicaraguans who today, as in the past, are seeking the democratic conditions that they have so long sought. They are seeking democracy and freedom, just as they sought democracy and freedom when they overthrew the previous dictator of Nicaragua—only to see him replaced by new military dictators.

Mr. President, as I said, we can understand that the elections in El Salvador cannot have been a happy occasion for the government of Nicaragua. The spectacle of thousands upon thousands of Salvadoran peasants and workers voting enthusiastically in a closely contested election represented a repudiation of the Nicaraguan-backed guerrillas, who had denounced and tried to sabotage the election. It represented a repudiation of the Nicaraguan style of democracy which substitutes the will of the government for the consent of the people. It represents an embarrassing contrast to the Sandinista-dominated and controlled so-called election process, now underway in Nicaragua.

Indeed, the nature of the conflict in Central America is illuminated by the policies of the government of El Salvador and Nicaragua as each searches for solutions to the conflicts which afflict their country. In response to a declaration by the armed opposition in Nicaragua that it was prepared—that is the Contras, the famous "counterrevolutionaries"—to lay down arms if it could participate in peaceful political competition in Nicaragua and help settle Nicaragua's political questions through the ballot box, the Nicaraguan government announced that such opponents would not be permitted to participate under any circumstances and would, instead, be tried in absentia as criminals. The government of El Salvador took exactly the opposite position and actually invited the armed opposition to participate in the election on the condition that they lay down their arms and agree to peaceful political competition. The government of Nicaragua continued to provide arms, supplies, training and other forms of assistance to Salvadoran guerrillas dedicated precisely to sabotaging the political process and imposing a dictatorship in El Salvador.

Since the beginning of this year, Nicaraguan-supported terrorists in El Salvador have assassinated three members of the Constituent Assembly, a military judge, and a campaign organizer. Under the slogan "Electoral farce no, popular war yes," the armed insurgents in El Salvador have done everything possible to disrupt the elections and reduce voter turnout. They disenfranchised thousands of voters by seizing and destroying their identity cards which are necessary for voting. They mined roads, threatened drivers, and threatened gas station owners selling fuel. In some places citizens were told there would be "lots of bombs going off," and that they had, therefore, best stay away from polling places. On election day the guerrillas attacked the towns of Jacuapa, Chinameca, El Triunfo, and Santa Clara as the voting was taking place. On election eve they killed soldiers stationed in Tejutepeque and prevented voting. Guerrilla sabotage caused about 80 percent of the country to be blacked out for over 12 hours immediately preceeding the opening of the polls. This loss of electrical power severely disrupted the final sorting and dispatch of voting materials and obviously had an effect on the timely arrival of voting materials to some polling places.

Nonetheless, despite all of this, some 1.4 million Salvadorans—over 75 percent of all eligible voters—cast their ballots. According to scores of first-hand reports by election observers, they voted with genuine enthusiasm. The observer delegation from Colombia called the election "an impressive demonstration of the will of the Salvadoran people to find a democratic solution." And their view was shared by most other observers.

Mr. President, a democratic solution is also the chief—indeed, the sole—objective of United States policy in Central America. Nothing more clearly illustrates the seriousness with which the United States has approached the problems in Central America, or the commitment of the American people to finding a democratic solution to those problems, than the report of the

National Bipartisan Commission on Central America. This Commission, chaired by former Secretary of State Henry Kissinger, consisting of twelve distinguished American citizens from both political parties, representing very diverse points of view, undertook an intensive six-month examination of the Central American crisis.

The Commission heard testimony from hundreds of expert witnesses. It made on-the-spot visits to each of the five Central American countries and to the four countries comprising the Contadora group. It reviewed voluminous documents. Its conclusions and recommendations are the product of as careful an examination of the problems in Central America that we are likely to have for some time. They form the basis of the Central America Democracy, Peace and Development Initiative Act of 1984 which President Reagan has submitted to the United States Congress.

This bill represents a far-reaching attempt to address the problems in Central America comprehensively. It identifies the United States firmly and unequivocally with the aspirations of the peoples of Central America for social and economic development, for democracy and human rights and for a peaceful solution to the conflicts now plaguing the region.

The fundamental conclusion of the Commission is that the roots of the crisis in Central America are both indigenous and foreign. The discontents are real, and for much of the population, conditions of life are miserable. While these conditions invite indigenous revolution, they have also been exploited by hostile outside forces—specifically, by Cuba, backed by the Soviet Union now operating through Nicaragua—which will turn any revolution they capture into a dictatorship, threatening the peace and stability of the region, robbing the people of their hopes for liberty.

The interrelationship of these problems is such, the Commission concluded, that neither the military nor the political nor the economic nor the social aspect of the crisis should be considered independently of the others. Without progress on the political, economic and social fronts, peace on the military front would be elusive and fragile. But unless the externally-supported insurgencies are checked and the violence curbed, progress on those other fronts will also be elusive and fragile. Progress in any one, therefore, is not enough. All the sources of the crisis must be addressed and be addressed simultaneously.

The distinguished President of Costa Rica, Luis Alberto Monge, has characterized the report of the National Bipartisan Commission on Central America as an "intervention against misery and ignorance. . . ." That surely was the intention of the Commission: to call upon the United States government and the American people to become fully engaged at the side of our Central American neighbors in the struggle against misery and ignorance.

In order to combat injustice and poverty, the Commission has proposed a series of bold measures to support agricultural development, education, health services, export promotion, land reform, housing, humanitarian relief, trade credit insurance, aid for small businesses and other activities. Because democracy is essential to effective development, special attention will be given to increasing scholarships, leadership training, educational exchanges, and support for the growth of democratic institutions.

A program of substantial assistance is proposed to revitalize the Central American Common Market and the Central American Bank for Economic Integration, which made a major contribution to the region's rapid economic growth in the 1960s and early 1970s and which today could stimulate increased intra-regional trade and economic activity.

To give structure, consistency and continuing direction to this sustained effort, the Commission proposed a high level meeting of U.S. officials with their Central American counterparts to consider the creation of the Central American Development Organization. This organization (CADO by acronym) would provide guidance and review as well as assistance for economic, social and political development programs of those Central American nations eligible to join by reason of their commitment to internal reform and democracy, as well as to external non-intervention. It is envisioned that other democracies outside the region would participate as well in this major effort to channel external assistance to the region.

The Commission also squarely confronted the dangers created by the unprecedented military build-up in Nicaragua, the regime's ideological commitment to the export of revolution and its military ties to the Soviet Union and Cuban—dangers which weigh heavily on the neighboring countries. I will not on this occasion, as I have said before, describe in detail this military build-up, or demonstrate the extent of Nicaragua's intervention in neighboring states or its militarization and military ties. All these points are thoroughly covered in the Commission's report. What I wish to emphasize here is the Commission's call for a vigorous diplomatic strategy and a negotiating effort designed to resolve the conflict and to include Nicaragua in a regional settlement that would ensure lasting security guarantees as well as national independence for all the nations of Central America. Such a settlement would be squarely based on the principles contained in the 21-point proposal of the Contadora group. These include:

- Respect for sovereignty and non-intervention.
- Verifiable commitments to non-aggression and an end to all attempts at subversion.
- Limitations on arms and sizes of armed forces.
- Prohibition of all military forces, bases or advisers of non-Central American countries.

- Commitment to internal pluralism and free elections in all countries.
- Provision for verification of all agreements.
- Establishment of an inter-government council to meet regularly and review compliance.
- Adherence to the overall agreement, to those 21 points, would be required for membership in the Central American Development Organization.

In drawing up these recommendations, the Commission drew heavily on its consultations with the leaders of the four Contadora countries. It declared that "The Contadora countries are engaged in a bold new experiment. They deserve the gratitude and encouragement of all the nations in the region." These are also the views of the United States government.

As the Commission repeatedly emphasized, all elements of the crisis must be addressed simultaneously. No short-cuts were discovered, no gimmicks, diplomatic or otherwise. Thus, as one element of the broad program, the report recommends increased military assistance under proper conditions to the governments of El Salvador and Honduras. That assistance will reinforce the diplomatic effort by helping to create the conditions under which peaceful settlements may be reached and the objective of a better life in freedom and national independence for all Central Americans successfully pursued.

Mr. President, in discussing Central America, there is a tendency sometimes to succumb to despair especially by those who know little about the region. But the Commission found everywhere a "hope for a democratic future and a readiness to sacrifice toward that end." I believe the election just held in El Salvador demonstrates as clearly as any single event could that the people of that country have not succumbed to despair and that they are ready to sacrifice for a better, brighter, democratic future. The report stated:

> The people of Central America have lived too long with poverty, deprivation and violence. The current turmoil must not be allowed to shatter their hopes for a brighter future.
>
> They have endured too many generations of misrule to let their aspirations for democratic political development be dashed in this generation on the rocks of fear, division and violence. Not least, their own security—and ours—must no longer be threatened by hostile powers which seek expansion of influence through the exploitation of misery.
>
> The crisis, thus, poses an urgent challenge to the United States. But that challenge in turn presents us with an opportunity—an opportunity to help the people of Central America translate their dreams of a better and a freer life into a reality.

That is our wish, Mr. President. It is our only wish. The rest is hard work, good will, fortitude, an uncompromising commitment to democratic values and practices and a respect for the principles embodied in the Charter of the United Nations.

Right of Reply

I will be very brief. First of all, in the interests of accuracy, I may say that I never suggested that Nicaragua had the most powerful army in South America. I only suggested that Nicaragua had the most powerful army in Central America, which of course includes, conventionally, five nations.

Second, I would like to say, regarding the Miskitos, who I do think long to come back to Nicaragua if only they could live in peace on the North Atlantic coast as they have for centuries and count on decent respect for their right to freedom and self-determination. They would be very happy. But, unfortunately, they continue to flee. Approximately a half million Nicaraguans have already fled the beneficent ministrations of the new dictatorship. Some 25,000 of those are Miskitos now in Honduras. More than 1,000 Miskitos are, as I have already said, fleeing Nicaragua this very day toward the Honduran border, suggesting that the practices—which have made these very peaceable people who seek only to be left alone to live their lives, flee—have not in fact improved.

Third, I find it very difficult to listen to the repeated accusations in this Council of the representative of Nicaragua and some of his associates concerning a purported U.S. penchant for dictatorship in Central America. It may come as a surprise to members of the Council having heard so many such accusations by the Nicaraguan representative to hear that Somoza was a Nicaraguan. He was not a North American. He was not only a Nicaraguan, but he was head of a government which consisted entirely of Nicaraguans and the son of another Somoza, who was also a Nicaraguan head of a government which was comprised entirely of Nicaraguans. During this whole period the United States expressed its own preferences for a commitment to democracy by living within democratic institutions and respecting democratic liberties in our own society.

I do not deny in this Council that my country has, from time to time, made mistakes in our policy vis-a-vis Central America or even in Nicaragua. I fear, in fact, that a close examination of the record would suggest that in 1979, the United States government acting in the best of faith did assist in the rise of power in Nicaragua of a new, repressive military dictatorship which has consolidated power in that society and governs today creating hundreds of thousands of refugees among Nicaraguans who flee their country still seeking the freedoms that they were seeking when they overthrew Somoza.

Finally, concerning those elections in Nicaragua which we heard about from my colleague who likes to read the *New York Times*, I, too, would like to read a piece from the *New York Times* which is written by one of his former colleagues, Arturo Cruz, who was, as I am sure members of the Council know, a member of the ruling junta of the Nicaraguan revolutionary government and their ambassador to the United States until he resigned out of dismay and disillusionment and disappointment with their government. He has since lived in exile and works for the establishment of democracy in Nicaragua as, indeed, he did before he left. He wrote in the *New York Times*, in a column which was titled, "Sandinista Democracy Unlikely," about the proposed elections in Nicaragua and he said:

> The revolutionary commanders' statement about the voting process foreshadows a mockery of elections. Sandinistas are determined to exclude leading dissident personalities like the former guerrilla leader, Eden Pastora Gomez, the former junta member, and Alfonso Robelo Callejas who is also the leader of an important political party. Under these constraining conditions, citizens with a sense of self-esteem will be neither candidates nor voters . . . Our erstwhile liberators, the Sandinistas, are becoming addicted to power. Having gallantly faced bullets in battle, they are now resorting to phony balloting just as our right-wing dictators did in the past . . .

CENTRAL AMERICA: THIS TIME WE KNOW WHAT'S HAPPENING

The whole scenario sounds like a grade B movie from the 1950s, but that, alas, does not mean it is not true. It's almost unbearably unfashionable to say so, but there is a plan to create a communist Central America which, if successful, will have momentous consequences for our security and that of our European allies, for Israel's international position, and for the unfortunate people of Central America. So far, Congress seems unwilling to make a serious effort to prevent—by means short of war—these human and strategic catastrophes.

Even though a very well organized lobby works indefatigably to confuse the moral, political and intellectual questions involved in U.S. policy to-

Washington Post Op-Ed, April 17, 1983.

ward Central America, there is growing clarity about the issues and the stakes. Indeed, what distinguishes the current debate about military and economic aid for Central America from similar disputes about China, Cuba, Vietnam and Nicaragua is that we have fewer illusions and more information.

We know by now what the government of Nicaragua is and what it intends—in El Salvador, Honduras, Costa Rica, New York, Jerusalem. We know who the guerrillas in El Salvador are, where and how they got their arms, what their plans are, and who their friends are.

As recently as July 1979 it was possible for American policymakers of optimistic disposition to suppose that, if they acted wisely and generously, Nicaragua would emerge from its bloody civil war with an independent, pluralist, socialist, neutralist government. To this end, the United States rushed some $24.6 million in emergency food, medical and reconstruction assistance to the FSLN on their triumph, provided $118 million direct economic assistance in the subsequent 18 months, and assisted the new government in securing, in addition, some $262 million from multilateral lending institutions (an amount almost double the amount the Somoza government had received in the preceding 20 years). But before the Carter administration left office in January 1981, the decision was made that Nicaragua no longer met U.S. requirements for assistance, its pattern of internal repression and external aggression being already clear. And during the subsequent two years, Nicaragua's facade of democratic intentions and national independence have been not ripped off, but cast aside.

Everyone who cares to know now understands that the government of Nicaragua has imposed a new dictatorship; that it has refused to hold the elections it promised; that it has seized control of all media except a lone newspaper that it subjects to heavy prior censorship; that it denied the bishops and priests of the Roman Catholic Church the right to say mass on television during Holy Week; that it insulted the pope; that it has stifled the private sector and independent trade unions; attacked the opposition; and driven the Miskito Indians out of their homelands—burning their villages, destroying their crops, forcing them into exile or into involuntary internment in camps far from home.

Persons interested in such questions understand, too, that Nicaragua's rulers have introduced into the country many thousands of Cuban teachers, trainers and supervisors, including at least 2,000 military advisers. The Sandinista rulers have denied their international supporters the comforts of ambiguity. They have explained who their friends are and what convictions guide them.

From Moscow and Managua they have announced their principles: "We guide ourselves by the scientific doctrines of the revolution, by Marxism-

Leninism," Minister of Defense Humberto Ortega explained to his army, ". . . our political force in Sandinismo and our doctrine in Marxist-Leninism." "Marxism-Leninism is a fundamental part of the Sandinista ideology," said another member of the junta, Victor Tirado Lopez. They have issued a new stamp with a picture of Karl Marx and excerpts from the Communist Manifesto.

Nicaragua's leaders are done with dissembling. They are proud of their ideology, proud of their monopoly of power, proud of their huge new military force (which has no peer in the region), proud of their role in Central America's guerrilla war, proud of their string of successes in international diplomacy. Those successes are impressive: a seat on the UN Security Council, a stymied regional diplomatic initiative, continued support from the Socialist International and a resounding victory at the Delhi Summit of the Non-Aligned Movement. Proud too of their friends, including: Libya, the PLO and, of course, Cuba, their constant companions. The PLO connection, acclaimed by Yasser Arafat at the revolution's first anniversary (". . . the Nicaraguan people's victory is the victory of the Palestinians. Anyone who threatens Nicaragua will have to face Palestinian combatants."), has spawned international progeny. This past week a Latin American preparatory meeting on Palestine has been held in Managua for the purpose of "obtaining governmental and nongovernmental support for the Palestinian cause" and "opposing" Israel's aggressive policy. According to Radio Sandino, delegates from some 20 nations and 10 UN organizations were expected.

Such conferences are but one manifestation of the junta's vocation for public diplomacy. Other examples may be observed on U.S. television and, especially, at the United Nations where, with dazzling chutzpah, Nicaragua's leaders last week pressed their demand for immunity from attack by anti-Sandinista Nicaraguans, at the same time they stepped up support for Salvador's guerrillas.

The character of El Salvador's guerrilla struggle is no more ambiguous than that of Nicaragua's government. Since the elections of March 1982, nobody even pretends that the FMLN enjoys popular support, is "really" a bunch of agrarian reformers, or a coalition that would, if victorious, usher in a more perfect democracy.

The fictions with which communist insurgents have conventionally clothed their conquest of power are not available to the partisans of the FMLN. The pretense that the FMLN is an indigenous guerrilla movement without significant foreign support has also been largely abandoned. Too many truckloads, planeloads, boatloads of arms from Cuba, Nicaragua and the Eastern bloc have been found; too many documents have been captured, too many pictures taken, too many bold announcements made from Managua. The facts about the FMLN are understood by people interested in these questions. It is a professional guerrilla operation directed from command and control centers in Nicaragua, armed with Soviet bloc arms delivered through Cuba and Nicaragua, bent on establishing in El Salvador the kind of one-party dictatorship linked to the Soviet Union that already exists in Nicaragua.

There has, moreover, been so much discussion among them of "revolution without frontiers," of "liberating" and "unifying" Central America, so many threats to Honduras, so much bullying of Costa Rica and guerrilla activity in Guatemala, that it is hardly possible seriously to doubt the regional character of Soviet/Cuban/Nicaraguan goals.

Yet to be fully faced is the relevance of these small, poor nations of the Central American isthmus to the United States, or the importance of Caribbean sea lanes to the Western Alliance. Neither is the extent of the Soviet investment—military, economic, cultural—in this hemisphere yet fully appreciated. But very reluctantly, more serious observers have come to acknowledge that, yes, the area's location gives it a certain irreducible relevance to our national interest. These serious observers grouse about the way the Reagan administration talks about the issues; they grouse about the government of El Salvador; but they understand.

The *Economist* noted last week that "The 'loss' of El Salvador could be a lethal foreign policy blow for America. . . ." and *The New Republic* made a similar observation.

There is also a growing, if grudging, acknowledgment that money—in the form of economic and military assistance—is quite probably the key to the viability of the region's non-communist governments. And two top aides of previous Democratic administrations, one a former assistant secretary of state, wrote in last week's *New York Times Magazine* that, "The area is of clear strategic and political importance to the United States . . ." so that "to stop American aid would be to deliver—yes, deliver—El Salvador into the hands of a guerrilla movement that is . . . allied externally with America's adversaries, and capable itself of the greatest brutality," and advised that ". . . abandonment is an option Democrats should reject."

Yet if few in or out of Congress advocated outright abandonment, a good many argued for such little assistance on such niggardly terms that the effect is almost sure to be the same.

From the perspective of hemispheric policy, it was an extraordinary week.

An official of the Soviet foreign office, Vadim Zagladin, reiterated Brezhnev's threat to install nuclear missiles in the Western Hemisphere five minutes from the United States. And a member of the Nicaraguan junta announced that, if asked, his government would consider installing Soviet nuclear missiles in Nicaragua.

In Managua, Nicaraguan officials made clear their determination to continue support for revolution in Central America while, at exactly the same time, their representatives at the United Nations demanded protection from an internal insurgency.

Meanwhile, the Democratic majority on the Latin American subcommittee of the House Committee on Foreign Affairs acted to deny the democratically elected government of El Salvador the military assistance it needs to stave off a very well armed and advised Marxist insurgency and, simultaneously, to deny a democratic Nicaraguan insurgency any support against a repressive, aggressive Marxist government—though the clear effect of such a policy would be to make the United States the enforcer of Brezhnev's doctrine of irreversible communist revolution.

If, as often suggested, the "Vietnam Syndrome" explains the extraordinary reluctance of America's political class to provide urgently needed assistance to endangered friendly governments in an area of clear national interest, in what does that syndrome consist? Obviously, the Vietnam experience did not make us isolationist. The U.S. government pursues, with the full consent of Congress, a foreign policy that involves us in the affairs of four continents. We support a large standing army and a huge defense establishment. We station troops in remote places, provide billions of dollars in economic and military assistance to governments of all sorts in Asia, Africa and the Middle East. Neither the moral nor military misgivings expressed with regard to Central America are evident with regard to these other regions.

Nobody talks about slippery slopes when we rush weapons to Thailand, trainers to Lebanon or economic aid to Africa or Asia. Nobody talks about human rights when there is murder and mayhem in Zimbabwe, though one can readily imagine the outcry if the bishops of El Salvador had issued a statement resembling that of the bishops of Zimbabwe.

Why?

Why is Congress so much more reluctant to assist an imperfect democratic government clearly important to our national interest than much less perfect governments in more remote regions?

What is it that Central America has in common with Vietnam that so repels liberals? Is it just the nature of the contest—the fact that, in both, well-financed communist guerrilla movements have simultaneously targeted the existing government and what is generally called "world public opinion"?

Is it because lobbies of the left have managed, in both cases, to make the anti-communist side seem unbearably unfashionable?

God knows there are parallels enough in the public discussion of Vietnam and Central America. In both cases, well-orchestrated international campaigns have focused mercilessly on the political and moral failings of the government. And in El Salvador, as in Vietnam, the introduction of elections and reforms, the reduction of human rights abuses and corruption have proved not to have much effect on the drumbeat of criticism. In El Salvador, as in Vietnam, Congress calls the U.S. commitment into doubt from quarter to quarter, "certification" to "certification," undermining the confidence of vulnerable allies in our reliability and their viability.

As with Vietnam, doubt is continuously voiced about whether the government of El Salvador, which struggles mightily to satisfy American demands, is morally worthy of American approval or even of survival.

But there are a few crucial differences too, and those differences involve what we know and when we know it. Not only do we know who Salvador's FMLN is, when we didn't know who the Vietcong were, we know now who the Vietcong were, how they came down from the north (20,000 in the early years alone), how they were supplied, how Western public opinion was manipulated into believing that the National Liberation Front created by decision of the North Vietnamese Communist party, was a spontaneous product of "deeper" social causes. We know all these things now because General Vo Nguyen Giap and his colleague, General Vo Bam, have told us about them.

We know too about human rights under those two Vietnamese regimes, about the labor camps and mass deportations. We know this at least in part because Stephen J. Morris' careful study has documented with endless, painful details that "The violation of human rights by the Communist party of Vietnam, in both the north and the south, was incomparably worse than the violation of human rights by the former Thieu government in South Vietnam. The difference was not one of degree but one of quality."

We know the Vietcong did not establish a broad-based government or a socialist democracy. We know what happened—and is still happening—in Cambodia. We do not enjoy thinking much about these matters, but we know about them just as surely as we know the character and the stakes of the contest in Central America.

The crucial difference between Vietnam and Central America is not the Pacific Ocean though that is important. The crucial difference is that the Congress that cut off aid to Vietnam could say it did not guess what would follow.

Pardon Me, But Am I That Hard-Liner the Anonymous Sources Are Talking About?

Time was I believed a leak was the unauthorized disclosure of confidential information about actual events—such as, for example, conversations within the executive branch. That was before I understood that a leak is the weapon of choice in Washington's unending internal wars—ideally suited to spreading disinformation about fictional events.

Undocumented allegations and anonymous sources link private ambitions to public policy in labyrinthine webs of personal and political relations. Two or three well-placed "sources" working with two or three well-placed journalists can create an issue, shape an interpretation, build or destroy a reputation. From the perspective of political science, it is fascinating. From the perspective of public office, it is frustrating beyond belief.

How do you correct the record when the discussions are all confidential? My interest is more than academic or personal. The paper triangle that links symbiotically anonymous and interested bureaucrats and politicians with dependent journalists is as much a threat to an informed public as the "iron triangle" of bureaucrats, politicians and the "interests" is to honest government.

During the past month or two, much of the U.S. national media have relied on undocumented leaks and unidentified sources to construct a political melodrama in which some bad guys—the "hard-liners"—are pitted against some good guys—the "moderates"—in a contest for control of U.S. policy toward El Salvador and the Central American region. According to this scenario, the good guys support political solutions, negotiations, regional dialogue, and bipartisan consensus, and are deeply concerned about "underlying economic and social problems." "Hard-liners," we are told, oppose these good things; they advocate military solutions, and are dead set against negotiations, regional dialogue and bipartisan consensus-building. Hard-liners *prefer* political polarization.

In the current scenario, hard-liners are frequently named Clark and Kirkpatrick, though sometimes they are called Casey, Weinberger, Stone or, even, Reagan. Their principal activity is giving bad advice to the president. Because my name is also Kirkpatrick and I hold almost none of the views attributed to that Kirkpatrick, I desire to clarify just what kind of evidence I have given in the weeks after the president asked me to visit Central

Washington Post Op-Ed, June 20, 1983.

America. I understand that it is not considered sporting to introduce into these Washington games verifiable facts or on-the-record statements of participants; but, then, I am not a thoroughly seasoned player and have not lost the predilections of my regular profession.

Obviously, I speak only for myself. I have not been present in most of the conversations of other participants. However, since I have often been cast by "sources" as the "hardest" and "most militant" of the hard-liners, my role seems relevant to the whole dramatic production, and the fact that my actual views and recommendations bear almost no relation to those attributed to me undermines, I should suppose, the credibility of this melodrama.

Interested persons might want to know that instead of opposing attention to economic and humanitarian dimensions of Central America's problems, bipartisan participation in policy-making, the Contadora process and the broadest possible participation in Salvador's elections, I have consistently made *opposite* recommendations. I have advocated greatly expanded humanitarian and economic assistance; bipartisan participation in formulating a new policy; unambiguous support for the Contadora process and regional dialogue; and maximum efforts to secure the broadest possible participation in Salvador's elections.

In my memorandum to the president on returning from Central America I took a very "hard line" on hunger, malnutrition, infant mortality, illiteracy, and economic underdevelopment.

"Congress," I wrote, "has not provided the resources or support needed in part, at least, because we have not worked with them to develop a bold, imaginative program which goes beyond preventing a communist victory in the very short run, to produce for the chronically deprived people of the area the reality of present progress and the promise of more to come."

I cited Congressman Mike Barnes' proposed "one-percent solution" to the region's problems (using one percent of the requested defense budget to finance an adequate economic effort). I recommended for inclusion in the speech to the joint session a program "so beneficial to the terribly poor, malnourished people of the region that the American people will be proud to support it . . ." and also recommended the establishment of "a national bipartisan commission [which would] examine how we should apply our talent and resources to foster health, growth, security and democracy among our neighbors in Central America and the Caribbean. . . ." I further explained to the president that this was an approach I had discussed with Senator Jackson and other Democrats.

Though current mythology suggests otherwise, new broad, bipartisan initiatives were resisted by the "good guys" themselves. So were efforts by the governments of Central America and the Contadora Four to get under way a process of negotiations for Latins only. President Herrera Campins last week described to the Venezuelan press the message he asked me to deliver to President Reagan: "Don't let your government torpedo our conference."

Reasonable people may feel the chances of success would be enhanced by our presence among the Contadora negotiators; they may think democracy would be better served by sticking with the San Jose approach. But the fact remains that Venezuela, Mexico, Panama, Colombia, et al., have desired an all-Latin conference, and our Central American friends have supported their effort. So have I. Far from believing that "the very mention of negotiations in El Salvador appeared a sign of weakness" (as charged by an anonymous source in The *Post* on June 12), against considerable official resistance, I argued from Latin America and in Washington that the United States should pose no obstacles to the Contadora negotiations, should make no demands that we be included, and should, instead, stand aside offering support as appropriate.

On all the above issues there has been a certain amount of disagreement within our government, though the sides are not those popularly perceived. On other important issues there is a clear public record to prove there has been no disagreement at all. No one has proposed sending U.S. troops into combat in Central America, no one has proposed abandoning Central America. No government official has supported a "two-track" approach where one track leads to negotiated power sharing in El Salvador; everyone has supported conversations to ensure elections with broad participation and security for all.

I have also advocated continued military assistance at levels adequate to meet and match guerrilla arms, but then so have all other participants in the executive department's policy dialogue.

Above all, I have argued in print and in person from well before President Reagan invited me to join his government, that the people and governments of Central America, the Caribbean and, indeed, South America are *important* to the United States; that our security and history bind us to the Americas just as surely as they bind us to Europe; and that it makes no sense at all for us to perceive and protect vital national interests in Europe, the Middle East, the Far East and Africa (where we provide large, continuing amounts of economic and military assistance and in some cases U.S. troops and trainers) while ignoring and neglecting friends and interests on our own borders. I have, moreover, insisted that the fact that the Central American peoples have suffered under dictators in the past is not a reason to consign them to repressive new dictators sponsored by the Soviet Union; it is, instead, a reason to help them escape to freedom.

What do all these views have in common with the struggle between the "hard-liners" and the "good guys"? An interesting question.

The fact is that "hard-liner" has become an all-purpose term of political abuse. In popular political mythology the hard-liner is the missing link between political Neanderthals and modern man. It is shorthand for a mindless, heartless approach to public policy. Along with other abusive terms, "hard-liner" should be eschewed in serious political discussion in favor of more meaningful ways of categorizing political actors—such as, for example, active and passive; innovative and conventional; smart and dumb; effective and ineffective; honest and dishonest; straightforward and devious; generous and niggardly; ambitious and contented; prudent and reckless; political and bureaucratic, and so forth.

Meanwhile, it is worth noting that if the "sources" were as good at managing public affairs as they are at managing the news, the world would be better governed; and that if journalists were as suspicious of their favorite anonymous sources as they are of, say, the president, we would be better informed.

CUBA AND THE CUBANS*

*With Carlos Ripoll

I am heartened to see this group of Cuban-Americans so deeply concerned not only with the face of their homeland, but also with the future of this country. I might say that I was not aware before I came that there might be among us tonight also Nicaraguans, Guatemalans, Salvadorans, and other citizens from Central America and the Caribbean. It is a very special pleasure, then, to meet with such a very large group of concerned citizens of the Americas, because that is what we all are, we are all concerned citizens of the Americas.

Most of my remarks this evening will be addressed by name to the Cubans, because this is an evening for the Cuban-American National Foundation, but I should say that their spirit is also profoundly relevant to all the Americas and to all the guests from all the Americas.

Only twenty-odd years ago, most of you in the audience who are Cubans were struggling with the difficult and urgent problems that daily confront those who escape tyrants and pursue freedom, who are compelled to settle

Address to the Cuban-American National Foundation, Miami, Florida, October 22, 1982.

in a foreign land. The Cubans who came here solved those pressing problems of survival, and more. Instead of remaining a burden on the communities in which they settled, Cuban refugees who have come to the United States have made major, indeed extraordinary, contributions to the vitality and the growth, not only of Miami, not only of Florida, but of the United States, and, indeed, of the Americas. Cubans, as everyone knows, are a great American success story.

Cuba and the United States have always been good friends. Leaving aside a few mistakes and a few misunderstandings, Cuba's history, like that of the United States, is characterized by commitment to liberty and justice. Only since Fidel Castro's consolidation of power have relations between Cuba and the United States been unfriendly, and that only because Cuba's ruling elite made them so.

The same small ruling group that has made its country into a colony of the Soviet Union, turning its back on Cuban history and ideals, has set Cuba and the United States at odds with one another. This at precisely the same time that it destroyed Cuba's independence and freedom. It is not the first time in our century that a small antidemocratic elite has betrayed its country's traditions, making refugees out of its people, and enemies of its friends. Similar developments occurred in the 1940's in Germany, Italy, Japan. Those nations were not our enemies until they had been perverted by insidious doctrines and organized into the great war-making machines. Once those doctrines were repudiated, as history tells, the American people reached out in friendship to help those nations rebuild, in freedom and independence. Their enemies and our enemies were the same.

Cuba's freedom and independence will be restored too, and that nation too will return to its own course, its own goals. Then we will have a fair chance to test that historic friendship between Cuba and the United States, to test our resolve, as President Reagan has said "to go beyond being a good neighbor to being a true friend and brother to Latin America."

I have no doubt that your English is better than my Spanish, but I believe that speaking about cultural pluralism is not enough. Cultural pluralism also must be practiced. We have practiced a bit of it this fall at the United Nations, when, for the first time in our history, a member of our delegation, the major of San Juan, Hernan Padilla, spoke on behalf of the United States, in the General Assembly, in Spanish. It was a historic first.

Tonight I should like to speak to you in your language as an expression of my high regard for its beauty and your culture.*

It is also as a citizen of this country that I am proud to be here among

---

*Following this point in the test, the speech was originally made in Spanish and was subsequently translated to English.

you, a citizen of this country whose greatest wealth is in the human beings that form part of it. We are largely descendants of men and women who came to his land to enjoy freedom, and to make use of the opportunities that the nation offered to them during those years of growth.

During the last century, the United States was enriched by the arrival of Germans, Italians, and Irish, among others; in this century, it has been enriched by the presence of millions of men and women who speak Spanish. You, the Cubans, are one of the most valuable acquisitions of this country.

It is most remarkable that in less than one generation you should have so adapted to our way of life. And it is even more remarkable that without giving up your love for Cuba, without abandoning the hope of returning to your homeland, you have achieved so many successes in this country. Those of us who are in public life are sometimes surprised to see the strength of your presence in the business world, in the worlds of science and art, in the labor force, and in so many other activities.

It seems to me very natural that, having become so happily integrated into our society, you might want to participate in the political process. That is one of the rights guaranteed by our Constitution, and it is one of the pillars that supports our democratic tradition. If commerce, industry, labor, and culture have all benefited from your presence, why should not politics derive the benefit of your participation? Just as each one of you chose his own road according to his performance and abilities, each one of you will be able to choose the candidate who will insure, for you, your children, your communities, and for the country as a whole, the course that you consider most beneficial.

All good Cubans who live here, from the humblest to the most fortunate, are a source of pride for the United States. They are an asset that could inspire us to write across the sky of Florida those words that you know so well: "Thank You, Fidel!"

I look upon the Cuban-American National Foundation with great pleasure as it works so effectively to inform public opinion, to convey to newspapers and other media, to the academic world, to labor and religious organizations, and to politicians, the information about Cuban matters that they have often sorely needed and not had.

The Cuban government has invented the most fabulous lies to justify its failure. Besides having demonstrated a total lack of creativity, besides showing that under communism the only thing that works well is terror, they have shown us an economy in shambles, agriculture that does not produce food, industry that manufactures few goods, science that does not discover, and education that does not educate. Every day we see the frustration of peasants and workers increase as the future of their country grows darker.

If I were to calculate in dollars and cents the loss that Cuba has suffered because so many useful Cubans have left, and because those who have remained feel no incentive to work (and thus produce less), I am sure that the result would show that the losses would amount to ten times more than all the aid that Russia has had to extend, for so many years, to the government in Havana. And that is in dollars and cents. In human terms, the loss is far greater.

The history of Cuba is one of the richest in this continent in its striving towards freedom. Few lands in America have had to pay so much, and to wait so long, in order to be free. Out of all proportion to its size and population, Cuba can count among its heroes men like Céspedes, Agramonte, Maceo, Gómez, and above all, that pride of the continent, José Martí.

We, in English-speaking America, know as well as our brothers to the South what efforts the Republic of Cuba had to exert to solve the problems it inherited from colonial times, and we know as well its efforts to establish itself in the world as a free, prosperous, and democratic country.

But today we look on with pain as that Cuba that loves freedom, democracy and progress is turned into a pawn of the Soviet Union; we look on with pain at her people enslaved; we look on with pain because that hardworking and prosperous Cuba has dropped from third place to one of the last in per capita income among the countries in the continent, because it is ruled by an alien ideology that has failed even at its very source. Suffice it to say that the index of productivity per inhabitant has diminished year by year, and that it now stands at a dismal 0.2 percent.

Cuba is today the country that perhaps shows most clearly the failure of the communist system. If the people lived even slightly better than they once did, one might look with a certain indulgence at the sacrifices that have been demanded of them. But when we see terror enthroned, when we see no activity that is not coerced, when we see the enormous number of victims (those who have died, those who have suffered and still suffer, languishing in jail, and even you yourselves, who have been forced to leave your homeland), when we see how high the price for so little return, we ask ourselves how some can dare speak of communism as a solution for the problems of the world.

Fidel Castro began his rule with a question that undermined the very basis of democracy, that cynical question: "Elections? What for?" And after 23 years of Fidel Castro, the people, if they could, would ask him: "Communism? What for?" The answer might be: communism, to suffer food and housing shortages; communism, to endure unconditional servitude to another state; communism, to drain off the country's scarce production; communism, to squander the lives of Cuban men in absurd expansionist adventures. "Communism? What for?" To turn schools into indoctrination centers, to reduce culture to an instrument of the party, to erradicate popular customs and beliefs, and to sow Marxism-Leninism in the minds of the young.

Were we to look at the government of Cuba in the light of the Universal Declaration of Human Rights, we would see how it has violated and continues to violate many of the articles of that convention. A country that denies basic rights to anyone whose opinions diverge from those of the ruling orthodoxy, a country that denies all opportunity to such people and exposes them to persecution and even to prison, goes against the very essence of the Declaration.

A country whose constitution openly denies basic human rights does not deserve the respect of its citizens or of the international community. To begin with, the socialist constitution of Cuba is nothing more than a document imposed by a small elite that controls the destiny of the country. It is a mockery of the will of the people, and contains only what is convenient to those in power. That is why it does not limit either the executive or the legislative branch. Instead it subjects the people to their will, and the legislative and executive branches, in turn, are subject to the will of one man. Dismissing the separation of powers as "bourgeois philosophy," the Cuban constitution concentrates all power in a single individual, which makes the system an undisguised tyranny.

The government of Fidel Castro cannot, for example, allow freedom of speech, one of the most important rights included in the Universal Declaration on Human Rights, and this absolute control over ideas has allowed it to hide for a very long time the abuses it has inflicted, and continues to inflict, on the Cuban people. That is why Cuban law is so severe on this matter, why it very clearly provides that nothing can be said, that nothing can be heard or read, that is not in the service of the "socialist state," that is to say, of whomever is in power.

In Cuba, secondary and higher education are restricted to those who follow the party line. This contradicts the principle of the Universal Declaration according to which a student's right to education can be conditioned only on his scholastic qualifications, and students cannot be discriminated against for any other reason where this right is concerned. Even the fortunate ones who manage to attend institutions of secondary and higher education never attain the goal of which the Declaration speaks, "the full development of human personality." Quite the contrary, what is achieved there is the opposite: their paths are narrowed to conform to dogma, and they are deprived of the richest roads of universal culture.

Since the Cuban government, like all totalitarian regimes, dominates all activities, one cannot speak of human rights in Cuba, but only of violations of those rights—and to speak of all of them would make this speech far too long. But in this country we are not blind to those violations, and we will not be remiss in speaking out when necessary. We now have the great joy that Armando Valladares, the poet who dared to incite Castro's anger from his wheelchair in jail, will soon be freed. His forthcoming release was achieved through the intervention of governments, of international press associations, and of intellectuals throughout the world. We must denounce human right violations in Cuba, loudly and clearly.

In speaking about the Cuban situation, we have used the word tyranny. And since I am speaking in Spanish, I would like to conclude with the oldest definition of that term in the Spanish language. I refer to the one given by Alfonso the Wise, the famous king of Castille, in the thirteenth century, in his treatise *Siete Partidas*, whose value has been recognized throughout the ages. In spite of all the changes that the world has undergone, his judgments are still of value. These are the words of the king: "A tyrant is a cruel lord who takes a land by force, deceit, or treason. The nature of tyrants is such that, after taking the land, they will do anything, no matter how harmful to it, in order to keep it. They love to do things that are profitable to them rather than to all, since they constantly live with the fear that they will lose what they govern." And he adds: "The wise men of antiquity said that to satisfy his desires most easily, a tyrant uses three ruses: first, he makes sure that those who follow him are fools and live in constant fear, so that they will not dare rise against him; second, he does whatever he can to ensure that his subjects do not trust one another, because those who live in strife will never dare to speak ill of him; third, he keeps the people impoverished by submerging them in great projects and interminable adventures, so that they will never think of doing anything against him."

King Alfonso concludes: "Above all, a tyrant always tries to corrupt the strong and to kill intelligence. He forbids his vassals to join in any kind of association and watches everything that goes on in his land; he trusts foreigners who serve him by choice to give him advice and care for his person more than he trusts the natives of his land, who serve him by obligation."

I do not have to point out to you the similarity between the tyrant of this definition and the Cuban regime, because the definition obviously applies to much of the regime's history. It covers the cult of terror and hypocrisy, the absurd production goals, the expansionist adventures, the handing over of the country's security system to foreigners, and all the other tricks that the tyrant uses to maintain himself in power.

With the exception of apprentice tyrants and those who are blind to the deceptions being practiced around them, everyone knows these truths, including the long suffering Cubans who live on the island. As Abraham Lincoln said: "You can fool all of the people part of the time, or you can fool part of the people all of the time, but you cannot fool all of the people all of the time."

KENNEDY-KHRUSHCHEV PACT
AND THE SANDINISTAS

We have arrived at another turning point in the history of the United States and the hemisphere. It will not be the first, it may not be the last. But its consequences will probably be far reaching and long lasting.

One of those turning points occurred in 1959 with the arrival of Fidel Castro and the hemisphere's first Marxist-Leninist regime.

Another was at the Bay of Pigs, when 1,400 Cuban civilians—trained, equipped and transported by the American government—were left stranded on the beach under enemy fire, denied the expected air cover, denied the expected chance to survive and prevail.

Another turning point occurred in 1962 when President John F. Kennedy began by confronting the Soviet plan to station missiles in Cuba and ended by granting a U.S. guarantee to Fidel Castro's harsh new dictatorship.

Another turning point for the Americas took place in 1979, when a period of unilateral U.S. disarmament, passivity, and accomodation ended in the establishment of new communist dictatorships in Grenada and Nicaragua. Who will forget the turning point marked by the liberation of Grenada in October of 1983? "Ahora somos tres," Fidel had shouted in Managua. "Ahora son dos," President Reagan communicated from the Situation Room.

Now the United States and the hemisphere confront another momentous decision: will we help the Nicaraguans fighting against the consolidation of another Marxist dictatorship in this hemisphere? Or will we leave

Address to the Cuban-American National Foundation, Miami, Florida, May 18, 1985.

them stranded in a border town called Las Vegas, thus consigning Nicaragua to totalitarian tyranny, Central America to subversion, intimidation and instability, and ourselves to unfamiliar and unwelcome dangers and defense burdens on our coasts and on our borders?

The evolution of Cuba and Nicaragua illuminates both the present and future. Think about the parallels.

As in Nicaragua, a broad coalition of Cubans overthrew a hated dictatorship in the name of democracy and social progress.

As in Nicaragua, the leaders of the Cuban revolution made some very clear promises to the people of Cuba:

• a promise to restore the 1940 constitution;
• a promise to provide an entirely civilian government;
• a promise of full democratic freedom (press, assembly, political activity); and
• a promise of honest, free elections within one year.

As in Nicaragua, a struggle broke out between communists and democrats inside the new government.

As in Nicaragua, the communists dissembled, hiding their identity, confusing the issues until they had driven the democrats from the government and into prison and exile.

As in Nicaragua, the government of Fidel Castro quickly entered into intimate economic and political relations with the Soviet Union.

As in Nicaragua, the consolidation of power by communists and the process of incorporation into the Soviet empire took place at a time when the U.S. was providing important economic support and trade.

As in Nicaragua, well-meaning Western liberals denied the reality of Cuban communists' beliefs, Soviet ties and repressive intentions, until they were no longer deniable—and then suggested it happened only because we drove them to it, by failing to "understand."

As in Nicaragua, they were wrong.

Marxist-Leninist Revolutions

"Inexorably," Fidel told TV interviewers in Spain, "we consider ourselves Marxist-Leninists"—and had been, he told Barbara Walters, since his law school days in the late 1940s.

"You cannot be a true revolutionary in Latin America without being a Marxist-Leninist," said true revolutionary Thomas Borge.

Our doctrine is Marxism-Leninism," said Humberto Ortega. "It is the scientific doctrine that guides the revolution."

As in Nicaragua, the promised freedom never came. An iron system of repression was imposed on the Cuban people that suppressed civil, political, cultural and religious freedom, ended economic development and made political prisoners of former comrades.

As in Nicaragua, Cuba's government acted quickly to introduce Soviet military power, lending its territory as a base for the projection of Soviet might in the hemisphere.

Soviet arms and technicians were accompanied into Cuba by assurances. "The armaments and military equipment sent to Cuba are designed exclusively for defensive purposes," the Soviet government announced. The thousands of Soviet military advisers moved into Cuba were there for purely defensive purposes, we were told.

The parallels between Cuba's development since 1959 and Nicaragua's development since July 1979 are many. But not complete.

Cuba is today a full member of the Soviet empire, "the world socialist system." Nicaragua has moved far down the path to incorporation. CIA Director William Casey said in a speech published in *The Washington Times* that U.S. analysts had identified 46 indicators of full consolidation of power by a Marxist-Leninist regime, of which Nicaragua has already accomplished 33.

What can Cuba's evolution tell us about what is planned for Nicaragua, Central America, and us?

I believe that events in Nicaragua stand today about where they stood in Cuba at the time of the Bay of Pigs.

Again troops trained and equipped by the U.S. confront the possibility of abandonment. Though their movement has made great progress, the Nicaraguan government is insecure. Its policies have disrupted all aspects of society, it has driven hundreds of thousands into exile. A rapid, urgent build-up of Soviet military strength is underway, Soviet bloc arms and technicians moved in a massive, continuous stream.

There is discussion in and out of the American government of the consequences of these events. In El Salvador, Honduras, Costa Rica, and Washington, governments and people debate whether it is or is not possible to "contain" a communist Nicaragua and prevent the spread of this pathology. Contadora talks and Manzanillo talks explore whether it is or is not possible to find a solution that will respect sovereignty and territorial integrity and security for all, whether it is possible to "tame" Nicaragua, whether it is possible to trade the security of Nicaragua for the security of El Salvador.

Meanwhile, arms arrive, repression intensifies, and the American Congress falters.

In the Shadow of the Missiles

In thinking about such present and future possibilities, I believe it is useful to recall the supreme effort undertaken to solve the "problem" of Cuba. I speak, of course, of the Kennedy-Khrushchev agreement negotiated in the shadow of the Cuban Missile Crisis in October 1962.

"Offensive missile sites" with "a nuclear strike capability" were discerned in Cuba. President John Kennedy informed the American people there had occurred a "[s]ecret, swift, and extraordinary build-up of communist missiles—in an area well known to have a special and historical relationship to the United States and the nations of the Western Hemisphere." He warned, "[T]he urgent transformation of Cuba into an important strategic base constitutes an explicit threat to the peace and security of all the Americas."

The U.S. "could not tolerate deliberate deception and offensive threats," President Kennedy concluded. "The threat," said Secretary of State Dean Rusk, "is to our hemisphere. . . . But the threat originates from outside the hemisphere."

The U.S. government, therefore, imposed a quarantine on all offensive military equipment under shipment to Cuba and announced that any such equipment from whatever nation or port would, if "found to contain cargoes of offensive weapons, be turned back." President Kennedy defined as prohibited material: "surface to surface missiles; bomber aircraft; bombs; air to surface rockets and guided missiles; warheads for any of the above weapons; [and] mechanical or electronic equipment to support or operate the above items."

It was the most serious direct confrontation between the U.S. and the USSR, before or since.

In the context of this confrontation, an agreement was negotiated on November 20, 1962. That agreement was described to the people by President Kennedy thus:

> Chairman Khrushchev, it will be recalled, agreed to remove from Cuba all weapons systems capable of offensive use, to halt the further introduction of such weapons into Cuba, and to permit appropriate United Nations observation and supervision to insure the carrying out and continuation of these commitments. We on our part agreed that once these adequate arrangements for verification had been established we would remove our naval quarantine and give assurances against an invasion of Cuba.
>
> As for our part if all offensive weapons systems are removed from Cuba and kept out of the hemisphere in the future, under adequate verification and safeguards, and if Cuba is not used for the export of aggressive communist

purposes, there will be peace in the Caribbean. And as I said in September, we shall neither initiate nor permit aggression in this hemisphere."

President Kennedy believed he had won a commitment that Cuba would not export subversion and revolution as well as a commitment that the Soviet Union would not install offensive weapons—or attempt to use Cuba as a forward base for Soviet military power. And it is clear that in exchange the United States agreed not to invade Cuba and to see to it that other governments in the hemisphere did not either.

In effect the United States became the guarantor of Cuba's communist government.

Since suggestions of just such a deal have been heard for Nicaragua, it is appropriate to consider how the Kennedy-Khrushchev agreement—more momentous than Salt I—has worked out 23 years later.

More Momentous than Salt I

Obviously, the U.S. has not invaded Cuba, nor encouraged or assisted others in doing so.

We kept our part of the bargain, as we regularly do.

What of the Soviets and Cubans? Have they kept their commitment?

A recent U.S. government document described the current Soviet presence in Cuba:

> The Soviets now have in Cuba 7,000 civilian advisers, a 2,800-man combat brigade, another 2,800 military advisers, plus about 2,100 technicians at the Lourdes electronic intelligence facility. Since 1969, the Soviet navy has deployed task forces to Cuba and the Caribbean 24 times. Soviet long-range naval reconnaissance aircraft are also deployed to Cuba. From there, they operate along with U.S. East Coast and in the Caribbean, shadowing carrier battle groups and spying on other U.S. military forces and installations. The Soviets also use Cuba as a stopover point for reconnaissance aircraft enroute to Angola.

> Cuba's strategic location makes it an ideal site for an intelligence facility directed against the United States. The Soviet Union established such a site at Lourdes near Havana in the mid-1960s. Lourdes today is the most sophisticated Soviet collection facility outside the Soviet Union itself. From this key listening post, the Soviets monitor U.S. commercial satellites, U.S. military and merchant shipping communications, and NASA space program activities at Cape Canaveral. Lourdes also enables the Soviets to eavesdrop on telephone conversations in the United States.

In addition, in clear violation of an agreement reached with Secretary of State Henry Kissinger, Cuba completed the submarine base at Cienfuegos, which has the capacity to service Soviet nuclear submarines (and has done so) and has an air base which can handle Backfire bombers and more than 200 jet fighters. The accumulation of Soviet military personnel is a clear violation of Cuba's "agreement" with President Carter, concluded at the time he discovered the Soviet combat brigade.

Cuba provides the clearest example of what integration into the Soviet empire means. Cuba provides bases that extend the reach of Soviet naval and air power and electronic surveillance. Cuba provides advisers and troops for Nicaragua, Angola, Ethiopia, Mozambique and South Yemen, among others. Cuba helps train guerrillas who operate throughout the world. Cuba mans and masterminds the drug and terror network that reaps chaos throughout Latin America and certain havoc on our own shores and in our country.

The Nicaraguan Buildup

In Nicaragua, a similar massive military build-up is underway. The same [United States] government report indicates:

> Several huge construction projects backed by the Soviet bloc represent the investment of hundreds of millions of dollars, including $70 million for nearly 40 new military facilities. In addition, Bulgaria, East Germany, and Cuba are building critical infrastructure facilities which will have important military use.

> The 10,000-foot runway at the Punta Huete airfield, when completed, will be the longest military runway in Central America. As the base took on the unmistakable signs of a military air base, such as protective earthen mounds (or revetments) for fighter aircraft, the Sandinsta air force commander admitted that it would be a military air base.

> When Punta Huete becomes operational, it will be able to accommodate any aircraft in the Soviet-bloc inventory. The potential threat to Nicaragua's neighbors would then increase dramatically. The recent acquisition of Mi-24/ HIND D attack helicopters, along with the existing inventory of Mi-8 troop-carrying helicopters, provides the Sandinistas with a powerful helicopter force. The Sandinista regime has declared repeatedly its intention to acquire combat aircraft, and Punta Huete would be a logical base from which such aircraft could operate. Nicaraguan jet pilots and mechanics have been trained in Eastern Europe and are reportedly now flying to Cuba. Sandinista acquisition of such jet aircraft would further destabilize the regional military balance; the United States has consistently made clear in diplomatic channels its concern about such weaponry.

The base at Punta Huete provides a Soviet base for long-range reconnaissance aircraft along the West Coast of the United States, comparable to such flights along the East Coast from Cuba. They could be readily supplemented by submarines. Electronic installation in Nicaragua already provides the Soviets important information on the Caribbean, Panama Canal traffic and the Pacific Coast.

Obviously, investment in Nicaragua indicates that Soviet leaders consider Nicaragua an important Soviet military resource. They have understood better than we the strategic potential of a presence on the U.S. border.

Anyone who argues that the U.S. should enter into an agreement which guarantees the Nicaraguan government must first explain why the Kennedy-Khrushchev agreement was in the interests of the U.S.—or the area—or the Cuban people. They must explain why Nicaragua will be more likely to keep an agreement than the government of Cuba, and why Nicaragua will be more likely to keep a new commitment than to keep its promise to the OAS to establish democracy.

It is not and cannot be our role to protect tyrants.

It must be our role to help others protect their freedom.

Certainly, this is the President's position:

> We must not break faith with those who are risking their lives on every continent, from Afghanistan to Nicaragua, to defy Soviet-supported aggression and secure rights which have been ours from birth. Support for freedom fighters is self defense.

Confronted with the expansion of the Soviet empire to the shores of the U.S., President Reagan has made clear his commitment to those who struggle to preserve their own independence. He said:

> Twenty-two years ago President John F. Kennedy went to the Berlin Wall and proclaimed that he, too, was a Berliner. Today, freedom-loving people around the world must say, I am a Berliner, I am a Jew in a world still threatened by anti-Semitism, I am an Afghan and I am a prisoner of the Gulag. I am a refugee in a crowded boat foundering off the coast of Vietnam. I am a Laotian, a Cambodian, a Cuban, and a Miskito Indian in Nicaragua. I, too, am a potential victim of totalitarianism.

The vote not to assist the Nicaraguan patriots was neither consistent with the president's policy nor with American traditions or interests. It was consistent only with the tradition of abandonment.

Even more shameful is the proposal of Congressmen Levin and Leach that would "prohibit private assistance" to Nicaraguan resistance.

It is only necessary to think of our own history, our own tradition, to think of how France helped the U.S. in our moment of need, of how in

Cuba the ladies of Havana donated 1,200,000 *livres* to George Washington, whose men were desperate.

Some say helping freedom fighters is a step down the road to war. It is the opposite. It is the assurance we will not face a threat in this hemisphere.

Some say Nicaragua's freedom fighters cannot win. I say they cannot lose . . . if we provide half the assistance Moscow provides the FSLN. Some say it is not consistent to support rebels in Nicaragua and not oppose them in El Salvador. But it is consistent to support a democratic government in El Salvador and democratic forces in Nicaragua.

If we are steadfast and true to our values and our interests, then democracy will prevail in Nicaragua. We will be able to say, *"Ahora, hay uno—y despunes, un dia, ninguno."**

THE BAY OF PIGS REVISITED

It is a pleasure to be here tonight with all of you. Let me just say that maybe if I had been a member of the DAR and had been reading your publications and resolutions as closely as I should have been, I wouldn't have been quite as deeply shocked as I was at what I found at the United Nations.

I will freely and willingly admit that there is almost nothing that I discovered and described about the United Nations that had not been described by the DAR before me. It is a fact that the United States had become a whipping boy at the United Nations. And it is a fact that the United Nations had become a place in which disputes among nations were more often exacerbated, deepened, and embittered than resolved. It is a fact that people had become accustomed to blaming America for all of the faults, sins and shortcomings and failures of everything in the world virtually. And it is a fact that on hearing it, I felt we really can't take this any longer. The United Nations teaches a very special kind of forbearance. I think it is very difficult to represent the United States in the United Nations. I have thought several times in the last 24 hours, that I thank God that it is not my responsibility to represent the United States in the United Nations. My sympathy and support are fully with our permanent represen-

*"Now, there is one—and later, one day, none."

Address before the 95th Continental Congress, Daughters of the American Revolution, Washington, D.C., April 15, 1986.

tative, Ambassador Vernon Walters. He is doing an eloquent job of defending the United States—last night, this morning, this afternoon—against an array of peaceloving nations such as Libya, Syria, Iran, Burkina Faso, South Yemen, the Soviet Union, Vietnam, Algeria—all those peaceloving nations who have been excoriating the United States just today.

It has been an exciting and important 24 hours. It is, of course, not the first time that the United States has struck at terrorists in North Africa, because it is not the first time that we Americans have been victimized by violent men operating from North African bases. It happened a long time ago, in the first years of our nationhood. Alexander Hamilton called the years between 1785 and 1789 the last stage of national humiliation. It was a period in which major powers in the world exploited our weakness. They doubted our capacity to survive, nor did we have their sympathy in that project. Almost all of those nations, we count our friends—British, French, Spanish, Prussians—almost all of them violated our sovereignty in those years. Frederick II of Prussia said, commenting on the miserable fight we presented to the world, "I'm much persuaded that this so-called independence of America will not amount to much." And most European leaders agreed. John Adams, who was then our ambassador to the Court of St. James, wrote that he was regarded and treated by the British as "little more than a cipher." No group exploited and mocked American weakness in those years more cruelly than did the Barbary pirates. They attacked American ships, seized sailors and sold them into slavery, and demanded ransom that the young American nation could not afford to pay. The distinguished American historian Richard Morris described the misery of American seaman in the dark dank dungeons of Algiers in those years. Morris wrote that the Americans held there were tattered and emaciated, that they were covered with vermin and that swarms of mosquitos preyed on them. In the morning they could be seen shackled, dragging heavy weights and walking on treadmills, their bare backs showing evidence of severe beatings. In the square, they were made to run to and fro so that prospective buyers could listen to their heartbeat against their bare chests. One by one they were sold off at prices varying according to their physical condition.

"Shall we wage war or pay tribute?" Secretary of State John Jay put that question to the Congress. The Congress would neither decide nor do either. Then as now, American efforts to find a basis for common action and cooperation with our friends in Europe failed. Then as now, the nations of Europe preferred to deal with the pirates under the table and pay tribute, each working on their own separate deal. Eventually, the United States became strong enough to confront the Barbary pirates. It was 1850, and it took a military victory against Algiers before the United States finally secured free transit for American merchant ships through the Mediterranean.

This is not a period of American history of which we are particularly proud, but it has important lessons to teach us, lessons of which we sometimes need to be reminded. Most important of these lessons is quite simply that a country and its citizens are respected when and only when that country is strong. A nation incapable of defending itself is at the mercy of others and all too often in foreign affairs, others turn out to be not very merciful. Afghanistan today is a pitiful example of what happens when a people must rely on the mercy of the Soviet Union. Their villages are destroyed, their crops burned, and their children shipped to the Soviet Union for a decade. Every aspect of their culture and their country is destroyed. History has many lessons to teach us about the blessings of our system based on freedom and about the human price of tyranny. It has lessons to teach us about the conduct of both our domestic and our foreign affairs. I believe it has some very particularly important lessons to teach us regarding the Nicaraguan freedom fighters today.

As I reflected on this situation, my mind turned back to another occasion when the United States made critical decisions about helping another band of Latin American freedom fighters who sought to prevent their own country's incorporation into the Soviet empire. I thought, of course, of the Bay of Pigs and that landing on April 17, 1961. This week marks the 25th anniversary of the landing at the Bay of Pigs. Many people present will remember when 1,400 Cubans, who had been trained by the United States at bases in Central America, landed on Cuba's beaches. On those beaches, they fought bravely until finally, out of ammunition and fuel, confronted with air superiority of Fidel Castro, they either died or were captured.

What went wrong at the Bay of Pigs was the subject of a great deal of inquiry and criticism at the time. It was clear that John Kennedy's decision to cancel the planned air strike of Castro's forces played a crucial role. Now the Bay of Pigs has taken a place alongside the Vietnam war as proof of the folly and failure of U.S. efforts to oppose the expansion of communism. Criticism of the United States for not doing enough has been replaced by criticism of the United States for having tried at all. The Bay of Pigs became "Exhibit B" in the liberal showcase of horrors about the disastrous consequences of trying to use American force or proxy forces to oppose consolidation of power by a communist leadership group. I have no desire tonight to reopen questions about whether the mission at the Bay of Pigs was doomed from the start or whether it failed as a consequence of President Kennedy's decisions. Certainly those decisions had important consequences. We will never know really whether Kennedy's decision to prohibit the second Cuban airstrike at Castro's airfields was crucial. Richard Bissell, the CIA official who was in charge of the Bay of Pigs operation, commented later, "Due to military operation, the invasion could have failed for a number of reasons." It did, in fact, fail because of their control of the air. We cannot be certain what would have happened had the brigade established their beachhead. But, we know what has happened because they did not.

Suppose they had prevailed.

Suppose we had prevailed.

Suppose Fidel Castro had not been permitted to consolidate power.

What difference would that have made to our world?

"Why," said a Nicaraguan refugee with whom I spoke yesterday, "I would be in Nicaragua today, not here in Washington. Without Cuba, there would be no communist Nicaragua."

How would the world have been different. First of all, it would have been different for the Cubans themselves. The most painful consequences of Fidel Castro's success have been suffered by the Cuban people, who before Fidel Castro enjoyed the highest per capita income in Latin America. For the Cuban people, communism and Castro meant repression, militarization, and stagnation. They have meant separated families and political prisons.

"The revolution begins today," Castro announced his very first day in power and proceeded to prove it by repealing the Cuban constitution, which was then, by the way, widely considered one of the most progressive and best constitutions in Latin America. He replaced it with a new so-called fundamental law as he quickly replaced the judiciary with "revolutionary tribunals." Promises of free elections that Fidel Castro made before his victory quickly gave way to a new slogan, "Revolution first, elections later." "Later" never came.

Fidel Castro's consolidation of power in Cuba meant a new tyranny to the people of Cuba, not new freedom. Bloc committees resembling Nazi Germany's surveillance bloc committees brought every Cuban family under surveillance. Harsh new laws brought every Cuban institution under state control. Political groups were merged into a single party—the Communist party—and otherwise forbidding. Catholic schools and all other private schools were closed. Labor unions were forced to submit to new communist leaders. Property was progressively expropriated by the government. Media—television, radio, the press—was brought wholly under communist control. New crimes were established and imposed on the helpless population. Opposition to the state, any aspect of the state, was punished by long years of imprisonment. Human rights violations—torture, beating—became a permanent feature of political life in revolutionary Cuba.

Control of all aspects of life made life more and more intolerable. And more and more Cubans fled as refugees. More than one million of a population of nine million left Cuba to come to the United States, to go to Venezuela or Costa Rica. Cubans have made a real contribution to the societies where they have settled including our own. But they have suffered a great deal in the process. Fidel Castro was not content, however, to be an absolute ruler of Cuba. He wanted to be more. He wanted to be a maximum leader on a global scale. So, he had a plan. His plan was first to follow the Marxist-Leninist blueprint and second to follow that blueprint right into the Soviet empire. He told a TV interviewer in Spain just two years ago, "Inexorably we consider ourselves to be Marxist-Leninist," although he had hid his Marxism-Leninism until after he came to power. Castro lost no time in aligning his country with the Soviet Union, not because the United States opposed his revolution—we ought to be clear about that because there is a lie that has been carefully cultivated to the effect that Castro opposed the United States because the United States opposed Castro. The fact is Castro aligned his country with the Soviet Union because he was implacably hostile to the United States. Soviet aid was quick in coming.

Each year the Soviets pump more than $4 billion of aid into Cuba. It is estimated that more than $6 billion in military aid have been received in the last decade.

Today, Cuba has the largest army in Latin America—more than 200,000 active duty military personnel and another 135,000 reservists. These forces are found not only in Cuba oppressing the Cuban people but in virtually every communist country in the world. Two-thirds of the communist forces stationed in the Third World today are Cubans. There are Cubans sent as military advisers and troops to Angola, Ethiopia, Mozambique, South Yemen, Nicaragua, Congo, Mali, Ghana, Guinea-Bissau, Algeria, Iraq, Syria, Lybia, Suriname, and of course there were Cubans on Grenada. There are now about five times as many Cuban soldiers in Africa alone as there were in Cuba's armed forces when Fidel Castro came to power.

Castro has made Cuba a major military power, although it is a relatively small island country.

What would be different if the Bay of Pigs liberation had succeeded? Well, those Cuban forces wouldn't be in Africa or South Yemen, or Asia, and they wouldn't be in Nicaragua. Those Cuban forces would be at home working at civilian jobs, contributing to their own economies and culture, and enjoying their own families. Nowhere has Cuba's commitment to international revolution been as important as here in the Americas. The realignment of the correlation of forces in this hemisphere has been Castro's very special goal. In that he has taken the greatest interest of all. Castro's role in training and supporting Latin America's terrorist and guerrilla groups has been tremendously important. It is estimated, for example, that more than 20,000 students from the Third World countries—a large number from Latin America—have graduated from Castro training camps and schools in the so-called "isle of youth." Most of Nicaragua's leadership has been trained in Cuba. Most of the guerrilla technicians and warriors of El Salvador's guerrillas have been trained in Cuba. Guatemala's Marxist leaders, Columbia's M-19 leaders, guerrillas of Ecuador, Peru, Bolivia, Suriname, and Guyana have been trained in Cuba.

We had the opportunity in Grenada, at the time of its liberation, to observe some of the Cuban workers building an airstrip, fortifying the island, organizing the revolution, and depriving the Grenadan people of self-government. Cuba promotes the spread and consolidation of Marxism in every nation of Latin America whenever and wherever it has the chance. Fidel Castro is driven always by an implacable hatred of the United States.

What difference would it have made if the Bay of Pigs had turned out differently? Latin America would have been spared much of the bloodshed and destruction of the past two and one-half decades—where, as in El Salvador, electric stations are dynamited, peasants murdered, and businessman kidnapped, there would have been peace and economic growth and development, as there was in Central America before Fidel Castro's trained guerrillas arrived in Nicaragua to spread their poison in the country and from there to El Salvador.

Today, Fidel Castro provides certain other benefits to the Soviet Union—some benefits of very special concern to us Americans. In Cuba, today, KGB personnel have installed and operate an electronic surveillance installation at Lourdes—eavesdropping on telephone conversations in the eastern part of the United States, and intercepting military and space communications. Today, in Cuba, some 2,800 Soviets (direct, real, honest to God) military personnel are still there in the famous combat brigade and another 2,800 military advisers help Cubans learn the weapons the Soviets ship them. And about 7,000 Soviet civilian advisers help with those various tasks. Today, in Cuba, the Soviet Union's long-range naval reconnaissance aircraft are frequently deployed to Cuban and to the Caribbean and Cuban service stations permit them to operate off our coast. The Soviet Union and Cuba's own military establishment today pose a very substantial, real threat to the maritime commerce in the sea routes in the Caribbean and the Gulf of Mexico.

If the Bay of Pigs brigade had succeeded on the those beaches 25 years ago, these real and present dangers to our American security and to the security of every independent nation in our hemisphere simply would not exist. The Bay of Pigs landing was perhaps badly planned. Certainly its chances of success were damaged by the progressive limits imposed on it. But, the Cubans who landed there were brave and their cause was just. It was a good thing for us to support them; unfortunately we just didn't support them enough. The price the United States, we Americans, pay in security, in increased military expense costs, defense costs, and increased risk is very high and the end is not in sight. The price that we and other people of the Americas would pay for the consolidation in Nicaragua of another communist power would be higher still because power is cumulative.

A communist Nicaragua helps Cuba reach further just as a communist Cuba helps the Soviet Union reach its military power into all parts of the waterways, airspaces, and land of our hemisphere. Only this week, new confirmation has been offered of Nicaragua's role in the firebombing of the Columbian Supreme Court in which most of the judges of that court were murdered in cold blood. The effects of the Sandinista consolidation of power would be more far-reaching because Nicaragua is not an island. Nicaragua's leaders are even more aggressive than Fidel Castro. Already, Nicaragua has begun the systematic export of subversion, oppression, guerrilla war, and relentless hostility to the other countries of Central America. "Our revolution was always internationalist from the moment Sandino fought his battle," one of the commandantes announced. They chant as they work in Nicaraguan fields, "When Sandinismo wins, El Salvador will follow." "We cannot cease being internationalists," another commandante shouted, "unless we cease being revolutionaries."

The internationalism that Nicaragua supports and implements is not a benign form of international cooperation. It doesn't mean joining together to accomplish worthwhile goals. Their internationalism means joining together with the enemies of America—joining, for example, with Libya about whom Tomas Borge said last year, "Our friendship with Libya is eternal." It is also mutual. Qaddafi has said the same about Nicaragua. Qaddafi has said, "Nicaragua is a great thing . . . it is fighting in America's own territorial waters."

It is very enlightening and disturbing to read Soviet military theory and doctrine. The Soviet Union's theorists believe that the next war will be a final showdown between the forces of capitalism and socialism. They believe it will be a coalition war and that the outcome will depend on the size and the unity and the cohesiveness of the coalition. Cuba was a very powerful addition to the Soviet coalition. Nicaragua would be a more powerful addition to the Soviet coalition. I regret to say, it is only necessary to look today at the United Nations to understand whose coalition is strongest, whose coalition has greater unity and more cohesion. Soviet allies line up like soldiers in back of Libya. U.S. allies scatter like autumn leaves in a whirlwind.

What should we do?

Try negotiations once more in Nicaragua?

I reflected a bit on this favorite argument of the opponents of the president's plan for supporting Nicaragua's freedom fighters. I thought about the effort at negotiations in Cuba. Remember the Kennedy-Khrushchev agreement? Remember that after the failure of the Bay of Pigs landing, the Soviet Union tried to install offensive nuclear missiles in Cuba? President Kennedy challenged them, imposing a United States blockade on the island of Cuba and creating the most dangerous direct confrontation between the United States and the Soviet Union since the Berlin Blockade or that there has been since.

That confrontation ended with a negotiation. It ended with a deal. One aspect of the deal was below the table and one above the table. The one that was below the table was the U.S. agreement to withdraw our missiles from Turkey provided that the Soviet Union kept quiet about it. The deal above the table is rather better known. The Soviets agreed to remove their offensive nuclear missiles and to halt their further introduction providing that the U.S. ended its naval quarantine and gave assurances that the United States would never again attempt or permit aggression against the government of Cuba—that we would never attempt to overthrow the government of Cuba or permit anyone else in the hemisphere to try to overthrow the government of Cuba. It was quite a promise we made.

President Kennedy believed and announced that in addition he had won a commitment that Cuba would not export subversion and revolution to the rest of this hemisphere. At the same time, we became in effect the guarantor of Cuba's communist government, Cuba's communist government agreed not to try to encourage any other communist states in the Americas. Obviously, we can see now how it has worked out. Obviously, the United States has not invaded Cuba or encouraged or assisted others in doing so. We kept our part of the bargain as we regularly keep our word. But, what of the Soviets and Cubans. Did they keep their commitment? It is only necessary to look at Nicaragua, El Salvador, the M-19 in Columbia, the Sindero Luminoso in Peru, the guerrillas in Bolivia, and those trying to reestablish a beachhead in Chile to know that bargain has not been kept. It is only necessary to look at the arsenals based in and around Cuba today to know that that bargain has not been kept. There is no more reason to suppose another deal negotiated another day would be in fact honored except in breach.

So, what should we do?

I believe that we should support those who fight for their own country's right to self-government and national independence and who incidentally fight for our security. I believe that it is terribly important for the Congress, in deciding on this issue tomorrow, to recall what John Adams said was its immediate dependence on the people and give the United States' security the benefit of the doubt.

I believe the American people should demand no less. And if we demand no less we will finally get no less.

We should all remember while respecting Congress' rights that though Congress makes the decisions it is we who will pay the bills and we will run the risks. So we pray on the eve of this momentous vote that Congressmen in making their decision will recall James Madison's deathbed counsel. "The advice nearest and dearest and deepest in my conviction," Madison said, "is that the Union of States be cherished, protected, and perpetuated."

TAKING POWER

I would like to begin with a text from an article that appeared in *Encounter Magazine* last fall called "Learning from Vietnam." The article was co-authored by Doan Van Toai and David Chanoff, and among many interesting observations in the article is the assertion "liberation war strategy calls for the creation of guerrilla fronts representing many shades of political feeling, within which the communists themselves are likely to be a minority." Second quotation: "If the Vietnam experience has taught liberation movement organizers anything, it is the value of maintaining a reformist, nationalist and non-aligned facade." The guerrilla movements in Central America today are distinguished in significant measure precisely because they have dropped the reformist, nationalist, non-aligned, democratic, broad-based facade, which has been conceived rather widely as a necessary prerequisite of a successful liberation war strategy.

As recently as 1979, when the Sandinistas undertook the last six months of their ultimately successful struggle against the Somoza regime, the Liberation Front, which achieved the victory over Somoza, was comprised of multiple groups. There were important persons from the private sector, like

Address before the Council on Foreign Relations, New York, New York, April 21, 1983.

Arturo Cruz, Alfonso Robelo and Jorge Salazar. There were religious leaders who had commanded the broadest support in the nation and who had become veritable symbols of opposition to Somoza. Archbishop Miguel Obando y Bravo is preeminent among those. There were the various armed tendencies within the FSLN.

In July of 1979, that broad front brought its case before the Organization of American States. At that time the OAS took an absolutely unprecedented step. For the first time in its history, the OAS passed a resolution calling for the replacement of a head of state. Interesting legal implications can be drawn from that act. The political bases of the act were clearly found in the apparently broad-based, reformist, pluralist, democratic character of the Liberation Front, and also some very specific commitments that the Front made to the OAS. Those commitments were made in a letter that is not often thought about today. The following are some passages from the letter written by the group acting for the FSLN before the OAS.

> Mr. Secretary-General of the Organization of the American States, we are pleased to make available to you and to the ministers of foreign affairs of the member states of the Organization, a document containing our plan to secure peace in our heroic long-suffering country at the moment when the people turnover the dictatorship. First, we have developed this plan on the basis of the resolution of the seventeenth meeting of consultations on June 23, 1979, a resolution that was historic in every sense of the word. It demands the immediate replacement of the genocidal Somoza dictatorship, which is now nearing its end, and backs the installation of a broadly represented democratic government in our country such as the one we have formed.
>
> While saying that the solution to this problem is exclusively within the jurisdiction of the people of Nicaragua, it appeals to a hemispheric solidarity to preserve our people's right to self-determination. We are presenting to the community of nations of this hemisphere, in connection with our plans to secure peace, the goals that here inspired our government ever since it was formed. They have been set forth in our documents and political declarations, and we wish to ratify them here today.
>
> 1 It is our firm intention to establish full observance of human rights in our country in accordance with the United Nations Declaration of the Rights of Man and the Charter of Human Rights of the OAS. Our observance of human rights has already been made plain by the way the Sandinista National Liberation Front has treated hundreds of prisoners of war. Our government thus invites the Inter-American Commission on Human Rights to visit our country as soon as we are installed in our national territory.
>
> 2 Our wish that our installation in Nicaragua come about through peaceful and orderly transition. The government of national reconstruction would take it as a gesture of solidarity if the foreign ministers of the hemisphere were to visit our country, and we do hereby extend to them a fraternal invitation to do so.

3 Our intention to embrace civil justice in our country, and to try those incriminated of crimes according to the regular law. The people have won themselves the right to let justice prevail for the first time in half a century and will do so within the framework of the law without a spirit of vengeance or indiscriminate reprisals.

4 Those who wish to do so may leave the country.

5 The plan to call the first free elections our country has known in this century, so that Nicaraguans can elect their representatives to the city councils, to a constituent assembly, and later elect the country's highest authorities.

Mr. Secretary-General, it is now up to the governments of the hemisphere to speak so that the solidarity with the struggle of our people is carried forward to make democracy and justice possible and Nicaragua can become fully effective. We ask that you transmit the text of this letter to the foreign ministers of the Organization of American States.

Yours most respectfully, Junta of the Government of National Reconstruction, Violetta de Chamorro, Sergio Ramirez Mercado, Alfonso Robelo-Callajas, Daniel Ortega Saavedra.

Those were the promises offered, the statement of intention presumably sincerely described. On the basis of those promises, and the expectation that those promises would be fulfilled, the United States, for example, rushed some $24.6 million in emergency food, medical and reconstruction assistance to the FSLN on their triumph. The U.S. also provided some $118 million in direct financial assistance in the subsequent 18 months. In addition, the United States firmly backed the applications of the new government of Nicaragua in the multilateral lending institutions and assisted them in securing some $262 million in aid from those institutions, an amount double that which the Somoza government had received in the preceding twenty years.

The United States was also helpful, as were other members of the OAS, in securing support from other Western and democratic countries. This was so successful that by November, 1982, the total amount of economic aid which the government of Nicaragua had received from Western governments was estimated authoritatively at $1.4 billion, as compared to about $.6 billion from the Eastern bloc.

This government, however, rather quickly began to shed some of its broad-based character. It became more and more narrow in composition and more and more repressive in its behavior. Of the five members of the Junta who made the application to the OAS and signed the letter I just read, two, Violetta Chamorro and Alfonso Robelo, resigned within the first year. Violetta Chamorro did so after it became clear that rigorous press censorship was to be the norm rather than the free press which had been anticipated; Alfonso Robelo resigned after it became clear that the policies of the junta were not those of the pluralistic democracy promised. Both of them were also unhappy with the decision announced during the first year to postpone and then postpone again elections, until finally the government announced just prior to the first anniversary of the revolution in July, 1980, that there would be no elections before 1985; that not even municipal elections would take place and that it would, furthermore, be illegal for parties to organize or to discuss candidacies for national elections before 1984. The elections, as the Sandinistas made clear, would not be the kind of elections that bourgeois democrats dream about, but the kind of elections that would serve the purposes of the revolution.

The Progressive Private Sector, COSEP, resigned in protest to these progressive restrictions on the political process, and not too long thereafter, its leader, Jorge Salazar, was gunned down as he travelled from one city to another. The opposition group that Alfonso Robelo had organized, the MND, was set upon repeatedly and his house attacked by the so-called "divine mobs" with which the junta attempts to protect itself and illustrate its seriousness of purpose.

Very soon it became clear that the Front was narrow. The process of attrition continued as person after person who had been initially associated with the Sandinista Front abandoned hope and usually went first into passivity and then into exile. Eden Pastora's departure was one landmark. The decision of both the first two Sandinista ambassadors to the United States were two other landmarks. The decision of Alfonso Robelo to join the directorate of the FDN constituted still another of those landmarks. Virtually, the entire group that had negotiated the $75 million loan from Washington went into exile.

So the revolution was not broad anymore. Neither was it independent anymore. It became clearer and clearer that the junta was ever more closely linked to the Soviet bloc. The landmark in this linkage was a trip in May, 1980, in which Moises Morales Hassan, Henri Ruiz and Carlos Colonel, among others, travelled to Moscow to sign a treaty between the FSLN and the Communist Party of the Soviet Union. Working with Bulgarian intermediaries the FSLN obtained assistance from the Soviet Union and the Eastern bloc under the condition that they would advance the plans of the Bulgarian team. While this happened the Russians would give the FSLN 80 percent military help and only 20 percent economic assistance. The Sandinista Front committed itself to spreading the revolution in Central America with the beneficent 80 percent. Once accomplished, it was understood the help from Moscow would then be reversed in ratio—that it would be 20 percent military assistance and 80 percent economic aid.

Adriana Guilan tells us the Bulgarian analysis of the Nicaragua situation was that Nicaraguan socialism was not viable in just one country, but that it would be made viable in a socialist Central America. The objective, therefore, should be a "revolution without frontiers," as the Sandinistas call it. The Bulgarians concluded that there were only two countries in the Soviet revolutionary bloc at the time in which the problems were not economic, but military and political. Those two countries were, interestingly enough, Nicaragua and Poland. The Bulgarian thesis was discussed and accepted in Managua. The struggle began. The Bulgarian team helped the FSLN establish its strategies for the consolidation of internal power, and they gave very clear-cut priority to the consolidation of power internally, over, for example, economic development. The plan included projects for bringing the Miskito Indians and the church, both of whom are notoriously independent, under control. Private enterprise also had to be controlled.

This process reached an apex about a year ago when the decision was made to impose a state of siege in Nicaragua. Under the state of siege, rule of civil law, to which the junta had explicitly committed itself to the OAS, was suspended indefinitely, and, indeed, still remains suspended today. At the same time, such basic rights as the right to organize free trade unions and bargain collectively and speak and meet freely were also rigorously postponed until some unstated future date. The colossal, rapid build-up of military power was under way.

It is very difficult for Americans to think of Nicaragua as a military power, yet Nicaragua is already a superpower in the isthmus compared, for example, to Costa Rica or to Panama. The military build-up in Nicaragua has been rapid and determined. It has included the development of some 25,000 active-duty forces and a reserve National Guard force, called "la Guardia" as in the Somoza tradition, of some 50,000 men under arms. There have been over 2,000 Cuban military and internal security advisors introduced into Nicaragua to engineer the development of a nation-wide internal secret police system. With a little help from some Eastern bloc countries, Nicaragua now has very sophisticated weaponry, including two battalions of Soviet T-55 tanks, amphibious ferries, helicopters and transport aircraft.

This makes Nicaragua's neighbors very uncomfortable. The president of Costa Rica, who is a marvelous, strong, thorough-going democrat, commented: "At this moment it is possible that the conditions for a consensus action within the OAS are not present. But yes, there is sufficient reason so that all the countries should be alert. Because of the possibility of a more direct intervention in the internal matters of other countries, a country dominated by the politics and interest of the Soviet Union in our Caribbean area is a danger for the other nations. Cuba has been, Nicaragua will be, when they definitely decide openly to take the road to international Marxism."

The President of Panama, Ricardo del Espriella, commented "When a country arms itself more than it needs to maintain internal order, its neighbors worry and can do the same. Nicaragua is arming itself and it is arming itself more than what is necessary to maintain order. This pushes other nations to do the same. This is not the solution, but we see with concern the excess of the Nicaraguan government's armaments. The decision to openly identify themselves with the Soviet Union, in fact, had almost been taken by the time that President Monjes spoke, that was something over a year ago."

Already Humberto Ortega was saying in public places, "We guide ourselves by the scientific doctrines of the revolution, by Marxism-Leninism. Our political force is Sandinismo, our doctrine is Marxist-Leninist" and Victor Lopez noted that "Marxism is a fundamental part of the Sandinist ideology." The government has issued a new stamp commemorating the 100th anniversary of the death of Karl Marx. It has a picture of Karl Marx and excerpts from the *Communist Manifesto*. Surely, it is a stamp collector's delight for pictorial originality.

The composition and policy of the government and political force in Nicaragua have become so clear, that it is impossible to deny its character. At the United Nations, the Nicaraguan government votes as well as speaks in support of the most extreme of the Soviet-sponsored violations of human rights, such as the occupation of Afghanistan and the use of chemical weapons in Cambodia. Clearly, the United States is confronting a disciplined member of the Soviet bloc, not simply an undisciplined fellow traveler.

Just as the character of the Nicaraguan regime became clearer, so did the character of the Salvadoran struggle. The Salvadoran struggle also began with the FMLN appearing to be a broad-based, reformist, neutralist, would-be pluralist group. I remember being here at the Council about a year ago when Ungo spoke. He took essentially that position and made those same points, and it was still possible for reasonably well-informed people to have at least a question about whether that was so. In the intervening months, the comforts of ambiguity have been deprived those who seek to support the FMLN in El Salvador without really facing its nature. The FMLN's character has been progressively, clearly announced by its own leadership, and also by the leadership of the FSLN. The interesting aspect is the extent to which the leadership of both these movements have cast aside the appearance which *The Encounter* article suggested was so useful to such movements, and indeed did prove useful to the FSLN in achieving power in Nicaragua.

Three days ago, an FMLN leader, Guitano Carpio, himself dead today, spoke at the funeral of Commandante Annamaria. In the course of that eulogy he said:

> Members of the directorate and all its working teams, some inside the coun-
> try, others outside the country (Nicaragua) are steadfastly at work, fully aware
> of the need to unite the internal struggle with the international solidarity and
> with the struggle of all peoples for the liberation of Central America and El
> Salvador. That is why we move from country to country. When I heard this
> blow of crushing news, I was, in fact, in Libya . . . From that far away place in
> the deserts of Africa, I immediately rushed here trying to get here on time for
> the funeral services of our late 'companiera.'

He went on to say, "that henceforth the world would understand that the
struggles of the FMLN and the FSLN had been fully united, that they were
one." "Two nations, two destinies, one army," was the way he put it.

The news that Carpio had committed suicide reached our Mission only
today. Later, there was the suggestion that he had committed suicide out of
unhappiness because of the death of Commandante Annamarie. I don't
know. I think there is an alternative hypothesis that suggests itself as at least
equally plausible and that may be that whoever killed Commandante Annamarie killed Guitano Carpio. But that is speculation.

The strategic importance of Central America to the United States and to
the West is only barely comprehended in this country. It has been better
understood by the Soviets for quite some time. Soviet offensives in the
hemisphere and in the Caribbean region have gone almost unobserved.
Robert Leiken noted in his book on the Soviet strategy in the Caribbean:

> The importance of the area to the United States cannot be overestimated.
> Current NATO contingency plans call for the bulk of relief troops and equip-
> ment to transit the Caribbean in a European war. A Soviet backfire bomber
> based in Murmansk with a 4,000 kilometer range now jeopardizes the mid-
> Atlantic routes. In World War II, more than 50 percent of the U.S. supplies to
> Europe and Africa were shipped from Mexican Gulf ports. Caribbean trade
> routes carry steadily mounting cargo of strategic and other raw materials, and
> the Caribbean serves as a trans-shipment point for raw materials flowing from
> the Middle East, southern Asia and Africa to the United States. About 25
> percent of imported U.S. oil is refined abroad, more than half of it in Carib-
> bean refineries. The combination of a Soviet naval presence in the Caribbean
> with a burgeoning Soviet-supplied Cuban navy regularly participating in
> joint exercises has created a major integrated defensive interdiction ca-
> pability for Soviet bloc power in the Caribbean.

The Nicaraguan government has confirmed reports that a Soviet floating
workshop designed for ship repair will be operating off Nicaragua's Pacific
coast, and so forth and so forth.

As I pointed out in an article I wrote for the *Washington Post* on Sunday,
"last week was an interesting one from the perspective of hemispheric
affairs. The Deputy Soviet Foreign Minister, Vadim Zagladin, reiterated

Brezhnev's threat to install nuclear missiles in the Western Hemisphere five minutes from the United States. A member of the Nicaraguan Junta, Daniel Ortega, announced that, if asked, his government would consider installing Soviet nuclear missiles in his country." We already know that there is going to be a Soviet workshop there to repair old ships. There is news already of a deep-water port under construction on the Atlantic side of Grenada, at Grenville, which is on the strategic side of the most strategic Atlantic sea lanes. The problem is clear. Our response is a good deal less clear.

VIOLENCE AND DECEPTION

Marxist-Leninist revolutions proceed through violence and deception; violence against targeted populations, deception of targeted populations, and of all who might help them. The deception constitutes a veil behind which the violence takes place. Thus, in Afghanistan today, invasion, occupation and unceasing war against the Afghan people have been accompanied by attacks on the United States for intervening in the internal affairs of Afghanistan. I shall never forget my surprise when the first General Assembly which I attended was addressed by Andrei Gromyko, who as foreign minister of the power which had, at that time, about 120,000 troops occupying Afghanistan, was attacking the United States for interfering in the internal affairs of Afghanistan.

There is an interesting effort underway in and around the United Nations to try to enhance the veils of deception, this time by re-defining the problem as one of how to end the resistance in Afghanistan. Thus, the question of how to secure Soviet withdrawal becomes how to secure guarantees that there will be no support for the Afghans' resistance.

The unique quality of the Soviet challenge to national independence, self-determination, self-government and freedom lies precisely in this all too familiar combination of violence and deception. The violence is more brutal, but the deception is more pervasive. Obfuscation saps the clarity of vision and purpose needed to resist conquest. Nicaragua provides us a very clear-cut, even classical, example of this interaction of violence and deception. Since I thought other people would talk more today about explicit

Address before the Ad-Hoc Committee for Democracy in Nicaragua, Washington, D.C., July 19, 1983.

Nicaraguan policy, I would like to focus briefly on some aspects of the deception.

First, there was the crucial, carefully cultivated deception concerning the commitments and intentions of the FSLN. Who among us does not remember the carefully cultivated image of the FSLN as a broadly-based, reformist group of democratic revolutionaries bound together by their democratic aspirations and intentions? Who does not remember their consistent efforts within and without Nicaragua to minimize the role and importance of anti-democratic elements within the FSLN, to dismiss concern about the flow of Cuban arms, the role of Cuban strategists and training, or the ties to the Soviet bloc? The centerpiece of this deception were the promises of FSLN leaders symbolized in the letter to the Organization of American States. These promises committed them to democratic elections, rule of law, respect for human rights and freedom. On the basis of these, the Organization of American States took the unprecedented action of asking a sitting head of state to resign.

A second example of deception by the FSLN is the exploitation of the symbols of nationalism. The FSLN leadership was and is today determined to subordinate the national identity, needs, aspirations and well-being of the Nicaraguan people to the international alliance of which they are members. These international priorities of the Sandinista government were quickly manifested after they took power. There was that first official visit in March, 1980 by four members of the Sandinista directorate—Moises Morales Hassan, Tomas Borge, Henry Hernandez Ruiz, Humberto Ortega Saavedra—to the Soviet Union, where they memorialized, in a joint communique, FSLN attachment to the global policies of the Soviet bloc including a clear declaration of support for the Soviet invasion and occupation of Afghanistan, and for Vietnam's occupation of Cambodia. This identification of Nicaragua's government with Soviet goals and policies can be readily observed at the United Nations where Sandinista representatives regularly align Nicaragua with such freedom-loving, popular democracies as those found in Vietnam, Afghanistan, Libya, and the Soviet Union itself.

Nowhere is the FSLN effort to identify itself with indigenous Nicaraguan nationalism as clear and as cynical as in its name. Through the name Sandinista, they attempt to associate themselves with the tradition in which they do not stand; a tradition which, in fact, they daily betray.

This question of obfuscation by symbolic identification with a tradition that is not theirs, is so basic, so classical, and so important, that it deserves our attention in a bit more detail. One distinguished, well-known commentator on the true Sandinista tradition was Pablo Joaquin Chomorro, the highly respected Nicaraguan writer, editor, and publisher of *La Prensa*, whose brutal, cold-blooded assassination, engineered by Anastasio

Somoza's government, was a death-knell for that government. Pablo Joaquin Chomorro wrote, concerning Sandino:

> Sandino should be exalted precisely as a contrast to the communists who obey signals from Russia and China. Sandino fought against the United States Marines but he did not bring Russian Cossacks to Nicaragua as Fidel Castro did in Cuba.

Another deception, also highly developed, which the Sandinistas, seek to have us believe is that they are arming themselves, militarizing their country, pressing teenagers and less into military service and attempting to turn the country into an enormous barracks only in response to external threats. They say it is because they are threatened from the outside that they are developing large armies and engaging in the importation of unprecedented quantities of heavy weapons, soliciting and accepting thousands of outside advisers.

The truth again is very different. The truth is that the militarization, like the "Cubanization" of Nicaragua, began almost immediately after the triumph of the FSLN four years ago, and it has proceeded apace. Before there was even a hint of external opposition, except for residual resistance among the Nicaraguan people, the FSLN junta had developed the largest army and largest militia Central America had ever seen. They imported more heavy arms into Nicaragua than any other country in Central America ever had, and they began submitting the entire population to military discipline and justifying a bloc system of nation-wide surveillance on grounds of an expected military invasion. During this period the United States, which had helped in their rise to power, provided economic assistance and help with international fiscal institutions. The Sandinistas were assuredly not surrounded by enemies.

Yet another deception with which the FSLN seeks to clothe its naked violence is that they intend to preserve and nurture a pluralist society in Nicaragua. They even pretend that Nicaraguan society respects pluralist values and institutions, when the educational system in Nicaragua has been thoroughly "coordinated," as they call it, under state control; when the private sector has been submitted to a control that leaves every action of an independent businessman at the mercy of the daily decisions of the state bureaucracy; when independent trade unions have essentially disappeared, deprived of the right to function; when opposition parties are harassed and terrorized, and their leaders arrested and driven out; when the Roman Catholic Church and its heroic Archbishop, Miguel Obando y Bravo, are submitted to controls and restraints unknown in the history of Central America; when even the Pope was not only insulted, but denied the opportunity for contact with those who desired to attend his mass; and when Nicaragua's indigenous people of the Atlantic coast are burned out of their villages, herded into exile in concentration camps, battered and threatened because they seek to pursue an alternative way of life. No one is left alone in the new Nicaragua. The lie that Nicaragua's government preserves pluralism is just that—a lie.

Yet another lie, of equal proportion, is that resistance to the Sandinista government is inspired by attachment to Somoza, and led by those seeking to restore a Somozista dictatorship to Nicaragua. The fact is that the resistance movement inside Nicaragua is led and peopled by those who believed the Sandinista lies; those who thought initially that they were fighting to establish a pluralist society, democratic institutions, a rule of law, and respect for human rights and freedom.

Then there is the lie of the irreversibility of what the junta calls "the revolution," but is really just a new dictatorship. This is a lie, like most of the lies I have mentioned, fabricated not in Managua but in Moscow. It holds that the "laws of history" insure that the seizure of power by this particular armed minority, the FSLN, can never be reversed. Once again, the truth is otherwise. This "Brezhnev doctrine" rests not on the laws of history but on the will and determination of some people. As such, it can be reversed by the will and determination of some other people.

Finally, the most vicious lie of all is that the FSLN should not be too harshly criticized for failing to establish democracy in Nicaragua, because the Nicaraguan people are not really capable of democracy, and have been too brainwashed to know their own interests, their own wills or preferences; that it is necessary to choose between bread and freedom, and in an underdeveloped country like Nicaragua one must choose bread over freedom. People who have lived under a dictator for 40 years are presumed incapable of living without a dictator.

The facts, of course, are otherwise. The Nicaraguan people proved in their resistance to Somoza that they were quite capable of acting independently of any government or any institutions which might have hoped or tried to mold their thoughts and wishes. Furthermore, experience demonstrates that one never needs to choose between bread and freedom; the two go hand in hand. Free people produce more bread than enslaved people. We all know the myth that poverty produces communism. I think a close reading of history suggests precisely the opposite. Communism produces poverty.

It is not true that after living 40 years under a dictator, the people of Nicaragua are incapable of living except under a dictator. The truth is that the people of Nicaragua are capable today of living as free people. I should like to emphasize in this regard that, what the United States government stands for, above all, is *power-sharing* in Nicaragua, with power shared freely by the people of Nicaragua through democratic institutions.

The United States government stands for power-sharing through democratic institutions in El Salvador, in Nicaragua, throughout Central America and, indeed, the world. We believe the people of Nicaragua should be permitted to decide their destiny, their government, their policies, their lives, under conditions of freedom. They have suffered too long under the method of violence. It is time for the people of Nicaragua to be permitted a politics based on consent.

CENTRAL AMERICA:
THE MORAL OF THE STORY

I not only believe that the events and developments in Nicaragua, El Salvador, Honduras, Costa Rica, and Guatemala were predictable; I know they were predictable. Quite frankly, I and some other people also predicted them. We predicted both the negative consequences of our policies in Nicaragua and the positive consequences of our policies in Nicaragua and the positive consequences of our policies in El Salvador, Honduras, and Guatemala. I don't say that to show that I was right; I say it to show that good theory can lead to good predictions, and bad theory leads to bad predictions and bad results. That is the important moral of the story of U.S. policy with regard to Nicaragua beginning about 1978.

What was likely to happen with the assumption of power of the Sandinista regime was predictable; and the relative success of democracy in El Salvador and the interest of the Salvadoran people in establishing democratic institutions was also predictable. I do not believe, of course, that the United States has full responsibility for what happened. However, I do believe that our policies were a necessary, though not sufficient, cause of the outcomes in those two countries—the dismal outcome in Nicaragua and the so far happy outcome in El Salvador. I would therefore underscore with all the conviction possible that there *are* lessons for the United States to learn from the recent history of these two countries and from American policy in these two countries.

I was almost amused recently to come across an unclassified telegram

Address at the Center for the Study of Foreign Affairs, Foreign Service Institute, Washington, D.C.,February 2, 1986.

which was sent by the secretary of state to all OECD capitals in early April 1982, summarizing the main points I had made in six speeches on Latin America during 1981. The situation was fairly clear then and is fairly clear now as you can see from these excerpts. I was saying:

> U.S. security interests in Central America and the Caribbean are vital. It is vital to our own security and to our ability to deploy our forces to more distant parts of the world. The crucial question for U.S. security is whether we're going to permit to develop on our southern shore and eastern flank military forces which would require, for the first time in our history, that we defend our own borders. If this becomes necessary, we will have less mobility elsewhere. What is diverted to the defense of our southern border is not available for the defense of anything else.

> The Soviet buildup in the hemisphere was already developed to an extent not generally appreciated. Soviets and Cubans have more military advisors in the southern part of the hemisphere than the United States does. They have given more money in security assistance over the past twenty years to nations in this hemisphere than has the United States.

> No matter how miserable the people of the region have been under traditional governments, they will be more miserable under communist governments. When we protect our own national security, we are engaging in a morally acceptable enterprise. It is even a moral imperative; above all, we have an obligation the United States.

> The section concerning El Salvador reads: The acceptable moral quality of the government of El Salvador (the first transitional government headed by Duarte before the first presidential elections) is attested by the willingness of its leaders to submit themselves to the judgment of the people in free elections. It is attested by its land reform program. In El Salvador murderous tradition must confront murderous revolutionaries with only the government working to end this brutality in attempting to pacify adversaries.

By 1981 El Salvador already constituted a sharp contrast to Nicaragua, where one could see one-party control clearly emerging. I said then that one could expect the same pattern of one-party control in case of an FMLN win in El Salvador. Each one of the propositions in that cable were, as late as 1981, very controversial. Today they seem like old hat to most people.

Concerning human rights in Nicaragua, the summary began:

> Human rights depend on restraint in the use of power. There is systematic repression in Nicaragua where the Sandinistas have moved to establish and then exercise control over all the segments of society. Since July 1979, there has been in Nicaragua a coup d'etat by installment, that is, incremental consolidation of one-party control. Marxist liberation has already produced its antithesis. There is an unremitting campaign of repression, efforts to eliminate diversity, eradicate autonomous social groups, and bring the entire

society under the control of the FSLN. It should no longer surprise us that tyranny calls itself liberation.

The Handwriting on the Wall

If I was fairly clear about this in 1979, certainly I was no clearer than the FSLN. Its members were writing much more clearly than I about their plans. The Sandinista leaders in Nicaragua understood very well how to use the middle class and the trade union representatives without permitting them to take control. We now know that Humberto Ortega was writing, as early as 1979, "It is necessary to include all in this great crusade. Although the pro-Yankee bourgeoisie may attempt to take control of such a movement from us, the secret is in our directing these changes ourselves." Daniel Ortega was equally frank about the popular front. "We assign a tactical and temporary character to this front," he wrote. And elsewhere he said, "We must use the trade unions and the bourgeois forces and we will take care that control does not slip from our hands into theirs."

So, what's the first moral of that whole story? The moral of that story was simply that we should have been paying close attention to who, among the Nicaraguans participating in the broad popular front, had the guns. There's no doubt who had the moral legitimacy. Obviously, the democrats in that broad popular front had the moral legitimacy. But, the FSLN had the guns, and they had great clarity about their purposes. The first moral is: Look for who controls the instrument of violence in any revolutionary front. Look at who's got the guns and who knows how to use them, look at who controls lines of supply because while the instruments of violence are of very little interest to sincere and dedicated democrats seeking to achieve and institutionalize democracy, they are of single-minded interest to any group seeking to seize power and exercise it as a minority through one-party control.

Dangers of Forming a Popular Front

In retrospect I would say that the second moral we might extract from Nicaragua was that it was very unfortunate that a broad popular front was joined by the democratic forces who comprised the majority of the anti-Somoza forces with the armed FSLN. The tragedy of Nicaragua is found there, in the fact that the FSLN were able to bring the democratic revolutionaries of Nicaragua into a common front. I believe the biggest single difference between the outcome in Nicaragua and in El Salvador was that in El Salvador there never was a popular front which included most of all of the democratic leadership in the same group with the armed Marxist revolutionaries. It could have happened. It was a close thing at a moment when the junta, under intense attack from the violent traditionalists of the right and the violent revolutionaries of the left began to split and people like Guillermo Ungo and Ruben Zamora split off and joined the armed Marxist–Leninist revolutionaries. But because major democratic groups and leaders, among whom Napolean Duarte is preeminent, refused to join with armed Leninists in a popular front, at the same time they fought off the armed attack from the violent traditionalist right, there was maintained in El Salvador a democratic center and democratic leadership. They offered an alternative. The leaders of El Salvador, of course, could profit by the experience of the leaders in Nicaragua, and they did. But they deserve credit for having had the tenacity and foresight not to make common cause, even in the darkest hours, with the violent Leninists or the violent traditionalist death-squad leadership.

I think that Lenin was probably right that in the case of a revolution the central question is: Who has the power? For democratic forces to join in a popular front with a minority of armed Leninists is to give them a kind of legitimacy at the moment of the seizure and consolidation of power. Those are the lessons, the morals, that can be extracted from that experience.

If we were to try to extract further morals, we could note that in a situation where there is a violent, armed insurgent force, it is very important that the institutions of the society that could constitute a counterforce not be destroyed in any process of change. It would have been important for there to be in Nicaragua some institutions, including some of the traditional armed forces, that could have constituted during a period of transition a counterforce to the FSLN. The presence in El Salvador of a military institution which continued to exist even while it underwent successive reforms in leadership, was very important and remains to this day very important in protecting that society against takeover by the FMLN, who have guns and organization. A disorganized and unarmed majority cannot protect itself against an armed, organized minority. That's, of course, the basic moral of this and every other Leninist revolution.

Role of U.S. Policy

U.S. policy can contribute by, first of all, always taking care to do no harm. I think our effort to influence events in any other society in the world ought to be a very cautious one. We are not good at this. Our record is very bad in fact. El Salvador—where we have provided continuing support to strong indigenous leaders who have insisted, often to the great irritation of American policy makers, on retaining the direction of their country's affairs in their own hands—is a shining example of a success of U.S. policy. Many aspects of American policy in Nicaragua were unfortunate and contributed to the negative results thereby hurrying, by trying to bring about reconciliation among groups about who we knew, in fact, relatively little and who were fundamentally incompatible, as later events proved.

The final moral is that outcomes in foreign policy are long-range, not short-range. The time frame in which we operate should be much longer than it is. We tend to be a very impatient people and we are impatient for results. If we had wanted to participate in the elimination of Somoza, which was surely a worthy goal, we should have been much more cautious. We should have worked only in the closest consultation with demonstrated indigenous Nicaraguan democratic leaders and not tried to hustle ourselves in and others out.

We need to be more careful to think not in terms of the next congressional appropriation cycle, or the next elections, but in terms of at least the next five to ten years. When we can learn to think in those longer terms, then we may achieve better results. If we continue our present policies in Central America, in the next five to ten years we can expect things to be just about as they are today. If nothing dramatic happens, like the development of an effective, strongly supported resistance force in Nicaragua, then we will see a continued consolidation of totalitarian power in Nicaragua. We will see the continuing consolidation of democratic institutions in the other countries in the region, and also continued efforts from Nicaragua to destabilize those governments. We will see continuing development of major Soviet military bases for the projections of Soviet military power in Nicaragua. We can expect to see new Soviet naval capabilities on our Pacific coast and in the Caribbean—facilities comparable to those already available in the other end of the Caribbean and off our Atlantic coast in Cuba. The Soviets operate in a very long time frame and our only hope of holding our own and helping the democrats in the hemisphere hold their own is to learn to think in terms of long-range continued threats.

REFLECTING ON THE FALKLANDS

Decisions cannot be made, and policies cannot be pursued, simply because they make us "feel good." The need for calculation and foresight, for the sober appraisal of the possible consequences of our actions is imper-

Address before the Calvin Bullock Forum, April 19, 1982.

ative in our society. We understand, in short, the supreme importance of prudence in the conduct both of business affairs and the affairs of state.

Of course, we are hardly alone in that understanding. Philosophers have long written about the importance of prudence. Aristotle equated prudence with "practical wisdom" and defined it as "that virtue of the understanding which enables men to come to wise decisions about the relations of happiness to goals of evils." Similarly, St. Thomas Aquinas defined prudence as "right reason about things to be done," and called it, "the principal of all the virtues." Yet despite the overwhelming philosophical consensus in its favor, prudence remains far and away the most unpopular of the political virtues, and those espousing it commonly find themselves the objects of severe censure. I myself have recently been criticized in the press for pursuing what I regarded as a prudent course during the current Falkland Islands crisis. That being the case, I thought a suitable topic would be the ramifications of the Falkland Islands crisis, and, more specifically the thinking behind the Reagan administration's handling of that crisis.

The immediate background to the crisis is well-known. On Friday, April 2, some 2,000 Argentine troops landed at three different points near Port Stanley, the capital of the Falkland Islands. A small detachment of Royal Marines resisted the Argentine forces until the British governor of the islands ordered them to surrender. The next day, Argentine forces landed on South Georgia, a dependency of the Falkland Islands, some 800 miles to the east, and overran British installations stationed there.

On April 2, the U.S. government issued a statement deploring Argentina's use of force to resolve the Falkland Islands dispute. On April 3, my colleague at the U.S. Mission to the UN, Ambassador Charles Lichenstein, cast the U.S. vote in favor of Security Council Resolution 502, which called for an end to hostilities and a withdrawal of the Argentine troops from the contested islands. As Ambassador Lichenstein stated in the Security Council, "We feel that the use of force to solve problems is deeply regrettable and will not produce a just and lasting settlement of the dispute."

The British reaction to the Argentine action was not long in coming. A naval task force was dispatched to the Falkland Islands on April 5. On April 12, Britain announced that its ships would fire upon any Argentine vessel remaining within a 200 mile radius of the Falklands.

The initial American *public* reaction to the Falkland Islands crisis was amused detachment, as though it were some kind of farce from a Gilbert and Sullivan opera. This tendency did not last very long. Soon, influential voices in the media began lining up behind the British. The *New York Times*, for example, declared that "the Thatcher government is entitled to an all out effort to persuade Argentina to back down." Similarly, the *Wash-*

ington Post editorialized that, "the U.S. has a large and strong interest in seeing British administration of the Falklands restored." The effort of this administration to maintain a modicum of neutrality between the British and the Argentines in order to be able to offer our good offices to both parties has been sharply questioned, if not criticized. Some have even suggested that the administration's failure to embrace the British cause wholeheartedly and unequivocally is further evidence of its preference for authoritarian non-democratic regimes.

Why, then, have we tried to maintain a modicum of neutrality between Britain and Argentina? Why has the U.S. invested its prestige in the delicate and enormously difficult task of trying to resolve the Falkland Islands crisis? And why, above all, are we behaving with such a singular degree of prudence and circumspection?

Some of the factors shaping the administration's policy have been reported in the press. The Falklands crisis involves two countries with whom the U.S. is obviously interested in maintaining good relations. Also, the crisis is an especially sensitive one because it involves an area of the world—the Western Hemisphere—where we Americans have a particularly vital stake. Finally, Argentina has threatened, in the event of war with Britain, to invoke the provisions of the 1947 Rio Treaty.

The provisions of this treaty and why this treaty is crucially important to this country's security interests are matters which have largely been ignored. I, however, would like to rectify this. The best way, I think, to do so is to read a passage from the conclusion of Robert F. Kennedy's 1969 memoir, *Thirteen Days*. That book deals with the Cuban missile crisis, in which Robert Kennedy, then the attorney general of the U.S., was a key participant. In the concluding chapter, Robert Kennedy tried to summarize the lessons learned by American policymakers from the Cuban missile crisis. He wrote:

> We have not always had the support of Latin American countries in everything we have done. Frequently, our patience has been sorely tried by the opposition of some of the larger South American countries to measures we felt to be in our common interest and worthy of their support. During the Cuban missile crisis, however, when it was an issue of the greatest importance, when the United States was being sorely tried, those countries came unanimously to our support and that support was essential.

> It was the vote of the Organization of American States that gave a legal basis for the quarantine. Their willingness to follow the leadership of the United States was a heavy and unexpected blow to Khrushchev. It had a major psychological and practical effect on the Russians and changed our position from that of an outlaw acting in violation of international law into a country acting in accordance with twenty allies legally protecting their position.

The Organization of American States acted as it did because of certain obligations its members had assumed—obligations codified in the Rio Treaty of 1947. That treaty, in other words, may have been instrumental in averting a nuclear showdown between the U.S. and the Soviet Union.

The Rio Treaty is the first collective security arrangement of the post-World War I era. Established in 1947, it served as a model for the subsequent NATO Treaty. The Rio Treaty contemplates collective action by all its signatories, including the U.S., in response to "an armed attack by any state against an American state;" by "an aggression which is not an armed attack;" by an "extracontinental or intercontinental conflict;" or by "any other fact or situation which might endanger the peace of America."

It would obviously be highly indiscreet of me to discuss what would happen if Argentina were to seek collective action against Britain under the terms of the Rio Treaty. I would like, however, to make the following observations:

1 The Rio treaty is important to U.S. security interests.
2 There are a number of countries, both in this hemisphere and outside it, who would like nothing better than to see the Rio Treaty become a dead letter.
3 A war between Britain and Argentina would provide the perfect pretext for those countries to try to undermine the hemispheric collective security arrangement existing under the Rio Treaty.
4 It is in the vital interests of this nation to forestall a situation from arising in which Argentina would invoke collective action under the Rio Treaty.
5 It therefore follows that the only role the U.S. can play in this crisis, consistent with our vital interests, is that of a mediator, i.e., someone trusted by both sides because he is perceived as being strictly neutral.

And that, of course, is precisely the role which Secretary Haig has been playing.

Seeking Peace in the Falklands

I should like to begin by expressing the appreciation of my government for your judicious and skillful leadership of the affairs of this Council in this deeply troubled time, as we seek a solution to the tragic conflict underway in the South Atlantic.

We desire to express in this public arena our gratitude to the Secretary General for his tireless and determined efforts to find a peaceful resolution to the conflict between the United Kingdom and Argentina. The Secretary General knows, as we should like the world as well to know, that he enjoyed the active support and cooperation of the United States in his search for a peaceful resolution of the conflict.

This conflict poses a particularly acute problem for persons and nations who love peace and also for this international body whose very raison d'etre is to promote and ensure the peaceful settlement of disputes.

The United States stands behind the principle that the use of force to settle disputes should not be allowed anywhere, and especially in this hemisphere where a significant number of territorial disputes remain to be solved diplomatically. For the United States, the Falkland crisis has been and still is a particularly agonizing, tragic event. As the whole world knows, we have a longstanding alliance and, beyond that, the closest relations of friendship with Great Britain, the country from which our political institutions, law and language derive. But we have not forgotten for a moment our close geographical, economic and political relations with our Latin neighbors. We do not only care about this hemisphere, we are part of this hemisphere, and we share many of the aspirations, goals and dreams of all nations of the Americas. Our own culture and society are deeply influenced by a growing Hispanic population. We can never turn our backs on, or be insensitive to, hemispheric goals and aspirations that we ourselves have promoted and defended.

That is why the United States tried so hard to avoid the conflict of the Falklands, why we are hoping so intensely to reduce and isolate it, and why we are eager and ready to back any realistic diplomatic initiative which will put a just end to it. And we especially mean to stay in close touch with our Latin neighbors while efforts are made to solve this tragic conflict, in order to restore peace and honor so that once again we can concentrate our efforts on the resolution of our problems. The quicker we put this tragic conflict behind us, the quicker we can begin building our future. And there,

Address before the Security Council, May 22, 1982.

as always, Latin America will find how deeply the U.S. is committed to the cause of peace and prosperity in our hemisphere.

Mr. President, as the fighting intensifies and the cost in lives mounts in the South Atlantic, I think we all share a sense of anguish that it has not yet been possible to prevent this tragic conflict.

We have all come to appreciate how deep the roots of the conflict are. Britain, in peaceful possession of the Falkland Islands for 150 years, has been passionately devoted to the proposition that the rights of the inhabitants should be respected in any future disposition of the Islands. No one can say that this attitude, coming from a country that has granted independence to more than 40 countries in a generation and a half, is a simple reflex to retain possession.

Yet we know too how deep is the Argentine commitment to recover islands they believe were taken from them by illegal force. This is not some sudden passion, but a long-sustained national concern that also stretches back 150 years, heightened by the sense of frustration at what Argentina feels were nearly 20 years of fruitless negotiation.

From the start it has been widely recognized that the conflict engages basic principles without which a peaceful international order cannot stand. Unless the principle is respected that force must not be used to settle disputes, the entire international community will be exposed to chaos and suffering. And unless the right of self-defense is granted, only those countries that use force first will have the protection of law.

The Security Council was profoundly right to reassert those principles in Resolution 502, which forms the indispensable framework in which a peaceful solution has been sought and will ultimately be found. It is of fundamental importance that both Argentina and Britain have accepted Resolution 502 in its entirety.

For the United States, the conflict has a special poignancy. We do not take—have never taken—any position on the underlying claims. Britain is a country to which we are bound by unique ties of friendship, values, and alliance. And Argentina is also an old friend, a country of immigrants and settlers like our own, a country with which we share the enormous human and national potential of the New World experience.

That a conflict of such dimensions should take place, and that it should occur here, in the Western Hemisphere—whose countries have long shared a particular commitment to each other, to their mutual welfare and to peace—causes us the deepest concern. This conflict, however urgent, cannot be permitted to obscure the common engagement of all American states to the rule of law and to the well-being of this hemisphere.

So it was natural that the United States should make a particular effort to help Argentina and Britain find a solution.

That effort began before April 2nd, when we offered to the two sides our good offices to help find a solution to the South Georgia incident.

After April 2nd, both President Galtieri and Prime Minister Thatcher asked the United States to see whether it could be of assistance. At President Reagan's direction, Secretary of State Haig undertook two rounds of intense discussions in both capitals. Finally, on April 27th, as prospects for more intense hostilities arose, we put forward a proposal. It represented our best estimate of what the two parties could reasonably be expected to accept. It was found squarely on Resolution 502 by providing for a cessation of hostilities, withdrawal of forces, and a political settlement of the dispute.

The British government indicated that it would seriously consider our proposal, although it presented certain real difficulties for it. However, the proposal was not acceptable to Argentina.

Immediately afterward, President Belaunde of Peru, after consultation with Secretary Haig, took the initiative to put forward a much simplified peace plan, also drawing on the fundamental elements of Resolution 502.

On May 5th a draft text was forwarded by Peru to Buenos Aires; we forwarded the same text to London.

Britain made clear that it could seriously consider the proposal. Argentina chose not to consider it, asking instead that the Secretary General use his good offices as, of course, it was his full privilege to do.

Mr. President, the tragic conflict before us also has special poignancy for the United Nations. It is precisely the kind of problem this organization was created to resolve. The Charter commits us

> to bring about by peaceful means, and in conformity with the principles of justice and international law, adjustment or settlement of international disputes or situations which might lead to a breach of the peace; to develop friendly relations among nations based on respect for the principle of equal rights and self-determination of peoples, and to take other appropriate measures to strengthen universal peace; to achieve international cooperation in solving international problems . . .; and to be a center for harmonizing the actions of nations in the attainment of these common ends.

The United Nations record in dealing with this conflict is commendable. The Security Council responded rapidly to the Argentine seizure of the Islands. The fact that both parties accepted Resolution 502 proves that it was a constructive response.

The Secretary General's determined and imaginative efforts were, of course, fervently welcomed by all of us. Again the elements of settlement seemed to be present or nearly present. Again peace eluded us. I believe the institutions of the United Nations have functioned in this crisis in the manner foreseen by its founders and its Charter. We can be proud of it; proud, especially, of the Secretary General.

We have already heard his account of his search for a formula that could resolve the conflict. I think all of us have been deeply impressed by the skill and sensitivity, by the judgment and fairness that the Secretary General brought to this task. That his effort has not so far succeeded does not mean that it has not realized important gains, notably in the establishment of a mutually acceptable concept of negotiations. The United States will wholeheartedly support any initiative that can help Argentina and Britain make peace with honor.

Despite all our efforts, the problem is not solved. Young men die in icy waters, on freezing beaches.

The dispute that appeared to many to be simple has nonetheless proved extraordinarily difficult to resolve. But we must not abandon the effort. Resolution 502, with its concept of linked and simultaneous cessation of hostilities, withdrawal of forces, and negotiations, must remain the framework of the search for peace. The problem is too important—for the rule of law, for the future of the Americas, for many of us who are friends of Britain and Argentina—not to make an all-out effort to settle this tragic conflict, so costly in every way.

Focusing on the Future

I should like once again to express the admiration and appreciation of my government for the skill and judgment with which you have conducted and are continuing to conduct the affairs of this Council while we are dealing with this terribly difficult problem.

Mr. President, the United States has already explained here that this conflict is particularly poignant and painful for us. We have already expressed our intense desire to reduce, to isolate, and to end this tragic conflict. I believe we have given evidence of the seriousness of our desire. My government in the person of the secretary of state made sustained efforts to avoid the conflict and subsequently offered full support to the efforts of Peru's President Belaunde and, of course, to the efforts of our distinguished Secretary General, Javier Perez de Cuellar.

The United States ardently desires an end to this tragic war. We welcome

Address before the Security Council, May 26, 1982.

this resolution and pledge our continued support for the Secretary General's efforts to find a just and enduring peace. I should like to take this opportunity to assure the distinguished representative of Panama and any other interested parties that my country has deep respect for all our neighbors in the hemisphere, that we desire greatly to live in peace with them, that we are ourselves part of this hemisphere, that we desire to put an end to this conflict so that we can get on with the business of living in peace in the hemisphere.

As I said earlier this week, the quicker we put this tragic conflict behind us the quicker we can begin building our future—and there, as always, the nations of Latin America will find how deeply the United States is committed to the cause of peace and prosperity for our hemisphere.

Changing Votes

The decision taken by this Council today is, I think we all understand, a terribly important one. It marks one more failure in a series of failed efforts to mediate a conflict that is more than 200 years old. One more failed attempt to substitute reason for force, negotiation for violence, words for bombs and bullets. Today's decision, then, marks one more step in a process of escalation whose end is not yet in sight. Phase one of this most recent conflict ended with the Argentine occupation of the Falklands. Phase two may well end with British reoccupation of the Falklands. Where, Mr. President, will phase three end?

Affirmed in the vote of the majority today is the will to negotiation and peace. Affirmed in the veto of my government, to which I will return momentarily, is the principle that force should not be allowed to triumph in international affairs.

Mr. President, one of my sons handed me this morning the poem of another man who disapproves Argentina's forcible act against the Falkland Islands. In some lines in a poem, called "An English Poem," the great Argentine writer, Borges, wrote:

> *I offer you my ancestors, my dead men,*
> *the ghosts that living men have honored in marble:*
> *my father's father killed in the frontier of Buenos Aires,*
> *two bullets through his lungs, bearded and dead,*

Address before the Security Council, June 4, 1982

wrapped by his soldiers in the hide of a cow;
my mother's grandfather—just twenty-four—
heading a charge of three hundred into Peru,
now ghosts on vanished horses.

Mr. President, the friends of Argentina, of the Americas, and of world peace, hope that Argentina will have few such offerings from this war and from the post-war period. We hope, I believe all of us here, that cooperation can be restored, friendships mended, urgent tasks recommenced, that building a new world in this New World can be begun again. My government worked hard for mediation of this conflict and peaceful settlement of this dispute. We have been rent by the clash of values, loyalties and friendships. That agonizing process of decision, Mr. President, continued down to the vote on this issue.

I am told that it is impossible for a government to change a vote once it is cast. But I have been requested by my government to record the fact that, were it possible to change our vote, we should like to change it from a veto, a "no" that is, to an abstention.

GRENADA: WHY AMERICA ACTED

The last remarks I made were by way of a right of reply. I should like now to address the issue before the Council tonight as briefly as possible because the hour is very late.

I would like to first address the question, what were the conditions which the Organization of Eastern Caribbean States, Jamaica, Barbados, and the United States felt justified the action which is being considered here tonight? Certainly the conditions were not any sort of abstract disapproval of the government of Prime Minister Bishop whom we have heard extolled tonight who had, of course, already been murdered in cold blood. We make no firm charges about who was complicit in the decisions to murder Prime Minister Bishop and his ministers in cold blood, though there is suggestive information concerning those questions. The facts are that on October 13th, Prime Minister Bishop was placed under house arrest and subsequently on October 19th, after he had been freed by a mass demonstration of Grenadans from house arrest and surrendered to the so-called Revolutionary Council, was then shot in cold blood along with five cabinet minis-

Address before the Security Council, October 26, 1983.

ters and twelve other political leaders who were killed at roughly the same time, creating one of the bloodiest struggles for power which the world has seen in some time.

The second question I would like to pose and respond very briefly to is, what are the objectives that the United States has in participating in this joint action? Those objectives are clear. The United States troops are involved for the purpose of protecting United States citizens, to facilitate the evacuation of those citizens who wish to leave, to provide support for the Eastern Caribbean forces as they assist the people of Grenada in restoring order and establishing functioning governmental institutions. Any continued political involvement in this cooperative effort will be guided wholly by the views of the Organization of Eastern Caribbean States and the government being formed in Grenada. We fully expect that the deliberations in the OAS which are scheduled to begin tomorrow will be constructive and may prove useful to the future of Grenada. The United States was also deeply concerned in evaluating the actual and potential danger to our citizens with the existence of a shoot-on-sight curfew. The shoot-on-sight curfew which threatened anyone who was seen in the streets in Grenada was, so far as we are able to determine, certainly the primary visible act of the so-called Revolutionary Council and constituted a clear and present danger to the security and safety and well-being of, among others, the Americans who had the misfortune to be in Grenada at the time these unfortunate events occurred. Also, it obviously constituted a clear and present danger to the well-being of Grenadans there.

Briefly, I should like to address the question what constitutes the legal basis upon which the United States based its action. We responded to an urgent appeal by the Organization of Eastern Caribbean States for assistance. The OECS took an action created under the treaty creating the organization itself and consistent with the provisions of that treaty for collective security. I would note that the OECS member states are not a party to the Rio Treaty. Their own organizational treaty is, in effect, the regional equivalent.

We believe that the support by the United States of the OECS is justified on a number of grounds. The OECS determined that, as I have said, conditions and institutions of authority had degenerated—a climate of fear, anxiety and acute danger to personal safety existed on the island. The OECS determined that a dangerous vacuum of authority constituted an unprecedented threat to the peace and security of the entire Eastern Caribbean. The United States government believed that this judgment by the Organization of Eastern Caribbean States was accurate and justified. The objectives of a collective security force organized by the OECS, we think, are equally clear. They have been stated publicly on several occasions by

OECS spokesmen and presumably will be restated here tomorrow. They have also been stated by U.S. government authorities including the president of the United States and Secretary of State Shultz today. Those objectives are to restore law and order, to help the people of Grenada to restore functioning institutions of government, to facilitate the departure of those who leave and most especially to put an end to the situation of acute threat to peace and security to the entire Eastern Caribbean region.

We believe that the action is reasonable and proportionate to the deterioration of the authority in Grenada and the threat that this posed to peace and security in the Eastern Caribbean. We believe it was consistent and is consistent with the purposes and principles of the charters of the United Nations and the Organization of American States since it aims only at the restoration of conditions of law and order fundamental to the enjoyment of basic human rights which were so clearly only in jeopardy but flagrantly violated in Grenada.

The United States is cooperating fully with the OECS countries in seeking a meeting of the OAS Permanent Council to review the situation. We expect, of course, to continue to cooperate with our colleagues on the Council and with the spokesmen for the OECS when they arrive here to continue this discussion tomorrow. Thank you Mr. President.

GRENADA: THE LAWFULNESS OF FORCE

Some of the speakers before this Council, in the past few days, have attempted to present the events of the past days as a classical invasion of a small country by an imperial power—a simple case of intervention in the internal affairs of others whose moral and legal character is easily discernible. After all, the United Nations Charter forbids the use of force to settle a dispute, and force has been used by the task force. The Charter forbids intervention in the internal affairs of states, and the task force is intervening in the affairs of Grenada. The Charter requires respect for the independence, sovereignty and territorial integrity of states, and when foreign forces land on an island state, it might not at first glance appear unreasonable to contend that the independence, sovereignty, and territorial integrity of the state are not being fully respected.

That is the purport, as I understand it, of the draft resolution now cir-

Address before the Security Council, October 27, 1983.

culating in this Council; that is the reasoning urged on the Council by an interesting array of speakers. It is presumably the reasoning that may lead some members of this Council, at least some of those members, to support the draft resolution.

It is a particular perspective. The perspective I have described begins with the landing of the task force in Grenada the day before yesterday; treats the prohibition against the use of force as an absolute, and the injunction against intervention in the internal affairs of other states as the only obligation of states under the Charter. The events of the past days pose no such morally or legally simple questions as has been suggested by that interesting array of speakers. The prohibitions against the use of force in the UN Charter are contextual, not absolute. They provide ample justification for the use of force against force in pursuit of the other values also inscribed in the Charter—freedom, democracy, peace. The Charter does not require that peoples submit supinely to terror, nor that their neighbors be indifferent to their terrorization.

The events in the Caribbean do not comprise a classical example of a large power invading a small, helpless nation. The impression that there is involved here a violation of the Charter which should be straightforwardly condemned by an outraged "world opinion" is not only a delusion, it is, as well, a snare, and will leave those caught within it a bit weaker, a bit more confused, a bit less able to defend themselves—a bit more of what Jean Francois Revel called in his most recent book, *Comment les Democraties Finissent*, "an obliging victim."

This is another way of saying that although the islands that we are meeting to discuss are small, the issues are as large as any ever discussed here. The use of force is indeed central to our deliberations, as are respect for the right of peoples to self-determination and non-intervention in the internal affairs of others. The most fundamental questions of legitimacy, human rights, and self defense are also present.

The intrusion of force into the public life of Grenada did not begin with the landing of a task force. From 1979, Grenada had been ruled by a government which came to power by coup, overthrowing a corrupt though elected predecessor. That government declined to submit to free elections. It succumbed to superior force more than two weeks ago when, with the complicity of certain powers, who have in the past three days nearly drowned us in crocodile tears over the death of Maurice Bishop and foreign intervention in Grenada's affairs, first arrested, then murdered Bishop and his ministers. Thus began, what can only be called an authentic reign of terror in Grenada. Tragically for them, the people of Grenada had already had large experience with political violence before the arrival of the task force.

The people of Grenada were also sadly accustomed to foreign intervention in their internal affairs. Let us speak frankly about this situation. Maurice Bishop was a man of strong ideological commitments. Those commitments identified him and allied him with Cuba, the Soviet Union, and the member states of that empire which invokes Marxist principles to justify tyranny. Bishop freely offered his island as a base for the protection of Soviet military power in this hemisphere. The familiar pattern of militarization and Cubanization was already far advanced in Grenada. More than three dozen Soviet officials have been detained in just the past three days. Truly enormous arsenals of Soviet weapons have been discovered in the last three days. The total number of Cuban military personnel in Grenada is still unknown, but it is clear that there were more than 1,000— more than one Cuban for every 100 Grenadans. Even this did not satisfy Prime Minister Bishop's friends. Maurice Bishop was not the victim of an ordinary power struggle. As Jamaica's Prime Minister Seaga put it:

> It became clear as events unfolded that this was . . . a well planned and orchestrated coup which was carried out with a savagery and brutality without predecent in the English-speaking Caribbean.
>
> On Wednesday, October 19, after having been released by a large crowd of his supporters, Mr. Bishop, his Minister of Education, Miss Jacqueline Creft, his Foreign Minister, Mr. Unison Whiteman, Mr. Norris Bain, Minister of Housing, Mr. Vincent Noel, leader of the Bank and General Workers Union, Mr. Fitzroy Bain, another trade union leader, had been brutally executed by Cuban-trained military officers who had seized power. We also learned subsequently that the People's Revolutionary Army had fired on a crowd of demonstrators which included many women and children and that several of these have not been accounted for and are presumed to have been killed. An eyewitness reports having seen the child attempting to jump to safety having his legs blown off.

Let us be clear in this chamber tonight, Grenada's internal affairs had fallen under the permanent intervention of one neighboring and one remote tyranny. Her people were helpless in the grip of terror.

Imagine, if you will, that here in New York tonight, just after we return home, some gunmen who had already proved that they would kill on a whim announced that anyone leaving his home, anyone appearing on the streets would be shot on sight. Imagine, if you will, that that condition lasted for four days and four nights, punctuated by the sounds of gunshots. Ask yourself whether friendly forces arriving from some nearby, democratic country to free us would be engaged in a violation of the United Nations Charter, in an unjustifiable intervention in the United States internal affairs, in an unjustified use of force.

Listen to the comments of the prime minister of Barbados:

> The pros and cons of the actions of the Caribbean governments will be long debated, so will those of President Reagan in coming to our aid. But I think that history will agree with the verdict of public opinion in the eastern Caribbean. There has seldom been in these islands such virtual unanimous support in the media and at political and popular levels for an action so potentially divisive. West Indians have shown that we have a view of our future that is democratic, peace-loving, devoted to constitutional and not arbitrary government. We have shown that we can cut through the sometimes artificial controversies generated by today's media and go right to the heart of things—what is best for our people. The United States and President Reagan have to their eternal credit concurred in our views and have come to the same conclusion as we have.

Mr. President, I know as well as you that such words may easily be dismissed as cynical. After all, are we not all accustomed to similar justifications when the Soviet Union invades Afghanistan or imposes a new government on the people of Poland or when Vietnam invades and occupies Cambodia. Why should anyone here suppose that this is not just one more cynical claim when we assert that the task force, of which we are members, is there to restore self-determination to the people of Grenada rather than to deny them self-determination? Mr. President, there is an easy test. The test is what comes after. We in the task force intend, as all of us have now made clear, to leave Grenada just as soon as law is restored and the instrumentalities of self-government—democratic government—have been put in place.

But all governments in our time claim to be democratic. They all say they are going to leave as soon as law is restored. What will there be to support the claim that the new government of Grenada will be any more an authentic expression of the will of the people of Grenada than was the gang of thugs from whom Grenada has just been delivered? Again, Mr. President, the answer is easy. There is a simple test. It will be clear that self-government has been restored to Grenada because freedom and the institutions through which free peoples express themselves will be clearly in evidence, a free press, free trade unions, free elections, and representative, responsible government.

It should not be difficult for any people, especially any democratic people, which has ever suffered a reign of terror from either foreign or domestic tyrants, to discern the difference between the force that liberates captive people from terror and the force that imposes terror on captive peoples. Neither the intellectual nor the moral nor the legal problems here involved are really very difficult.

Mr. President, because of the repeated discussions and questions here in this chamber concerning the legal basis of this intervention, I should like to address now, briefly, once again this matter of the legal foundation for U.S. action in Grenada.

It was, indeed, a unique combination of circumstances prevailing in Grenada that led the United States to respond positively to the OECS request that we assist them in their decision to undertake collective action to secure peace and stability in the Caribbean region. Those circumstances included danger to innocent U.S. nationals, the absence of a minimally responsible government in Grenada, and the danger posed to the OECS by the relatively awesome military might those responsible for the murder of the Bishop government now had at their disposal. The United States' response, we believe, was fully compatible with relevant international law and practice.

I turn briefly to each of these points. First, the defense of innocent nationals: The United States concern for the safety of its nationals was real and compelling and had absolutely nothing to do with any inclination to "gunboat diplomacy." As pointed out by Prime Minister Seaga in his address to Jamaica's Parliament on October 25, "madmen" wiped out the whole government of Grenada, murdered its leading citizens, and imposed a twenty-four hour, shoot-on-sight curfew against its own citizenry.

The madmen responsible for the coup in Grenada did not put their captured adversaries on trial; they simply murdered them in cold-blood. In these circumstances it was fully reasonable for the United States to conclude that these madmen might decide, at any moment, to hold hostage the 1,000 American citizens on that island. American nationals, scattered throughout the island, were denied the right of free exit, as students returning last night testified to repeatedly. The airport was closed and entry by humanitarian organizations and others concerned with their welfare was prevented.

The United States—having recently been the victim of, as well as the witness to, revolutionary violence in Iran, where, in contravention of all international conventions and the express ruling of the International Court of Justice, U.S. diplomatic personnel were held hostage—could not be expected to sit idly by while the lives of our citizens were again threatened.

Of course, it goes without saying that the United States does not advocate that in normal circumstances concern for the safety of a state's nationals in a foreign country may justify military measures against that country. But normal circumstances presuppose the existence of a government which, regardless of the democratic, non-democratic or anti-democratic nature of the system which it pursues, is nevertheless recognized as minimally responsible for not wantonly endangering the lives of its citizens, foreign nations and the security of neighboring states in the region. Where, however, terrorists murder the leading citizenry and leadership of their own country, a situation may well arise whereby no new government replaces the former order, but anarchy prevails. In these circumstances the general rule of international law permits military action for protecting endangered nationals. Such was the situation in Grenada.

The second point I would like to address briefly is that this was, indeed, a unique situation in which there existed a vacuum of responsible governmental authority. The revulsion shared by the international community over the cold-blooded murder of Mr. Bishop's government was nearly universal in scope. The consequences of the coup, however, were not restricted to Grenada. Though a small island, Grenada, because of its massive build-up of arms and material, had been capable of gravely affecting the security of the entire Caribbean region. Those most immediately affected by the situation prevailing in Grenada were, of course, Grenada's neighboring countries, all of whom were members of the OECS, the Caribbean regional organization.

Aware that terrorists were in control of Grenada, it became incumbent upon the states of the OECS to assess the military capability at their disposal and the dangers presented to the security of all the states in the Caribbean region. In assessing this danger, the states of the OECS, most of whom have no army at all or armies of less than 200 men, concluded that the military potential of Grenada in the hands of the madmen who engineered the coup had reached threatening proportions. For example, although Jamaica's population exceeds by twenty-fold that of Grenada, Grenada's army—its indigenous forces alone—exceeded by one and one-half times the size of Jamaica's armed forces. Moreover, a new airstrip was in the final stages of completion by over 600 armed Cubans. In the words of Jamaica's Prime Minister Seaga:

> In the hands of sane men the airstrip would have offered no threat, but against the background of the insanity of the past two weeks it would be a logical staging area for countries whose interests are similar, who have ambitions for using Grenada as a center for subversion, sabotage, and infiltration within the area and against member states of the Organization of Eastern Caribbean States.

It was in this context that the OECS, viewing with the greatest alarm this combination of brutal men with awesome might, decided to undertake collective action pursuant to its charter. Such action fully comported with relevant provisions of the UN Charter, which accords regional organizations the authority to undertake collective action. When asked to assist this effort, the United States, whose own nationals and vital interests were independently affected, joined the effort to restore minimal conditions of law and order in Grenada and eliminate the threat posed to the security of the entire region.

The third legal point I should like to address briefly concerns collective regional action. Dominica, Barbados, Jamaica and other Caribbean states have already made clear the factors which impelled them to invoke their regional treaty arrangements for collective action. As pointed out by their representatives here, the issue was not revolution. This hemisphere has seen many revolutions and many members of the OECS, like the United States itself, were born of revolution. Each of us in this hemisphere celebrates an independence day.

Nor was it an issue of the type of government Grenada possessed. While the government of Maurice Bishop, which had never secured a mandate from its electorate, was an anomaly and an unwelcome anomaly in the democratic Caribbean Sea, no thought was ever given by the OECS to influencing a change of that government. No effort, may I add, was ever undertaken by the United States to in any way affect the composition or character of that government.

Rather, the OECS was spurred to action because, as a result of the murder of Mr. Bishop and almost his entire cabinet, the military power which Grenada had amassed with Cuban and Soviet backing had fallen into the hands of individuals who could reasonably be expected to wield that awesome power against its neighbors. That the coup leaders had no arguable claim to bring the responsible government was indeed made clear by their own declarations, the failure of other states to recognize them as a legitimate government, and by the fact that the governor-general of Grenada, the sole, remaining symbol of governmental authority on the island, invited OECS action.

In the context of these very particular, very unusual, perhaps unique circumstances, the United States decided to accede to the request of the OECS for aiding its collective efforts aimed at securing peace and stability in the Caribbean region. Mr. President, let me close by once again quoting Prime Minister Seaga, who I believe has given the best justification, finally, of this decision of Jamaica's and of ours to accede in the request of the OECS for assistance in their effort to establish collective security for the region. Prime Minister Seaga said:

> It is the inescapable fact that revolution breeds revolution because it makes no allowance to institutionalized opposition and for change of administrations peacefully. During the past week we witnessed . . . not only a revolution spawning its own destruction, but a brutal military take-over of a civilian government. It may be felt that these matters do not concern us, but most certainly they do. If a whole government can be wiped out overnight, either

by political or military extremists, and the governments of the Caribbean remain silent and passive, then no government elected by the people can be safe from madmen of one type or another who would seek to replace a government of the people, elected by the people, with one selected by whichever chosen few of whatever nature.

If we ignore the occurrence of brutal military take-overs or political overthrows of governments, we would immediately give heart to every subversive group within the region to engineer disorder and instability as a means of overthrow. No democratic system of government would have a chance of carrying out the programs of development which it was elected to implement if in its midst was a group of subversives, anarchists, and terrorists bent on the destruction of the foundations of stability which underpin the whole system of democracy. The far-reaching consequences of such neglect on our part would be awesome and would have the effect of creating an unsure and insecure future for all of us.

For the sake of the democratic system of government, which we all agree to be the one which allows the maximum freedom of choice to a people and protects their right to elect a government of their choice, we cannot ignore the events which defeat these purposes wherever they occur in the English-speaking Caribbean.

It behooves this chamber, Mr. President, as well as the English-speaking Caribbean, not to ignore events which defeat the purposes for which this organization was founded. Those purposes are the promotion of human freedom and human rights, of self-determination, the protection of national independence, and the promotion of development. This chamber is not incapable of making distinctions between policies which serve those purposes and policies which undermine them. No government in this chamber is incapable of making such distinctions. We very much hope that those governments in this chamber who do indeed endorse and support the principles of the Charter of the United Nations will reflect carefully on the most profound and important issues involved here so of them it will never be said they knew not what they did.

A QUESTION OF PRIORITIES

The United States does not oppose the inscription of the situation in Grenada under Rule 15 as an additional item for consideration by the General Assembly during the current session. The United States does not

Address before the 38th General Assembly, November 2, 1983.

object to debate of this issue. To the contrary, we welcome a full, judicious discussion of all the facts pertaining to the situation in Grenada. Convinced that an understanding of the situation will support the action of the Organization of Eastern Caribbean States and its associates, including the government of the United States, the United States therefore, particularly and most especially, regrets the decision of this body to terminate debate before it had ever begun, to deny the Assembly the right either to discuss or to review the facts before it made its decisions. The United States very deeply hopes that the Assembly will not repeat this decision in dealing with other important matters concerning international peace and security.

The United States is convinced that the facts, understanding of the facts, will support our actions. We believe that the use of force by the task force was lawful under international law and the UN Charter because it was undertaken to protect American nationals from a clear and present danger, because it was a legitimate exercise of regional collective security, because it was carried out with due concern for lawful procedures and carried out in the service of values of the Charter, including the restoration of the rule of law, self-determination, sovereignty, democracy, and respect for the human rights of the people of Grenada.

The United States did object to giving special priority to the consideration of this item, not because we do not think it important, obviously, we think it is very important, but because the situation that now prevails in Grenada is not more urgent than other matters still to be considered by the Assembly, matters that also involve the basic values of the Charter and, even more human lives; matters such as the situation in Lebanon and the Middle East, Southern Africa, Central America, Afghanistan, the war between Iran and Iraq, and other issues that will not come before the Assembly at all, such as the aggression against Chad or the repression of the Polish people, or the persecution of Andrei Sakharov, Anatoly Shcharansky, Jose Pujals, Ricardo Bofil, Eloy Gutierrez Menoyo and other beleaguered defenders of human rights now held prisoner in some country which not only votes to deny debate in this Assembly but represses discussion and dissent at home.

Moreover, the United States deemed it hypocritical and politically tendentious to turn the Assembly's urgent attention to the situation in Grenada only after the real emergency in that country had passed, that is to say, only after Grenada had been rescued from the murderous elements that had taken over the country, threatening the people of that country and the neighboring states as well. But the issue was brought before us without debate, it was forced to a vote without debate, and so we are left to consider only retrospectively the issues raised in the resolution.

First, it is necessary to consider the situation that prevailed in Grenada before the intervention of October 25 to decide whether that situation was such as to warrant the use of force in a manner consistent with the Charter of the United Nations. Examination of those facts permits us to decide whether the principle of self-determination was violated or whether it was upheld; whether the sovereignty of Grenada was destroyed or whether it is being restored; whether the people of Grenada were victimized or whether they were in fact and quite truly liberated; whether the cause of peace was damaged or was served. These only appeared to be difficult questions. The difficulties disappear when the questions are addressed not in the abstract but in the context of the concrete circumstances that led the small, peaceful, democratic island states of the Caribbean not merely to sanction the intervention but to request it and to participate in it.

Mr. President, the test of law lies not in the assertion of abstract principles but in the application of universal norms to specific situations. A court that cannot distinquish between lawful and criminal use of force—between force used to protect the innocent and force used to victimize the innocent—is not worthy to sit in judgment on anyone. The failure to preserve such distinction does not preserve law as an instrument of justice and peace, but erodes the moral and legal foundations of civilized existence. There was, of course, first the question of force, the question of violence. There was, as I have already referred, the death, the murder of Maurice Bishop, his deputies, his cabinet ministers, people randomly shot in the crowds around Bishop. In these murders there were no courts, no trials, no judgments, only murder.

Mr. President, the full facts concerning these murders will become clear, will be presented to the world in due time. Expressing horror at these brutal and vicious murders, Prime Minister Tom Adams of Barbados said that the division in the Caribbean now goes far beyond ideological pluralism and is the difference between barbarians and human beings.

Mr. President, the United States, in the course of its participation in the collective regional security action in Grenada, has, along with its colleagues in that action, come into the possession of documents captured on Grenada and these documents are being analyzed. Among these documents are five very interesting secret military assistance agreements between Grenada, the Soviet Union, Cuba, and North Korea, executed between 1980 and 1982, which provide for the training of Grenadan soldiers in Cuba and the Soviet Union, and the assignment of Cuban and Soviet advisers and trainers in Grenada. Among these documents are agreements for the delivery, free of charge, of millions of dollars in military supplies, 20,000 uniforms, 4,500 rifles and submachine guns, 58 armored vehicles, 7,000 mines, and so forth.

Mr. President, the United States will be presenting photographs of the weapons actually found in seven warehouses in Grenada and those just discovered on the adjoining island.

Mr. President, the United States believes, as some nations have suggested, that a parallel can be drawn between the action in Grenada and the Soviet action in Afghanistan—a very meaningful parallel. Just as Maurice Bishop was murdered in Grenada because he tried to free himself from the Soviet stranglehold, so too was Mohammed Daud murdered in Afghanistan. And after him, Hafizollah Amin was murdered in Afghanistan. They, too, discovered that the only thing more dangerous than embracing the Soviet bear is trying to break loose from its deathly grip. They too learned that the price of trying to "reverse" Soviet conquest is violent death. This, and this alone, is the parallel between Grenada and Afghanistan. The difference is that the people of Grenada have now been spared the cruel fate of the people of Afghanistan.

The United States is proud to have participated with its Eastern Caribbean friends in the liberation of the people of Grenada, in the restoration of their sovereignty, their right to self-determination, their human rights, their rights to democratic government, and for that reason, proud to have voted today against the resolution that deplored this positive and constructive event. Thank you, Mr. President.

GAG RULE

It is particularly sad, if symbolically appropriate, that the action on this issue concerning Grenada in this body should be accompanied by attempts to stifle free discussion of the issue and to reject an amendment which calls for free elections. It is particularly appropriate that the effort to stifle free elections should be made by a country which calls itself Democratic Yemen. It is particularly appropriate that the representative of Libya should raise questions about how the governor-general of Grenada and the Organization of Eastern Caribbean States would be able to organize free elections—since the government of Libya is singularly unqualified on the subject of free elections.

The motion by Democratic Yemen to bloc consideration of this resolution has been described as irresistible. If indeed this body finds irresistible two proposals by "Democratic" Yemen, that debate be stifled and that an

Address before the 38th General Assembly, November 2, 1983.

amendment proposing free elections for a liberated people should be rejected, then we have arrived at a moment of truth.

Has it come to this, Mr. President—that this organization founded in the wake of a great war against tyrants—comprising, from the moment of its birth, nations liberated by force from the troops and quisling governments of tyrants—should here deplore the rescue of the people of Grenada from the grip of a small band of murderous men whose clear intention was to secure the permanent subjugation of Grenada and its people, putting this small but strategically located island at the disposal of foreign tyrants. Mr. President, if yesterday's victims of yesterday's tyrants and tomorrow's victims of tomorrow's tyrants should join in deploring the liberation of today's victims from today's tyrants and should do so in an organization founded precisely to ensure that there be no more victims, no more tyrants, then we have arrived at the end of the dreams and the hopes of the Founding Generation.

Mr. President, free discussion, free elections, rule of law, due process of law are precisely the questions at issue in Grenada, precisely the questions at issue in this body today. Maurice Bishop and his cabinet were murdered without a trial, without a right to defend themselves, without a court, without a judge—they were murdered in cold blood. If this body today attempts to stifle discussion of the issues involved in the establishment of democracy in Grenada after a terrible experience with lawlessness and tyranny, then the majority here is an accomplice to the death of the dreams we all bring to this great Assembly.

THE UN AND GRENADA: A SPEECH NEVER DELIVERED*

*With Carl Gershman

The United States did not oppose the inscription of "The Situation in Grenada" under Rule 15 as an additional item for consideration by the General Assembly during the current session. The United States does not object to debate of this issue. To the contrary, we welcome a full, judicious

Published in the *Strategic Review*, Winter 1984.

consideration of all the facts pertaining to the situation in Grenada, convinced that an understanding of the situation will support the actions of the Organization of Eastern Caribbean States and its associates, including the United States; that the use of force by the task force was lawful under international law and the UN Charter because it was undertaken to protect U.S. nationals from a clear and present danger, because it was legitimate exercise of regional collective security, and because it was carried out with due concern for lawful procedures in the service of the values of the Charter—including the restoration of the rule of law, self-determination, sovereignty, democracy and respect for the human rights of the people of Grenada.

We did object to giving special priority to the consideration of this item, not because we do not deem it important—obviously we do—but because the situation that now prevails in Grenada is not *more* urgent than other matters still to be considered by the Assembly—matters that involve the same basic values of the Charter and even more human lives, such as the situation in Lebanon, South Africa, Central America, Afghanistan, the war between Iran and Iraq—or other issues that will not come before the Assembly at all, such as the aggression against Chad, or the repression of the Polish people, or the persecution of Andrei Sakharov, Anatoly Shcharansky, Jose Pujals, Ricardo Bofil, Eloy Gutierrez Menoyo and other beleaguered defenders of human rights. Moreover, we deemed it hypocritical and politically tendentious to turn the Assembly's urgent attention to the situation in Grenada only after the real emergency in that country had passed—which is to say, only after Grenada had been rescued from the murderous elements that had taken over the country, threatening the people of that country and the neighboring states as well.

Application of Universal Norms

But now the issue is before us, so let us consider it in all its aspects. Let us consider all the issues raised in this resolution. Let us consider the situation that prevailed in Grenada before the intervention of October 25th. Let us consider whether that situation was such as to warrant the use of force in a manner consistent with the Charter of the United Nations. Let us consider whether the principle of self-determination was violated or upheld. Let us consider whether the sovereignty of Grenada was destroyed or restored. Let us consider whether the people of Grenada were victimized or liberated. Let us consider whether the cause of peace was damaged or served.

These may appear to be difficult questions, but the difficulties disappear when they are addressed not in the abstract, but in the context of the concrete circumstances that led small, peaceful, democratic island states of the Caribbean not merely to sanction the intervention but to request and to participate in it. The test of law lies not in the assertion of abstract principles, but in the application of universal norms to specific situations. A court that cannot distinguish between lawful and criminal use of force, between force used to protect the innocent and force used to victimize them, is not worthy to sit in judgment. The failure to draw such distinctions will not preserve law as an instrument of justice and peace, but will erode the moral and legal—and ultimately political—foundations of civilized existence.

An Authentic Reign of Terror

First there is the question of force. The intrusion of force into the public life of Grenada did not begin with the intervention of October 25th. From 1979 Grenada had been ruled by a government that came to power by coup, overthrowing a corrupt, though elected, predecessor. The government of Maurice Bishop was initially welcomed by Grenadans. Initially it promised to hold elections and respect basic human rights. These promises were honored in the breach, as the government attempted to impose a Castro-style dictatorship with Cuban and Soviet aid. Eventually, when Bishop sought to free himself from the Cuban-Soviet grip, he was arrested by his Cuban-trained deputy, Bernard Coard, and shot in cold blood on October 19th along with other members of his cabinet and political leaders. At least 18 deaths were confirmed and many more were reported, including those of women and children. There was no court, no trial, nor judgment, only murder. Expressing "horror at these brutal and vicious murders," Prime Minister Tom Adams of Barbados said that the division in the Caribbean now went "far beyond ideological pluralism" and "is the difference between barbarians and human beings."

In the wake of these murders, the People's Revolutionary Army announced the dissolution of the government and the formation of a 16-member Revolutionary Military Council with General Hudson Austin as the nominal head. This group was not a government—it indicated that it would subsequently announce a government—but literally a gang of murderers who imposed an authentic reign of terror upon the Grenadian people. It decreed a 24-hour curfew, warning that violators would be shot on sight, and closed the airport, thereby entrapping nearly 1,000 U.S. citizens—each and every one a potential hostage. Although the Military Council gave assurances that the airport would be opened on October 24th and foreigners allowed to depart, it failed to fulfill that assurance. The threat of violence against these American citizens, and against the people of Grenada, was real and imminent.

Infrastructure for Hostility Against Neighboring States

Grenada's neighbors also feared for their security. During the period of his rule, Bishop had permitted Grenada to be transformed into a base for the protection of Soviet and Cuban military power in the Western Hemisphere. The instruments of violence and deception assembled during Bishop's tenure now fell into the hands of Bishop's murderous successors, presumably even more pliant tools of Soviet and Cuban designs. Here is how this new threat was viewed by Prime Minister Edward Seaga of Jamaica, one of Grenada's Caribbean neighbors. The danger, he told the Jamaican Parliament on October 25th, arose "from the capacity of the leadership which seized power to use the armed capabilities and military infrastructure of Grenada for acts of hostility against neighboring states." He went on:

> The size and sophistication of the armed force of Grenada can be measured by a comparison with those of Jamaica. Grenada, having only one-twentieth of the population of Jamaica, had mobilized an army that was one and a half times as large as the Jamaica Defense Force. Some of Grenada's neighbors have no army at all; others have armies of less than 200 men.

> The new airstrip, in the final stages of completion by Cubans, added another capability which in the hands of sane men would have offered no threat, but against the background of the insanity of the past two weeks would be a logical staging area for countries whose interests are similar, and who have ambitions for using Grenada as a center for subversion, sabotage and infiltration within the area and against member states of the Organization of Eastern Caribbean States.

> Again, the powerful broadcasting station in Grenada, standing on its own, although capable of reaching from one end of the Caribbean to the other and far exceeding the power of any station in Jamaica, would in itself not necessarily be a threat, but in the hands of extremists of a military or ideological nature, both of whom exist in Grenada, constitutes a potent weapon for subverting neighboring states.

> While Maurice Bishop was alive, there was some indication that these capabilities could and would be used in this subversive manner against neighboring states, as there were complaints regarding training of a paramilitary nature taking place in Grenada among citizens of neighboring countries known for their own subversive interests.

> However, whatever may have been the threat, it was minimal in the hands of Maurice Bishop, who was a moderate in comparison with the military and political leaders of the regime which overthrew him. A totally different picture emerges when this array of military and subversive capability came to be at the disposal of one of the most extremist groups of men to assume control of any country in recent times. Few countries can have claimed the experience of having its entire cabinet wiped out in the manner in which that of

Grenada was exterminated. Who then can blame the Eastern Caribbean states for perceiving this combination of awesome might and brutal men, who apparently had no concept of where to stop in taking human life, as a prelude to hostile action being taken beyond their own borders by those in power in Grenada?

Warehouses Packed With Arms

Prime Minister Seaga made these comments on the basis of the perceived threat emanating from Grenada but *before* the full scope of the Soviet and Cuban military capability on the island had been uncovered. These fears, as he subsequently said, were amply confirmed by what was found on the island, including "thousands of crates filled with millions of rounds of ammunition and a large number of other crates of Russian AK-47 submachine guns. Heavy artillery capable of firing 2,000 rounds per minute, anti-tank weapons and anti-aircraft installations . . . embedded in the hillside around Point Salines have been uncovered. . . ." He went on:

> There is no longer any mystery, therefore, about what was going on at the Cuban-built airport at Point Salines. The airport has turned out to be nothing less than a sophisticated military camp. All the signs and directions are in Spanish, none in English. Facilities are present throughout for the storage of arms, and there is no evidence of provision being made for any normal commercial or civilian traffic. The installation is filled with places to hang rifles—even in the sanitary conveniences. The six warehouses packed with arms and other discoveries speak more eloquently than any words could of a Grenada that was being converted into a fortress and a base camp for hostile activities against its neighbors and within the region.

The prime minister does not speak of the weapons found in the small island of Carriacou adjoining Grenada, where only yesterday were uncovered 700 rifles and 38 Soviet-made AK-47s, rocket-propelled grenades, 150 cases of ammunition, two jeeps, a truck, a generator, radio equipment and a dozen cases of TNT. Less than a mile from Grenada's "tourist" airport, six warehouses were found which contained material of a similar variety, but in far larger numbers—enough to outfit two brigades, or 8,000 men, according to U.S. military officials.

Secret Treaties for Covert Supply of Arms

Mr. President, these discoveries revealed only what had already been emplaced in Grenada. They do not speak of the buildup that was envisioned through 1985 and agreed to in five secret treaties, three with the Soviet Union, one with Cuba and one with North Korea, which alone had agreed to supply $12 million worth of arms. These secret treaties provide for the covert supply of arms to Grenada from the Soviet Union, to be transshipped through Cuba—a pattern that is also being followed in Central America. The arms included millions of rounds of ammunition, sniper rifles, armored vehicles, naval patrol craft from North Korea, anti-aircraft guns, anti-tank guns, mortars, thousands of automatic rifles, hand grenades and land-mines, and 18,000 military uniforms—18,000 military uniforms for a country with a population of only 100,000. In addition, the treaties provided for assistance in the creation of a force run by the Ministry of Interior and for surveillance equipment and other items used by the KGB. They also provided for training Grenadans in the Soviet Union.

Mr. President, the United Nations was established to beat swords into plowshares. In Grenada, the Soviet Union and its proxies beat plowshares into AK-47s, machine guns and heavy artillery.

Direct Appeal to the OECS

Is there any reasonable basis for concluding that the fears of Grenada's neighbors were unfounded? Can any prudent judgment question the urgent appeal from the Organization of Eastern Carribbean States for assistance in meeting this threat to their security?

The OECS, a subregional body established to promote regional cooperation and collective security, determined that the collapse of government and the disintegration of public order in Grenada posed a threat to the security and stability of the region. As a consequence, the OECS members decided to take necessary measures in response to this threat, in accordance with Article 8 of the OECS treaty. They sought the assistance of friendly foreign states to participate in a collective security force. The United States, together with Barbados and Jamaica, agreed with the OECS assessment of the gravity of the situation and offered to contribute forces to a collective action in support of this regional measure. The governor-general of Grenada made a confidential, direct appeal to the OECS to take action to restore order on the island. As the sole remaining authoritative representative of government in Grenada, his appeal for action carried exceptional moral and legal weight.

Listen to the governor-general's description of his request and his thoughts about it, as expressed in a BBC interview:

> *Q*: Does it not seem a little strange that the Governor General of a Commonwealth country should ask America to intervene rather than Britain?
>
> *A*: Well, I thought the Americans would do it much faster and more decisively. At first, I was against invasion of the country. But things deteriorated

very rapidly. You see, when the military took over, they quickly came to me and acknowledged my authority as representative of the Queen, in the same way as the People's Revolutionary Government did when they overthrew the elected government. And at first I thought they were the right people. I was impressed. But within a very short time I thought things deteriorated rapidly. For example, I still need to know what became of the bodies of people who were killed on that day, including the bodies of Prime Minister Bishop and three cabinet ministers. I know that these bodies have never been handed over to relatives, and I am advised that these bodies were never taken to the hospital or any of the two undertakers in town.

Q: What was the moment you decided that an invasion was necessary?

A: I think I decided so on Sunday the 23rd, late Sunday evening.

Q: But the British say that on that day you told them you still didn't want one; that was early in the day, wasn't it?

A: I did see somebody earlier in the day, and they said you know invasion was the last thing they wanted, and I said it in my speech. But if it came to that, I would give every support; and later on, as things deteriorated, I thought, because people were scared, you know, I had several calls from responsible people in Grenada that something should be done. "Mr. Governor-General, we are depending on you [that] something be done. People in Grenada cannot do it, you must get help from outside." What I did ask for was not an invasion, but help from outside.

Q: Do you regret that the British were not associated with America in coming in?

A: I would not like to comment on this. I'm afraid in my position I would not like to blame any country for anything or to express such regrets. But what I can say is that we were very, very grateful that these other countries came to our rescue and they came just on time.

Q: Did you invite Britain to take part?

A: No, I did not invite Britain to take part, and I asked for help from the OECS countries. I also asked the OECS to ask America whether they can help. And then I confirmed this in writing myself to the President of the USA.

Q: How long, sir, do you think the Americans should remain here?

A: I would like—and I speak for the people who have to live and work in Grenada—I would like them to remain here as long as it is necessary. This I cannot say at the moment. I cannot say two weeks or three weeks or two months. I don't know.

And Governor-General Scoon said, further, in his radio speech to the people:

Innocent men, women and children were also killed or injured. To say the least, I was deeply saddened, and I shall like to extend heartfelt sympathy to the bereaved families. The killing of Prime Minister Bishop and the subsequent control of our country by the People's Revolutionary Army so horrified not only Grenadans but the entire Caribbean, the Commonwealth and beyond that certain Caribbean states with the support of the United States of America decided to come to our aid in the restoration of peace and order. Of course, intervention by foreign troops is the last thing one would want for one's country. But in our case, it has happened in deteriorating circumstances, repugnant to the vast majority.

Consistent with the Charter of the UN and of the OAS

Mr. President, collective action in response to the kind of dangerous situation that existed in Grenada is consistent with the Charter of the United Nations and with the Charter of the Organization of American States. Both charters expressly recognize the competence of regional security bodies in ensuring peace and stability. The OECS states are not parties to the Rio Treaty, and the OECS treaty, which concerns itself in part with matters of collective security, is their regional security arrangement.

Article 22 of the OAS Charter states that measures taken pursuant to collective security agreements do not violate the OAS Charter provisions prohibiting intervention and the use of force. Similarly, Article 52 of the UN Charter expressly permits regional arrangements for the maintenance of peace and security consistent with the purposes and principles of the United Nations. The actions and objectives of the collective security force, in the circumstances I have described, are consistent with those purposes and principles.

The OECS states, in taking lawful collective action, were free to call upon other concerned states, including the United States, for assistance in their effort to maintain the peace and security of the Caribbean. Assistance given in response to their request is itself lawful. Moreover, U.S. cooperation with the collective security force permitted the safe evacuation of endangered U.S. citizens. Such humanitarian action is justified by well-established principles of international law.

Mr. President, the extent of the danger faced by U.S. citizens in Grenada was vividly illustrated by the numerous photographs of American students kissing the ground after deplanning in the United States. "We thought we could be potential hostages," said one. "We just wanted to get out if we could." Said another, who talked to Grenadans about leaving: "They said they were afraid and they would leave if they could. If they feel that way about their own government, I don't see how I could trust it." Let me also quote, if I may, from a letter that was sent to President Reagan by 65 students last Thursday:

We the students of St. George's University School of Medicine at Kingstown

Medical College, St. Vincent, would like to express our appreciation of your concern for the safety of our fellow students in Grenada. . . . Having spent the past two years in Grenada and being in almost daily contact with American students there during the recent unrest, we support your decision. . . ."

An Intervention Popular Throughout the Region

There is no question, Mr. President, that the intervention in Grenada was immensely popular throughout the Caribbean region. The Prime Minister of Barbados, Tom Adams, said: "There has seldom been in these islands such virtual unanimous support in the media and at political and popular levels for an action so potentially divisive." The Jamaican columnist and opinion analyst, Dr. Carl Stone, wrote that the intervention in Grenada "is both popular here in Jamaica and in the rest of the Caribbean because of the feelings about the murderous butchers of St. George's." James Nelson Goodsell, the Latin American correspondent for the *Christian Science Monitor,* reported: "At the recent Inter-American Press Association meeting in Lima, Peru, there was virtually unanimous backing by Caribbean editors for the combined U.S.-Caribbean invasion of Grenada."

Mr. Goodsell's finding was amply confirmed by reactions in the region to the intervention. Mark A. Conyers, the managing editor of the *Trinidad Guardian,* said: "I thoroughly agree with the forces' landing. You have to protect Caribbean democracy. There must be an elected government in Grenada, and this landing should help bring that about." An editorial in the *Bridgetown Advocate* noted: "If we are really serious about the concept of sovereignty, what has been done has given the Grenadans a real chance to recapture their true sovereignty as a people." This point was echoed in *El Universal* of Caracas, which said that the action in Grenada was "taken to end totalitarian intervention in the Republic of Grenada, and it will guarantee that island's people the right to freedom and to elect their governments democratically." An editorial on October 27th in Colombia's leading daily, *Il Tiempo,* noted that the Cubans in Grenada were not simply workers and teachers "but a group armed to the teeth, capable of direct combat in a direct and efficient manner. . . . Now Fidel orders the Cubans dug in on the island to resist until the end, by which he virtually admits that they had already invaded the island by other means and that now they refuse to allow themselves to be pushed away."

The Views of the People of Grenada

I could go on citing regional opinion, but the views that count most are the views of the people of Grenada. Let me quote from Alister Hughes, the

Agence France Presse and CANA correspondent and the sole independent news link between Grenada and the outside world until his arrest on October 19th: "I don't regard it as an invasion, but a rescue operation. I haven't met any Grenadan who had expressed any other view." He added: "Thank God they came. If someone had not come in and done something, I hesitate to say what the situation in Grenada would be now."

TV interviews conducted by the Canadian Broadcasting Corporation found the people in the streets of St. George uniformly favorable to the intervention, a reaction also found by *Washington Post* reporter Ed Cody. The Governor General himself, Paul Scoon, said: "The people of Grenada, the people who live and work here, . . . I am well advised have welcomed the presence of these troops as a positive step forward in the restoration not only of peace and order but also of full sovereignty that's enabling our democratic institutions to function according to the expressed wishes of the Grenadan people at the earliest possible time."

Self-Determination Involves Respect for Fundamental Freedoms

The governor-general has, of course, raised here the central issue, the issue of democracy, the issue that is at the heart of the principle of self-government and self-determination. It is the governor-general's intention, which we fully support, that the people of Grenada will exercise their right of self-government and self-determination through the instrumentalities of free elections and free institutions. How, then, has their right of self-determination been violated, as some claim?

The states which make this claim presumably believe that the Grenadian people enjoyed self-determination before October 25th, which is to say, when they were subjected to a brutal reign of terror. The fact that these states include the Soviet Union, Cuba, and Nicaragua and others of their imperial vocation should not be at all surprising, since they do not, in fact, see any contradiction between self-determination and totalitarianism, between self-determination and the seizure of power by armed minorities, between self-determination and the subversion of democratic neighbors, between self-determination and absorption into the Soviet empire.

Self-determination involves respect for "human rights and fundamental freedoms," as stated in Article 55 of the Charter, and it is expressed through "self-government" that takes due account, as Article 76 states, of "the freely expressed wishes of the people concerned." Is there anyone here who can reasonably believe and credibly assert that the prospect for the full enjoyment of this right by the Grenadian people was not immensely better after October 25th than it was before that date? The Grenadian people do not take that view, nor do their neighbors who are closest to their situation.

Life is already returning to usual in Grenada. People are moving freely on the streets after having been confined for ten days.

The governor-general and the people of Grenada know precisely what it plans and how it proposes to achieve its goals. The governor-general is planning for a nonpolitical interim administration to prepare elections and return to democracy.

In the same broadcast quoted earlier, the governor-general announced that 400 soldiers and national policemen from the Eastern Caribbean countries that took part in the landing would be formed into a security force. The governor-general has ordered remaining members of the People's Revolutionary Army and the militia to stop fighting and has officially disbanded the armed forces.

The proof of the pudding, of course, is finally in the eating. It is one thing to rescue people from murderers and another for those same people to hold free elections. The latter does not necessarily follow from the former, although surely free elections and democratic life can hardly exist under conditions of terror. But let there be no question that it is the profound hope of the people of the United States that the Grenadian people shall soon enjoy freedom, democracy and stability. We trust that this hope is shared by those who invoke the principle of self-determination in their objection to the means used to rescue the Grenadian people.

Force Used to Liberate and Force Used to Impose Terror

There are those who say—let us be blunt—that the use of force by the United States in Grenada is equivalent to the use of force by the Soviet Union in Afghanistan or Eastern Europe. Let me just pose the following questions in response: Is there no distinction to be drawn between force used to liberate captive people from terror and force used to impose terror on captive people? Is Solidarity in Poland to be equated with the Revolutionary Military Council in Grenada? Is "socialism with a human face" in Czechoslovakia of the Prague Spring the same as communism armed to the teeth in the Grenada of Bishop's killers?

There is, let me say, a parallel to be drawn between Grenada and Afghanistan—a very meaningful parallel. Just as Maurice Bishop was murdered in Grenada because he tried to free himself from the Soviet stranglehold, so, too, was Mohammed Daud murdered in Afghanistan and after him Hafizollah Amin. Let me here also remind the representative of South Yemen that on June 26, 1978, the President of South Yemen, Selim Rubai Ali, and two of his followeres were executed for precisely the same reason. They, too, discovered that the only thing more dangerous than embracing the Soviet bear is trying to break loose from its deadly grip. They, too, learned that the price of trying to reverse the course of history—the inexorable course of history, in the Soviet view—is violent death. This, and this alone, is the parallel between Grenada and Afghanistan. The difference is that the people of Grenada have now been spared the cruel fate of the people of Afghanistan.

Speaking before the OAS, the representative of St. Lucia said that the United States is only "guilty of responding positively to a formal request for assistance from some of the Eastern Caribbean states who wish only to maintain their security and protect their people from the totalitarian grip which seeks to place a stranglehold on the Caribbean." There are others in this world who, if not now similarly threatened by the totalitarian grip of the Soviet Union and its proxies—who specialize in gaining power through subversion and terror and then consolidating totalitarian control—may well be so threatened in the future. In voting on this resolution, we ask them to consider what they would do were they to be in the position of the Eastern Caribbean states? What would they want done were their country subjected to the kind of terror that prevailed in Grenada? Would they, too, want assistance? And would they, too, appeal for rescue? And if they would—which would be entirely consistent with a desire to preserve and defend one's nation—we ask just one more question: How can they reconcile that position with a vote in favor of the resolution now before us?

End of the Dreams and Hopes of the UN?

Has it come to this: That this organization, founded in the wake of a great war against tyrants, comprising from the moment of its birth nations liberated by force from the troops and quisling governments of tyrants, should meet here to deplore the rescue of the people of Grenada from the grip of a small band of murderous men whose clear intention was to secure the permanent subjugation of Grenada and its people and put this small but strategically located island at the disposal of foreign tyrants?

If yesterday's victims of yesterday's tyrants should join today in "deploring" the liberation of today's victim from today's tyrants—and should do so in an organization founded precisely to ensure that there be no more victims, no more tyrants—it would surely mark the end of the dreams and hopes of the United Nations.

4
Aggression in Asia

THE SOVIET INVASION OF AFGHANISTAN*

*With Carl Gershman and Rosanne Klass

The Soviet invasion of Afghanistan, launched on Christmas Eve nearly two years ago, was a momentous event that altered the climate and, indeed, the course of world politics. The invasion was a grave violation of the United Nations Charter, which enjoins all Members to "refrain in their international relations from the threat or use of force against the territorial integrity or political independence of any state." As such, the Soviet invasion of Afghanistan shook the very foundations of world order.

The far-reaching consequences of this event should by now be apparent to all of us. It had a shattering effect upon the prospects for the continued stability of South Asia and the Persian Gulf, deepening anxieties throughout this vital region and raising the specter of a wider conflict. It also severely aggravated tensions between East and West. More than any single event in recent years, the Soviet invasion impelled a widespread reassessment of the world situation based upon a new and more sober appreciation of the danger that the policies of the Soviet Union now pose to global stability and world peace. The invasion thus marked a watershed in the postwar era, bringing to a definitive conclusion a period of optimism concerning the evolution of Soviet policy and intentions.

Nowhere, of course, have the consequences been more immediately or harshly felt than in Afghanistan itself. No sector of Afghan society has been spared the consequences of the Soviet occupation and the ruthless effort to impose upon the Afghan people a Communist totalitarian system—an

Address before the UN General Assembly, November 18, 1981.

effort that began in 1978 with the initial Communist coup overthrowing the Daoud government. Almost three million people, about one-fifth of the entire Afghan population, have been forced to flee their country and now constitute the largest single refugee group in the world. Tens of thousands of people have been killed. Afghanistan's educated class has been decimated. Whole villages have been destroyed, their inhabitants killed or forced to flee. Mosques have been desecrated and religious leaders jailed or murdered. Schools have been turned into centers of political indoctrination. The country's economic and social infrastructure of roads, power and communication networks, hospitals, and educational institutions has been badly damaged and in many instances completely destroyed.

It is rarely noted that Afghanistan made significant economic and social progress during the decade of democratic freedoms and representative government brought about by the 1964 constitution. All this—and more—has now been undone.

There have been many attempts in the past to conquer Afghanistan. But nothing in the country's long history—with the possible exception of the devastating attacks more than 750 years ago by Genghis Khan—resembles the destruction wreaked in Afghanistan since 1978.

The Soviet Union and the Kabul regime have tried to conceal this destruction by sealing the country off from journalists and other foreign observers, and from humanitarian organizations such as the International Red Cross. Nevertheless, the truth about the situation there and about the terrible human suffering is becoming known to the world.

How far the Soviets are willing to go in their war against Afghanistan is indicated by the kind of weapons they have used there, including little boobytrap mines which the Soviets scatter by the thousands along the paths used by refugees and other civilians. These mines are frequently disguised as ordinary household items or toys. Children, naturally the least wary, are the ones most likely to pick them up. If they do, they risk being killed or having their limbs blown off.

On April 10 of this year, the Soviet Union signed an international convention prohibiting the use of such weapons. At the time, its Permanent Representative to the United Nations called the convention "an illustrative example of the possibility of reaching agreements on measures aimed at curbing the arms race." The real "illustrative example," however, is contained in the Soviets' continued use in Afghanistan of the kind of anti-personnel weapons prohibited in the treaty. It is an example that illustrates both the character of the Soviet Union's involvement in Afghanistan and its attitude—in this instance, at least—toward a treaty obligation. In this connection, there are many reports from refugees and other victims of the Soviet invasion that lethal and incapacitating chemical weapons are being used in Afghanistan, in violation of both the Geneva Protocol of 1925 and the Biological Weapons Convention of 1972.

It is not possible to justify the Soviet actions in Afghanistan according to any meaningful interpretation of international law. The sole exception to the proscription against the use of force in international relations is provided for in Article 51 of the Charter, which affirms "the inherent right of individual or collective self-defense if an armed attack occurs against a Member of the United Nations." But not even the Soviet Union itself has suggested that it has been the victim of an armed attack.

Moreover, it is hard to imagine how Afghanistan might conceivably have posed a threat to the Soviet Union. For decades the Soviet Union had proclaimed to the whole world, repeatedly, that its relations with Afghanistan were a model of peaceful co-existence, a prime example of neighborly relations between a small country and a big country, each with different systems of government and social structures, but living together in peace without interference. Since 1921 the two countries had signed numerous treaties, affirming and reaffirming Moscow's respect for Afghanistan's independence and territorial integrity and promising non-interference in Afghan affairs. It should not be forgotten, furthermore, that Afghanistan was a member of the Non-Aligned Movement and was not involved in any relationships that Moscow might look upon with concern.

How, then, could it have posed a threat? The argument is advanced that the Soviet Union felt threatened by the turmoil inside Afghanistan. But aside from student riots fomented by Babrak Karmal and his followers in 1965 and a brief period of unrest following the bloodless Daoud coup in 1973, there was no turmoil at all in Afghanistan before April 27, 1978— before, that is to say, the Communists violently seized power in Kabul and, with the help of growing numbers of Soviet "advisers," began forcibly to impose upon the people of Afghanistan a foreign ideology and a total-itarian system.

It is also suggested by apologists for the invasion that the Soviet Union feared that a tide of Islamic fundamentalism might sweep from Afghanistan into its Central Asian provinces. But even if this were true, it would hardly justify the Soviet invasion. In fact, the Afghans are a devout people, but they have not tried to impose their beliefs on others and histor-ically they have allowed minority faiths to live peacefully within their midst. This attitude of tolerance is characteristic of the Afghans except when their faith itself is attacked, as it now is by Communism. They are *not* tolerant, nor should they be, of an attack upon their freedom, indepen-dence, and identity, of which their religion is an important part. But there should be no doubt whatsoever that the threat in this instance is *to*—not from—the people of Afghanistan.

The Soviet Union also claims, of course, that its forces were invited in by the Kabul regime, which invoked *its* right to self-defense under Article 51. But so far, neither the Soviet Union nor the Kabul regime has produced a shred of evidence to prove that such an invitation was ever issued. It is hard to imagine what kind of evidence they *could* produce since, as we know, the invasion *preceded* the installation of Babrak Karmal, who wasn't even in Afghanistan at the time his predecessor was overthrown and killed by invading Soviet troops. Of late, Babrak Karmal has taken the line that the invitation was issued by the Afghan Communist Party. This, of course, is actually an admission that the invitation was not issued by any government.

The Kabul regime, moreover, has no legitimacy whatsoever in the eyes of the Afghan people. It exists only by virtue of Soviet actions and is, in fact, merely an appendage of Moscow. Soviet personnel direct virtually all aspects of its administration, including the Ministries of Foreign Affairs, Defense, Interior, Information and Culture, Justice, and Economic Planning. Since 1979, Soviet personnel have also commanded the Afghan army down to the brigade level and sometimes down to the company level. The Soviets even control Afghanistan's natural resources, in particular natural gas, which are extracted in a one-sided barter arrangement in exchange for goods used to sustain the Kabul regime.

Suspicions have been raised that the Kabul regime may also have acceded, in a treaty signed earlier this year, to the annexation by the Soviet Union of at least a part of the Wakhan corridor, the narrow strip of land that joins Afghanistan with China. A *de facto* annexation has already taken place since the area—from which the indigenous Kirghiz tribes have been forced to flee—is now under the control of the Soviet army.

Given the Kabul regime's utter subservience to Moscow, it is hardly surprising that it should have no base of support among the Afghan people. It is propped up by 85,000 Soviet troops. Yet the freedom fighters—poorly armed and trained, and virtually defenseless against some of the most sophisticated weapons in the Soviet arsenal—have been able to deny the Soviets control of perhaps 90 percent of the countryside and have made them contest many of the most important cities. In a desperate attempt to stem the disintegration of the Afghan army, the regime has offered many times normal pay to former enlisted men. Yet still they do not turn up, while draft-age men continue to slip out of the cities to join the resistance and whole units of the army desert *en masse*. The regime has repeatedly offered an amnesty to refugees who would return to Afghanistan from exile. Yet every week the refugee centers in Pakistan and Iran swell by the thousands.

What is clear today was clear in 1979. Then, as now, the Kabul regime was not threatened by an outside power, justifying defense under Article

51, but was in fact threatened by a popular uprising, a *spontaneous* popular uprising, of the nation—of the people in whom nationhood inheres and *solely* inheres in the absence of a legitimate government. It was an uprising against a regime that had slaughtered its own people, destroyed their homes, sent almost half a million people fleeing into exile, and delivered the country to an alien force—an uprising that continues to this very day against the present regime and its Soviet masters.

It is this uprising, and this uprising alone, that is justified to invoke the right of self-defense, for it is defending the independence and very existence of the Afghan nation against a foreign and brutal domination.

Small wonder, then, that the Soviet Union is doing whatever it can to obscure the truth about Afghanistan. There is no other way to understand the charge—repeated by the Soviet Foreign Minister before this body in September—that the real source of the conflict in Afghanistan is foreign interference by the United States and China. This charge is ludicrous but also revealing, for it shows the lengths the Soviet Union is forced to go to conceal the real nature of its policy.

There are only two realities in Afghanistan today: the Soviet occupation and the Afghan nation, and neither is compatible with the other. The Soviet Union can conquer Afghanistan only by eliminating the Afghan nation. This the world must not permit to happen, for if Afghanistan is vanquished, no independent nation will be safe.

The draft resolution now before us, like its predecessors, seeks an end to the occupation of Afghanistan. It calls for:

- Immediate withdrawal of all foreign troops;
- Restoration of the sovereignty, territorial integrity and non-alignment of Afghanistan;
- Restoration of the right of the Afghan people to choose their own form of government and economic and social system, free from outside intervention, coercion or restraint; and
- Return of the refugees to their homeland.

My government is firmly committed to these terms.

The struggle of the Afghan nation for survival is consistent with the basic and most cherished purposes of the United Nations, which are to protect national independence and to maintain world peace.

It is only fitting, therefore, that the United Nations should affirm the basic and most cherished purpose of the Afghan nation, which is to regain its ancient homeland so that it may once again be independent and live at peace.

THE MEANING OF THE AFGHAN STRUGGLE*

*With Carl Gershman and Rosanne Klass

Once again the issue of Afghanistan is before the General Assembly. Once again, in what is now a familiar exercise, one representative after another will come before this body to decry the Soviet invasion of Afghanistan and the continuing and increasingly brutal attempt to subjugate the Afghan people. And once again we will consider, and hopefully adopt by another overwhelming majority, a resolution calling for the withdrawal of the Soviet occupation force, respect for Afghanistan's right of self-determination, restoration of Afghan independence and nonalignment, and the return of the Afghan refugees to their homes in safety and honor.

The familiarity of this exercise must not be allowed to detract in any way from its extraordinary significance. Of all the issues before this Assembly, none has more far-reaching implications than the issue of Afghanistan. The aggression committed by the Soviet Union in Afghanistan and its proxies elsewhere has had and continues to have a great impact upon the climate and course of East-West relations. Such aggression ominously affects the entire fabric of international relations and the future of the state system based upon respect for the principles of territorial integrity, national independence, and political sovereignty. These actions bear directly upon the capacity of states, especially those most vulnerable, to retain their unique identities and to fulfill their aspirations in peace and security.

The Afghan people are fighting for their own survival, but their struggle has a much broader meaning. If a small, relatively defenseless, nonaligned country like Afghanistan is allowed to be invaded, brutalized, and subjugated, what other similarly vulnerable country can feel secure? If the fiercely independent and incredibly courageous people of Afghanistan are uprooted, economically ravaged, culturally annihilated, and eventually subdued, the survival of other peoples—even those equally resilient—will be endangered.

The effort to subjugate the Afghan people and to impose upon them a form of alien and totalitarian rule has been marked by a degree of violence against the population that is exceeded in the recent past only by the terrible tragedy in Cambodia. The crimes against the Afghan people have

Address before the UN General Assembly, November 24, 1982.

taken place far from the eye of world publicity, behind a tight curtain of totalitarian disinformation and thought control. Still, the story of the brutality has come out—as it often does in such situations—from refugee accounts and, from reports of journalists and doctors who have ventured into the country.

One measure of the extent of the violence inflicted upon the Afghan people is the number of refugees uprooted from their homes and forced to flee to neighboring countries. When the illegitimate regime of Babrak Karmal was installed as a result of the Soviet invasion, the number of refugees in Pakistan had already reached 400,000. These refugees had fled the reign of terror unleashed against Afghanistan by the earlier Communist regimes of Taraki and Amin. Babrak promised an end to the methods of terror used by his predecessors. But in the less than three years of his rule, the number of Afghan refugees in Pakistan and Iran has increased nearly tenfold to over 3 million, almost one-quarter of the estimated 1978 population of Afghanistan. This is the largest single refugee mass in the world for any one national group.

Even these figures fail to convey the full extent of the dislocation and suffering of Afghanistan, since there have been many hundreds of thousands of internal refugees who have fled from the rural areas where the fighting has been most intense. The depopulation of the countryside, it appears, has been the deliberate goal of Soviet scorched earth policies in rural areas controlled by the resistance. As a result of the fighting in these provinces, many farmers have been unable to gather their crops and there is a danger this winter of famine.

The last General Assembly called upon the Soviet Union to withdraw its forces from Afghanistan. Far from respecting the decision of the Assembly, the Soviets over the past year have augmented their forces in Afghanistan to approximately 105,000, and they have conducted their most ruthless, wide-ranging, and systematic offensive of the entire war. The heightened aggressiveness of the Soviet forces became evident in January when the Soviets bombarded, shelled and occupied the resistance stronghold of Qandahar, Afghanistan's second largest city located some 250 miles southeast of Kabul. The brutal action in Qandahar, which resulted in high civilian casualties, was repeated two months later in Herat and Mazar-E-Sharif, and later in the spring against the northeastern town of Tashkurghan. In the early summer the town of Aq Gozar in the far northwest was rendered unfit for human habitation by systematic air and tank strikes.

As brutal as these attacks have been, the main thrust of the Soviet offensive took place closer to Kabul in the spring and summer of this year. The principal targets were villages in the Panjsher and Logar Valleys and the Shomali region, and districts near Kabul, particularly the mountain town of Paghman located only twelve miles northwest of the capital. These attacks have been marked by indiscriminate bombardments of villages resulting in thousands of civilian casualties, many of them women and children. Survivors also relate that Soviet troops, frustrated in their search for resistance fighters, have committed numerous acts of terrorism against civilians.

In Qandahar, for example, accounts of rape and plunder by Soviet troops following last January's bombing shocked and alienated even the most enthusiastic apologists of the Babrak regime. According to eyewitness reports from the Shomali region, in one village all males over the age of ten were shot in the presence of their female relatives. The Swedish journalist Borje Almquist, who visited the Logar Province in July and August, has described similar incidents in that area, as indeed such incidents have been reported from all over Afghanistan. According to Almquist, women, children and old men were dragged into the street and executed, while civilians with their hands tied behind their backs were used instead of sand sacks for protection in street fighting. He also reported the burning of harvests, the poisoning of food and drinking water, and the plundering of homes and shops.

The Soviets also continue to use antipersonnel "butterfly bombs" and boobytrapped objects such as toys, cigarette packs and pens, in gross violation of an international convention outlawing such weapons which they themselves signed in 1981. Earlier this year a team of French doctors which had returned from as far inland as the central highlands of Hazarajat charged that the Soviets scatter such mines over fields, villages, and mountain paths, causing heavy casualties among inhabitants, especially among children who are the least wary. "We have treated many children whose hands and feet are blown up by such mines," said Dr. Claude Malhuret, a member of the French medical team. He also revealed that the Soviets, fearing that the French doctors might speak about what they had seen, destroyed their hospitals in an attempt to drive them out of the country.

Boobytrap mines are not the only outlawed weapons used by the Soviets against the people of Afghanistan. They continue to use chemical weapons in violation of both the Geneva Protocol of 1925 and the 1972 Biological Weapons Convention which they, along with 110 other countries, have ratified. Earlier this year the United States listed 47 known chemical attacks in Afghanistan. They began as early as 6 months before the invasion and have resulted in over 3,000 deaths. These attacks have continued. Just last September a Soviet soldier captured by the resistance, Anatoly Sakharov, said that he knew of three types of chemical agents used by the Soviets in Afghanistan. His testimony about the effects of one of them, a particularly deadly agent which he called "smirch," corresponds closely to reports given to the UN experts team by doctors working with refugees in Pakistan. The doctors noted that on several occasions after attacks on villages, "bodies had quickly decomposed, and limbs had separated from each other when touched." Sakharov also described a chemical attack on resistance fighters in which the Soviet soldiers had been ordered to use gasmasks.

Next week the United States will make public an updated report on chemical and biological weapons which will contain new information regarding the Soviet Union's continued use of these illegal weapons in Afghanistan as well as in Laos and Kampuchea.

Nothing more clearly demonstrates the courage and resilience of the Afghan freedom fighters, or the Afghan people's universal hatred of the Soviet occupation, than the fact that the resistance forces remain intact and active throughout the country despite the massive violence that the Soviets have used against them. In the Panjsher and in Paghman, for example, the Soviets were able to establish footholds as the Mujahidin melted into the hills. But as soon as the main invading force withdrew, the resistance overran the newly established government outposts and regained control of these positions. Similarly, savage bombardments in the Shomali temporarily drove the Mujahidin back from the main roads but in no way broke their organization. Even in the devastated city of Qandahar the freedom fighters have been able to mount operations against the occupying forces, the most notable being a spectacular jailbreak and freeing of prisoners last August. Destroyed Soviet tanks and transport vehicles litter the roadsides throughout Afghanistan, testimony to the Soviets' continuing inability to establish security in the countryside or control over the population.

The most glaring and revealing failure of the Soviets has been their inability to build the various branches of their puppet regime's armed forces into effective units that could take over the brunt of the fighting. To date it appears that no progress has been made in this key area. Recent measures to overcome the critical manpower shortage in the Afghan army—including the toughest draft decree yet issued, indiscriminate arrests and beatings of those resisting conscription, and incentive payscales for recruits almost equal to sub-cabinet salaries—have been fruitless. As a consequence, press gangs have returned to the streets of Kabul and provincial cities, and young men have been forcibly conscripted in house-to-house searches. The futility of these various measures was demonstrated during the summer fighting when large-scale defections, surrenders, and desertions by Afghan soldiers led to a net loss of military personnel.

The failure of the Soviets to break the resistance by military means, and the self-evident fact that the Soviet aggressors and their Afghan proxies are rejected by the Afghan people, have not caused the Soviets to relent in their desire ultimately to subjugate the country. Instead, they show every sign of pursuing a long-term strategy, looking on the one hand to the gradual wearing down of the resistance through attrition, and on the other hand to the military, economic, and social integration of Afghanistan into the Soviet sphere.

The Soviets have already taken significant steps in this direction. They have consolidated their military, transport, and communications infrastructure, including the expansion of existing air fields and the completion of the bridge across the Amu Darya River. They have tightened their grip on the strategic Wakhan corridor which rests on Pakistan's northernmost border and links Afghanistan with China, and they have tied Afghanistan's economy tightly to those of the Soviet Bloc through a proliferation of economic and trade agreements.

Perhaps most significant is the Soviet effort to reshape Afghan culture and to replace the decimated intellectual and middle classes with a new elite trained in the Soviet mold. Thousands of Afghans, including even children between the ages of six and nine, are being trained in the Soviet Union and other bloc countries, while the Afghan educational system itself is being restructured along Soviet lines. The Sovietization of Kabul University is made evident by the presence of Soviet advisers at all levels of administration and instruction and in the preference given to party activists in admissions. The curriculum of Afghanistan's primary education system has been redrawn to promote indoctrination in Marxist-Leninist ideology and to prepare young Afghans for further study in the Soviet Union.

It is in the light of these policies—and the continuing, escalating, savage Soviet military involvement—that we must view Moscow's repeated claim that the Great Saur Revolution of April 1978 is "irreversible." But what, one may legitimately ask, gives the Soviet Union the right to insist that the violent overthrow of a nonaligned government constitutes an "irreversible" revolution? According to what tenet of international law, on the basis of which article of the United Nations Charter, do they base their position? One would think that it is the Afghan people, and only the Afghan people, who have the right to determine whether the events of 1978 are or are not "irreversible."

In fact, the Afghan people made their decision—long ago. They rejected a revolution whose chief accomplishment before the Soviet invasion was the arrest, torture, and execution of tens of thousands of Moslem clerics, teachers, civil servants, doctors and engineers. They rejected a revolution whose cruelty and sadistic violence is best symbolized by the mass burial pits outside Pol-e Charkhi prison and the massacre at Kerala. They rejected a revolution which systematically assaulted Islam and Afghan nationhood and turned their proud country over to its predatory northern neighbor.

They expressed this rejection in the form of a spontaneous, countrywide resistance movement. By invading Afghanistan in order to crush this resistance and maintain in power a hated, Marxist regime, Moscow took a momentous step which signaled the expanding scope of its political and territorial ambitions. In effect, for the first time it was claiming the right to apply the Brezhnev Doctrine to a previously nonaligned, Third World Country.

The world has not permitted this act of expansion and aggression to go unchallenged. It has rejected the claim advanced by Soviet propaganda that it is providing "fraternal assistance" to Afghanistan with its "limited military contingent." These words ominously echo assurances which were given to Afghanistan itself sixty years ago when it protested the entry of Soviet troops into two of its neighbors, the independent Moslem states of Khiva and Bokhara. Let me quote from a letter which the Soviet Ambassador in Kabul sent to the Afghan Ministry of Foreign Affairs on February 20, 1922:

> Concerning the question of the independent status of Khiva and Bokhara, this has been provided for in the treaty agreed to and signed by the two governments of Russia and Afghanistan. The Government which I represent has always recognized and respected the independence of the two Governments of Khiva and Bokhara. The presence of a limited contingent of troops belonging to my Government is due to temporary requirements expressed and made known to us by the Bokharan Government. This arrangement has been agreed to with the provision that whenever the Bokharan Government so requests, not a single Russian soldier will remain on Bokharan soil. The extension of our friendly assistance in no way constitutes an interference against the independence of the sovereign State of Bokhara.

Today, sixty years later, the Soviet Union provides the same justification and the same assurances with respect to its invasion of Afghanistan. It is useful, therefore, to reflect upon the ultimate fate of Khiva and Bokhara. Two years after the Soviet Ambassador gave his assurances to the Government of Afghanistan, the Soviet Union annexed Khiva and Bokhara. Their languages, Turkish and Persian, were abolished and replaced by pseudo-languages fabricated by Soviet linguists. These languages, Uzbek and Tadzhik, were mere dialects of Turkish and Persian, but were transcribed into Latin and later Cyrillic script. Mosques were closed or changed into museums and Koranic education was abolished. The surviving members of the local factions the Soviets had supported with their invasion were executed on charges of "bourgeois nationalist deviationism" and replaced by young bureaucrats trained in new Soviet schools.

Is history repeating itself today in the case of Afghanistan? If we are to judge from Soviet actions to date, it is hard not to conclude that they intend that history *shall* repeat itself, if not through the formal annexation of Afghanistan, then through its *de facto* absorption into the Soviet empire. And if this is allowed to happen, can anyone be reasonably assured that this will be the end of the process, that there are not future Khivas and Bokharas and Afghanistans that await a similar fate?

It is not, therefore, simply moral considerations and human solidarity that link us to the fate of the Afghan people. At stake in their struggle is respect for the principles of the United Nations Charter, the principles of the non-use of force, respect for the territorial integrity, national independence, and political sovereignty of states. Without this respect, world politics would succumb to anarchy and domination by the most ruthless, expansionist predator.

We cannot—we must not—permit this to happen.

The Soviet leaders undoubtedly believed when they launched their invasion of Afghanistan that they could deal with the international reaction by waiting patiently for the world's outrage to subside. The General Assembly can take great credit for frustrating this strategy. Passage of time has not served the aggressor. Indeed, the adoption of resolutions on Afghanistan by increasingly large majorities over the last three years shows that the world's outrage is growing.

We now have an opportunity to reaffirm once again our commitment to the liberation of Afghanistan. In so doing, we can help remind those in the Kremlin who ordered the Soviet invasion that their strategy has failed. We cannot afford, either as individual states with our own security concerns, or as a world organization dedicated to maintaining world peace, for the Soviet leaders to have any doubts on this score.

The resolution before us today offers an honorable course for ending the Afghanistan crisis. Its objective is a peaceful, negotiated settlement leading to the withdrawal of Soviet forces, the restoration of Afghan self-determination, independence, and nonalignment, and the return of the refugees to their homeland. By adopting this resolution, the United Nations General Assembly will be impressing on the Soviets the necessity to negotiate an end to their misadventure. Hopefully, this will speed the day when real negotiations on a settlement can begin.

In this context, the United States wishes to express its appreciation to Secretary General Perez de Cuellar for his effort to probe the opportunities for a settlement which would implement the General Assembly resolutions. We support these efforts and urge the Soviets to cooperate with them. We also recognize, as the Secretary General said in his report to the General Assembly this year, that "time is of the essence." If the Soviets truly desire to negotiate, they must come forward quickly or the rest of the world will be forced to conclude that they have no serious interest in reaching a settlement.

The alternative to a negotiated settlement is a continuation of the conflict, with far-reaching and long-lasting consequences for world peace. The Afghan people, unbowed and unbroken despite repeated and relentless hammer blows, have shown that they will not submit to aggression—not now and not ever. They have proved themselves to be a strong, proud, heroic people. With our support and solidarity, they shall also once again become a sovereign and independent people, permitted, as President Harry Truman once said, to work out their own destiny in their own way. This is all that they seek. It is all that we, the member States of the United Nations, seek for them.

UNLAWFUL USE OF FORCE*

*With Carl Gershman and Rosanne Klass

The present debate in the United Nations on the situation in Afghanistan marks the fifth time that the General Assembly has met to consider the Soviet Union's invasion of that country and its continuing effort to subjugate the Afghan people by force. The fact that our deliberations, by this time, follow an established pattern must not be allowed to detract in any way from the urgency and the extraordinary significance of the issue before us.

On one level, the continuing war conducted by the Soviet Union against the people of Afghanistan poses a challenge to the ability of the United Nations effectively to defend the bedrock Charter principle prohibiting aggression against the territorial integrity and political independence of member states. But on another level, the continuation of the war, which will shortly enter its fifth year, is a tribute to the heroism of the people of Afghanistan.

As of today, November 22nd, the Soviet war against the Afghan people has been fought 35 days longer than the Soviet Union's participation in the

Address before the UN General Assembly, November 22, 1983.

struggle against Nazi Germany during World War II—what the Soviets call the "great patriotic war." The fact that the Afghan people have been able to resist an adversary so much more powerful militarily and so ruthless in its use of force is testimony to their fierce pride and unsurpassed courage. But this war, which is truly Afghanistan's great patriotic war against the Soviet Union, has taken a devastating toll on the Afghan people, hundreds of thousands of whom have been killed and millions of whom have been forced to flee their homeland.

It has been said that Afghanistan can be destroyed but cannot be conquered. Unable to subdue the Afghan freedom fighters, the Soviet forces have launched ruthless campaigns against the general populace—leveling entire villages, burning harvests, killing livestock and taking cruel reprisals against Afghan civilians. Areas that once exported foodstuffs now suffer food shortages and, in some cases, actual starvation.

The chronicle of the rising level of violence inflicted by Soviet occupation forces against Afghan civilians recalls images of Guernica and Lidice. This violence, which has included torture, mass executions, rape and civilian massacres, has been painstakingly documented and strongly condemned by independent international humanitarian groups, including the Permanent Tribunal of the Peoples, which met last December in Paris, and the International Conference on Afghanistan, which was held in Oslo in March.

Of all the dozens of witnesses who testified at the Paris meeting—among them journalists, doctors, experts on weaponry, representatives of humanitarian groups who had secretly visited Afghanistan, Afghan victims and other eyewitnesses—none presented more compelling testimony than three men from a village in the Logar valley near Kabul. They described in harrowing detail how Soviet troops entered the village on September 13, 1982 and deliberately burned to death 105 villagers, including many small children, who had taken refuge in an underground irrigation tunnel. According to one of the witnesses, the Soviet troops "burst into applause" after successfully sealing up and igniting the tunnel. The witnesses charged that incidents of equal brutality had occurred in other villages.

The report of the Oslo Conference, which was presented to the recent meeting of the United Nations Sub-Commission on Prevention of Discrimination and Protection of Minorities, contains many factual accounts and eyewitness testimonies of flagrant violations of basic human rights, including mass killings perpetrated by Soviet forces in Afghanistan.

The main Soviet military efforts in 1983 have included a ruthless bombing and ground campaign in the western city of Herat during the spring and summer and attacks on villages near Kabul and along the Pakistan border near Qandahar, Gazni and Jalalabad. The bombing attacks resulted in heavy civilian casualties but relatively few losses among the *mujahidin.* Herat, for example, was hit by some fifty sorties in a day in April, but the city still remains in the hands of the resistance.

Among the many reports of violence against civilians was the execution by Soviet forces in July of 20 elders in the provincial capital of Ghazni to avenge the deaths of several Soviet personnel. In October, reprisals were launched against villages near Kandahar, Afghanistan's second largest city, resulting in the death of some 100 civilians.

More recently, several hundred men, women and children were reportedly killed as a result of the Soviets' savage destruction of the small handicraft-producing town of Istalef north of Kabul. At least half the town was levelled by artillery shelling, aerial bombardments and torching by Soviet troops. Shocking but credible reports have been received from numerous sources of Soviet soldiers killing women and children with bayonets. A respected Istalef religious figure is said to have been summarily shot after a personal complaint.

Wartime devastation and the violence directed against the civilian population have forced a massive exodus of Afghans from their homes. Over three million Afghans have fled their country, while tens of thousands more are displaced within Afghanistan itself. Pakistan, which provides asylum to well over two million refugees, has handled its burden in a humane manner which is truly admirable. The United Nations High Commissioner for Refugees deserves special recognition for tireless efforts to lessen the burden by providing shelter, food and medical care to the refugees.

Finding themselves unable to defeat the Afghan resistance in its native mountainous terrain, Soviet forces have cruelly used chemical weapons and toxin weapons against freedom fighters and civilians alike in contravention of international law and agreements—and human decency. Victims tell of long and painful sickness and death following Soviet chemical attacks. Their accounts conform with those of Hmong tribesmen in Laos and Kampuchean resistance fighters who report similar attacks by Soviet surrogates in Indochina.

The Soviets also continue to use boobytrapped mines disguised as toys, cigarette packs, pens and other household objects in violation of an international convention which they signed in 1981 prohibiting the use of such cruel weapons.

The increased Soviet brutality against Afghan civilians makes a mockery of Soviet propaganda which portrays the Soviet Union as the protector of Afghanistan and Babrak Karmal as the beloved and democratically chosen leader of the Afghan nation. In fact, the Soviet invasion and occupation of Afghanistan is a clear—indeed, blatant—example of imperialist expansion, the fulfillment of a long-standing Soviet, and before that Tsarist, goal of obtaining warm-water ports on the Indian Ocean. In its effort to add Afghanistan to its collection of conquered Central Asian Khanates, Moscow unilaterally invaded the country (in December, 1979) and installed a puppet regime there. Moscow's claim that it was invited by an established government was concocted after its invasion. The Soviet Union has, in fact, never produced a shred of concrete evidence supporting its claim that an invitation was issued, and its first action in Afghanistan after the invasion was the murder, by a special Soviet assault team, of then-president Hafizullah Amin, in whose name they claimed to be acting.

The Soviet assertion that it sent its forces into Afghanistan to beat back American, Chinese and other foreign invaders is equally absurd and unsubstantiated. Not a single American or Chinese soldier has ever been found there. In a recent interview, a Soviet soldier who defected to the *mujahidin* said that he and other Soviet soldiers sent to Afghanistan were told that they would be defending the Soviet southern border against such foreign invaders. "But one or two months after I arrived in Afghanistan," he said, "I realized that I was deceived. We didn't see any Chinese or Americans." He added: "I didn't want to be part of this dirty war in Afghanistan. None of the Soviet soldiers wants to be here ... the Soviet Union should pull out its forces, because innocent people are dying on both sides."

Moscow's argument that it is fighting "outside interference" has validity only if one considers the Afghan people to be outsiders in their own country. Meanwhile, four years after the Soviet invasion, Moscow is still attempting to make Afghanistan a subservient satellite, with 105,000 Soviet troops wreaking death and destruction upon an unyielding Afghan citizenry.

Real Soviet intentions toward Afghanistan are futher underscored by its efforts to absorb the country economically and culturally into the Soviet empire. Afghanistan's natural resources, including natural gas, copper and iron ore, are being shipped to the Soviet Union to offset the cost of the occupation. New road and rail links connect Afghanistan with the Soviet Union, while the power grid in northern Afghanistan is now integrated with that of Soviet Central Asia. The effort to reshape Afghanistan's traditional culture in a Marxist-Leninist mold continues apace. In addition to the Sovietization of Afghanistan's educational institutions, thousands of young Aghans, including children aged 6 to 9, have been sent to the Soviet Union and other Bloc countries for training and indoctrination.

Such efforts to reshape Afghan culture are one indication of the total absence of popular support for the Soviet occupation, as well as for the puppet regime of Babrak Karmal which has no following apart from the tiny, splintered and despised Communist party. As a result, the Soviets and their surrogates have had to exert control through brute force and terror. The Afghan secret police, known as the Khad, is modeled after the Soviet KGB and is under Soviet direction. During the 20-month period of Communist rule preceding the Soviet invasion, the Khad and its Soviet advisers were responsible for thousands of executions, as many as 32,000 in Pul-i-Charki prison alone, according to the Paris-based International Federation for Human Rights which has conducted extensive interviews with survivors of the terror campaign. The Khad remains the most pervasive and systematic violator of human rights in areas under regime control. Through surveillance, arrest, imprisonment and torture, the Khad has instilled a pervasive atmosphere of terror.

Amnesty International recently reported that torture is used systematically by the Khad. Victims range from 16-year-old girls to persons in their sixties. Amnesty's interviews with former prisoners reveal that hundreds of students from Kabul University and high schools have been tortured during the past three years. Amnesty renewed an appeal to Babrak Karmal, which has still gone unanswered, to put an end to the torture.

With the Soviet invasion of 1979, a totalitarian, one-party state ruled by the Afghan Communists has given way to a totalitarian apparatus completely controlled by the Soviet Union. Soviet military and civilian advisers sit in almost all ministries and make or approve every decision in the name of the regime. So weak and isolated is the Soviet client regime that its tenuous control extends only over parts of some major cities. The Afghan army continues to elude Soviet and regime efforts to make it an effective fighting force. Wracked by desertions and low morale, the army remains at half its pre-1979 level, despite the use of hated press-gangs to conscript males, many in their early teens, and incentive pay scales for recruits almost equal to sub-Cabinet salaries. Defections to the resistance in fact *equal* inductions into the army.

Afghans tell of Alexander the Great defining the hero as "he who does not ask the number of his foe, but asks as to where his foe is." This description epitomizes the Afghan *mujahidin.* Enjoying widespread support among the Afghan people, the *mujahidin* have heroically held the Soviet Union at bay for four years in a tenacious defense of their homeland, their religion and their right to self-determination as a people. They have not been deterred by the military and technological superiority of the Soviet forces or by the violence that these forces have used without restraint against the population of Afghanistan. On the contrary, fully three-quarters of the Afghan countryside and populace and a third of the district capitals remain under the control of the resistance. Indeed, Moscow's efforts to subjugate Afghanistan have fostered a new sense of Afghan nationhood based partly on common ties to Islam and, increasingly, on the

Afghan nation's unbending determination to resist Soviet aggression and domination.

Nothing more clearly illuminates the aggressive nature of the invasion of Afghanistan and the utter fraudulence of the Soviet arguments defending the invasion than the universal revulsion this action has occasioned among the Afghan people. Had the reaction of the Afghan people been different— had they, for example, welcomed the Soviet troops as liberators—then surely the judgment of the international community regarding the Soviet action would, and should, be different. The norms embodied in the United Nations Charter become meaningful in their application to specific situations. It is not possible to distinguish between the lawful and the criminal use of force without first carefully examining the reasons for the use of force, the manner and duration of its use and the result.

In this respect, the use of force by the Soviet Union in Afghanistan is without legal foundation and lacks any reasonable moral or political justification. As we have already seen, the use of force by the Soviet Union was not undertaken at the request of any lawful authority within Afghanistan and resulted, in fact, in the murder of the existing president. Similarly, the countries of the region neither requested nor welcomed the action but regarded it as a blatant act of aggression and a threat to their own security and to regional stability. Nor was there evidence of any foreign involvement in Afghanistan posing a threat to Soviet security. Moreover, the Soviet action could not be justified in terms of liberating the Afghan people from internal oppression or alien domination. As the attitude and the actions of the Afghan people clearly demonstrate, the Soviet Union is an oppressor and a foreign aggressor, not a liberator. There are no reports of Afghans welcoming Soviet forces with cries of "God bless Andropov!"

On all other counts, the Soviet invasion violates the norms of international law and the fundamental principles of the UN Charter. The Soviet Union has used force without restraint and without regard to civilian casualties. It has deliberately attacked the civilian population in an effort to depopulate areas of resistance strength. Nor has it allowed the International Committee of the Red Cross or any other international humanitarian organization to establish a presence in Afghanistan or to fulfill its international function. It has not only forbidden such organizations to work in Afghanistan; it has deliberately bombed hospitals established by French doctors in an effort to drive them out of the country.

Regarding the duration of the Soviet presence in Afghanistan, the Soviet forces have already been there for four years, and Moscow gives no sign that it has any intention of withdrawing these forces in the foreseeable future. Finally, the result of the Soviet invasion is the clear and unambiguous denial of the right of the people of Afghanistan to self-determination. The argument put forward by Moscow that the Afghan people exercised their right of self-determination through the so-called Great Saur Revolution of April 1978, thus precluding the need for free elections, is ludicrous on the face of it. The argument is meaningful only to the extent that it reveals Moscow's Orwellian interpretation of self-determination as absorption into the Soviet Empire.

A careful examination of these issues not only helps clarify the illegal and, indeed, the immoral character of the Soviet invasion of Afghanistan but also exposes as intellectually pernicious and morally obfuscating any equation of this invasion with the rescue operation undertaken by the United States and six Caribbean nations in Grenada. I have no intention of discussing the issue of Grenada at this time beyond noting that on each and every point mentioned above—the attitude of the people concerned, the legal authority of the action undertaken, the stability and security of the region, the clear threat posed by foreign involvement, the effort to avoid civilian casualties, cooperation with humanitarian agencies, the announced intention to withdraw forces with deliberate speed and by a certain date, the intention to hold free elections in a manner consistent with the principle of self-determination, as well as the additional factor of the safety of innocent U.S. civilians whose lives were endangered—on all of these points and more, Grenada was as different from Afghanistan as day is from night, as liberation from enslavement, as independence from subjugation.

The failure to make such distinctions will not, as some may feel, preserve the integrity of the principle of non-use of force. Rather, it will undermine international law as an instrument for the resolution of conflict in a manner consistent with the purposes and principles of the United Nations Charter.

It is on the basis of these purposes and principles that we support the resolution before us today. This resolution outlines a fair and comprehensive solution to the situation in Afghanistan. It calls for the complete withdrawal of foreign troops from Afghanistan; the right of the Afghan people to choose their own form of government; the restoration of Afghanistan's political independence and nonaligned status; and the rights of the refugees to return to their homes in safety and honor.

My government supports these principles. It supports as well the search for a negotiated political settlement to end the tragedy the Afghan people now endure. We firmly believe that a peaceful settlement is possible, and we strongly support the efforts of the Secretary-General to find such a settlement. Indeed, the Secretary-General and his personal representative for Afghanistan negotiations, Diego Cordovez, deserve to be commended for their sustained effort to bring about an end to the Soviet occupation of

Afghanistan. We have been pleased to hear of the progress made in the UN talks, and my government will continue to support them in the context of the four fundamental principles outlined in the resolution before us today. The Soviet Union, and it alone, can insure the success of these talks by committing itself to a timetable for the total withdrawal of its troops from Afghanistan.

The elements for a fair and just settlement are in place. They have been repeatedly endorsed by the large majority of nations. The world awaits a Soviet act of good faith. The world hopes for a peaceful and free Afghanistan—an Afghanistan in which the people of that country, and they alone, shall determine their country's destiny. Surely if any people in the world has earned the right to self-determination through courage, determination, sacrifice and faith, it is the people of Afghanistan. In an age of cynicism and un-belief, they are authentic heroes. For their courage and resilience, they deserve our admiration. For their just cause, they deserve our support. And for their defense of rights which all people cherish and which constitute the foundation of world peace, they deserve our undying gratitude.

WHAT HAPPENED IN AFGHANISTAN?*

*With Carl Gershman, Rosanne Klass and Mary Tedeschi

Mr. President, the occupation of Afghanistan approaches the end of its fifth year. In the succession of special sessions and debates, this General Assembly has time and again called for an end to the occupation of this beautiful land of ancient caravans. Time and again, we have called for the withdrawal of invading forces, for the right of the people of Afghanistan to determine their own future. Yet even after five years and all these efforts, the situation remains virtually as it was in the first year of occupation—a human disaster and a military impasse. For the Soviets, the war against the Afghanistan people, the Afghan nation, has now lasted longer than the second World War, but still the Afghan people are not subjugated.

So, after five long and difficult years, the struggle in Afghanistan con-

Address before the UN General Assembly, November 14, 1984.

tinues. But we should not be too surprised at the will and determination of the Afghan people. Since at least the time of Alexander the Great, the Afghan people have demonstrated their extraordinary willingness to bear hardships and make sacrifices in long and bitter resistance against foreign invaders in all directions. They are, perhaps, the original national libera- tion movement in the true and most meaningful sense of that term. Their struggle to liberate their nation will go on.

What has happened in Afghanistan during these five tragic years? The regime of Babrak Karmal—installed by the Soviet Union during the De- cember 1979 invasion, after another communist prime minister Hafizullah Amin and all his family had been killed—has remained unpopular, weak, divided within itself. It has been able neither to increase its support throughout the country nor to win the allegiance of the Afghan people. When Babrak Karmal assumed the leadership of the government in Kabul, his strategy appeared to be to seek to gain public sympathy by blaming the evils endured by the Afghans on the previous government. Yet, he was increasingly rejected by the Afghan nation and its leaders personally. He also sought to reconcile the estranged Parcham and Khalq factions within the People's Democratic Party of Afghanistan, to institute conciliatory domestic policies, to release many political prisoners and ease political repression, to downplay the role of the Soviet armed forces and advisors, to strengthen the Afghan army, and to lay the foundation for the transforma- tion of the Afghan social and economic systems by Sovietizing the Afghan educational system and sending Afghan exchange students to the Soviet Union for training. The goal, it would appear, was a docile, client state.

What has happened in Afghanistan in the past five years? At the most general level, we may say that the goal of the occupying forces and of their puppet government has not been achieved, and few of the strategies of that government have had any success at all. Most have been total failures. Hostility to the regime of Babrak Karmal has grown, rather than dimin- ished. The overwhelming majority of the Afghan people oppose the alien system he seeks to impose. The tide of resistance continues to rise.

The People's Democratic Party of Afghanistan, the political facade be- hind which the Soviet Union attempts to exercise political control, remains fractured. Political intimidation and assassination remain facts of political life in Kabul, often blamed on the resistance in an effort to cover up the inability of the leadership of the party to bring the two factions together and to govern effectively. No matter what domestic policies are adopted, the Government of Afghanistan is unable to implement them beyond Ka- bul and a few other cities. The city of Kabul itself remains under virtual siege despite the enormous concentration of troops there. The authority of the Government of Afghanistan simply does not extend beyond these few strongholds. In fact, in one major city it is reported that the governor, to go to his office for a few hours a day, must travel in a convoyed armoured personnel carrier.

Repression has intensified after the release of some political prisoners in the early months of 1980—there are more political prisoners than ever before. The secret police, known as KHAD, are ubiquitous. The role of the Soviet advisors in every aspect of the Afghan government has increased to the point that every major decision appears to be made by Soviet advisors, not by Afghans. During the heavy fighting in the summer of 1984, the Soviet forces were forced to take over an increasingly large share of the fighting, largely because the Afghan army, rent by disloyalty, desertions, defections and indiscipline, lacks the will to fight.

What has happened to Afghanistan? Its economy has been virtually destroyed. That economy already stagnated after the April 1978 coup, but since Afghanistan has experienced wrenching economic disruption and destruction. Two years ago in April 1983, Prime Minister Sultan Ali Kashman admitted at an economic seminar in Kabul that about 24 billion Afghanis, some 432 million dollars in damage, had already been done to that country. This is one-half the total amount set for developing the country's economy during the twenty years before April 1978. Agricultural production has also declined, necessitating the importation of large amounts of grain. Severe food shortages exist in various areas of Afghanistan, in part because food has been deliberately burned and livestock destroyed. Most educated and skilled Afghans, along with millions of their fellow men, have fled as refugees to Pakistan, Iran and other parts of Afghanistan. Valleys and villages have been deserted, factories are idle, and the agricultural infrastructure developed over centuries has deeply deteriorated. The effects of all this destruction are now emerging throughout the country. Afghan Aid, a charitable organization, recently provided the results of its investigation of over 5,000 children in 30 Afghan provinces. The report estimates that half a million Afghans are in imminent danger of starvation. According to Dr. Frances D'Souza, director of the study, conditions in the developed areas of the country have been severely damaged, the standard of living for most Afghans has fallen drastically, malnutrition is widespread. Still, Afghans have not given up their fight to rid their country of foreign domination.

The human devastation more than equals the economic devastation. Violation of human rights abounds. The regime has continued its attempts to control political expression and also the flow of information. It has relentlessly pursued its efforts to Sovietize Afghan political life and the social fabric of the country. Arbitrary arrests, detention and torture continue to be commonly practiced by the ubiquitous security and police forces. Due process is completely absent for persons accused of political crimes. Homes are searched and robbed by armed soldiers without warrants. "Press gangs" roam the streets looking for recruits into the Afghan army. Kabul saw a new wave of executions of suspected mujahidin over the summer. In the countryside, the Soviets have increased their policy of arbitrary retaliation against villages suspected of harboring mujahidin fighters. Tales of brutality to children, to ordinary civilians are ubiquitous too.

What has happened to Afghanistan? Information is not easy to come by. No humanitarian organizations are permitted to operate in Afghanistan. The International Committee of the Red Cross has not been allowed in Kabul since 1982. Selected journalists, who report favorably on the Soviet Union and the Afghanistan regime, are permitted to operate in the country. Other journalists do not fare as well, and are subject to capture and imprisonment, without the usual international norms of trial and consular access. The experience of the French journalist, Abouchar, has recently demonstrated the hazards of attempting to function as a journalist in this environment. Two other French journalists were told in Islamabad only last month: "I warn you, and through you, all your journalist colleagues, stop trying to penetrate Afghanistan with the so-called guerrillas. From now on, the bandits and the so-called journalists accompanying them will be killed."

Since last spring, Soviet forces have launched major operations throughout the country. In late April, the sixth major offensive in the Panjsher Valley was launched using, for the first time since World War II, high-level, saturation bombing from airplanes based in the Soviet Union, driving out inhabitants, emptying valleys, swelling the tides of refugees already forced to flee their homes.

What has happened in Afghanistan? As of 1983 there were a million and a half Afghan refugees in Iran. Some four million others have fled to Pakistan, and an estimated two million more are displaced within Afghanistan itself. Thus in five years, almost half the population have fled from their homes and sought refuge in internal or external exile. What accounts for this mass exodus, which one member of the International Rescue Committee called "refugee movement that is historically unparalleled?" What accounts for it is what has happened in Afghanistan. Throughout the country, fighting and skirmishes of heavily armed occupation troops against virtually unarmed civilians continue. But in spite of Soviet air power and increased involvement of Soviet military forces, the will of the mujahidin has not been broken. Intense fighting raged throughout the summer. Recent visitors describe Andahar, Afghanistan's second largest city, as a living cemetery; Harat as a ghost town.

But nowhere has the strength and resilience of the Afghan resistance been more apparent than in Kabul, where, during September and into October, the mujahidin have become increasingly effective in challenging Soviet control of the Afghan capital, a virtual armed camp. In Afghanistan, we see confirmed the truth of political philosophers who have observed that conquest cannot serve as the stable base for the possession and exercise of political power. Rousseau said it: "the strongest man is never strong enough to be always master unless he transforms his power into right and obedience and to duty." Conquest is achieved by force and violence, by armies wielding weapons, by invasion and occupation, but the transformation of might into right is achieved by persuasion, by persuasion of a claim to legitimate rule. In Afghanistan, we see again that rulers may achieve power by force, but that simple possession of power does not obligate submission—it may even obligate resistance. The Afghan people—invaded, overrun, murdered, occupied—resist. Their resistance is a modern legend. Slated for incorporation, absorption, secularization, the Afghan people refuse to acquiesce in the destruction of their society, culture, themselves as a nation.

What has happened in Afghanistan? Why were the Afghan people subjected to this terrible suffering to begin with? Why did the Soviet Union invade Afghanistan anyway? Obviously, the people and Government of Afghanistan constituted no threat to the security of the U.S.S.R. Indeed, it is difficult to imagine how an independent Afghanistan could conceivably have posed a threat to the Soviet Union. For decades, relations between the Soviet Union and Afghanistan had been a model of peaceful co-existence of two countries with different social and political systems. Afghanistan, a member of the non-aligned movement, had no ties to other governments which might have caused concern to Moscow. It neither sought nor received weapons from Soviet adversaries. It did not seek to proselytize a fundamentalist revolution among neighboring peoples. Violence and anarchy in Afghanistan did not threaten the peace of the region. Indeed, there was no turmoil in Afghanistan before April 27, 1978, when a violent coup marked the beginning of the effort to impose on the people of Afghanistan a foreign ideology and an alien way of life. There was no invitation, no request for Soviet help from the Afghan government, whose leader was murdered by invading forces. There was no welcome from the Afghan people, and five years later there has been no withdrawal of occupying forces.

Why did the Soviet Union invade Afghanistan in the first place? Perhaps history best explains it. Those who believe the Soviet Union is, at base, a contemporary embodiment of historic Russian goals, see the Afghan policy in that light. Since the time of the czars, it is said by those who argue along that line, Russian leaders have pursued the dream of a warm-water port on the Indian Ocean. Domination of Afghanistan is, thus, essential to the fulfillment of historic territorial aspirations. A century ago, Afghans recognized these territorial aspirations. Abdur Rahman, Amir of Afghanistan, wrote: "The Russian policy in Asia is that, in any way, rightly or wrongly, friendly or unfriendly, with peace or war, the Islamic kingdoms should be washed away ..." If contemporary Soviets do, as some people believe, live out old age aspirations in Afghanistan, so do contemporary Afghans. Afghans live out historic Afghan predictions in their resistance to conquest. Rahman also wrote of his people one hundred years ago: "Whether trained soldiers or simple peasants, (they) would all sacrifice every drop of blood till the last man was killed, in fighting for their God, their Prophet, their religion, their homes, their families, their nation, ... their liberty and independence." Day after day, contemporary occupying armies experience the fulfillment of Rahman's prophecy that day after day contemporary Afghans realize.

For five long years, the Afghan people, who are surely among the most courageous and independent in the world, have demonstrated their determination to remain a people. What can the rest of us learn from this harsh experience? We can note and remember the incredible courage and endurance of the Afghan people. We can affirm that their battle is not lost, that their struggle is alive in Afghanistan's valleys, and mountains, and in this world body.

The proposed resolution and expected vote in this Assembly are a reflection of the views of us all against the outrage that continues in Afghanistan. What can we do to help? We can remember the needs of the Afghan people, of the Afghan refugees in Pakistan. We can remember what that government—the Government of Pakistan—has done to ease the plight of the Afghan refugees. We can applaud the humanitarian work of the United Nations High Commissioner on Refugees, of the World Food Program, of private voluntary agencies who labor without recess to assist the millions of refugees. We can support their efforts. We can note and appreciate the contributions of all those volunteers, of the Government of Pakistan, of the United Nations and other bodies to the survival of the Afghan refugees huddled on the borders. We can vote for the resolution that is offered here in this body.

It is not too difficult to conceive a solution for Afghanistan's problems. In fact, the basis for our solution is present in the resolution on which we will vote in this body. The United States supports the resolution on Afghanistan before us. We believe its four major elements offer the basis for a negotiated settlement that will be just and viable, one in which the legitimate security interests of all the parties will be protected.

These elements are the immediate withdrawal of foreign troops; the preservation of the sovereignty, territorial integrity, political independence, non-aligned character of Afghanistan; the right of the Afghan people to determine their own form of government and to choose their economic, political and social system free from outside intervention, subversion, coercion or constraint; and the creation of the necessary conditions which would enable the Afghan refugees to return voluntarily to their homes. We believe this is a basis for an honorable solution which serves the interests of all parties.

What else can we do? We can support the steady and untiring efforts of the Secretary-General and his personal representative, Mr. Diego Cordovez. They have made progress in defining a settlement and how it might come about. As President Reagan said in his address to this body on September 24 of this year, the United States strongly supports the efforts of the Secretary-General and his personal representative. We welcome the announcement that those efforts will resume in 1985. We support, too, the strong efforts the Government of Pakistan has made to seek a solution through this medium. We believe that these efforts offer the base for hope that a negotiated political settlement can be found which will end the terrible war against the Afghan people. We believe that the people of Afghanistan, of Pakistan, the people of the Soviet Union would profit greatly from such a peaceful solution. We very much hope that the processes here in the General Assembly contribute to that end.

THE FATE OF AFGHANISTAN*

*With Carl Gershman and Rosanne Klass

Summary

The Soviet occupation of Afghanistan and the Afghan resistance to it continue, as they have over the past five years, but with a difference. Both sides are stronger; the fighting is more intense. Changes in Soviet force

Congressional Task Force on Afghanistan, Washington, D.C., March 11, 1985.

profile and tactics are the result of the Red Army and associated Soviet elements (the air force and KGB units) taking a greater role in the fighting. The armed forces of the Democratic Republic of Afghanistan (DRA) remain ineffective and unreliable, frustrating Soviet efforts to build it up. The mujahideen exhibit continued improvement in armaments, coordination, and capability. Over the past six months, compared to the winter season in previous years, fighting within Afghanistan, and cross-border violations by Soviet or DRA forces against Pakistan and Iran have increased. There is a good reason to expect that combat in Afghanistan will continue to intensify over the next several months. The costs are bearable to the Soviet Union.

Soviet strategy

Moscow's primary thrust has been to seek a military solution to the problem of maintaining a totally pro-Soviet regime in Afghanistan. The Soviets are aware that they are far from such a solution and are clearly prepared to conduct a very long struggle. They understand that the only reliable military forces are Soviet ones, but they hope in the long run to transfer more of the fighting burden to Afghans. Some Soviet officials appear to believe that control of the country—aside from key cities—cannot be gained by Soviet forces as presently committed, but Moscow is apparently not at this time prepared to make the substantially larger commitment that would be needed for victory. Soviet military activities in Afghanistan for the past several years has consequently represented a search for more effective tactics rather than a campaign for an early victory.

Soviet forces in Afghanistan have increased over the last year by about 10,000 to approximately 110,000-115,000. These troops are supported by some 30,000-35,000 active duty troops across the border in the Soviet Union and under a command based in Tashkent. These arrangements facilitate the occasional operational use of forces, and increased use of aircraft, based in the U.S.S.R. The bombers which carpet bombed the Panjshir Valley during last spring's offensive were staged directly from the Soviet Union.

In addition to the marginal numerical increase, Soviet forces in Afghanistan have been strengthened by the deployment of troops better suited to counter insurgency operations, improved equipment and firepower, and upgraded air support. Spetznaz (special forces) are making their presence felt by their unconventional attacks on the mujahideen. Military police-type units are being utilized for screening traffic on the highways and for urban patrol duties in Kabul. Hardware improvements have included the arrival of more artillery and rocket launchers, including some not previously used in Afghanistan. The Soviets have been further strengthening and hardening their bases and facilities, and improving their logistical network—investments indicative of a readiness to remain in Afghanistan for some time to come.

Refinement of Tactics

Soviet forces are displaying more organizational and tactical flexibility and operational presence. The realization that the pursuit of the mujahideen will remain a Soviet responsibility until, if ever, an effective Afghan military can be developed, has produced more activity by Soviet forces in 1984 than at any time since immediately after the invasion. The Panjshir 7 offensive last spring, confirmed this new role. In the last six months the Soviets have taken the initiative in smaller actions as well. Spetznaz and other forces have conducted ambushes of mujahideen supply columns and encampments, sometimes operating at night. Airdropped flares facilitate these nighttime sweeps. Heliborne assaults have become more common.

The Afghan Military remains worse than useless in the counter-insurgency. It is still a major source of munitions for the mujahideen, who have adjusted their tactics to enable them to derive the greatest benefit in deserters and arms transfers. More regime garrisons would have been overrun by the guerrillas if they weren't perceived as a non-threatening source of supplies. Troops desert at every opportunity, sometimes en masse. One Afghan division reportedly lost 900 men, including officers, at a single stroke. Problems of replacing the deserters and the insufficiency of press-ganging caused the DRA to offer reduced terms to volunteers. An ill fated scheme to recruit high school students backfired, as over half failed their exams in order to avoid going to the army.

Most important, despite concentrated efforts such as training in the Soviet Union, the Soviets have been unable to build a large ideologically committed cadre in the DRA Armed Forces to whom they could eventually hand over the protection of the regime. The majority of leftists in the military belong to the Khalq faction of the Peoples Democratic Party of Afghanistan (PDPA). Even their loyalty is suspect due to their dissatisfaction with the Soviet-installed Parcham ruling faction and resentment of the heavyhandedness of the Soviet advisors.

Partly to mollify Khalqi officers, but also probably as a mark of their general dissatisfaction with the performance of the DRS military, the Soviets removed the Minister of Defense. Abdul Zader, a Parcham leaning pragmatist was replaced in December 1984 by Nazar Mohammed, identified with the Khalq. Mohammed had trained in the Soviet Union and in fact had spent most of the past two years there, despite being nominally Air Force Commander, possibly to keep him out of the intraparty strife.

Combat over the past years has been concentrated in or around the major cities, in the Panjshir Valley, and in border areas, particularly near the Pakistani frontier. Security of Kabul remained the focus of regime concern. The mujahideen were able to reduce security through assassinations, small group attacks on regime posts, and frequent rocketing of the city. However, by imposing heavy security, the regime and the Soviets were able to forestall any resistance activity in the capital on the fifth anniversary of the Soviet invasion or during the January 1985 celebrations of the 20th anniversary of the founding of the PDPA.

The mujahideen downed several aircraft, including a Soviet IL-76 heavy transport. The Soviets suspended IL-76 flights and have adopted defensive measures for all aircraft coming into Kabul. The city's sky is regularly lit by flares ejected from Soviet/Afghan aircraft, in the hope of thwarting the heat-seeking SAMS. The resistance exploded a bomb at Kabul airport, killing 31, mostly Afghan students bound for Moscow.

In the Panjshir Valley, Soviet and Afghan forces conducted offensives in November and in December. These have been sometimes called Panjshir 8 and (less frequently) 9, although they were much smaller in size and scope than the April campaign. The main objectives were to consolidate control of the lower valley taken last spring, to capture Mosood or to keep him off balance and to make it more difficult for him to attack the highway which links Kabul to the Soviet Union. The highway has usually remained open, as a relative abundance of goods in Kabul will testify.

The other major theatre was near the Pakistani border, in the provinces of Paktia and Paktika in the southeast and Kunar in the northeast. The Soviets have made a major effort to control resistance infiltration routes, thus far with little success. In Kunar, Barikot remains surrounded, and subject to constant mujahideen fire from the surrounding hills. Further south in Paktia, major battles have raged around Jaji (Ali Khel), Chamkani and other nearby posts. DRA troops rarely venture out of garrison, much less interdict supply efforts, substantial operations by Soviet forces have had little more success.

Border Violations

One result of the fighting near the border is a continuing high level of Soviet/Afghan violations of Pakistani territory by reconnaissance flights, bombing attacks and shellings. There have been dozens of incidents over the past six months and hundreds of casualties. The incursions of early mid August may have been a form of pressure, associated with a whole range of general pressures, exerted on Pakistan to be more flexible in the August session of the Geneva talks, and the increased violations as a whole may be construed as general pressure on Pakistan. Nevertheless, it appears that the bulk of the violations (both overflights and attacks) are tactically related to combat in adjacent areas of Afghanistan.

Developments in the Resistance

Operational cooperation among the diverse fighting groups inside Afghanistan continues, but despite a variety of efforts, the parties in Peshawar are as divided as ever. The leaders of the moderate alliance retain their support, derived from their traditional religious legitimacy and tribal affinity, inside Afghanistan. The fundamentalist parties field more, and in general better fighters. Neither alignment appears disposed to cooperate with the other, though there is increasing evidence of some tactical alliances between fighting units in Afghanistan.

Each side experienced a major initiative, designed to foster unity. Moderate alliance agreement on a role for ex-king Zahir Shah is not shared by the fundamentalist groups. A broad based *loyah jirga*, or council was apparently planned after the haj, but had to be called off, for lack of consensus, particularly on a role for the King. The idea of a *jirga*, however, remains alive. Attempts to promote Sayyaf as the supreme leader of the resistance have not worked. Sayyaf faces opposition within his own fundamentalist alliance.

Inside Afghanistan, operational cooperation even between associates of the fundamentalist and moderate parties, was especially evident in Paktiya, Kandahar, and Balkh provinces, and elsewhere throughout the country. Fighting between groups continues, resulting, for example, in the disruption of supplies to the Panjshir. In the Hazarajat, pro-Khomeni groups, with Iranian support, have managed to wrest overall control from traditionalist, more broadly based Shi'a factions. Foci of resistance related to or under a single command have been forming and expanding, regardless of party affiliation, throughout the country.

Regime Highlights

The Karmal regime neglected to note the fifth anniversary of its installation (and the Soviet Invasion), but instead concentrated on the 20th anniversary of the founding of the PDPA, celebrated in Kabul the third week of January. Honored guests included the Chairman of the Communist Party of Uzbekistan (the official Soviet representative), mid-level officials from a variety of pro-Moscow Communist Parties, and an emissary from newly elected Rajiv Ghandi.

The most important regime change was the replacement of Defense Minister Abdul Qader with General Nazar Mohammed. Interfactional maneuvering continued, amidst rumors of a crackdown on the Khalq.

Economic and Social Developments

Afghan trade and aid are ever more oriented toward the Soviet Union, although a variety of goods from many countries can still be bought in the Kabul Bazaar. Scattered reductions in precipitation, and the effects of the war, including some instances of deliberate Soviet/regime destruction of crops and agricultural infrastructure, have caused food shortages in some areas. Reduction in rural incomes due to drops in cash crop production, and limitations of the distribution system, particularly in areas outside regime control have exaggerated the problems, where they exist. Relative to the reduced population, overall food production is not significantly diminished and the snowpack for next year appears adequate for traditional agriculture purposes.

The U.S.S.R. continues its attempt to mold an Afghanistan in its own image. This long term Sovietization process is focussed on institutions and youth, and will take decades to have an effect. In the last six months the Soviets have expanded their programs to train Afghans in the U.S.S.R. One program will take thousands of Afghans below 10 years of age to the Soviet Union for up to 13 years of schooling. The first batch of nearly 1000, mostly war orphans, departed this fall.

International Developments

The fifth anniversary of the Soviet invasion was observed throughout the world. With the concommitant increase in press attention this produced an increase in international public awareness of the Afghan problem. One result was the increase in public pressure for concerned governments to provide humanitarian and other assistance to the Afghans.

Another important development was the capture by the DRA of French journalist Jacques Abouchar, who had been travelling with the mujahideen. Pressure from the French government, media, and the French Communist Party culminated in Abouchar's release, the episode proving an embarrassment to Kabul. Shortly thereafter, the Soviets and Afghans warned journalists with imprisonment and death for covering the war from the resistance side.

In November, the United Nations voted, by the biggest margin yet, for the annual Pakistan-sponsored resolution calling for the withdrawal of foreign forces from Afghanistan, self-determination, non-alignment, and the return of the refugees. In December the Organization of the Islamic Conference voted a similar package, couched more forcefully and naming the U.S.S.R. Both fora called for a negotiated settlement. Still, the war continues. Soviet policy shows no signs of change.

Soviet Policy

Moscow has from the outset looked upon diplomatic activities as an adjunct to military operations. Diplomacy presently centers upon the UN-sponsored "proximity" meetings in Geneva, the last in August 1984 and the next scheduled for May 1985, delayed because of Pakistan elections. The Soviet position regarding this process has not changed. Moscow insists that prior cessation of "outside interference" in support of the mujahideen is a precondition for any Soviet troop withdrawal and it stands firm that the question of troop withdrawal is a bilateral issue to be discussed only with its Afghan client. The Kabul regime itself is not subject to international discussion.

The Soviets have been willing to keep the UN effort going because it enables them to hold at bay international demands for a negotiated settlement and to maintain the claim that the key to the Afghan problem lies in stanching the flow of supplies to the mujahideen through Pakistan and Iran. There appears to be little present chance that Moscow will alter its terms.

From Moscow's viewpoint, the most serious international problem relating to Afghanistan is the continuing and growing strength of the mujahideen. It is to be expected that Soviet pressures against Pakistan will continue, both in the form of the diplomatic pressures of which the UN talks are a part and in the form of cross-border bombings and other military action.

Moscow probably considers the diplomatic consequences of the Afghan war to be reasonably acceptable. Many of the sanctions imposed by various countries after the invasion have been lifted; if Moscow still suffers from some international isolation it is a factor of ineffective Kremlin leadership and not the result of any embargo imposed from outside.

The Afghan war has created some domestic problems for the Soviets, but none appear to be unmanageable. The economic burden of the war does not appear to be unacceptable. Direct military expenditures pertaining to Afghanistan probably amount to less than one percent of the Soviet military expenditures, and even this is offset by gains in combat experience, equipment testing, and the like. Related economic assistance to the Babrak regime has probably not yet reached the levels granted to the major client states of Cuba and Vietnam.

There have been occasional reports of efforts by potential conscripts to avoid service in Afghanistan but this and related problems caused by the growing number of casualties and returning veterans are probably also manageable under the Soviet system. There has been a very slow growth in Soviet media coverage of the Afghan war, recently resorting to patriotic literary allusions and even occasionally featuring articles describing individual heroism in combat. This coverage seems of late to be preparing the populace for a long and bloody haul in Afghanistan. However, the principal image conveyed to the Soviet citizen is still one of a limited deployment whose role is more in civic action and humanitarian assistance than in combat.

Soviet Goals

To understand what the Afghan war means to the Soviet Union and why they remain it is necessary to understand why they invaded to begin with.

Why did the Soviet Union invade Afghanistan?

Not to eliminate a threat to the security of the Soviet Union. No threat existed. For decades the Soviet Union had described its relations with Afghanistan as a model of peaceful co-existence, as proof of how the Soviet Union could live next to small neighbors without interference.

Not to prevent the threat of Muslim fundamentalism from spreading to the Soviet Union's Central Asian provinces. The traditional Islam of Afghanistan did not threaten either the Soviets or the Afghan communist regimes. As long as the government left traditional patterns undisturbed, the Afghans remained indifferent to this form of government.

Not to install a communist government. A communist government had already been installed when the April 1978 coup eliminated the Daoud regime and brought the Khelqi Communist to power.

That regime could not be faulted for lack of zeal since it had set about trying to transform the Afghan society. It is true that the effort produced opposition and resistance from traditional Afghanistan. That resistance occurred moreover at a time of an unprecedented period of Soviet expansion when Soviet analysts were convinced the world forces had shifted in their favor.

Imperial Expansion

It is difficult to avoid the conclusion that the Soviet Union invaded Afghanistan because they intended to incorporate that country. Following the fall of Saigon the expansion of Soviet influence proceeded rapidly in Asia, Africa, Central America, creating new satellites and client states in far flung places such as Angola, Mozambique, Ethiopia, Benin, South Yemen.

This expansion proceeded through subversion and proxy forces not through the direct use of Soviet military forces. The Soviet invasion of Afghanistan was the first direct use of Soviet military forces outside the Soviet bloc since World War II. For the first time since World War II the Soviet Union invaded an independent country. That invasion, launched on Christmas Eve of 1979, altered the climate and the course of world politics, severely aggravated tensions between East and West, and had an important effect on the prospects for continuing stability in South Asia and the Persian Gulf.

The invasion has rent the fabric of Afghanistan, driving nearly half the population of Afghanistan into internal or external exile, devastating the Afghan economy, threatening now to produce a famine of major proportion. It has also tied down approximately 150,000 Soviet troops in Afghanistan and across the border. In spite of a large Soviet investment of men and material and relentless pulverization of Afghan society, the Afghan army remains utterly unreliable and its mujahideen forces have improved their organization capabilities and effectiveness. Soviet casualties have been high, and their objective still eludes them. This has left some observers—especially American observers—speculating that the Soviet Union may be stuck in its own "Vietnam," a quagmire that spreads its resources, bleeds its army, and promises failure.

A Soviet "Vietnam"?

There are, I believe, fundamental flaws in the various "Vietnam" analogies.

First, "Vietnam" was a problem for the United States because of the response of American public opinion to the continued war. Vivid information on the casualties was not only available, it was virtually inescapable; criticism of U.S. government policy was not only possible, it was ubiquitous; organized opposition was widespread and effective; periodic elections provided an opportunity to express popular dissatisfaction with Vietnam policy.

All these conditions depend on democracy and a democratic political culture. None prevails in the Soviet Union.

Second, there is a profound difference in Soviet and American time frames. If the goal of Soviet strategy is transformation of Afghan society and politics, they have already made substantial progress. What Louis Dupree has called "migratory genocide" and the "rubbleization" of

Afghanistan is advanced. Chemical weapons, carpet bombing, pillage, destruction of irrigation networks, destruction of crops, levelling of villages, have had the effect of expelling, disorganizing, demoralizing the population. A massive program of separating eight-and nine-year-old children from their parents and sending them to the Soviet Union for "education" is preparing a new generation.

The Soviets have sometimes been clear about their goals, and about their long range character. "Time changes everything," one official noted. "In another ten or twenty years the new generation of Afghans will view our presence differently."

The short range time frames in which we think about foreign policy are profoundly ill-suited to understanding Soviet goals. Our assumptions about public opinion and foreign policy are equally misleading, and our own lack of interest in territorial expansion makes it difficult for us to imagine Soviet goals and policies in Afghanistan.

It seems likely that the Soviet goal in Afghanistan is incorporation of Afghanistan and achievement of a warm water port and geopolitical access to Iran and Pakistan. The Soviet claim is that it is providing "fraternal assistance" to Afghanistan with its "limited military contingent." Some observers hear in these assurances an ominous echo of those given by the Soviet Union to two of Afghanistan's neighbors who were once the independent Moslem states of Khiva and Bokara and are now part of the Soviet Union.

They have already taken significant steps in the direction of the military, economic and social integration of Afghanistan into the Soviet sphere. Soviet military officers are learning the Baluchi language.

The Soviets have consolidated their military, transport, and communications infrastructure, including the expansion of existing air fields and the completion of the bridge across the Amu Darya River. They have tightened their grip on the strategic Wakhan corridor which rests on Pakistan's northernmost border and links Afghanistan with China, and they have tied Afghanistan's economy tightly to those of the Soviet Bloc through a proliferation of economic and trade agreements.

Perhaps most significant is the Soviet effort to reshape Afghan culture and to replace the decimated intellectual and middle classes with a new elite trained in the Soviet mold. Thousands of Afghans, including even children between the ages of six and nine, are being trained in the Soviet Union and other bloc countries, while the Afghan education system itself is being restructured along Soviet lines. The Sovietization of Kabul University is made evident by the presence of Soviet advisers at all levels of administration and instruction and in the preference given the party activists in admissions. The curriculum of Afghanistan's primary education system has been redrawn to promote indoctrination in Marxist-Leninist ideology and to prepare young Afghans for further study in the Soviet Union.

Afghanistan would not be the only prize. Babrak Karmal promised in May 1982 that before long the Afghan Army would be capable of playing a role "not only in Afghanistan, but in the region as well." Some strategists, including Rosanne Klass, believe "There can no longer be any doubt that Soviet moves in Afghanistan since 1978 have been aimed at creating a strategic base from which to control Iran, Pakistan, the Persian Gulf and the Indian Ocean." "If Pakistan can be collapsed, or neutralized and detached from Washington, by threats," Klass wrote, "the Soviet Union will effectively dominate the vast area from the Horn of Africa to the Strait of Malacca without having fired a shot."

The major Soviet air bases have been built in Afghanistan; more are in the works. All are aimed at Pakistan and beyond.

The Reasons for Assistance

The fate of Afghanistan is profoundly important—for humanitarian reasons, political reasons, and for geo-strategic reasons.

The Afghan people have been gassed, bombed, buried, driven from their homes, and now they may be starved. "Aid workers with experience in famines" the *Economist* reported, "say that Afghanistan is sliding toward disaster." "About 500,000 people in Afghanistan are in imminent danger of starvation," Dr. Frances D'Souza reported to Freedom House.

Obviously, there are important valid humanitarian reasons for assisting Afghanis, inside and outside Afghanistan.

The resistance of the Afghan nation to incorporation, its struggle to survive, is a challenge to the carefully cultivated image of Soviet invincibility. Soviet triumph in Afghanistan is not inevitable. Defeat of the mujahideen is not inevitable. The expansion of Soviet power in the region is not inevitable.

The final consequences of Soviet goals and Afghan resistance are not known and are not even predictable. But it is clear that support for the survival of the Afghan people is a moral and a geo-political necessity. And it is also clear that victory or surrender are not the only alternatives facing the Soviet Union.

The UN General Assembly's resolution passed last year by the largest margin ever contains four major elements offering the basis for a negotiated settlement that will be just and viable, one in which the legitimate security interests of all the parties will be protected.

The elements are the immediate withdrawal of foreign troops; the preservation of the sovereignty, territorial integrity, political independence, non-aligned character of Afghanistan; the right of the Afghan people to determine their own form of government and to choose their economic, political and social system free from outside intervention, subversion, coercion or constraint; and the creation of the necessary conditions which would enable the Afghan refugees to return voluntarily to their homes. We believe this is a basis for an honorable solution which serves the interests of all parties.

The United States supports the efforts of the Secretary-General and his personal representative, Mr. Diego Cordovez. We support, too, the efforts the Government of Pakistan has made to seek a solution through this medium. We believe that these efforts offer the basis for hope that a negotiated political settlement can be found which will end the terrible war against the Afghan people. We believe that the people of Afghanistan, of Pakistan, the people of the Soviet Union would profit greatly from such a peaceful solution.

Cambodia's Right to Self-Determination*

*With Carl Gershman

Our purpose in meeting here today is both clear and urgent:

- to uphold the right of the Kampuchean people, as of all people, to self-determination;
- to restore Kampuchea's sovereign identity and national independence;
- to bring stability, peace, and development to Southeast Asia, an area that has suffered destruction, violence and death for too long.

In each of its two preceding sessions the General Assembly, by overwhelming majorities, has found the Socialist Republic of Vietnam in violation of fundamental provisions of the United Nations Charter—the inviolability of the sovereignty, independence, and territorial integrity of

Address before the UN General Assembly, October 19, 1981.

nations, non-interference in the internal affairs of other nations, and the inadmissability of the threat or use of force in international relations. A conference mandated by last year's Assembly has reaffirmed these findings, and proposed a program to restore Kampuchea's independence, its territorial integrity and sovereignty, and to allow Kampuchean people freely to choose their own form of government.

Almost three years have passed since the Socialist Republic of Vietnam, supported and financed by the Soviet Union, first invaded and occupied Kampuchea, and nearly 200,000 Vietnamese troops still occupy that grief-stricken country. The people of Kampuchea, ravaged by a succession of horrors, including three decades of war and the savage devastation of Pol Pot, must now endure conquest and occupation by their historic adversaries. Vietnamese forces and administrators stand above the law. They deny all human rights to the conquered Khmer people. Vietnamese penetration of the country is broad and deep. Vietnamese advisors work in Phnom Penh and in rural areas, each Khmer province has a sister province in Vietnam to "assist" it. All ministries have Vietnamese advisors who hold final decision-making power. Kampucheans willing to work for the Vietnamese puppet regime have been paid in internationally-provided relief commodities; rural Khmer not employed by the regime are left to fend for themselves. Naturally, economic breakdown has accompanied Vietnam's alien, imperialistic government. An unofficial landbridge spanning the Thai-Kampuchean border, and established over the objections of Vietnamese authorities, has rescued some one million Khmer from starvation.

But while the people of Kampuchea are the principal victims of Vietnam's aggression, they are not the only victims. The people of Vietnam itself, indeed all the people of Southeast Asia, suffer from the oppressive tyranny of the Vietnamese government. The pursuit of an unpopular war has caused widespread misery within Vietnam; and imperialist adventures have necessitated escalation of the already scandalous level of oppression inside Vietnam. Not surprisingly, then, thousands of Vietnamese continue to flee their country each month, risking pirates, storms, and rejection, citing government repression, unreasonable controls on daily life, stepped up military conscription and deteriorating economic conditions as their reasons for leaving. Once again misery and insecurity engulf the region, and the people of non-communist Southeast Asia, having only recently emerged from a conflict of 30 years' duration, face a precarious future as their governments divert resources sorely needed for development to stregnthen their defenses against the possibility of further Vietnamese expansionism.

Vietnam's aggression also confronts the rest of us here in the United Nations with a grave challenge. If Vietnam can invade, subjugate, and occupy a neighboring state, by brute force and with impunity, and retain the prize of its aggression, then the security of all members of this Assembly is substantially diminished. Aggression feeds on aggression: It is the great lesson and the warning of history. It is hardly necessary to note that aggression is no more tolerable because its perpetrators claim to have been "invited in" by a regime that did not exist until it was set up by those same aggressors. Vietnam's actions threaten to establish an ominous precedent whose consequences should be of especial concern to the smaller, non-aligned members of this body.

How has the Socialist Republic of Vietnam justified this travesty against the Kampuchean people? What defense has it offered for this threat to its other neighbors in Southeast Asia, this affront to the vital principles of international order, reaffirmed in this case specifically by two General Assemblies? It has answered as tyrants always do: with a great lie, for tyranny abhors truth and is sustained only by lies.

Representatives of Vietnam have responded to the clearly expressed will of the overwhelming majority of the members of this organization by accusing that majority of interference in Kampuchean affairs. They have rejected the legitimate role of the United Nations in seeking a solution to this international tragedy, and have attempted to portray Vietnam's aggression as a rescue mission undertaken at the behest of the Heng Samrin regime. Vietnamese efforts to justify their invasion and occupation of Kampuchea are both disingenuous and incredible, and only serve to bring their nation into further disrepute.

Vietnam's claim to have acted at the behest of the Heng Samrin regime is absurd on its face. The Heng Samrin regime, which according to Hanoi invited Vietnamese forces into Kampuchea, and whose permission Hanoi piously claims is required in order to withdraw Vietnamese forces from Kampuchea, is, of course, a Vietnamese creation whose power is maintained by Vietnamese weapons. That government did not even exist at the time of the invasion; its so-called invitation to the Socialist Republic of Vietnam had to be issued retroactively, after the Vietnamese forces had already invaded and occupied Kampuchea. In this as in other respects, the Vietnamese invasion of Kampuchea is strikingly, tragically analogous to the Soviet invasion of Afghanistan. Indeed, the new imperialism can be recognized everywhere by its aggressiveness, its violence, its contempt for truth.

Vietnam's attempt to pose as the liberator of the Kampuchean people is a particularly clumsy masquerade that has fooled no one. All of us remember that it was precisely that government of Vietnam that assisted the accession of the Pol Pot regime to power in the first place. All of us remember that, at a time when many of our governments were bitterly critical of the Pol Pot regime for its notorious human rights violations, it was the government of Vietnam that staunchly defended Pol Pot's human rights record. In this and in other forums, Vietnam persisted in its defense of the Pol Pot regime, right up to its invasion of Kampuchea late in 1978. Thus, Vietnam's contention that its invasion of Kampuchea was prompted by a solicitude for the human rights of the Kampuchean people is the kind of falsehood that is as offensive as it is egregious.

Instead of rescuing the Kampuchean people from oppression, the Vietnamese have demonstrated a cruel, cynical disregard for their welfare. It was Vietnam's invasion which precipitated a massive famine throughout Kampuchea, bringing starvation and further devastation to a people that already had suffered all too much. It was Vietnamese-imposed authorities who then endeavored, first to deny the very fact of the famine to potential donors of relief outside of Kampuchea, and then to obstruct the efforts of international organizations and other donors to provide desperately needed relief to the people of Kampuchea. This callous policy has forced hundreds of thousands of Khmer to flee their ancestral homes for Thailand, and for the border no-man's land. By in effect hurling these Khmer on their neighbor's doorstep, Vietnam and its Kampuchean puppet regime have abdicated the most basic responsibilities of government. That the refugees who have left Kampuchea for Thailand, or for the relative safety of the Thailand-Kampuchea border, remain there for fear of returning to Vietnam-dominated Kampuchea, is the clearest possible demonstration of the true character of Vietnam's self-styled "liberation."

It is a marvelous tribute to the United Nations that its specialized agencies have been able to meet this massive humanitarian challenge. When I visited the border camps last August, I felt and have said repeatedly that seeing their good work made me proud of the United Nations and proud of my country's contribution to the agencies that carry it out. I was, therefore, especially pleased when that great honor, the Nobel Prize for Peace, was awarded to the Office of the United Nations High Commissioner for Refugees. The High Commissioner, Mr. Paul Hartling, and those who assist him deserve the gratitude of the international community for their efforts on behalf of the victims of war and political tyranny.

Reviewing the arguments advanced by Hanoi to justify its aggression, one can only marvel at their lameness, their utter lack of plausibility. In fact, no arguments, however artfully constructed, could possibly obscure the reality that the government of Vietnam, financed and supported by the Soviet Union, has conquered a member-state of this organization. It refused to comply with repeated General Assembly resolutions calling on it to withdraw its forces. It refused to attend the International Conference on Kampuchea mandated by the General Assembly to seek a solution to the

Kampuchean problem. It profoundly compromised its own integrity and independence by making itself an instrument of Soviet ambition in Asia.

Mr. President, a majority of the nations of the world have clearly asserted and reiterated that they will not acquiesce in Vietnam's aggression. Neither will they forget it. They have rejected Vietnam's threadbare rationalizations, and have formulated a concrete program to restore Kampuchea's independence, territorial integrity and sovereignty, a program which will allow the Kampuchean people to choose their own government. The declaration of the International Conference on Kampuchea, held last July, judiciously addresses the needs of all parties, and provides a reasonable, practical and wholly honorable basis for a negotiated settlement of the Kampuchean problem:

It calls for a UN-supervised withdrawal of all foreign forces from Kampuchea.

It makes full provision for the legitimate security needs of all the countries of the region, including Vietnam.

It contains safeguards to insure that armed Kampuchean factions would be unable to prevent, disrupt, intimidate or coerce the outcome of free elections.

It emphasizes the need for an independent Kampuchea to remain neutral and non-aligned.

And it calls upon the government of Vietnam to participate in the negotiating process that can lead to a peaceful solution to the Kampuchean problem and a restoration of peace and stability to Southeast Asia.

In addition, through its ad hoc committee, and through the possibility of its reconvening whenever needed, the Conference represents a continuing mechanism to negotiate a settlement in Kampuchea.

Mr. President, the declaration of the International Conference on Kampuchea was formulated by the countries of the region with the advice and unanimous approval of the delegations present, who comprise a majority of the United Nations membership. We believe the General Assembly should now formally express its strong support for the declaration by its vote on the present resolution. We call upon the government of Vietnam and its Soviet patron to heed this Assembly's urgent plea for justice and compassion, and to join in negotiations designed to resolve the tragic plight of the people in Kampuchea and end the threat to the peace and stability of Southeast Asia. Surely, the Kampuchean people, and all the people of Southeast Asia, are entitled to more from life than endless conflict and constant turmoil. Surely they deserve our unremitting efforts to restore peace, independence and security to their strife-torn region.

Mr. President, the principles of self-determination, of national independence, of non-aggression—the principles on which this organization was founded—have never been more centrally involved than here, in the continuing occupation of Kampuchea. The integrity of the United Nations as well as the well-being of the Kampuchean people are therefore involved here this morning.

REJECTING PUPPET STATES

The United States continues to support the credentials of Democratic Kampuchea on technical grounds. Democratic Kampuchea's credentials are clearly in compliance with the General Assembly's rules of procedure. This fact has been recognized by the Secretary General in his report to the Credentials Committee, which has accepted the Khmer credentials. The past three General Assemblies also have affirmed this.

The United States support for Democratic Kampuchea's credentials is based on the ground that, in the absence of a superior claimant, there is no basis for rejection of Democratic Kampuchea's credentials, which have been accepted since 1975. There is no superior claimant. Certainly the Heng Samrin regime is not a superior claimant. It was created by Vietnam's invasion of Kampuchea four years ago, and is sustained by Vietnam's occupation force. It is controlled by Vietnamese officials both in Phnom Penh and in Hanoi. The Vietnam which would have us reject Democratic Kampuchea's credentials is also, we would underscore, the Vietnam which continues to defy three successive General Assembly resolutions on Kampuchea as well as the Declaration of the International Conference on Kampuchea, all of which call for the withdrawal of her troops and the end of her occupation of Kampuchea.

Support by the United States for the credentials of Democratic Kampuchea does not diminish our concern for human rights violations in Kampuchea, particularly from 1975 to 1978 during Khmer Rouge rule. The United States has repeatedly spoken against these heinous abuses and gross misrule of the Khmer Rouge and will continue to disassociate itself from those responsible for them.

However, this year the United States welcomes the broadened base on which Democratic Kampuchea rests as a result of the formation last June of the Coalition of Democratic Kampuchea. Now, with the inclusion of Prince Sihanouk as President and Mr. Son Sann as Prime Minister, the

Address before the 37th General Assembly, October 25, 1982.

Coalition of Democratic Kampuchea is clearly more representative of the Kampuchean nation.

We welcome the participation of Prince Sihanouk and Prime Minister Son Sann in the deliberations of the General Assembly. We have been impressed with the response given to this new leadership by the Khmer people who have an alternative to the grim choice between the Khmer Rouge and a regime imposed by Vietnam. The inauguration of the Coalition also constitutes a major step in implementing the General Assembly's basic policy for a resolution of the Kampuchean crisis—that embodied in the Declaration of the International Conference on Kampuchea held in July, 1981 and in GA resolutions 34/22, 35/6 and 36/5.

Prince Sihanouk, in addressing this assembly three weeks ago, put succinctly Kampuchea's plea to the United Nations:

> We ask but restoration of our national sovereignty, our territorial integrity, and once that is achieved, we solemnly commit ourselves to live in perfect, peaceful co-existence with all our neighbors, and amongst the first with Vietnam, as will all other countries who respect us, no matter what their political and social systems may be. Is this an unreasonable demand, an impossible pretension?

My government believes it is neither unreasonable nor impossible. It is rather the minimum that this body must support in line with its own past commitments, with the principles of the United Nations Charter, and with the peace and stability of Southeast Asia.

CAMBODIA'S TRAGEDY

A principle purpose of this United Nations is to preserve the right to self-determination, independence, security and sovereignty of all nations. The Charter is clear, so is the history of the United Nations in emphasizing and encouraging self-determination and independence of nations. The United Nations can, indeed, be proud of its role in advancing self-determination for millions of people and in working to preserve the independence of all nations. There is no principle that was more widely shared or more basic than that one nation should not use force to invade and subjugate another people.

Address before the 39th General Assembly, October 30, 1984.

The people of Cambodia, however, continue in occupation by a foreign power, denied their right to self-determination and independence by the Socialist Republic of Vietnam, which invaded and continues illegally to occupy Cambodia. Five times the world community has called on Vietnam to withdraw its illegal expeditionary force and to restore to the Khmer people their right to seek their own destiny under a freely chosen government without outside interference. The overwhelming margins which have supported the General Assembly's call for withdrawal of foreign forces reflect the concern of the great majority of the world's nations at the continuing tragedy in Cambodia.

What has occurred in the wake of these resolutions:

Hanoi, aided and abetted by the Soviet Union, ignores those resolutions, continuing its illegal occupation of Cambodia and its oppression of the Cambodian people in violation of the Charter of the United Nations and in defiance of the expressed will of the General Assembly, offering to the Cambodian people no opportunity for self-determination or self-government. The need to address the situation in Cambodia for the sixth time is testimony to the stubborn policy of military conquest and colonization being pursued by the Socialist Republic of Vietnam.

During the past two decades, Cambodia's people have endured unmatched suffering. Hanoi's use of Cambodian territory in its war against the South and the war between the Khmer Republic and the Communist Khmer Rouge, aided by Hanoi, destroyed Cambodia's economy. Khmer Rouge victory in 1975 brought a horror the world still struggles to comprehend. Systematic political murder and starvation took the lives of more than one million Cambodians and nearly destroyed an ancient culture.

The Socialist Republic of Vietnam must bear a full measure of responsibility for the tragic tyranny of the Khmer Rouge. Vietnam's support was critical to the Khmer Rouge victory in 1975. Hanoi's claim that it invaded Cambodia to liberate the Khmer people from Pol Pot and that it remains there only to prevent his return to power is a transparent deception. Vietnam deposed Pol Pot only when it became apparent that it could not dominate and control the Khmer Rouge. No one laments the demise of the Khmer Rouge, a regime detested universally. But Hanoi did not invade Cambodia for the purpose of returning Cambodia to its people. Instead, Vietnam did so in order to install a puppet regime largely comprising former followers of Pol Pot, including the hated Heng Samrin himself.

Now, the Cambodian people are threatened with the loss of their homeland and the extinction of their culture. Thousands of Vietnamese nationals have settled throughout Cambodia, abetted and encouraged by Hanoi. Independent observers have estimated their number to exceed 500,000. Vietnam's clients in Phnom Penh have been instructed to assist

Vietnamese, both former residents and new immigrants, in any way possible and to consult with their Vietnamese superiors before taking any action affecting Vietnamese settlers. Vietnamese immigrants are also given extraterritorial status and many have reportedly received Cambodian citizenship. This officially sanctioned Vietnamese immigration raises serious questions about Hanoi's long-term intentions towards Cambodia. It will be the ultimate tragedy if Cambodia, decimated by war and famine, should now be extinguished as an entity, overrun, submerged and colonized by its expansionist neighbor.

Nearly 250,000 Khmer civilians remain encamped along the Thai-Cambodian border, unable or unwilling to return to their homes. Assistance to them remains an international responsibility. The United States will continue to do its share and urges other nations to continue their support for this program of humanitarian assistance. We offer our sincere appreciation to the Secretary-General and his Special Representative for Humanitarian Assistance to the Kampuchean People, Dr. Tatsuro Kunugi for their efforts on behalf of the Khmer people uprooted by invasion and war. The staffs of the United Nations Border Relief Operations, the World Food Program, the United Nations High Commissioner for Refugees, and other specialized United Nations agencies, the International Committee of the Red Cross, and the various voluntary organizations continue their important and untiring work in providing emergency food and medical care to the displaced Cambodian people, often under dangerous conditions caused by Vietnamese attacks. Their efforts have earned the commendations of the international community and our admiration. Special thanks are also due to the Royal Thai government for its aid to the Khmer people, particularly during the fighting earlier this year.

Vietnam's invasion and occupation of Cambodia is a challenge to the United Nations system and to the international community. The challenge is to induce Vietnam to withdraw its army and to restore Cambodia's independence, sovereignty, and neutrality without permitting a return to power of the Khmer Rouge. The members of the Association of South-East Asian Nations (ASEAN) have provided the world the leadership to meet that challenge here at the United Nations and beyond.

The 1981 UN sponsored International Conference on Kampuchea, in its final declaration, worked out the principles which must guide a settlement of the Cambodian problem: a cease-fire and withdrawal of all foreign forces under UN supervision; free elections under international auspices; and arrangements to insure that armed groups do not interfere in free elections and respect the results of those elections. Ninety-four nations participated in that conference. Its principles have been endorsed by five successive resolutions of the General Assembly. They provide the best basis for meeting the challenge posed by the Cambodian crisis. The United States supports these principles and extends its appreciation to Mr. Willibald Pahr, Chairman of the International Conference on Kampuchea, and to Ambassador Massamba Sarre and his colleagues of the ad hoc Committee for their continuing efforts in seeking a settlement in Cambodia.

The United States affirms its support for Mr. Pahr's recent proposal to internationalize the temple complex surrounding Angkor Wat so that these ruins can be restored free from the danger of war. Mr. Pahr's proposals merit international support. The ruins at Angkor Wat and Angkor Thom represent the greatest achievements left by classical Khmer civilization and are a cultural treasure of importance to the entire world. Their destruction through neglect and war would be a tragic loss to us all. Despite political concerns, the ASEAN nations have endorsed Mr. Pahr's initiative. Unfortunately, Phnom Penh and its Vietnamese masters have denounced the proposal. It is not surprising that Hanoi shows no interest in preserving these relics of Cambodia's glorious cultural heritage. But it is sad that Hanoi's Cambodian clients are unable to assert enough independence even to save the enduring symbol of Khmer civilization.

Vietnam, unfortunately, rejects the reasonable proposals of the ICK (the International Conference on Kampuchea), insisting that the situation in Cambodia is irreversible. ASEAN has sought to work out the framework of a settlement which preserves the legitimate security concerns of Cambodia's neighbors, including Vietnam, as long as the key elements of Vietnamese withdrawal and free elections are preserved. The September, 1983 ASEAN "Appeal for Kampuchean Independence," proposed a territorially-phased Vietnamese withdrawal, coupled with an international peace-keeping force and reconstruction aid in the areas vacated, as part of a Vietnamese commitment to a complete withdrawal and elections. Hanoi rejects this proposal, insisting that it will maintain its clients in Phnom Penh for as long as necessary until the world finally accepts its domination of Cambodia. Hanoi ultimately seeks, then, the legitimization of its client regime.

But that regime clearly does not represent the Cambodian people and its pretensions to do so have been repeatedly rejected by the people of Cambodia, by its neighbors and by the General Assembly. Vietnam no longer offers its clients as claimants to Cambodia's seat at this Assembly. Their regime remains dependent on Vietnamese soldiers and Vietnamese officials to remain in place. The growing appeal of the nationalist organizations led by Prince Norodom Sihanouk and former Prime Minister Son Sann is indicative of the fact that the Khmer people are unwilling to accept a regime established on the bayonets of a foreign army. The United States welcomes the presence in this debate of Prince Sihanouk and Son Sann. They and the organizations they lead are the true embodiment of Khmer nationalism and the hopes of Cambodians for a future which is neither Khmer Rouge nor Vietnamese.

To what lengths will Vietnam's rulers go to impose their will on others? The war in Cambodia, and the confrontation with China it has engendered, have drained Vietnam's economy. With a per capita income far lower than any of its ASEAN neighbors, indeed, one of the lowest in the world, Vietnam supports the world's third largest standing army. Unable to pay the costs itself, Vietnam has turned increasingly to the Soviet Union for assistance. Massive Soviet aid meets Hanoi's military needs but cannot meet the needs of the Vietnam people, thousands of whom have risked their lives to flee in small boats rather than remain in a Vietnam oppressed and destitute. Other nations have reduced their aid because of their opposition to Vietnam's occupation of Cambodia. Moscow has traded on its aid to increase its military presence in Vietnam, establishing now a major air and naval base at Cam Ranh Bay and underlining the falseness of Vietnam's claim to be a non-aligned nation.

Even Vietnam's rulers have begun to realize that their efforts to control Cambodia have failed and that they face an increasingly difficult situation. In recent months Hanoi has tried to demonstrate to the world its willingness to reach a political settlement. In speeches and interviews, the Vietnamese Foreign Minister has hinted at Hanoi's willingness to negotiate a settlement at a conference and its willingness to consider peacekeeping activities in Cambodia.

Genuine Vietnamese willingness to negotiate a settlement in Cambodia based upon the principles of the International Conference on Kampuchea and successive resolutions of the United Nations would be a welcome development, above all, for the Cambodian people. But Hanoi apparently still views a political settlement simply as a means, one more tactic, to legitimize its client regime and secure it against the threat from the Cambodian resistance. Then, Vietnam says, it will withdraw the "bulk" of its army. The world rejects this concept of a settlement and will continue to reject it.

It should be noted that Vietnam put on its "peace mask" in March of this year during its Foreign Minister's trip to Indonesia and Australia. Days after his return to Hanoi, the Vietnamese army launched its dry season offensive along the Thai-Cambodian border. In March and April of this year, Vietnamese forces launched a series of assaults, backed by armor and heavy artillery, against the civilian encampments, there forcing more than 80,000 people to flee to safety inside Thailand. Nearly 50,000 of these civilians still remain in temporary encampments, unable to return because of the ever-present threat of Vietnamese shelling or attack. Even as Hanoi talks of a settlement and negotiations today, the Vietnamese army is building up its forces near Thailand, threatening the civilian encampments which house 250,000 Cambodians. New units have moved up near the border and artillery fire continues to threaten the residents of these camps. It is an ominous harbinger for the coming dry season, which may begin only days after this General Assembly completes its work. The world will mark Vietnam's actions in Cambodia as well as hear its words.

In time, the Cambodians' quiet, heroic determination will convince its leaders that they cannot subjugate the Khmer people. We hope that realization will lead to a settlement of the Cambodia problem to the satisfaction of all parties, most importantly the Cambodian people. The way to a fair and just settlement has been shown by the international community. The General Assembly resolutions on Cambodia, the 1981 International Conference on Kampuchea and ASEAN's "Appeal for Kampuchean Independence" all outline a basis for a comprehensive settlement for Cambodia involving complete withdrawal of foreign forces, UN supervised free elections and non-intervention and non-interference in Cambodian internal affairs. Such a settlement would guarantee a free and neutral Cambodia and constitute a threat to none of its neighbors. It would also end Vietnam's international isolation, restore Vietnam's dignity and freedom of action and permit Vietnam to turn to the task of building its own economy and uplifting the living conditions of the long-suffering Vietnamese people.

The United States looks forward to that day, and in the meanwhile, offers its full support to the efforts of the Secretary-General and his representatives, to the ASEAN countries and, above all, to the people of Cambodia in their struggle.

THE UNITED STATES AND ASIA

Those two great indicators of one nation's involvement with another, war and trade, provide all the proof that is needed that American ties to Asia have become so multifarious in this century, so complex, so intertwined, that they are today already part of the national fabric.

Three times in the last half century, more than in any other part of the world, the United States has fought a bloody war in Asia. Asia's role in our trade is no less important. In 1980, for the first time in our history, U.S. trade with the countries of Asia surpassed trade with any other region in

Address before the Asia Society, New York, New York, April 14, 1981.

the world, including Western Europe. Making policy toward Asia is, then, one of the primary tasks of any American administration. It is rendered more delicate by the memory, still vivid for many Americans, of the bitterly controversial questions that have surrounded aspects of our Asian policy three times since World War II: Who "lost" China and how? Who involved us in a "no-win war" in Korea? Who was responsible for our disasters in the Vietnam War?

Obviously, Asian policy can arouse intense passions and has; it can produce lethal political folly and has. How then should we think about the distant lands that are so important to our prosperity, our politics, and our peace?

I am not a specialist on Asia. I have no special responsibilities for Asian policy in this administration. The comments that follow, therefore, take Asia as an example of a more general orientation which I believe informs our approach to foreign policy. That general orientation begins and ends with the concrete. It eschews the abstractions that mystify relations among nations.

George Orwell noted that the whole tendency of modern prose is away from concreteness. We of the Reagan administration propose to try to reverse that tendency. We agree with the famous European philosopher of the past century who held that the concrete is the real and the real is the concrete. The more complicated the reality, we believe, the more intense the temptation toward, and the greater the cost of, oversimplification.

The language of contemporary politics is filled with abstractions that complicate the intellectual problems they purport to illuminate. None of the verbal prisms through which we view reality are the source of greater distortions than those simple, putatively geographic concepts, North and South, East and West. Many of the difficulties that engulf the contemporary world ensue when we attempt to understand the world and make policy by way of these metaphysical and meta-empirical terms. Nowhere is their power to distort reality and delude us more evident than in their application to Asia.

The first striking point about the notions of North and South, East and West is, of course, that although they purport to describe geographic categories, they do not do so. Not all the countries south of the equator fall into the category termed "the South." Australia and New Zealand are good examples of exceptions. Certainly, Asia itself does not fit neatly in the geographic category "South."

It may be argued that I am belaboring the obvious, that everyone knows that North applies not to geography but to a condition of development defined, above all, in economic terms and that, understood in this fashion, Asia is still *under*developed. But that too is not true.

Some Asian countries feature a subsistence level, land-based economy, low mobility—social and geographic—and the poverty and primitive technology associated with what are often termed "underdeveloped" societies. The Brandt Commission identified as the world's poorest countries some twenty-nine nations, several of which lie in southern Asia. The OECD defines southern Asia as including eight nations—India, Bangladesh, Pakistan, Burma, Afghanistan, Sri Lanka, Nepal, and Bhutan—where the average income is about $150 per capita. Although some notable successes in economic development have been registered in these countries, too many people live in these parts of Asia for a good life to be possible with their existing technologies, and many live barely above the level of subsistence, utterly vulnerable to every natural disaster.

The concept of South might have been modeled on these nations, and they are an important part of Asia. Yet they are no more Asian than the countries of the region that have achieved an advanced stage of industrialization, large exports of manufactured products, and a wide enough distribution to have an important internal market. I speak, of course, especially of Japan, Singapore, Hong Kong, Taiwan, Korea. The meteoric rise of Japan to the status of an economic giant with a gross national product surpassing $1 trillion is well known to all—a fact, by the way, that proves that democratic capitalism is not irrelevant to all except Western countries. It has now become clear, moreover, that the Japanese achievement was not an anomaly with no relevance for the rest of the region.

South Korea's 10 percent annual income growth from 1962 to 1976 is unprecedented and unequaled. Korea's extraordinary increase in exports was accompanied by distribution policies that encouraged the dramatic expansion of internal markets. Singapore, whose per capita income now stands at approximately $2,700 a year, and Hong Kong, which is not far behind, are nations in which the dynamics of continuing progress have been securely established. In consequence, their futures appear as bright as their past. These nations are as different from the stereotype of "South" as nations could be. There is almost no policy imaginable that would be equally relevant to all the Asian nations we have so far mentioned, and we have not even yet referred to China. Although progress has been most dramatic in Japan, Singapore, Hong Kong, Taiwan, and South Korea, notable strides have also been made in Malaysia, Thailand, Indonesia, and the Philippines. It should be emphasized, moreover, that the social, cultural, political differences are, if anything, even more pronounced than the economic ones. But if Asia is neither North nor South, still less is it East or West.

Whether we focus on how they organize their economies or on their relations to the Soviet Union, we are forced to recognize the diversity of the Asian nations and the undesirability of thinking about policy toward them in terms of an East-West dichotomy. Some of those nations—Afghanistan,

Vietnam, Laos, Kampuchea—are indeed linked to the Soviet Union. Moreover, 80,000 Soviet troops in Afghanistan and many thousands of Vietnamese in Kampuchea guarantee that these nations will remain linked to the political empire that is so often termed "East." But east of them lies China, which also features a command economy and is not integrated into the Soviet empire. To the contrary, China provides in itself a particularly striking example of the inappropriateness of trying to deal with Asia in terms of any simple East-West dichotomy. Although a socialist country, it has in recent years allowed a much greater scope to market forces within its economy and increasingly has recognized the indispensability of productive economic relations with the market areas of other nations and has planned for rapid modernization. Over 55 percent of China's trade is now going to the United States and Western Europe, to Japan and the non-Communist countries of Southeast Asia.

The United States, of course, welcomes the steps that the Chinese have taken toward liberalizing their economic and political systems and welcomes their expanding ties with us and the other nations of our region. Indeed, the Reagan administration has committed itself to a relationship with the People's Republic of China based on the Shanghai communiqué and the communiqué normalizing relations between the two countries. Given the mutual good will of the American and the Chinese people, the relationships which have begun so recently will continue to expand and develop, while we maintain our cordial relationship with Taiwan on the basis of the Taiwan Relations Act.

Suppose then that we agree that these simple concepts, North and South, East and West, do not apply to the lands ranging from Iran in western Asia to Japan in the Far East, lands that are the home of 2.5 billion people comprising, incredibly enough, 56 percent of the world's population. Suppose we agree that the remarkable diversity of these nations makes it difficult to set forth any valid generalizations about the Asian continent, except that it is different from some other parts of the world. Suppose we agree that sensible policy cannot rely on these categories. What then should we do to rid ourselves of this misleading intellectual framework? How are we to make language describe rather than distort reality?

The answer must be to ground our thinking and our policies in what Edmund Burke described as "due attention to the concrete circumstances which give to every political principle, its color and discriminating effect." To purge ourselves of disabling, distorting, and ultimately defeating intellectual habits we should recommit ourselves to knowing what we mean. The reward should be clearer thinking and better policy, for, as Orwell also said, thinking more clearly is the prerequisite to political regeneration. In this administration we are firmly committed to clearing away the trampled intellectual underbrush that blocks the path to political regeneration.

5
Coping in Africa

The Problem of Namibia

Because a free press is indeed the absolutely essential ingredient of a free society, absolutely essential to democratic institutions, it is a very special pleasure to be associated with the celebration of the responsible coverage by a free press of the multifarious events in the world.

Since my very recent university experience has been mentioned, I may note that the transition from the classroom to the cabinet, from the critic to the criticized, from a strictly private person to a not so private person, is traumatic as well as dramatic. I often feel, to paraphrase both the president and the late W.C. Fields, that altogether I think I'd rather be at Georgetown. However, I'm not. Instead, I am at the United Nations, which is a very odd place. I'm trying to learn a new language there.

As everybody in this room also knows, I'm sure, all professions have their own language or, if you prefer, their own jargon. They develop distinctive words and phrases and acronyms to describe their distinctive activities and problems. As a newcomer to the United Nations and to the diplomatic world, one moreover who cares as much as you do about words, I'm aware of the importance of learning the rudiments of that new language of the new profession and world in which I am involved—new modes of communication as well. Indians prefer smoke signals, Victorians wrote letters, teen-agers rely on telephones; with diplomats, I've learned, nothing is regarded as having really happened unless it's been sent and received by cable; and I've also learned that those cables are collectively called "the traffic" and that reading "the traffic" is a very important activity of diplomats and related persons. I now start reading "the traffic" at about 7:30 every morning. "The traffic" communicates in a language of its own that features very odd abbreviations. I read, for example, within the first

Address before the Overseas Press Club, New York, New York, April 29, 1981.

day or two that I was at the United Nations, a cable which said "See GOL ASAP." I thought to myself, "Who in the world is GOL ASAP, and how will I know where to find him?" It took me a little while to figure out that GOL ASAP meant " government of Lebanon as soon as possible." It's an example of the problem. There isn't even a glossary or a vocabulary list that goes on the back of the cables. You just learn as you go.

I also have learned that, among other things, the United Nations, and diplomatic missions and diplomats in general, do not become "involved" in issues or active in relation to them, they are "seized" of them. Now, in the beginning I found this very odd. It's an interesting expression, as anybody interested in words knows, because being "seized" by something suggests that it's not something one wills, not something that happens by a deliberate act, but something that one is struck by, if you will, like a fit, possessed by some sort of outside force, which operates independently of anyone's desires. More and more, I may say, that seems to me to describe accurately the condition of that world body in which I now reside vis-à-vis certain issues which claim the attention of all of us there and develop a life of their own.

Right now, as we say at the United Nations, we are seized of the Namibia question, which has riveted the attention of that world body for at least a week, most intensively the last week. It has become the occasion on which some twenty-five or so—depending on the day you count them—foreign ministers descended from Algiers, where they had (among other things) received and discussed *The Council on Namibia Report,* which (among other things) called for severe, comprehensive, mandatory sanctions against South Africa for having blocked the Geneva Conference of last January, which it was hoped would bring independence to Namibia under the United Nations plan embodied in Resolution 435. Another interesting thing about reading United Nations documents is that they almost always include references to at least seven other resolutions, which, if you take documentation seriously, involves you in a process of infinite regression. Tonight I am not going to tell you about all the other resolutions to which you get referred if you look up Resolution 435. If you are really interested, you can check them for yourselves.

There are various interesting aspects of the current discussion, but two are especially so. One is that, like the other discussions I have witnessed more than participated in, in my brief time there, this one seems, first, to have moved beyond the control of virtually all the key participants; and second, it seems to have at best an ambiguous relationship with the putative goal of the exercise, which is to achieve independence for Namibia. It's a fascinating process—watching a United Nations initiative take on a life of its own. It reminds me a bit of watching someone throw a basketball in a fast-moving game. Once the ball is in the air, it develops a momentum of its own and frequently has an unpredictable outcome decided by the skills of the players and by unpredictable interactions among them.

The United States and I, seized of the issue of Namibia, are confronted by two quite different questions. The first is, What can we do or should we do to help bring independence to Namibia? And the second question is, What can we do and should we do *in the United Nations* in relation to the Namibia debate? The distinction between the two questions is important.

The United Nations, like most political arenas, structures whatever passes through it. I don't have to tell a group of journalists that the medium often shapes the message. The United Nations, which was established as a problem-solving institution, of course, sometimes becomes part of the problem. In the past few days I have become almost convinced that it would be easier to create an independent, stable, democratic Namibia than to participate constructively in this United Nations debate, which presumably has that as its goal. I will come back to this matter, but first I'd like to touch on a prior question which occurs to me as I take part in this extraordinary process.

The question is, Why, of all the issues the nations in the world might confront and deal with, why is the United Nations seized with Namibia? Why is the United Nations not dealing, for example, with the Libyan invasion of Chad, which deeply disturbs and threatens neighboring countries, or with the Soviet threat to Poland? Why is the United Nations not dealing with the more than a million destitute and desperate African refugees? Why is it not dealing with the destruction of Lebanon? Why does it focus so much attention, so intensively, on a territory with fewer inhabitants than there are refugees in Africa today?

It is an interesting question. The reason apparently is that the United Nations is an institution that specializes in certain kinds of issues, among which "decolonialization" is central. In fact, it specializes in certain kinds of decolonialization. Another qualification for becoming a major issue, one that remains in the forefront of United Nations attention, seems to be that the issue not be seriously linked to a major concern of a major power. It is probably relatively safer for the United Nations to focus on the "continuing illegal occupation" of Namibia (as they say there) than on the continuing illegal occupation of Afghanistan. So be it. We must, at least for now, play it as it lays; so we are seized with Namibia.

What *is* Namibia anyway? As I am sure everybody here knows, it is a large, ethnically heterogeneous territory, rich in minerals, poor in political experience. Namibia has been an intermittent matter of concern to the United Nations since 1947. It has a white population that comprises about

12 percent of the total and one dominant tribe, the Ovambo, who comprise about 47 percent of the total population. It has a tiny black and colored middle class. It is a society in which most of what is worth having is securely held in the hands of the Afrikaaner, the German, the English, that is, the white population.

As everyone knows, Namibia is still ruled by South Africa, a medium-sized power which, though important in Africa, does not constitute a major threat in the international arena to anyone except its immediate neighbors, whom it worries a great deal, and some of its own population, whom it worries in a different way. But it is not a major power, and that, surely, is one reason it is safer for the United Nations to focus on it than on Afghanistan.

Vis-à-vis Namibia, the Reagan administration confronted on arriving in office a failed conference, a ruptured negotiation. We were not in a position to start from scratch on this issue, but neither could we merely continue. In approaching this issue we formulated goals. Our principal goal, as we have stated repeatedly, is independence for Namibia. The United States is not a colonial power. We are committed to national independence and self-determination for all people. We desire independence for all African states, indeed for all the states in the world, among which we would like to see an authentically independent Namibia. That is not our only goal. Namibia has the largest known uranium deposits in the world, and a second goal we have is to prevent this mineral-rich territory from being permitted to slide into the Soviet sphere of influence, which has expanded markedly in Africa. A related strategic goal is to keep the vital waterways around Namibia out of hostile hands. A third goal we think about in connection with Namibia is that dealing with the problem of Namibia should not inhibit our good relations with surrounding African nations or our good relations with our allies with whom we associate on this problem in the Western Contact Group.

Our goals are complicated by the presence of more than 30,000 Cuban troops in neighboring Angola. Although many argue that the independence of Namibia will more or less automatically produce Soviet-Cuban withdrawal from Angola—why would the Cubans stay, it is asked, if the MPLA no longer needed to worry about South Africa?—we doubt it. We tend rather to believe that the Cuban troops remain in Angola because of UNITA's resistance to the MPLA as much as because of fear of South Africa's coming over its border. We think they stay in the area, also, because the Soviets desire a forward position there. In sum, then, the United States has multiple goals vis-à-vis the region; achieving those goals is complicated by the very high feelings of the various parties to the conflict.

Being a political scientist whose profession is the analysis of political problems, I am led next to identify the actors who are involved in this problem. One of these actors is SWAPO. Now SWAPO, as everyone knows, is a coalition whose ethnic base is the Ovambo, who constitute about one-half of the Namibian population. SWAPO is the oldest, best-established party devoted to independence in Namibia. Like a great many "national liberation movements," SWAPO is a mixed bag, which contains some merely nationalist elements, some persons who are simply dissatisfied with the present government, some persons of undefined ideology, and some who are enthusiastic supporters of Marxism-Leninism and closely tied, by training and connections, to the Soviet Union, which is the principal source of arms to the movement.

There are other political parties in Namibia, including the DTA or Turn-halle Alliance, a predominantly white and multiracial party historically tied to South Africa. Neither it nor any of the other parties seems to be as strong as SWAPO, though one cannot accurately estimate the popular strength of a group in the absence of either free elections or careful opinion polls. Since neither is available here, we have no reliable information about the popular support for these groups. We do know, however, that there is a powerful tendency in the politics of Africa for party preference to follow tribal identification.

South Africa, of course, is also a major party to this conflict. It too is an ethnically heterogeneous, mineral-rich nation—the most powerful in the area—which is a democracy on top and an authoritarian system on the bottom. It is a democracy for the whites and an authoritarian system for everyone else. South Africa's white population identifies strongly with Europe and cares about being accepted as a civilized Western nation by other Western powers. That concern, indeed, constitutes an important factor in the equation. South Africa is rich, strong, tough, and—in the purest sense of the word—racist, because it makes access to values depend on race. Still, it features a rule of law which is, of course, a protection to the population, a restraint on government, and a lever for peaceable change.

The United Nations is another party to the negotiations. It is a would-be referee with somewhat tarnished credentials. Since 1973, when the United Nations General Assembly passed a resolution designating SWAPO the sole authentic representative of the Namibian people, the United Nations has tried to serve both as a partisan for one side and as an impartial mediator. SWAPO has enjoyed permanent observer status in the United Nations, and the United Nations has dispensed millions of dollars in financial support for SWAPO under one or another of its programs. Its Council on Namibia travels all over the world "raising consciousness" on the issue. In the past the United Nations has claimed that only the General Assembly was committed to SWAPO. Recently, however, the United Nations Security

Council acted to deny the DTA the opportunity even to be heard in the Security Council—while hearing SWAPO. The United Nations contains people who are presumably capable of behaving in a fair and evenhanded fashion if they set their minds to it, but the body itself has clear-cut public commitments to one of the parties.

Other parties to these interactions are the other nations of the Contact Group—France, the United Kingdom, Canada, the Federal Republic of Germany—all of whom have very large investments in Africa, which give them a special stake in staying on good terms with as many leaders of as many African nations as possible, and a proclivity, now quite strong, for believing that "colonial" questions become more dangerous the longer they are permitted to fester.

A very important counter in this whole drama with which the United Nations is seized is Resolution 435, which has acquired the status of a sacred text. United Nations resolutions seem to take on a life of their own even though they may be viewed as quite unsatisfactory by all parties concerned with them. The fact that they have finally become a matter of consensus, if even a consensus of the moment, gives them a special status in this body, one of whose principal activities is seeking consensus. Resolution 435 provides for independence for Namibia and for free elections to be conducted under United Nations supervision. In fact, this resolution is filled with gaps. It leaves unanswered questions concerning what kind of regime will emerge and even who will govern Namibia during the period before a government is elected.

We, the United States, are another actor in this drama. What kind of government would we like? What kind of settlement would we like? One thing we would like is a framework that provides more stability than 435 alone. We would like some constitutional guarantees.

What will we, the United States, accept? We will accept anything that will achieve our goals, which, as I have said, are nothing less than an independent, stable, democratic Namibia which cannot readily be incorporated into the expanding Soviet sphere of influence. Does that mean we will accept Resolution 435? Of course it does, provided that it is completed or, augmented, so that a way is found also to provide the basic minimums of civilized government. Those basic minimums include protection for minorities and a framework that would protect Namibia's independence once it is won. Those do seem to us to be among the minimum requisites of civilized government, and we are reluctant to be parties to the construction of any government anywhere that does not provide them.

What is going to happen in that glass house where everyone throws stones? We, the United States, are going to go right on working with the problem, with our allies, with the front-line states, with South Africa, with the United Nations, and with the other interested parties. We are, I think it is fair to say, flexible, determined, and optimistic about the means of achieving those goals. I, who am by temperament not given to optimism, am quite optimistic about the possibilities today of achieving an independent, stable, democratic Namibia provided that the dynamics of interaction inside the Security Council do not destroy what diplomacy achieves. But God alone knows what we will be able to achieve in the Security Council. Immanuel Kant described the categories through which we perceive reality and their effect on what we perceive. I think that the glasses through which we perceive reality at the United Nations frequently distort the objects being examined. Perhaps the time has come to seek a new oculist.

UNIVERSALITY

The United States believes that South Africa's credentials should not be rejected and opposes the denial of South Africa's right to participate in the General Assembly.

Mr. President, the questions of procedure involved here have substantive implications of great import to the United Nations. In 1974 the United States made plain its strong opposition to the ruling of the General Assembly that by rejecting the credentials of the delegation of South Africa the General Assembly had, in effect, decided to refuse to allow the South African delegation to participate in its work. This afternoon the United States delegation reiterates its position. Involved here are the most fundamental questions of membership and the rights of membership. The fact that South Africa's intention to resume its seat today was not known is irrelevant to the exercise of these rights. Neither is it relevant that South Africa is in arrears in the payment of its financial assessments. Only the Charter of the United Nations is relevant. The provisions and requirements of that Charter should be our only guide. Under the law of Article V and VI of that Charter, a member state may be suspended or expelled from the United Nations only upon the recommendation of the Security Council as confirmed by the General Assembly. Yet depriving a member state of the right to participate in the work of the only universal, parliamentary organ of the United Nations is a principal consequence of suspension and

Address before the 35th General Assembly, March 2, 1981.

expulsion. And that is also the consequence of denying a state the right to participate in the General Assembly. Consequently, the right of participation can only be denied in accordance with Articles V and VI of the Charter.

The Security Council has never recommended that the Assembly should suspend or expel South Africa. For this reason, the General Assembly's action in 1974 was without legal foundation. On so fundamental a question as rights of membership the passing of time has not given the Assembly a better legal basis for doing in 1981 what it did improperly in 1974. No one has shown that South Africa's credentials fail to meet the requirements of the Rules of Procedure. To refuse to consider those credentials as required by the rules is to use the guise of credentials to try to accomplish a suspension that lies beyond the powers of the General Assembly.

Fair Play for Namibia

In considering this vote I should like to emphasize that the United States believes it a very important matter of principle that all individuals with relevant information to impart to the Security Council be permitted to speak under Rule 39 of the Security Council's provisional rules of procedure. We believe there are two important issues here. One is whether the United Nations, through the Security Council, is and should be willing to listen to a party to any important question before it, assuming that the application has been made according to the rules of the body. And second is whether it matters whether the United Nations and the Security Council through which it acts is willing to listen to any such group.

It seems to us that no one here tonight requests of the Security Council that it agree with the analysis or the position of the DTA, and no one asks that anyone in the Security Council support the positions or the arguments which will be made by the representatives of the DTA. We ask merely that the Security Council hear the representatives of this group of Namibians.

We do not purport to know how many Namibians support this party or any other party. We will not know the answer to that question unless or until free elections are held in that country, if indeed they can ever be arranged. We only know that some Namibians support this party and the question therefore seems to us whether the members of the Security Coun-

Address before the Security Council, April 21, 1981.

cil should stifle in this arena the expression of the DTA's opinion merely because the majority of this Council expects to disagree with that opinion. Is a majority of the Security Council ever justified in refusing even to listen to an argument of a group which some of its members desire to have heard. We think not.

We think further that the stakes here are very high. By its actions on such a fundamental matter of principle—those principles seem to me to be the most fundamental: fairness, democratic spirit, evenhandedness—the United Nations and the Security Council defines itself. The Security Council damages its capacity to act as a forum, as a peacemaker, as an impartial mediator who can be trusted to treat all parties fairly. If the Security Council were to deny the DTA the right even to be heard then the Security Council, it seems to me, damages precisely those principles on which the United Nations itself is based—the principles of reason, discussion, representation. It is as easy to damage these principles of reason, discussion, representation as it is easy to silence dissent.

I hope the members of the Security Council will consider very carefully before they vote which course, listening to the DTA or not listening to the DTA, will be most consistent with the principles of the United Nations and the peace and independence of Namibia.

Solving the Problem of Namibia

I have thought repeatedly as I followed these discussions about the goal of this meeting. It seems to me that it is time that we focus again on the goal of this meeting and this special session of the Security Council. Presumably that goal is to produce an independent, stable, self-governing Namibia. As I understand it there is no disagreement on that goal.

A number of charges have been made in the past few days and I have followed with interest those charges. There have been charges that the western countries, the Contact Group, have failed to achieve the goal of an independent, stable, self-governing Namibia. There have been charges that the western countries, the Contact Group, have failed to bring South Africa to her knees. There have been charges that the western countries are responsible somehow for the continuation of racism and colonialism in Namibia, in South Africa, indeed in Africa. It has been suggested that

Address before the Security Council, April 23, 1981.

because the Western Contact Group, like the African countries, like the Comcon eastern bloc, have substantial economic relations with South Africa, they are somehow responsible for the continuation of repression in South Africa.

I have asked myself repeatedly in the course of these negotiations and discussions how the charges which are being made here relate to the accomplishment of the goal on which we are presumably all agreed—the goal of an independent, stable, democratic Namibia. Repeatedly it has been suggested in the course of the past few days that because we have not already succeeded we should not try again, that we should try some other course than the continuing search for an internationally acceptable peace arrived at through peaceable negotiation, an internationally acceptable independent Namibia arrived at through international negotiation. It has been suggested, for example, that we should adopt some other course, such as make a declaration or commit ourselves to comprehensive compulsory sanctions. But, Mr. President, I think that if we are realistic—and if we are not realistic we waste our time and that of everyone else present—if we are realistic then we will understand that resolutions do not solve problems, sanctions do not solve problems, declarations do not make peace, declarations do not secure independence.

Is it not past time that we consider here realistically the practical, actual alternatives to a continuing search for an internationally acceptable solution in Namibia?

Mr. President, my government has no other objective than to achieve authentic independence and self-government for Namibia and indeed I believe that all the Western Contact Group has no other objective than this. We have no territorial objectives in Africa. We have no aspiration to station thousands of our troops in African countries. We have no desire to send armed surrogates to subvert the independence of the new states of Africa. We have no desire to divide this body or to divert its attention from the problem of self-government for Namibia to the creation of divisive diversions here.

Mr. President, solving problems is much more difficult than adopting resolutions, but the problem of an independent, stable, self-governing, democratic Namibia will be solved because it must be solved and it will be solved eventually only by the forces of arms or by the exercise of reason. No one has spoken much here about the true alternatives to the continued search for a negotiated, internationally acceptable solution to the Namibia problem, but I think it is past time that we face those alternatives squarely. And I should like on behalf of my government to pledge ourselves to the continued effort, at the maximum of our abilities and our ingenuity, independently and with our colleagues in the Contact Group and with our associates here in the United Nations, the unflagging search for an internationally acceptable, truly, authentically independent, stable, democratic Namibia.

No to Economic Sanctions

In the previous discussions it was suggested that here in public consultations the world could observe the attitudes of Security Council members toward Namibia, most especially toward the independence of Namibia. But, the votes which have been registered here did not reflect attitudes toward Namibia, least of all toward the achievement of an independent, stable, democratic Namibia. Those votes reflected, rather, the views of members about quite different questions. Neither did those votes reflect intentions of members concerning the future, or their future actions, concerning the independence of Namibia.

Mr. President, the voting here today in no way affects the determination of the United States or our firm intention to make every possible effort to find a way to achieve an early, internationally accepted independence for Namibia. My Government has set that as a prime goal. We have already undertaken consultations in Africa and we have met at high level with other members of the Contact Group in London. With these actions we continued a process begun years ago by our predecessors. We will continue that process in the next few days with discussions of the Namibia problem at the Ministerial level with our colleagues in the Contact Group in Rome. The next step will be the preparation of specific proposals which we would hope to discuss with the parties concerned in the near future.

In view of our efforts, Mr. President, we regret that it was felt necessary by some to press the sanctions issue in the Council, here, at this time. I asked you here last week whether sanctions were a realistic alternative to future efforts to resolve the issue peacefully by negotiation. While I understand the frustration of the African countries with the length of time involved in pursuing our common goal, my Government does not believe, and I do not believe, that frustration is cause for us now to abandon the search for effective means of achieving that goal.

Following the meeting of the Contact Group in London last week my Government participated in a joint statement that Security Council Reso-

Address before the Security Council, April 30, 1981.

lution 435 continues to provide a solid basis for a transition to an independent, stable Namibia. Throughout the past week we have repeatedly restated that view. My Government is firmly committed to make every effort to achieve an internationally accepted, lasting settlement in Namibia which will bring Namibia finally the stability, democracy, and independence she deserves.

It is for that reason that we could not support the drafts contained in documents S/14459 through S/14463. Each of those drafts, one way or another, relates to sanctions and therefore represents what we are persuaded is the wrong course toward the achievement of our common goal for independence for Namibia. We do not believe economic sanctions are an effective means of influencing political policy. We believe the study of history supports our view that they were not effective when applied against Italy in the 1930's nor against Rhodesia in the 1970's. I might mention, Mr. President, that my Government's low regard for economic sanctions as an instrument of policy was reflected in our recent decision concerning the grain embargo.

I feel I should make special mention of the resolution contained in S/14462 which would have imposed an arms embargo on South Africa. There is already such an embargo in existence as mandated by Resolution 418. The United States voted for Resolution 418 and supports the measures imposed under that resolution. We will continue to enforce the embargo. We do not at this time accept the need to adopt, in addition to 418, the provisions of S/14462.

I would like to close, Mr. President, with an appeal to all present, and to the governments of the Front Line States and to South Africa, to strengthen their own efforts to find a peaceful, negotiated solution to the Namibia problem. The people of Namibia have a right to self-determination to be achieved by free and fair elections. The parties most directly involved have agreed to those principles for a solution. We must all now find a way to implement those principles. I pledge the commitment of the highest levels of my Government to this effort. I pledge our solidarity with the people of Namibia in the search for independence.

THE PROMISE OF NAMIBIA'S
INDEPENDENCE

The events of this past weekend, in Pretoria and Maputo, are a bloody reminder, if any was needed, of the consequences of violence, and of the very real potential that today exists throughout southern Africa for the further escalation of that violence. As is all too often the case, the victims of these most recent tragic events include many who were entirely innocent and blameless. The United States deplores such acts of violence, from whatever quarter, whether perpetrated in the name of change, or in opposition to it. Violence cannot solve the pressing problems of the region. On the contrary, by creating new victims, new grievances and new grounds for anger and hatred, such acts can only increase the danger of new and greater violence, in an ever escalating cycle. Ultimately, we must count among the wounded of these acts all those who seek and hope for peaceful change through negotiation and dialogue.

My government has for the past several years been seeking to assist the governments of the region to find peaceful ways to address and to resolve mutual problems. We have been encouraged by the purposeful high-level dialogue between Mozambique and South Africa, a dialogue which the events of last weekend must not be permitted to place in jeopardy. We have made known to both South Africa and Mozambique—and, indeed, to all governments of the region—our willingness to help. We have stressed our conviction that the problem of cross-border violence, if allowed to go unresolved, will seriously endanger prospects for both stability and peaceful change.

Let it be clearly understood that the United States deplores violent cross-border activities in southern Africa, in whatever direction and for whatever stated goal. Similarly, we categorically reaffirm the principle that all states have a duty to refrain from tolerating or acquiescing in organized activities within their territory by guerrillas or dissidents planning acts of violence in the territory of another state. There can be no double standard for southern Africa. Cross-border violence cannot be condoned, whether it be in the form of a bomb placed in a crowded square in Pretoria by externally based organizations, or of the continuing violation of Angola's territorial integrity by South African forces.

Mr. President, the Security Council also bears a solemn responsibility to uphold the principles of non-violence and the settlement of disputes by

Address before the Security Council, May 25, 1983.

peaceful means. Those principles are especially pertinent to the issue which this meeting of the Council has been convened to consider.

The United States welcomes the opportunity afforded by this meeting to participate in a review of the efforts that are being made to bring about the independence of Namibia, in accordance with decisions previously taken by the Council. As all are aware, the United Nations, and in particular the Security Council, bears a unique responsibility for furthering the interests of the people of Namibia and their aspirations for peace, justice and independence. It has been two years since the Council last met to examine the question of Namibia, and it is therefore appropriate that it should wish to review what has transpired in the intervening period.

The participation in this debate of so many distinguished foreign ministers testifies to the importance and the urgency which the international community as a whole attaches to the attainment by the people of Namibia of their justly deserved and too long delayed independence. I especially welcome the presence here of the foreign ministers of the Front Line States, with which governments of the Western Contact Group have enjoyed an active, constructive and vital partnership in our efforts to hasten Namibia's independence.

Finally, I welcome this opportunity to report to you on the role that my government, in partnership with the other members of the Western Contact Group, has sought to play in helping to promote a peaceful, negotiated settlement for the earliest possible attainment of Namibia's independence.

Before doing so, however, I wish to pay a special tribute to the Secretary General. I know first hand his deeply felt commitment to the attainment of Namibia's independence. I have been impressed by his dedication and objectivity, and have full confidence in his ability to carry out the responsibilities assigned to him under Security Council Resolution 435. I am also aware of the efforts he and his staff have made to ensure that all is in readiness for the day when agreement is reached for implementation of the UN settlement plan.

I also wish to thank the Secretary-General for his report, which provides an accurate summation of what has transpired since the Council last met on this issue in April, 1981. It is not necessary to recapitulate what he has already set out. I would, however, like to recall the very different circumstances that prevailed at the time of that last meeting.

The tone and the outcome of that debate were very much a reflection of the widespread disappointment over the failure of the Pre-Implementation Meeting in Geneva to reach agreement on a date for the start of the ceasefire envisaged in Security Council Resolution 435. The Pre-Implementation Meeting ended only a few days before the Administration, of which I am now a member, took office in Washington. It became one of the urgent tasks of the new American government to assess, jointly with its Contact Group partners, the reasons for the failure of the Geneva meeting.

It would be fair to say that the new American government was the recipient of a great deal of advice at that time. I will be frank in telling you that there were those who advised strongly against a continuing U.S. role in pursuit of a negotiated settlement of the Namibian problem. It was said that the obstacles to a peaceful settlement were too great to be overcome, and that the interests of the United States in the region did not justify the tremendous commitment of time and energy that would be required. Needless to say, those responsible for formulating the policies of this Administration did not share these views. Although mindful of the great difficulties involved, they were also aware of the efforts that had already been made, and of the opportunity which existed to resolve through peaceful negotiations, this pressing issue. They were in this regard sensitive to the cardinal importance attached to Namibia's early independence by the nations of Africa. These goals, Mr. President, more than justified a rededication of efforts which the Contact Group had first undertaken four years earlier.

At the same time, we were anxious in our renewed approach to the problem to avoid, if at all possible, the frustrations of the past. We sought an approach that would not result in the same disappointment so keenly felt—above all by the people of Namibia—following the failure of the Geneva Pre-Implementation Meeting. With this firmly in mind, we undertook a fresh round of consultations, first with our Contact partners, and then with the other concerned parties: the Front Line States, the South African Government, SWAPO, and the Namibian political parties that would also participate in the UN-supervised elections envisaged in Resolution 435.

In the course of these consultations several facts became abundantly clear:

- First, we were assured of the interest and the desire of all those directly concerned that the negotiations should continue.
- Secondly, it was clear that in the absence of a peaceful negotiated settlement leading to Namibia's independence, the situation of armed conflict and instability in the region would only worsen, with unacceptable consequences for all the inhabitants of the region.
- Finally, we were assured by those with the greatest stake in the success of the negotiations that the Contact Group had a continuing and important role to play in helping to bring about a peaceful settlement.

On the basis of this assessment, the foreign ministers of the Contact

Group met in May of 1981 and decided to redouble their efforts to bring about a negotiated settlement. They reaffirmed their conviction that only a settlement under the aegis of the United Nations would find broad international acceptance, and that Security Council Resolution 435 continued to provide the basis for Namibia's peaceful transition to independence. Bearing in mind the difficulties that had arisen at the Pre-Implementation Meeting in Geneva, the Contact Group foreign ministers further decided to develop specific proposals that would address directly the concerns that had thus far prevented the implementation of Resolution 435. They considered that the purpose of these proposals should be to give all concerned greater confidence as regards the future of an independent Namibia.

Since the relaunching of their negotiating efforts in the spring of 1981, the members of the Contact Group have worked closely and intensively with all the parties concerned. It is a matter of the greatest regret to us, as I know it is to all of those here, that the promise of Namibia's independence has not yet been realized. At the same time, however, I believe it would be a mistake to discount the progress that has been achieved toward the implementation of Resolution 435 since the Council last met to review the situation.

- First, it is important to note that all parties concerned have reaffirmed their acceptance of Resolution 435. That resolution, and the settlement plan it endorsed, remains the only agreed and recognized basis for an internationally acceptable settlement of the Namibia question.
- All parties have committed themselves to constitutional principles which will serve as a guide to the elected Constituent Assembly in drafting a democratic constitution for an independent Namibia. This agreement, which was confirmed to the Secretary-General in July of last year and which is noted in his report to the Security Council, has helped to reassure all those who will participate in the UN-supervised elections of the democratic future of an independent Namibia.
- Substantial progress has also been made in resolving the issues which were responsible for the unsuccessful outcome of the Geneva Pre-Implementation Meeting. In particular, through intensive consultations which took place in New York and Washington last summer, involving representatives of the Front Line States, SWAPO, South Africa and of the UN Secretariat, understandings were reached that will assure all parties to the elections of the fairness and impartiality of the process leading to Namibia's independence.
- Finally, through their own consultations with the parties concerned, the Secretary-General and his staff have made substantial progress in resolving outstanding questions concerning the composition and deployment of the military component of UNTAG. Here I would like once again to express our appreciation to the Secretary-General for the determined

efforts he has made to ensure that all is in readiness for the implementation of the UN settlement plan.

Because of the substantial progress that has been made over the past two years, only two major issues remain to be resolved in preparation for the implementation of Resolution 435. These are: the choice of the electoral system to be employed in the elections, which all parties are agreed must be settled in accordance with the provisions of Resolution 435, and in a manner that does not cause delay; and final, technical matters concerning the composition of the military component of UNTAG.

Mr. President, while the United States is pleased with the record of what has been achieved over the past two years, we are by no means satisfied. Indeed, none of us can rest content until the goal which we seek has been attained. But the fact that much has been achieved justifies continued commitment to the course.

Apart from the specific accomplishments I have just mentioned there has been the development of an atmosphere of confidence which we hope will make it possible for the parties concerned to make the important political decisions necessary to go forward with the implementation of Resolution 435. We have been especially gratified by the constructive and flexible attitude displayed by the concerned parties, which has made possible the progress that has been achieved to date.

We share the concern that the factors relating to the regional situation in southern Africa, which are, however, outside the scope of the mandate of the Contact Group, have not yet permitted implementation of the United Nations plan. We believe that these issues should be resolved rapidly, in a manner consistent with the sovereignty of all states concerned, so that the people of Namibia can exercise their right of self-determination. The Ministers have accordingly decided that the Contact Group should continue its work with all urgency.

We are convinced, now more than ever before, that with the continued good faith and cooperation of all concerned, our shared objective of a negotiated settlement leading to a stable, democratic, prosperous and independent Namibia will be realized.

Here, Mr. President, I would like to say a word about the role and the objectives of my government in these negotiations.

I wish to stress above all that the United States neither desires nor seeks any special advantage or position for itself in these negotiations.

It is not our intention, nor is it within our power, to impose our own views or wishes on those whose interests and aspirations are most directly involved.

We fully respect the fact that the political decisions needed to proceed with the implementation of the UN settlement plan are sovereign decisions that can only be taken by the governments most immediately and directly concerned.

Furthermore, we recognize that those who must take those decisions will wish to assure themselves that their own interests and security will be respected and protected.

In the sometimes thankless role that we have assumed our sole objective has been to assist the parties in overcoming the difficulties that have to date prevented the implementation of Security Council Resolution 435 and the attainment of Namibia's independence.

Finally, Mr. President, I wish to assure all those here assembled that the United States will continue to work for Namibia's transition to stable and prosperous independence once an agreement has been achieved. With other members of the United Nations, we are prepared to contribute a fair share to ensure the effectiveness of the United Nations Transition Assistance Group. We also stand ready to cooperate with others in providing the assistance that will be essential to giving all Namibians the opportunity to lead peaceful and productive lives.

I am keenly aware of the sense of frustration felt by members of this body because the aspirations of the people of Namibia have not been realized. We share that frustration, and we have sympathy for the people of Namibia, and the region, who suffer from the continuing conflict. We will not, however, allow our feelings of frustration to lead us to despair. Our common efforts will succeed. The only alternative to the continued, vigorous pursuit of a peaceful, negotiated settlement, is a more dangerous and ever more destructive escalation of the violence that the people of Namibia and those throughout the region have known too well too long.

Those of us who are priviliged to participate in the decisions of this body have a special responsibility to do all we can to help achieve Namibian independence peacefully and promptly. We are ready to work closely with other members of the Council, and with the parties concerned, to achieve such an outcome, which we know will also enhance the prospects for peace, security, and economic development throughout the region.

THE WILL FOR SETTLEMENT IN NAMIBIA

The tragic events of Beirut of yesterday, testified to the dangerous point to which international issues can grow if left to fester unresolved. Unfortunately, the people of Southern Africa are no strangers to such unhappy, indeed, tragic scenes. It is our special responsibility as members of this august body to confront the problems of our world in a timely, realistic and responsible manner. This isn't easy for many factors work against anyone who assumes seriously the task of peace-maker. Certainly the members of the Council and the leaders of the Front Line States, as well as of the Contact Group, have expended great efforts in the search for a way to bring Namibia to a peaceful independence. And we have come very close in our goal, but we have not yet succeeded. Meanwhile, our frustrations mount and the call for violent solutions grows louder. In times like these, I believe that a special value attaches to clear assessment to the skills of diplomacy and statesmanship of our political leaders. It is our responsibility to help the people of the world to see better where we are, how far we have come, so that they will renew their commitment to the goal of a prompt and peaceful settlement of this terribly troubled and important issue and not from despair, cast aside the agreements already so painfully reached.

It is for these reasons that the United States especially welcomes this opportunity for the Security Council, once again, to exercise its responsibility for Namibia and to review developments in the negotiations being conducted pursuant to United Nations Security Council Resolution 435 since the Council's last discussion in May.

On that occasion, the Council was able to hear directly from the principal parties to the negotiations regarding the progress that has been achieved and to address frankly what remains to be done in order to bring about implementation of the UN settlement plan. On that basis, the Council was able to act unanimously, through the adoption of Resolution 532, to ask that the Secretary-General lend his personal, good offices to consultations with the parties aimed at identifying a basis for the movement towards Namibia's rightful independence.

My government welcomed the Secretary-General's sincere, constructive and skillful approach to his mandate under Resolution 532. I should like once again to express the deep appreciation of the United States for the dedication and objectivity shown by the Secretary-General and his staff, which have so thoroughly characterized their commitment to the Namibia settlement process and which have, in fact and very significantly, gained the

Address before the Security Council, October 24, 1983.

confidence of all sides of the conflict. The Secretary-General's achievements have been noteworthy. My government welcomes his interest and continued active involvement to reach our common goal.

In his August 29 report to the Council, the Secretary-General described in detail his discussions in South Africa, Namibia, and Angola, underscoring both the very significant achievements of his trip and the obstacle that still stands in the way of a settlement. The United States attaches the highest importance to the results of the Secretary-General's discussions with the South African government. In the course of those talks, very real progress was made on issues that had, until then, remained unresolved over the years. Notably, all questions regarding UNTAG that had a direct bearing on implementation of Resolution 435 have now been cleared up. The South African government has also affirmed its commitment to indicate at an early date prior to implementation its choice of an electoral system. We regard this as important forward progress. The South African government also stated unequivocally that it now has no question or reservations regarding the impartiality of the United Nations in the settlement process. These are significant accomplishments which have contributed in important ways to building a climate conducive to a peaceful settlement of the Namibia conflict.

Similarly, my government welcomes the Secretary-General's report that SWAPO President Nujoma in his meeting with the Secretary-General in Luanda, reaffirmed that his organization stands ready to sign a ceasefire and to move forward on implementation on the basis of the agreements that have been reached.

Mr. President, although the Secretary-General's initiative in southern Africa measurably advanced the negotiations, his report to the Security Council also made clear that there does remain one issue standing in the way of implementation of Resolution 435: South Africa's position regarding the withdrawal of Cuban forces from Angola. This put into focus the frustration widespread in Africa, felt most sharply among the Front Line States who have worked so long and so hard on the Namibia process, that an issue outside the scope of Resolution 435 is delaying our common objective. It is obviously a matter of frustration. The United States and its partners in the Contact Group share that frustration. However, my government remains firmly convinced that this obstacle can and should be resolved—that this can be done with perseverance and good will, that we will be able to overcome this obstacle.

The United States remains firmly committed to the objective of Namibian independence pursuant to Resolution 435. Our attachment to freedom—manifested in our foreign and domestic policies since our own independence struggle more than two centuries ago—permits no other course. Our continuing concern in these negotiations has been that this goal be approached realistically—practically. We must recognize that, as a practical matter, implementation of Resolution 435 will take place only if the fundamental concerns of all parties are addressed. To that end, we have devoted our energy to the search for a solution based on reciprocity, with full mutual respect for security and sovereignty on all sides, with Namibia's independence as its only acceptable result. We will remain engaged in this effort as long as it appears that there is a chance for a peaceful solution.

Mr. President, the problem of cross-border violence in southern Africa is of deep concern to us all. We are working toward a peaceful resolution of the region's differences and have urged and will continue to urge military restraint. We do not believe there are military solutions to the conflicts afflicting the states of this troubled region. Our policies are premised on the belief that negotiated solutions are both possible and essential. As we have said in the past, cross-border violence cannot be condoned, whether it be in the form of a bomb placed in a crowded square in Pretoria by externally based organizations or in the form of the continuing violation of the territorial integrity of Angola by South African forces.

Mr. President, many speakers in this debate have stated their concern over the amount of time it has taken to move the negotiations as far as they have come. The truth is that the complex issues directly relating to the United Nations plan have required the most delicate negotiation. With the results of the Secretary-General's trip, there is today virtually complete agreement on the basis for implementation of Resolution 435. It is also equally clear that there can be no final resolution of the Namibia question without the cooperation of the parties most directly involved.

Mr. President, during the May debate, the position of my government regarding these negotiations was made clear to the Council. There has been progress since then, as the Secretary-General's report makes clear. At the same time our basic position has not changed.

Mr. President, while Namibian independence is not yet within our grasp, it is within sight, doubling our impatience, but also redoubling our commitment. The United States is convinced that the will for a settlement is present on all sides in no small part based on recognition of the imminent, dangerous alternative of an escalating cycle of destructive violence. The future of the people of Namibia, for whom the United Nations and this Council bear unique responsibility, depends on our working together to keep the negotiating process firmly on track. The United States continues to stand ready to work closely with other members of the Council and with other parties to hasten the day when an independent Namibia can take its place among us as a sovereign state. Until that day, it is to each of us to think how best we can contribute to that achievement.

ACHIEVING NAMIBIA'S INDEPENDENCE

As we hope everyone in this chamber is aware, the United States, in cooperation with partners in the Contact Group and with our colleagues in the Front Line states, has been engaged in the effort to bring independence to Namibia through the elimination of the illegal South African occupation of that territory. Our effort has not slackened; to the contrary, it has intensified markedly of late as the exchanges between the United States and various parties in southern Africa have mounted in intensity.

The United States government has tried hard to demonstrate at the highest levels our continuing commitment to good relations with Africa and, in particular, to achieving the independence of Namibia in the shortest possible time in accordance with UN Security Council Resolution 435. President Reagan has underscored the fact that this is a major goal of his administration. We hope that with the continued cooperation of our friends and partners in and outside the region, the goal will be achieved. Because of the sensitive nature of our involvement in this effort, we have consistently held the view that it is inappropriate for the United States government to take a position on the substance of the resolutions before us. We will, therefore, abstain on these resolutions again this year.

The citation by name of member states and, in particular, of the United States in certain sections of these resolutions constitutes an unfair and regrettable exception to the long established practices and norms of the United Nations and this body. The United Nations was founded to promote peace and greater mutual understanding among nations, despite their differences. It was founded to promote discussion. In pursuit of these goals, it is essential that this Assembly consistently respect basic principles of civility, fairness and factual accuracy. We feel very strongly that direct, hostile and unfair references to particular member states in UN resolutions are contrary to these basic principles and detrimental to our common purposes in the organization. We have, therefore, moved to strike such language from these resolutions, as the Fourth Committee did in similar instances. Our amendments received the support of the majority of that body, and we hope that the important principle involved will receive similar support now.

Some delegations have asked us how we can oppose such a phrase as "on account of the veto of the United States of America." "Is this," they ask, "not simply a statement of fact?" It is a fact that the United States exercised its veto on the 31st of August, in 1981, as it is a fact that other states have

Address before the 39th General Assembly, December 12, 1984.

exercised vetoes to defeat Security Council resolutions since then. Yet the names of those states have not been cited in resolutions before this body, despite the fact that blatant and ongoing aggression in Afghanistan and Kampuchea were involved. More objectionable, still, is the argument made in the same paragraph, that, as a result of the veto of the United States, armed aggression against Angola continues. That is to say, the resolution maintains that the United States is the direct cause of this aggression. That is not true. This assertion is not only demonstrably untrue, it ignores the successful efforts undertaken by the United States to achieve an end to the South African intervention.

Another paragraph which similarly ignores these efforts and which we have proposed to delete, denounces the establishment of the United States Liaison Office at Windhoek as a violation of General Assembly and Security Council resolutions and of the advisory opinion of the International Court of Justice. Delegations should be aware, however, that the United States Liaison Office was opened as a direct result of the agreements entered into between Angola and South Africa at Lusaka in February of this year. According to the communique of that meeting, the parties agreed that a small number of American representatives would participate in the activities of the Joint Monitoring Commission at the request of the parties in order to facilitate the withdrawal of South African troops from southern Angola. To this end, and with the agreement of the governments directly involved, the United States government opened a small office, which had to be near enough to the disengagement process to work effectively with the parties involved. Though located in Windhoek, this office is in no way accredited either to the South African government or to the authorities in Namibia. It has no diplomatic or consular function; it implies no recognition of the legitimacy of the South African presence in Namibia. Our action is, therefore, entirely consistent with the resolutions passed by the UN General Assembly and Security Council.

Mr. President, the issue posed by our proposed amendments is, in fact, quite a simple one. Does the General Assembly wish to see its resolutions on the serious and urgent matter of Namibia abused for purposes which not only make no contribution to the effort to bring about Namibian independence, but are calculated to discourage those engaged in that effort? Our amendments aim to eliminate just this abuse. We have not proposed to alter in any way the substance of the resolutions before us. Therefore, whatever a govenment's substantive views may be—whether your government's wish to support the resolutions, abstain or vote against them—you should feel free to support these amendments. We appeal to all, therefore, to join together in reaffirming our respect for the principles of civility, basic fairness and respect for accuracy, which have shaped our accepted practices and which should govern all our deliberations and decisions here.

ESCALATING VIOLENCE IN SOUTHERN AFRICA

My country, together with a good many others, has been deeply involved for a number of years in the quest for peace in southern Africa and the quest for independence for Namibia, and the quest for the pacification of that troubled area. We remain today deeply involved in that quest. This effort has been and remains an issue of high priority for the United States. In the course of our quest we have consulted closely with Angola, South Africa and other interested states in and out of the region, who also seek peace in the region. The Namibian political parties, our Contact Group partners, other African governments, the Secretary-General—all of us have spoken together again and again in the search for peace in this troubled region. The Secretary-General's role in this process has been particularly constructive. We are all indebted to him for his constructive involvement in this search for peace in the region.

Mr. President, the South African commitment to begin a disengagement of its "forces which from time to time conduct military operations against SWAPO in Angola, on January 31, 1984," was announced in a letter of December 15th and represents, in our judgment, a major new step in this arduous process. We welcome this public announcement of a readiness to disengage its forces. We believe this step has the potential to contribute substantially to a climate that could facilitate further movement in southern African negotiations, and we hope that conditions on the ground will permit a cease-fire as soon as possible.

A durable settlement of the problems of southern Africa clearly depends on mutual respect for the essential principles of sovereignty and territorial integrity of all states in the region. We further believe that such a settlement, if it is to be achieved, must take account of the security of all in the region. We would, therefore, hope that once a cease-fire comes into effect it would extend beyond the initial 30-day period proposed by the South African government, in order that these conditions have a chance to take hold.

Address before the Security Council, December 20, 1983.

The South African announcement underscores the validity of the effort in which we and our Contact Group partners have been and are involved. We continue to believe this effort provides the best hope of bringing lasting peace to the area. The questions before us now are essentially these: Do we seize on this significant new development, this hopeful and encouraging first step, and allow it to be considered and tested by those most directly involved? Or do we reject it out of hand as meaningless and choose instead to engage in this forum in fruitless recriminations? The alternatives are clear and so should the answer be clear—to all who genuinely seek peace in the region.

The position of my government is, in any case, clear: We are deeply concerned with the escalating cycle of violence in southern Africa. We are particularly disturbed about the problem of cross-border violence. We have urged and will continue to urge military restraint and respect for national boundaries. We do not believe there are military solutions to the conflicts in southern Africa. The policies of the United States are grounded in the belief that negotiated solutions are both possible and essential. Cross-border violence cannot be condoned, whether it be in the form of terrorist attacks by externally-based organizations or a violation of the territorial integrity of Angola by South African forces. Neither contributes to the process of building a structure of peace which is so ardently desired by all those who live in the region.

Our own effort to pursue peace in southern Africa is moving forward actively through contacts with the states most directly involved. We are in close and regular touch with the states of the region. We will do nothing which will jeopardize this delicate and, we believe, hopeful peace process. Our position in this debate is shaped primarily by our commitment to achieving results in the ongoing negotiations.

Mr. President, each of us must decide whether to pursue the new hope toward peaceful reconciliation, or to bury it in mistrust and condemnations. For my government the choice is clear: We do not intend to let this opportunity pass us by. Thus, we have abstained on the draft resolution.

THE RIGHT TO FULL CITIZENSHIP

I ask for the right of reply in order to address certain questions that were raised in the form of assertions by the previous speaker with regard to the views and values and conduct of the Government of the United States. I should like to make just a few points, and very briefly, in order to set at rest any questions which any member of the Council may have concerning our commitments relevant to the resolution in the matter before us.

First, I will affirm as clearly and unequivocally as possible, as I have on many occasions in this Council on behalf of the United States, that the United States Government deplores apartheid, condemns apartheid as we condemn all denial of full citizenship and rights of full citizenship and of democracy to all citizens of all countries, unequivocally.

Second, I should like to underscore that the United States does, indeed, condemn the constitution now before us for consideration, and all constitutions that are not, and do not provide full adult suffrage and free elections, as we deplore all constitutions of all governments that do not feature democratic elections in which all adult citizens may participate under conditions of free speech, access to media, free assembly, majority rule, and with protection of minority rights. The United States, indeed, deplores all governments, everywhere, which are not governments based on consent deriving from the right of all citizens to participate in the processes of their government. We do not approve of any government in which blocs or, indeed, any other category of citizens whatsoever are disenfranchised. We oppose, indeed, deplore all governments which deprive any category of their citizens of their full rights. We especially deplore the keeping of political prisoners. And we call on all governments to release their political prisoners. We wholly affirm the words of former Secretary of State George C. Marshall—one of our most distinguished military and diplomatic leaders of all times—when he said that governments which systematically violate the rights of their own citizens are, indeed, not likely to respect the rights of others anywhere else in the world.

I would like to assure the previous speaker, and, indeed, all other members of the Council, that the Council can count on United States support for any resolution which espouses the rights of members under the Charter of the United Nations, which are consistent with the principles of the Charter, providing only that the members of the Council are ready to apply those principles and guarantee those rights to all other people in all other societies represented here today.

Address before the Security Council, August 16, 1984.

APARTHEID: A WRONG IN ITSELF

In abstaining today the United States interposed no obstacle to the resolution adopted by this Council, though some excesses of language prevented us from joining the Council in voting affirmatively.

My government abhors apartheid. We have expressed this abhorrence on many occasions. We have also repeatedly expressed our conviction that denial of equal rights to all citizens, all South African citizens, is wrong in itself and the source of great unrest and disturbance in South African society. My government is distressed and concerned with the violence that has swept South Africa recently.

We fully support the demands expressed in the resolution for equal rights, majority rule and respect for minority rights for all South African citizens of all colors and races. Indeed, Mr. President, the United States government strongly supports the demand for equal rights and freedom, opportunity, self-government and self-determination for all citizens of all countries. We do not believe that the problems of South Africa will be resolved until all South African citizens enjoy their full rights as citizens in a self-governing society.

The United States government's priorities in southern Africa remain those of the search for peace and concrete progress toward our common goals in South Africa and the region as a whole.

May I take this occasion, Mr. President, to add that this session has given us the opportunity and a very welcome opportunity indeed, to hear the eloquent views of a great exponent of human rights. We always listen to Bishop Desmond Tutu with attention. Our respect for him has been expressed many times, on many occasions. At this point it is perhaps most appropriate for me to quote the words of President Reagan, who has written to Bishop Tutu, saying:

> Dear Bishop Tutu: Please accept my congratulations and those of the American people on being named the 1984 recipient of the Nobel Peace Prize in recognition of your efforts on behalf of peaceful change in South Africa. All Americans join me in recognizing your labors in seeking to promote non-violent change away from apartheid, toward a form of government based on consent of the governed and toward a society that offers equal rights and opportunities to all its citizens, without regard to race. The United States has heard the appeal for justice voiced by South Africans who suffer under apartheid rule. We continue to urge the South African Government to engage in a meaningful dialogue with all its citizens aimed at accomplishing a peaceful transition away from apartheid. We applaud you in being selected for this

Address before the Security Council, October 23, 1984.

honor, and assure you that we share these goals. Sincerely, yours. Ronald Reagan.

LIBYA'S FALSE CHARGES

I have, today, addressed the following letter to you for circulation as an official document in the Security Council:

> The Government of the United States rejects the false and malicious charges of the Government of Libya and calls the attention of the Council to yet another example of a threat to international peace and security posed by the policies of the Libyan Government.
>
> Furious that its plans for illegal, violent action were frustrated, the Government of Libya comes now to the Security Council with lying complaints against the United States. In fact, the United States committed none of the acts charged by the Government of Libya.
>
> The United States dispatched no offensive aircraft into the region, violated no Libyan airspace. As a matter of fact, neither the U.S. Carrier Nimitz nor its aircraft entered waters or airspace claimed by Libya on the days in question, although we have every right to enter these international waters, recognized as such under international law. We also have every right to conduct, under appropriate circumstances, training exercises with friendly governments.
>
> The United States affirms its rights under international law and the Charter of the United Nations and intends to exercise them.
>
> Naturally, the Government of Libya would prefer that no obstacles—however legal—be interposed to its plots and expansionist projects. But peace-loving nations cannot accommodate Libya's designs on its neighbors.
>
> In calling attention to Libya's false charges, the United States notes that such lies mock the serious work of building international peace, just as Libya's repeated efforts to interfere in the affairs of its neighbors destroys security in the region.

Mr. President, the United States did not seek this confrontation in the United Nations Security Council with the Government of Libya, but we welcome the opportunity thus presented to put *facts* on the record (not the fabrications of Colonel Qadhafi's spokesman) and to assign *responsibility*

Address before the Security Council, February 22, 1983.

for this grave threat to international peace and security where that responsibility belongs.

I speak, of course, of the Government of Qadhafi's Libya. And I wish to put this threat, which seems for the moment to have receded, in the context of Libyan-sponsored worldwide terrorism and adventurism directed against its neighbors—indeed, throughout northern, eastern, and central Africa. This pattern of lawless expansionism constitutes a continuing threat to the peace and security in the region and beyond.

My government and the American people have never sought, and do not now seek any confrontation with the government or people of Libya. We have never engaged, and do not now engage in any acts of provocation. But we are deeply sensitive to threats to international peace, to our own security, and to the security and national independence of Libya's neighbors. And let there be no doubt: we will respond as appropriate to Libyan threats.

Briefly, I wish to recall the salient events that led to this situation.

Last Friday, February 18, official Sudanese radio announced the discovery of a Libyan-backed coup plot against the government of President Jaaffir Nimeiri. It announced the apprehension of Libyan-sponsored dissidents and infiltrators. It also reported that the Government of Sudan had been closely watching concentrations of Libyan bombers and fighters in southeast Libya close to the Sudanese and Egyptian borders.

This concentration of Libyan aircraft had been of particular concern to the Sudanese. In view of the successful steps which the Sudan has now taken to deal with this latest Libyan effort to destabilize one of its neighbors, we are now able to put the spotlight of world attention on events in the region.

We follow Qadhafi's irresponsible incursions into the affairs of his neighbors closely and with deep concern. We have been aware for some time of his efforts directed against President Nimeiri. We were also aware of the concentrations of Libyan aircraft which were of concern to the Sudanese and Egyptians. Because of the situation, we moved up the date of an AWACS training exercise which had already been scheduled about a month hence, and sent our AWACS and tanker aircraft into Egypt. We have also had U.S. naval forces deployed in the eastern Mediterranean. Their presence in international waters sometimes seems to have a deterring effect on Libyan adventurism in the region.

The desired result seems to have been achieved, at least for the present. The statement on Sudanese radio, and yesterday's statement by the Sudanese Assembly, speak for themselves. We can be reassured by the bold and decisive manner in which the Sudanese dealt with the threat of Libyan expansionism.

Fortunately, Mr. President, the most recent threat has receded. But the pattern of Libyan misconduct is longstanding.

Colonel Qadhafi conducts a virulent, hostile foreign policy which respects the territorial integrity, national independence, right to peace and security and self-determination of no one. Because of a relative lack of conventional military power, Colonel Qadhafi has tried to accomplish his goals through a combination of economic and military aid to radical governments; bribery of officials; help to international terrorists by providing sanctuary, funds, weapons, planning, assassination of exiled opponents; and planned assassination of target-government officials; and assistance to guerrilla groups working to overthrow established governments.

The Qadhafi regime has been engaged in these activities almost since it took power. For example, in 1972, Libya provided sanctuary to the perpetrators of the Munich Olympics murders. Qadhafi also gave refuge to the terrorists who held hostages at the 1975 Vienna OPEC meeting. Libya has been used as a "safe" area in which terrorist groups have planned acts to be committed in many of Europe's capitals. The infamous "Carlos" has operated out of Libya over several years. The weapons found on the French terrorists Breguet and Kopp had been sold to the Libyan Army. It was their release which Carlos demanded.

Assassination has been an important Libyan tool, and the proof of Libya's utilization of this tool is not hard to come by. The 1980-81 murders of a dozen exiled Libyans, primarily in Western European capitals, have been reported by the international press in detail. Less widely known are a 1975 plot to murder the Prime Minister of a neighboring country; plans to kill American Ambassadors in several Middle Eastern countries and at least one European capital; and a November 1981 attempt to plant explosives in the American Embassy Club in Khartoum, which explosives were concealed in stereo speakers, designed to detonate on a Saturday evening when scores of people would have been present and killed.

A major facet of Libyan foreign policy has been and remains subversion and destabilization of independent governments in the Middle East, Africa and elsewhere. Chad has been a recent principal victim of the aggressive policy of Libya. Currently, Libyan intentions toward Chad are a major concern. Colonel Qadhafi has brought large numbers of Chadian followers to Libya, trained and equipped them and is moving them into the northern parts of Chad. Other efforts to increase its own strength in that area are underway. Most disturbing was the mid-January deployment of a dozen Libyan SU-22 ground-attack fighters to the Aouzou Airbase in northern Chad, apparently in preparation of a Libyan option to provide air cover to an assault by dissidents and infiltrators against the Chadian government and Chadian-held population centers. A Libyan team of approximately eighty "advisors" in another African republic may be assisting anti-government Chadians there. Libya has a long record of training guerrillas, supplying weapons, plotting subversion and destabilization of its North African neighbors.

In the Horn of Africa, Libya continues to try to overthrow the governments of Sudan and Somalia. A number of Libyans are in Ethiopia advising Somali and Sudanese guerrillas. Libyan aircraft and ships continue to train guerrillas and to supply arms, ammunition, explosives and material to the Somali Salvation Front and to Sudanese rebels. Also, Libya's deliveries of increasingly advanced weapons to warring tribes in the Sudan have contributed to death and violence in that region.

Elsewhere, Libya delivers military equipment and is involving itself increasingly, for example, in this hemisphere, always on behalf of military dictatorships, always opposed to democratic regimes and movements.

Mr. President, that is the pattern of Libyan misconduct, worldwide. It constitutes, as I have said, a grave threat to international peace and security. The culprit in this proceeding is identified beyond any reasonable doubt or question.

Mr. President, what has happened to Libya may happen to other states, the representative of Libya has suggested. I should like to say that we hope so. We hope that what happened to Libya will happen to other states. We hope that all states with aggressive designs on their neighbors will be discouraged by the lawful response of others and thus to desist in their unlawful plans. My Government rests *its* case on the factual record—and its adherence to the principles of the United Nations Charter, in the cause of international peace and security.

LIBYA IN THE SUDAN: RECRUITING, ORGANIZING, PROMOTING VIOLENCE

I would like to begin by congratulating you on your accession to the Presidency, expressing the confidence which my country and its government has in your judgment and in your skill and the sense of justice with which you can be relied upon to conduct the affairs of this Council and indeed our satisfaction with the efficiency and fairness with which you have already this month conducted the affairs of this Council.

Address before the Security Council, March 27, 1984.

I have already expressed, I think, my government's great satisfaction and approval of the skill and style and effectiveness with which your predecessor, the distinguished representative of Pakistan, served as President of our Council last month.

I should also, like other speakers today, like to express the deep grief of my government and myself at the untimely and unexpected death of President Sekou Toure of Guinea and our profound sympathy to the government and the people of that country. President Sekou Toure's distinction as an African leader, a leader in the struggle for independence, a distinguished nation builder, is very well known. We share that worldwide evaluation of his great gifts. We are certain the world will be poorer for his departure.

Mr. President, we are here today to consider yet another sad development in the contemporary history of Africa. We are here today to consider another episode in Colonel Qaddafi's escalating war against the world, the unprovoked attack against Sudan on March 16. Despite the web of lies and fabrications presented to this Council this morning, the facts surrounding the dismal attack are clear. Ample evidence is available to support these facts.

On March 15, two Libyan TU-22 bombers flew from their home base at Umm Aitiqah, in Tripoli, to Kafra. On March 16, one of these TU-22s conducted an unprovoked attack on Sudan's second largest city, Omdurman, which is well within the combat radius of Libya's TU-22s. This bombing attack, which was conducted from a very low altitude, was witnessed by several qualified observers. The radio station was damaged and five persons were killed. The bombs utilized were an export model of a Soviet 500 KG general purpose, high explosive bomb M-62 with AVU series impact detonating nose fuse. Flying over northwest Sudan the TU-22 bomber returned to Libya. The next day, both TU-22s, which had deployed to Kafra, had returned to their home base at Umm Aitiqah.

The TU-22 is a very distinctive plane. It looks like no other aircraft in the region. Libya is the only country in the region which possesses these Soviet-built TU-22 bombers. There is no way to disguise any other plane to look like a TU-22. Its range is entirely adequate to make the trip from Kafra to Omdurman. It was closely observed both in traveling and in bombing. It was photographed.

The facts are clear, despite a certain international effort to obscure them. Truth is not a matter of political will, nor can reality be obscured by the will to confuse, humiliate, destroy.

The Libyans have demonstrated in the last decade that they are masters of violence; today they demonstrate they are promising apprentices in deception. Their leader speaks frankly about his commitments and his plans. His representative today has sacrificed candor to strategic obfuscation.

An innocent auditor hearing the Libyan representative this morning might have thought that the Sudan threatens its neighbors and conspires against them. Having misfired with its bombs, Libya's representative took up the weapons of lies, taunting his neighbor for his poverty, flaunting Libya's oil revenues as if they reflected national virtue. It was the first time in my years at this Council that I have heard a Third World country reproached and shamed for being poor.

Efforts to sow doubt about the identity, origin and ownership of the plane serve as one more example of the practice of wrapping aggression in lies designed to obscure the aggressor's role and deprive the victim of deserved sympathy and redress. It has become a familiar pattern: a violent assault; a denial of complicity; a suggestion that the violence is of purely internal origin; a vicious attack on anyone who seeks to aid the victim; Soviet weapons, Libyan planes, dead civilians, disinformation and intimidation.

What happened is clear. It is also possible to understand *why*. Col. Qaddafi denies the bombing at Omdurman but he admits freely and frankly his plans. "The battle has now become overt and not covert" between him and his enemies, he told the world on the March 2nd anniversary of his current regime.

The speech on that occasion is fascinating. It deserves attention.

In it, Col. Qaddafi brags, celebrates, gloats, threatens. He is full of self-congratulation for those who worked to subvert the independence of Lebanon and its legitimate government.

"We worked for months, day and night; we and the Syrians and the Palestinians and the Lebanese . . . have been working . . . to achieve this victory." (So much for the theory of purely Lebanese dissension.)

If things do not go as desired he comments, "the struggle will continue with guns, with machine guns, with bombs . . . until the last man and woman." (So much for the idea of a political rather than a military solution in Lebanon.)

He gloats: "A great victory," he says was achieved against America, France, Italy, Britain. Listen to his words: "The defeat which the Americans suffered in Lebanon is not less than its defeat in Vietnam, and the strike which was directed against the French forces in Lebanon is not less than the historic strike which was directed against it at Dien Bien Phu." President Reagan, he said, "lost his nerve," was "forced to concede defeat," to "flee like a rat."

Col. Qaddafi invoked Arab nationalism to justify his attack on Arab nations.

Col. Qaddafi affirmed in the clearest words his intentions with regard to Sudan:

> We tell the agents in Sudan that we are allied with the popular revolution in southern Sudan for the sake of liberating Sudan inch by inch, just as Lebanon was liberated. The United States cannot save that mean man who is hiding in Khartoum. This is because we and the revolutionary force in Ethiopia, in the Arab homeland, the revolution in Libya has decided to ally itself with the revolution in southern Sudan for the sake of liberating Sudan inch by inch.
>
> The morale of the popular masses has strengthened as a result of America's defeat in Lebanon. The morale of the popular masses has strengthened as a result of America's defeat in Lebanon at the hands of the Lebanese popular resistance and the steadfastness of Syria and the Iranian-Libyan revolutionary alliance with the Lebanese revolution.
>
> The peoples will march forward and will develop the people's war of liberation in Sudan and tomorrow in Egypt and in every part that America seeks to dominate, to use for serving the interests of the American people.

Col. Qaddafi threatens war "on a hundred fronts all over the earth." "We must escalate the people's liberation war in Latin America and in Central America so that we may force America to fight there . . ." and in Lebanon, Sudan, Somalia, Chad, Southern Africa.

He celebrates violence: "Let the masses march begin to give a push forward to the revolution, and consolidate the concept of the master people and commanding people . . ." "All shall carry arms . . ." "We carry the shovel in one hand and the gun in the other." Women will not be kept from military training, and anyone who opposes women's military training is "an agent of imperialism . . . , whether he knows it or not."

Even in this violent age we are not accustomed to hearing such bold assertions of the intention to use violence, worldwide, to achieve political goals. The practice of terror and violence is more familiar in our time than is its frank affirmation.

But in the case of Col. Qaddafi, such frank affirmation of violence is not new. As we pointed out three years ago, he is quite forthright. On March 2nd of 1981, he said: "It is the duty of the Libyan people constantly to liquidate their opponents . . . the physical and final liquidation of the opponents of popular authority must continue at home and abroad, everywhere." The announcement made in Tripoli in August, 1981, of the desire to "undertake the physical liquidation of" hostile individuals "beginning with Ronald Reagan" defies either response or comment. But the words of March, 1984, echo and expand them.

They were not idle words. They were part of a new, violent phase. Despite certain foreign policy "successes" and his continued ostensible accommodation with a few of the moderate Arab states, Col. Qaddafi has within the past few months begun to devote more energy to using terrorism and subversion against his domestic and foreign enemies.

The outright use of terror was observed on March 10 in two widely separated areas—Britain and Chad—followed by the bombing of Omdurman radio/television station on March 16.

Twenty-six persons were wounded when several bombs exploded and others were defused in London and Manchester on March 10 and 12. On March 10, two bombs planted in the hold of a French passenger jet en route from Brazzaville to Bangui to N'Djamena to Paris destroyed the aircraft on the ground at N'Djamena. Twenty-five people were wounded.

In his pursuit of expanded power and influence, Col. Qaddafi has repeatedly employed tactics of assassination and violence, demonstrating that he is unconstrained by international law as by accepted standards of international conduct. He has sought the assassination of moderate leaders and Libyan exiles by financing known terrorists and by providing terrorist training in Libya on a continuing basis. The habits are of long standing.

The appeals of hatred, however, have their limits. After 10 years in power, Col. Qaddafi had still largely failed to stir the popular support he continually evokes. He had established "revolutionary committees" in 1977— groups charged with injecting the appropriate revolutionary fervor into the existing "people's committees" and into the armed forces—but they have never been particularly active. In 1980, Col. Qaddafi sought to use them to orchestrate massive purges and corruption trials involving thousands of arrests, including influential businessman, high government officials, and senior military officers. Those arrested were tried before special tribunals composed of revolutionary committee members and sentenced; some, after dramatic televised "confessions," were released; others vanished. At the same time, the regime launched a campaign to intimidate dissidents abroad. Libyan hit squads embarked on a series of murders of exiled Libyans in an overall effort to enforce their views at all costs. Eleven people were killed, four in Rome, two in London, and one each in Bonn, Beirut, Athens, Milan, and Manchester; several others were wounded, including a student in the United States and two children in England. In October, 1982, Qaddafi once again publicly warned Libyan exiles to "repent" and return home or face renewal of the murder campaign.

Virtually all African and Arab moderate regimes are targets of Libyan-supported subversion. Unable to persuade or bribe other states into submitting to a Qaddafi-led "Islamic revolution," unable to use his army to force stronger states to submit to his will, Qaddafi has armed, funded and trained a wide range of dissident groups to achieve his ends. Subversion has become the principal tool by which he hopes to fulfill his ambitions.

Libyan subversive activities range far beyond neighboring states. Libya is a potential source of funds, arms and safe-haven for virtually any group claiming to be anti-Israel or anti-United States. His focus is on the Middle East and Africa, but he has been active in Europe and the Far East, and has recently supported anti-U.S. regimes and subversive groups in Latin America.

In some cases, Libyan activity takes the form of handouts to individuals or small groups of dissidents. In several instances, it has involved sustained support, with substantial payments and deliveries of military equipment. Subversive groups also frequently receive military training in Libya, where thousands of dissidents are being trained either in special camps created for the purpose or at Libyan bases. Most of the dissidents come from countries neighboring Libya, but they are also drawn from further afield. The training program relies heavily on foreign instructors, including Soviets, Palestinians, Cubans and East Germans as well as Tunisians, Egyptians, and other foreigners who help train dissidents from their own country or region. Subversion continues to be Col. Qaddafi's principal *modus operandi* to expand his domain and gain wider African influence, although he is increasingly prone to use military intervention as well. The Sudan is an early intended victim.

Beyond Sudan and Chad, the most immediate objects of Libya's aggressions, lie Egypt and Algeria, Niger, Tunisia, Morocco, Mauritius, Somalia, Togo, Central African Republic, Liberia, Upper Volta and every independent nation in Africa. All have at one time or another inspired the ambitions of this ambitious ruler. Each has at one time or another been a target. The independence of his neighbors is felt by Col. Qaddafi as a personal affront.

Libya's record of subversion, assassination, terror is clear. It is grim. It challenges civilization. The Libyan record provides an interesting example of the difference between ideology and process. Col. Qaddafi's creed of Islamic unity masks an overriding ambition for the expansion of Libyan territory and of his own power.

In organizing, promoting, recruiting, perpetuating violence and terror— against airline passengers, diplomats, civilian passers-by, heads of state, neighboring peoples—with its pursuit of political goals by the methods of violence, Libya works to destroy the distinctions between war and peace, between civilian and combatant, between politics and crime.

The world should take careful note of these words and acts of the Libyan government. They clarify the threats to peace, independence, self-government with which so many countries must live—the threats to peace and security with which we are all burdened.

Meanwhile we should offer the Sudan our support in its efforts to secure from this Council protection against aggression to which the Charter entitles it.

6
America and Her Allies

THE UNITED NATIONS AND NATO

It is a year of anniversaries:

Last week the world watched while the leaders of the Western democracies commemorated the end of World War II in Europe and talked about trade, or more accurately talked about talking about trade.

The president visited battlefields, cemeteries, parliaments, and reminded us all of how far we in the Atlantic Alliance have come in the past 40 years since the defeat and surrender of Adolf Hitler's Third Reich.

It is also the fortieth anniversary of the founding of the United Nations, which was constructed in the ashes of war.

These events remind us of the period just after World War II when the United States was not only stronger than anyone but very nearly stronger than everyone—and of the efforts we made then to shape a peaceful world.

Two quite different U.S. initiatives were undertaken in the years immediately after World War II: the founding of the United Nations and the construction of the Atlantic Alliance—the Marshall Plan, the Greek-Turkey doctrine and the founding of NATO.

Each represented an effort to establish international order.

In each the U.S. was the principal architect and builder.

The assumptions and the consequences of each are very different from each other.

What can we learn from the undoubted successes of U.S. policy fashioned in the wake of World War II for Europe and Japan that will help in dealing with today's problems of a powerful expansionist Soviet empire in a shambling world?

The United Nations was built in the very ashes of war. It represented the hopes, above all, of American leaders—that after the terrible carnage or

Washington Times, June 26, 1985.

hardship of World War II it would be possible to establish a world organization that, in the words of the UN Charter, would

> save succeeding generations from the scourge of war by requiring that members act in accordance with the principle of respect for the sovereign equality of all states, peaceful resolution of disputes, the non-use or threat of force, and non-intervention in internal affairs.

The founding of the United Nations represented the crowning achievement of the effort to eliminate war by judicial means.

We Americans had been dreaming that dream for a long time. We had already tried to outlaw war three times in this century with The Hague Convention in 1907, the League of Nations in 1919, and the Kellog Briand Pact of 1928. Now we are trying again. Obviously we believed it should be possible to control the dangerous and violent aspirations of governments by some system of law and restraints.

George Kennan put it this way:

> To the American mind, it is implausible that people should have positive aspirations, and ones that they regard as legitimate, more important to them than the peacefulness and orderliness of international life. From this standpoint, it is not apparent why other peoples should not join us in accepting the rules of the game in international politics, just as we accept such rules in the competition of sport in order that the game may not become too cruel and too destructive . . .

The United Nations was based on the assumption that nations would value peace above territorial acquisitions, that they would submit disputes to international adjudication, that they would keep agreements and live by the principles of the UN Charter, and that if an *outlaw* arose, who refused to live by those legal rules, the other nations would quite literally function as a world policemen—and call the outlaw to order.

The fact that the UN Charter had been violated, even before it was ratified, made not much difference to the initial enthusiasm. Even that great realist Harry S. Truman pledged that henceforth the UN would be the foundation of U.S. foreign policy. Yet, the conditions permitting optimism did not last long.

It is difficult to remember how bad things were: how devastated the cities and the economies, people, how aggressive the Soviet's and how unruly the indigenous communist parties in Italy and France. It is easy, too, to forget the absence of democratic institutions and a democratic tradition in Germany and Italy.

The shadow of the Red Army exercised more power over the fate of

Eastern Europe than did the principles of the UN Charter. And by the time that the democratic government of Czechoslavakia had succumbed to a violent coup, President Harry Truman concluded that the principles of non-intervention and non-use of force required some reinforcement by means not foreseen or provided in the Charter.

The ensuing decades of European peace, stability, and economic development, have so transformed the security and well-being of Europe that it is easy to forget the reality of destabilization, intimidation and outright aggression in the late 1940s. Events in Poland, Hungary, Finland, and Czechoslovakia dramatized the character as well as the reality of the danger confronting Greece and Italy and their prospects for democracies in Europe.

Truman thought that Western Europe was about to be swallowed by the Soviet advance. He called a special session of Congress and solemnly warned the Congress:

> Since the close of the hostilities, the Soviet Union and its agents have destroyed the independence and democratic character of a whole series of nations in Eastern and Central Europe.
>
> It is this ruthless course of action, and the design to extend it to the remaining free nations of Europe, that have brought about the critical situation in Europe today.
>
> The tragic death of the Republic of Czechoslovakia has sent a shock throughout the civilized world. Now pressure is being brought to bear on Finland, to the hazard of the entire Scandinavian peninsula. Greece is under direct military attack from rebels actively supported by her Communist-dominated neighbors. In Italy, a determined and aggressive effort is being made by a Communist minority to take control of that country. The methods vary, but the pattern is all too clear.

The identification of our security with countries beyond our borders, beyond the Atlantic, remained unsettling to Americans. It is difficult today to recall how great a departure from traditional American practice NATO was.

It was hotly disputed and feared by some. The comments of the late Senator Robert A. Taft of Ohio, who warned against ratification of the North Atlantic Treaty, manifested these rational American concerns. Addressing the U.S. Senate in 1949, Taft said:

> By executing a treaty of this kind, we put ourselves at the mercy of the foreign policies of eleven other nations, and do so for a period of twenty years . . . The Monroe Doctrine left us free to determine the merits of each dispute which might arise and to judge the justice and the wisdom of war in the light of the

circumstances at the time. The present treaty obligates us to go to war if certain facts occur.

The Alliance was forged as a direct response to the actual, imminent danger to Western Europe of Soviet subversion and aggression. No amount of historical revisionism can explain away facts of Soviet expansion into Europe. Truman described these to the Congress in a speech to a joint session on March 17, 1948:

> On April 4, 1949, I stood by Secretary of State Dean Acheson as he signed his name, on behalf of the United States, to a treaty which was the first peace time military alliance concluded by the United States since the adoption of the Constitution.

Signing the North Atlantic Treaty was, as Truman noted, "one more step in the evolution of U.S. foreign policy, along with the United Nations Charter, the Greek-Turkish Aid Program and the Marshall Plan."

NATO is the great success story of the century. The United Nations has become a largely impotent arena of global politics unable to make peace or keep peace.

In Germany, France, Italy, the president spoke from the scene of America's greatest success ever in foreign policy. Forty years of peace had followed . . . the longest period of peace Western Europe had enjoyed in more than two centuries.

The security and stability of Europe is so great, the alliance has been so successful that there has not even been a Europe-centered East/West confrontation since 1962. Moreover, the relative cooperation and cohesion among European states that have repeatedly fought one another has been remarkable. And within this framework of security, stability and cooperation the politics, economics and cultures of all alliance members have flourished.

What exists in Western Europe is exactly what we had hoped and worked and contributed to—prosperous, independent, democratic nations strengthened by cooperation with each other and with us.

What can we learn from these two post war experiences?

One of which failed, one which succeeded, for obviously the United Nations did not produce the desired result.

Someone estimated before the outbreak of the Iran/Iraq war that there had been some 41 wars since the founding of the UN in which more than 10,000,000 people had been killed with very conventional weapons. Not one of those wars has taken place in Europe. Europe is the *only* continent into which the Soviet empire has not made inroads in the last two decades.

The UN's basic concept of a *universal* organization and a universal commitment to keep peace and prevent aggressors from profiting by their aggressions did not prevent war. Instead I think it led the U.S. into two wars: Korea and Vietnam.

In Korea, we fought as part of a UN force. The UN flag still flies over the DMZ. In Vietnam, I believe, the U.S. committed its forces because of the conviction that we must not permit violence and aggression to succeed. The U.S., that is, would not permit an outlaw nation to achieve its goals.

While the Korean outcome, undertaken in the wake of war, was positive, I think it is clear that the Vietnam war was by realistic standards—a mistake.

Our fighting men were brave and loyal—they deserve all honor. But the war, undertaken in the role of world policemen was not a practical investment of American resources and above all—of American lives. Our interests were not directly involved. The principle of a universal commitment was not internalized as a basic value.

NATO, needless to say, was constructed on principles very different than those of the UN. It would not have been necessary to have a defensive alliance if we could have counted on others being bound by a commitment not to use force or to respect the sovereignty, territorial integrity and right to self-determination by democratic means.

Obviously, the principles of alliance and cooperation of which NATO is a product have proved a far more solid basis for peace than any of the alternative efforts at collective security. For this reason alone NATO deserves scrutiny and reflection.

NATO—with its permanent headquarters, and forces, unified commands, regular consultations and exercises, its missiles—embodies one approach to a potential military threat: its approach is to counter potential force with force. Not because its members are belligerent. Not because they seek war. Not because they do not value peace or seek peace through their foreign policies. Not because they are not willing to take risks for peace.

Still, the very existence of NATO proves its members are not willing to take the ultimate risk: of betting their independence on the Soviet Union's good intentions. No one says of our largest military commitment: look for a political solution to a potential threat, not a military one.

NATO has other characteristics that are vitally important to its survival and success:

1. It comprises democracies, which is to say its members share fundamental political moral values, and a Western democratic tradition.
2. It is a *long* range undertaking. Its members do not expect that the problem or the need for support will either disappear or be eliminated in the short run. No one says as about El Salvador: we invested in that project last year and now you are back asking for more.

3. The U.S. stake in NATO is widely recognized. It is so clear that serious American political leaders do not question what's in it for us, or whether we have a vital interest that justifies our involvement. We all think we know: the industrial strength of Europe is too great to permit it to fall to potential adversaries. Besides, our cultural and historical ties are too strong and Europe too central to our civilization, and our identity. And, with two previous wars in this century, we have too great a vested interest there.

NATO accepts that there are limits to our resources, our altruism. That is true. But, Europe is not the only area of the world in which vital interests and values are involved.

PROBLEMS OF THE ALLIANCE

It is sometimes said, by cynics, that the United Nations is a microcosm of the world. On my most pessimistic days, I fear this may be the case. If it is, we are in even worse trouble than most of you here dream, as regards the alliance or almost anything else.

At the United Nations, the alliance is not very strong. At the United Nations, the United States frequently stands alone on controversial issues, some of which are very important to us, some of which are very important to others. At the United Nations, our European allies often prefer a posture of nonalignment between us and the Group of 77 on the so-called North-South issues, which consume much of the time of that organization. On some other issues, they vote with our adversaries. Just this past week, the United States cast a lone veto in the Security Council on an obnoxious Golan Heights resolution. We voted no. The Soviets, Arabs, and miscellaneous others voted yes. Some five of our closest associates abstained. That's a common pattern on Middle Eastern and some other questions. A more ominous pattern was manifest on the El Salvador resolution in the last General Assembly. The resolution on El Salvador reaffirmed the Franco-Mexican communiqué, which opposed elections and supported the "negotiated" settlement advocated by the guerrillas. The resolution was cosponsored by five of our NATO partners. Nine of the European Ten finally supported it. Only the United Kingdom abstained. Abandoned by

Address before the Committee for the Free World, New York, New York, January 23, 1982.

our allies on this issue of great importance to us, we voted with some twenty Latin nations, including most of the Latin democracies.

At the United Nations, the NATO countries vote together mainly on administrative and budgetary matters, on which we are also joined by the Soviet Union, and on some—but not all—of the most egregious of the Soviet propaganda resolutions. If we regarded voting at the United Nations as the litmus test of the alliance, we would have to conclude that the alliance was not in very good shape.

I shall argue here today that that is not a fair or even a relevant test; that the alliance is in better shape than this test would reveal; and that just as the lack of allied agreement should not lead us to despair, neither should it constrain the United States. The allies' failure to join us on issues not central to the defense of Europe should not threaten the alliance. Neither should our unilateral action on such issues. Like cooperation, independence must be mutual.

Much of the contemporary discussion about crisis in the alliance is an example of what Edward Banfield, in his *Unheavenly City,* called "crisis mongering," to which, he argued, Americans are particularly prone. Freud wrote about World War I that he was less disappointed than many of his contemporaries with what the war revealed about human nature because he had never expected so much of it. Having never expected so much from the Western alliance, I am less dismayed by its performance.

To deal adequately with the question of whether there is a crisis in the Atlantic alliance and, if so, what are its characteristics and what we might do about it, it is necessary to go back to basics: What was the alliance supposed to be, anyway? In judging a tool, one should ask, What is the tool for? Is it able to accomplish the task for which it was intended? It is that question—what NATO is for—that I want to address in my remarks today.

I propose to begin where the Atlantic alliance began—at the end of World War II—and desire to remind us all that NATO represented a dramatic abandonment of the traditional American posture, stated by George Washington, who advised us to steer clear of "permanent alliances with any portion of the foreign world." In particular, he advised us not to entangle ourselves and our "peace and prosperity in the toils of European ambition, rivalship, interest, humor, or caprice." The conviction that the United States should avoid permanent alliances dominated the U.S. role in foreign affairs until World War II. As one historian noted, until the end of World War II and the emergence of the cold war, "the general public, the Congress and most public leaders believed that alliances caused wars instead of preventing them, and they opposed any such arrangements for the United States."

It follows, then, that for the United States NATO was not a preferred pattern of relating to the postwar world. It was not an arrangement that American leaders regarded as an ideal instrument for bringing peace to the world. On the contrary, the Atlantic alliance was founded on the shattered hopes for a very different structure of peace. In 1945 American leaders did not envision, and certainly did not wish for, the division of Europe that compelled the establishment of the Atlantic alliance. They cherished a vision of "one world" governed by the democratic principles embodied in the Atlantic Charter. Speaking to a joint session of Congress on March 1, 1945, President Roosevelt said that the Yalta Conference had been a success because it spelled "the end of the system of unilateral action, exclusive alliances and spheres of influence, and balances of power and all the other expedients which have been tried for centuries and have always failed." "We propose," he said, "to substitute for all these, a universal organization in which all peace-loving nations will finally have a chance to join." This universal organization on which Roosevelt based his hopes for peace was, of course, none other than the United Nations. This perspective, we know today, was idealistic to the point of utopianism, impatient with the constraints of international diplomacy and with the methods of the past. It was distinctly American. And it was doomed from the start.

These optimistic universalist plans were based on the even more optimistic assumption that the world order would be made up of democratic governments. Today, in the shadow of the Soviet-ordered repression in Poland, it is easy to forget that Yalta reaffirmed the principles of the Atlantic Charter, recognizing "the right of all people to choose the form of government under which they will live," and, in the case of Poland specifically, pledged that "free and unfettered elections" would be held "as soon as possible on the basis of universal suffrage and secret ballot." Roosevelt and Churchill no doubt took these words very seriously. But Stalin, who once wrote that "good words are a mask for the concealment of bad deeds," clearly did not. A Soviet puppet regime was already in place in Warsaw. The Red Army had occupied all of Eastern Europe, with the exception of most of Czechoslovakia. Words and dreams could neither conceal nor change this reality.

Stalin used words to great effect at Yalta. He argued that Poland was a question of both honor and security: honor because of past Russian grievances against Poland and security because Poland was a neighbor and had been a corridor for attack against Russia. This was, of course, the kind of falsification of history to which we have since become accustomed. It was Poland that had grievances against Russia, not Russia which had grievances against Poland. Stalin's falsification of history, however, concealed the real reason for the failure of the U.S. vision of the United Nations and for the division of the postwar world. The real reason was Soviet imperialism. The consolidation of the Soviet hold over Eastern Europe—lowering of the Iron Curtain—necessitated the creation of NATO as one of a system of defensive alliances, designed as protection against Soviet expansion in Europe.

The American alliance system, of which NATO is only the most highly developed example, is thus rooted in the cold war. It was a specific response to the Soviets' effort to gain control of the governments of Greece and Turkey and other governments in Eastern Europe over whom they had not been able to consolidate power immediately following the war. The Inter-American Treaty of Reciprocal Assistance, the so-called Rio Treaty, which was signed almost two years earlier than the NATO Treaty, in September 1947, established a mutual collective security agreement for the Western Hemisphere. NATO was explicitly concerned with mutual security arrangements in Western Europe.

NATO was established for the specific purpose of protecting Western Europe against being overrun or subverted by the Soviet Union. Neither Yalta nor the NATO Treaty was intended to ratify or recognize the division of Europe, much less to legitimize the consignment of the eastern half of Europe to the Soviet sphere. On the contrary, the NATO Treaty opened with a reaffirmation of the United Nations Charter, which itself was based on the democratic principles of the Atlantic Charter. The Truman Doctrine also signified the refusal of the United States to acquiesce in the spread of Soviet totalitarianism in Europe and its determination to regard the evolution of Europe as a matter of concern for U.S. security.

Although the Atlantic alliance recognized that the nations of Western Europe shared with the United States an attachment to democracy and an aversion to nondemocratic institutions, the NATO alliance never was regarded by its members as having the responsibility for rolling back communism or even for acting in concert to encourage the independence of Eastern Europe. In Hungary in 1956 and Czechoslovakia in 1968, NATO was confronted with clear-cut, brutal Soviet invasions aimed at smashing indigenous national liberation movements in those two countries. But in neither case did the countries of the Atlantic alliance act, nor was their inaction generally regarded as a betrayal of the alliance, whose purposes were perceived as less broad even than the defense of freedom *in Europe.* But although the Atlantic alliance committed NATO neither to containing communism outside Western Europe nor to helping Eastern Europe peoples liberate themselves, it was not devoid of ideological content. Its ideological purposes derived from the democratic character of the governments it was pledged to protect. But no additional ideological content can be attributed to it, I believe, without either distortion or exaggeration or both.

I should also like to emphasize that since 1949 the members of NATO have pursued independent national policies, except on matters of common concern to the alliance, that is, matters involving the security of Western Europe. Little effort has been made to consult or to coordinate national policies oriented toward other goals. France and Britain, the Netherlands, Belgium, for example, had colonial empires of which they more or less peaceably, more or less traumatically, divested themselves after World War II. The process of decolonization went on without significant mutual consultation, no matter how violent or difficult it became. France's long war in Indochina did not trigger alliance support, even though the "national liberation" movement she fought had important and relatively clear ties to the Soviet Union. Neither did anyone propose that France's long struggle in Algeria concerned NATO or that Belgium's problems in the Congo were the business of the Atlantic alliance. The pursuit of national foreign policy goals outside the Atlantic alliance was the norm. It was not regarded as disloyal or threatening to the alliance.

A greater strain was put on relations within the alliance when one of its partners actively opposed the policies of others. When the United States, for example, joined the Soviet Union in opposing the British-French-Israeli invasion of Egypt in the Suez adventure, that temporarily strained the alliance. When John Kennedy quietly supported national liberation movements in northern Africa against France's colonial rule, that was hardly welcomed by the French—but it was not regarded as a violation of the Atlantic alliance.

The United States' own understanding of the limits of commonality among members of the alliance has been manifest in various important initiatives. The Kennedy administration saw the prospect of Soviet missiles in Cuba as a serious threat to the security of the United States. However, it had recourse not to NATO but to the OAS and the Rio Treaty and took pains to brief the OAS ambassadors carefully and urgently before Kennedy's announcement of the U.S. response. Secretary of State Dean Rusk called a special meeting of the OAS, at which he invoked the Rio Treaty to justify U.S. actions.

This is one example—there are others—of the United States acting, and assuming it had the right to act, independently of the NATO alliance to protect its national interests. We did not consult in advance with European allies on that occasion. Instead, we informed them about the same time we were informing the world. NATO partners responded in various ways. President de Gaulle, a man who appreciated boldness and nationalism in foreign affairs, announced: "If there be a war, I will be with you, but there will be no war." Konrad Adenauer was also quick to express support. Britain and Italy had misgivings. Harold Macmillan pledged Britain's support at the United Nations but not in the Atlantic. And so forth.

The point is that collective action by NATO was neither expected, sought, nor forthcoming. It was generally understood that, like other members of the alliance, the United States had interests that lay outside the concerns and commitments of the Atlantic alliance, which she could pursue without prior consultation but with the hope of understanding and support from her European friends in such cases.

It is important to remember also, in considering the alliance, that it has proved very flexible; otherwise it wouldn't have survived for thirty-three years. One dramatic piece of evidence of that flexibility, of course, occurred when Charles de Gaulle announced on January 14, 1963, his new plan for France's national defense. De Gaulle, who had written that England is an island, France the edge of a continent, America another world, brusquely redefined and limited France's relationship to the alliance. Since then, as everyone knows, France has concentrated on the development of her own national defense, coordinating her relations and role within NATO with her national purposes. But this candid, forthright affirmation of French national identity and purpose has not ended France's role as a member of the Atlantic alliance. Neither then nor later was it argued that the pursuit of national policies independently of the alliance constitutes betrayal of the alliance.

In assessing the present difficulties, the so-called crisis of the alliance, it is terribly important to understand that NATO has demonstrated unity only when it has confronted a possible threat to European security. During the Korean War, for example, Western Europeans were reluctant to join the police action in Korea, even though that war was carried out under the banner of the United Nations. The European contribution to the U.S. effort in Vietnam was even less. The NATO powers in both instances demonstrated that they did not see the Atlantic alliance as a party to a global effort to contain communism and that they did not accept American leadership beyond the very important, but quite specific, purpose of providing for the security of Western Europe.

Emphasizing this point in no way demeans or diminishes the importance of the NATO alliance to the United States or to its various members. It does, I hope, demystify a bit that relationship, which, from time to time, becomes overloaded with sentimental rhetoric and grandiose expectations.

As human institutions go, NATO has been a colossal success. I do not think there can be any question that since NATO was founded, nearly thirty-three years ago, the parties to the treaty have fulfilled their goal of safeguarding "the freedom, common heritage and civilization of their peoples, founded on the principles of democracy, individual liberty and the rule of law." Even neutral states in Europe have been able to maintain their freedom and independence by virtue of NATO's stabilizing influence. NATO has been a great success. It remains one. It was never intended to be an all-purpose instrument. It should, therefore, not be criticized for failing to be one.

Why then is there so much discussion in places like this of the crisis in the alliance? Partly, I believe, because as memory of the history and purposes of the Atlantic alliance grows dim, there is a tendency both to romanticize the alliance and to overload it with exaggerated expectations and demands concerning what it might be and do. Furthermore, the relative eclipse of other mutual security treaties, which were constructed to provide for hemispheric security and containment, encouraged some to treat NATO as though it were *the* instrument of our foreign policy.

The ultimate antidote for this delusion should be the fact that the most critical international involvements of the United States in the post–World War II period—the Korean and the Vietnam wars and the Cuban missile crisis—have not directly involved the Atlantic alliance. This fact testifies neither to the success nor to the failure of NATO but to its nonrelevance to some major aspects of U.S. foreign policy. More realistic expectations of the alliance will surely lead to a more positive assessment of its performance.

Another reason for contemporary concern about the condition of the alliance is, I believe, the certain knowledge that as the social and economic, political, and military environments of NATO change, these changes may affect the alliance itself. Most dramatic and important among the changes is the evolution of economic independence between East and West associated with détente. The Polish crisis has dramatized the potentially negative effects on the alliance of interdependence, by focusing attention on the different views of the NATO partners concerning economic policy. Concern about the long-range effects of these environmental changes on the alliance is, I believe, reasonable and realistic.

A third source of concern about the present and future of the alliance lies, I believe, in the conviction of people like us that ideas and culture matter, that they have consequences for politics and for foreign policy, and, indeed, that they ultimately shape the world. We are, therefore, naturally worried when, for the first time, we hear significant numbers of people on both sides of the Atlantic questioning the value of the alliance. The fact that many Americans ask today whether an American alliance with Europe still serves *our* interests is itself indicative of the evolution of intra-alliance doubts in the United States, and it is every bit as important as the more widely publicized mass demonstrations in Europe for disarmament. The trends toward isolationism, globalism, and unilateralism in the United States, toward neutralism and pacifism in Europe, are equally reflections of unease about the alliance. Some Europeans are focusing on risks involved in alliance with the United States, risks that draw them, they fear, into conflicts that they might otherwise avoid; while Americans are saying that alliance with Europe imposes burdens and constraints on American foreign policy that can, perhaps, no longer be justified by the advantages of collective security in Europe.

European and American complaints against the alliance have not yet been translated into significantly different policies. We hope that they will not be. But as pressures and mutual recriminations mount, the time is fast approaching for a reaffirmation of the place of the alliance in a U.S. and Western strategy for defense and security. Obviously, Europe cannot insist on American support against the Soviet Union in Europe while at the same time supporting pro-Soviet forces outside Europe that may endanger U.S. security (as in Central America).

The growth of neutralism, isolationism, unilateralism—whatever one calls it—on both sides of the Atlantic constitutes an independent strain on the alliance and illuminates the fact that the alliance must be defended at the level of ideas. The defense of freedom is finally grounded in an appreciation of its value. No government, no foreign policy, is more important to the defense of freedom than are the writers, teachers, communication specialists, researchers—whose responsibility it is to document, illustrate, and explain the human consequences of freedom and unfreedom.

WHO PROFITS MOST FROM THE ALLIANCE?*

*With Mark Salter

How important are the changed circumstances which confront the Atlantic Alliance thirty-five years after its founding? How basic? How threatening or liberating? Is this relationship among the nations of the Atlantic Alliance still necessary, and if so, to whom and for what?

Certain facts—known to persons present—need, nonetheless, to be mentioned to set the questions and discussion in context.

First, the fact that, from the U.S. perspective, the Alliance represented a

National Committee on American Foreign Policy, New York, New York, April 30,1984.

sharp departure from traditional U.S. attitudes and behavior. In his memoirs, President Harry Truman wrote:

> On April 4, 1949, I stood by Secretary of State Dean Acheson as he signed his name, on behalf of the United States, to a treaty which was the first peacetime military alliance concluded by the United States since the adoption of the Constitution.

Signing the North Atlantic Treaty was, as Truman noted, "one more step in the evolution of U.S. foreign policy, along with the United Nations Charter, the Greek-Turkish Aid Program and the Marshall Plan." It was also a specific violation of the nation's traditional policy of refusing permanent alliances.

The identification of our security with countries beyond our borders, beyond the Atlantic, remained unsettling to Americans. The comments of the late Senator Robert A. Taft of Ohio, who warned against ratification of the North Atlantic Treaty, manifested these traditional American concerns. Addressing the U.S. Senate in 1949, Taft said:

> By executing a treaty of this kind, we put ourselves at the mercy of the foreign policies of eleven other nations, and do so for a period of twenty years. . . . The Monroe Doctrine left us free to determine the merits of each dispute which might arise and to judge the justice and the wisdom of war in the light of the circumstances at the time. The present treaty obligates us to go to war if certain facts occur.

Although there was a growing sense of global interdependence in the postwar U.S., we still approached international commitments with caution and only with the expectation that they would be temporary in duration. The founding fathers of the Alliance did not intend to establish a permanent security system. Rather, they hoped to allow the war-weakened democracies of Western Europe a security framework within which they could take refuge from Soviet threats and subversion until, with massive American aid, they repaired their devastated economies and rebuilt their defenses, thereby impairing the Soviet's ability to challenge their security.

The second point I desire to emphasize is again well known. Yet more and more often its importance is underestimated with the passage of time. It is that the Alliance was forged as a direct response to the actual, imminent danger to Western Europe of Soviet subversion and aggression. No amount of historical revisionism can explain away facts of Soviet expansion into Europe. Truman described these to the Congress in a speech to a joint session on March 17, 1948:

> Since the close of the hostilities, the Soviet Union and its agents have destroyed the independence and democratic character of a whole series of nations in Eastern and Central Europe.
>
> It is this ruthless course of action, and the design to extend it to the remaining free nations of Europe, that have brought about the critical situation in Europe today.
>
> The tragic death of the Republic of Czechoslovakia has sent a shock throughout the civilized world. Now pressure is being brought to bear on Finland, to the hazard of the entire Scandinavian peninsula. Greece is under direct military attack from rebels actively supported by her Communist dominated neighbors. In Italy, a determined and aggressive effort is being made by a Communist minority to take control of that country. The methods vary, but the pattern is all too clear.

The ensuing decades of European peace, stability, and economic development, have so transformed the security and well-being of Europe that it is easy to forget the reality of destabilization, intimidation and outright aggression in the late 1940s. The Soviet threat to which the Alliance was a response constituted a large part of the "Red Scare" of the times. Events in Poland, Hungary, Finland, Czechoslovakia, dramatized the character as well as the reality of the danger confronting Greece and Italy and the prospects for democracies in Europe.

The third point that I desire to underscore is that despite, or perhaps because of, its duration and patent success, the Alliance has repeatedly, even chronically, been perceived as undergoing some sort of crisis which threatened to transform if not destroy it.

We err if we think that the Alliance, having once enjoyed a golden age of nearly uniform judgments on all things important, has now lapsed into a progressively problematic relationship. In his *Fire in the Ashes*, published in 1953, Theodore White wrote of the passing of a period marked by great closeness and constructive cooperation and the entry into a period of new problems and new misunderstandings that challenge whether we can deal with these misunderstandings at all.

The same sense that the solutions to the problems of the postwar Soviet threat to Europe were being overtaken by events was expressed by Arthur Schlesinger's comments in *The Kennedy Years*:

> By 1960 the economic dependence on the United States had largely disappeared. Western Europe had been growing twice as fast as America for a decade; it had been drawing gold reserves from America; it had been outproducing America in coal.

Americans were flocking across the Atlantic to learn the secrets of the economic miracle. And, at the same time, the military dependence had taken new and perplexing forms. If the prospect of a Soviet invasion of Western Europe had ever been real, few Europeans believed it any longer. Moreover, the Soviet nuclear achievement, putting the United States for the first time in its history under the threat of devastating attack, had devalued the American deterrent in European eyes. These developments meant that the conditions which had given rise to the Marshall Plan and NATO were substantially gone. The new Europe would not be content to remain an economic or military satellite of America. The problem now was to work out the next phase in the Atlantic relationship.

Hans Morgenthau expressed the same concern that basic premises and characteristics of the Alliance could not remain unchanged in a rapidly changing world. He wrote in 1962:

> NATO was created as, and is still today officially considered to be, the shield that protects Western Europe from a Soviet attack on land. Yet it has never been clear how NATO could perform that function with the forces actually at its disposal or how it could have performed that function even with the much larger forces which its official spokesmen from time to time declared to be indispensable. Nor has it been clear how such a military organization, top-heavy as it is with collective agencies for the making of decisions, would operate effectively in case of war.

> These are some of the doubts which arise from within NATO itself. There are others which concern the relations between NATO and the overall political and military purposes of the Western alliance and, more particularly, of the United States. What is the place of NATO within the overall military strategy of the United States? What functions could NATO perform for the European communities and a more closely integrated Atlantic community? What impact is the impending diffusion of nuclear weapons likely to have upon the policies and the very existence of NATO? And what of the probable replacement of the manned bomber and bases supporting it by long-distance missiles? These are some of the questions which the Western governments should have raised long ago and answered.

That was twenty-two years ago. Today the search for definitive answers to those questions and others continues. Henry Kissinger has recently advised us that the problems facing the Alliance today may require "a remedy that is fundamental, even radical." He suggests that the time may have arrived for Europe to assume the responsibility for its own defense against conventional attack, time to draw down or withdraw entirely the 300,000 U.S. troops in Germany. Recently, James Schlesinger and Helmut Schmidt had a widely reported public dialogue in which they too questioned the validity of using long-established NATO security arrangements to face the challenges of today. And perhaps the most basic question of all has been raised by *La Stampa*'s Arrigo Levi: "Can one generation's experiences be bequeathed to the next?"

The fact is that there has never been a time in the thirty-five year life of NATO when everyone has been entirely satisfied with its performance. We have disagreed as to the nature of the Soviet threat and anguished over how to deal with it. We have disagreed about policies outside the area of the Alliance. Diversity of the interests and views of the members in matters outside the treaty area has resulted in some dramatic conflicts inside the Alliance. It is hard to remember, retrospectively, the passion associated with the Suez crisis of 1956, with European decolonization and with France's withdrawal from NATO in 1966. Yet even a casual review of Alliance history reveals disagreements so frequent and so widespread that they have sometimes obscured the fact that we have continued to share a general sense of the reality of a potential Soviet threat to the security of Western Europe and a belief that the Atlantic Alliance is the best available option for protection from that threat. The permanence of the debate is instructive. It compels us to examine the reasons for the longevity of the Alliance in defiance of the doubts and challenges that have plagued it and the chronic problems of divisive democracies trying in peacetime to make and maintain common policies with regard to a potential military treat.

The problems are to a significant degree a consequence and a reflection of the Alliance success. The persistence of the Alliance over three and one half decades demonstrates that it is a much more flexible instrument than it is usually conceived as being. Established as a framework for the participation of the United States in the defense of Europe, it has been a colossal success. Many things have changed since 1949. But most important is the reality of two generations of peace and prosperity in Western Europe, which has not. The relative cohesion among European states that have fought one another for centuries is, itself, a remarkable occurence. Its effect on the security and stability of Europe are also remarkable. There has not even been a significant European-centered, East/West confrontation since the last Berlin crisis in 1962. Within this relative stability, the economies and cultures of all Alliance members have flourished.

Indeed, European stability has been so uninterrupted it now seems unremarkable and is frequently viewed with indifference. A decade ago, the late Raymond Aron labeled this development "the routinization of the Atlantic Alliance," by which he meant that the Alliance ". . . no longer arouses enthusiasm or hostility. Aron suggested that, while "we may imagine a system that is better, we cannot dismiss as of marginal importance NATO's protection of Western European security against Soviet attack and subversion. Whatever the feasible alternatives to Atlantic security arrangements are, there is no evidence that they could hope to fulfill their basic purposes as successfully as the current arrangement has done.

However, it is never clear that what is will continue to be, or even that what is successful will survive. It is not necessary to be a Hegelian or a Marxist to be impressed with the tendency of solutions to become problems, requiring new solutions. Obviously, there are strains within the Alliance. Some of these are deeply rooted.

The U.S. and its partners share certain characteristics of democracies that create problems for maintaining permanent military alliances. The dynamics of electoral politics predispose democracies to focus on short-range problems and short-range solutions. Moreover, democracies, reflecting as they do the concerns of ordinary citizens, are in their very nature predisposed to seek and to expect peace, not war; to resent military expenditures and to evade long-range planning. The very fact of four decades of peace in Europe makes the need for maintaining the Alliance less plausible.

There are also the geopolitical realities in which the American tradition of isolationism and universalism are alike based. "An island continent," Walter Lippmann called us, "separated by two oceans from Europe and Asia, separated, too, by history and demography: Most Americans came here seeking relief from their former conditions and are in some sense ambivalent about permanent involvement in the affairs of other nations." Geographic realities give the Western Hemisphere irreducible importance to America and the westward course of American destiny links us to the Pacific states. We cannot transcend nor ignore these realities.

Larry Eagleburger recently predicted what he perceived as "the shift of the center of gravity of U.S. foreign policy from the transatlantic relationship toward the Pacific basin and particularly Japan." Besides the growing importance of Pacific states in the world economy, he cites the Europeans having "become so concerned with their own problems that it has tended to make it ever more difficult to get Western Europe to look outside its borders" as the reason underlying this perceived shift.

Certainly, the U.S. involvement with the nations of the Pacific is long-standing. We have been going west throughout our history. Our trade with that region has surpassed that with Europe and is growing at a faster rate.

There is also the special relationship with our Hemisphere and the other nations of the Americas. Geography, demography and history alike link our security and destiny with the Americas.

Beyond geography, there is, of course, history and identity. The United States has historical and demographic ties to the Pacific, Africa, Latin America, but strongest historical and demographic ties to Europe.

Indeed, one could say that the Atlantic Community is as old as the European discovery of America. We are part of what is called "Western Civilization." That Greco-Roman, Judeo-Christian approach to life defines us just as surely as it defines Europe. We are the heirs of the liberal, demo-

cratic tradition born of the efforts of Englishmen and other Europeans to
make just government dependent on the consent of the governed. To be an
American means to be part of that civilization. It does not mean that we
are European. It does not mean we are Euro-Centric. But we share a
civilization with Europe, a heritage, an identity that defines our destiny at
the same time it links our destiny to Europe. This sense of identification
reinforced those who sought successfully to involve the United States in
World War I and II. And there are less readily categorized ways in which
our national interest links us to Europe.

Hans Morgenthau, writing in 1951, explained how U.S. national interests led us to participate in the politics of the old world.

> Since a threat to our national interest in the Western Hemisphere can only
> come from outside it—historically from Europe—we have always striven to
> prevent the development of conditions in Europe which would be conducive
> to a European nation's interfering in the affairs of the Western Hemisphere or
> contemplating a direct attack upon the United States. These conditions
> would be most likely to arise if a European nation, its predominance un-
> challenged within Europe, could look across the sea for conquest without fear
> of being menaced at the center of its power; that is, in Europe itself.
>
> It is for that reason that the United States has consistently pursued policies
> aiming at the maintenance of the balance of power in Europe. It has opposed
> whatever European nation—be it Great Britain, France, Germany or Rus-
> sia—was likely to gain ascendancy over its European competitors which
> would have jeopardized the hemispheric predominance and eventually the
> very independence of the United States. Conversely, it has supported what-
> ever European nation appeared capable of restoring the balance of power by
> offering successful resistance to the would-be conqueror.

A balance of power?

A would-be conqueror?

Revisionists affirm these concerns were ever-illusory and join a larger
chorus of voices that question their contemporary realism.

Two questions, each important, must be addressed.

One concerns reality: does the Soviet threat to the peace, national independence and freedom of Western Europe, which stimulated NATO's formation, *still* exist? The answer seems to me to be found in the sponsorship
by the Soviet Union of subversion, coups, insurgency, invasion, incorporation in other continents, and the new unilateral vulnerabilities created for
Western Europe by Soviet deployment of new generations of missiles targeted on Western Europe. *Le Monde* last week commented in an editorial
on "le style Tchernenko."

> The observers who have been wondering if the new Soviet leadership installed

last February would harden the policy followed previously have now new evidence. Events of the last days in Afghanistan confirm the warnings of the leaders of Afghanistan's resistance: Moscow has mounted a new form of combat much more massive and brutal, devoid of any of the subtleties which Andropov demonstrated.

Afghanistan is not Europe. The rulers of the Soviet Union are capable of differentiated response. But their continued boycott of INF talks, the demand for superiority present in the adamant insistence on removal of Euromissiles, seem to underscore many other indications that Soviet hegemony over Western Europe remains a realistic concern. The most powerful argument for the persistence of the Alliance is the persistence of the threat of peace, national independence, freedom which stimulated its formation in the first place, a threat symbolized today in the SS-20s and their various cousins.

Freedom from fear is not tantamount to freedom from danger, Lawrence Martin has reminded us, adding:

> It is the difficult task of Western strategists . . . to preserve the real safety of their nations in an environment of conflict which the nations would rather ignore and a price in money, and in blood, which the peoples would, quite reasonably, rather not pay."

Between threat and threat-perception lies the whole subjective world with its well-known possibilities for deceit, exaggeration, hopes, fears, illusions, concerning both self and others. There lies, too, the domain of value and choice.

The objective persistence of threat does not guarantee the persistence of its perception and constant perception does not guarantee constant response.

The Europe of the late forties was vulnerable and *felt* vulnerable. The recent experience with conquest and despotism had left a clear, deeply felt, widely held sense of the superiority of freedom, the horror of subjection. The U.S. of the late forties enjoyed clear military and economic superiority, felt the confidence, community and purpose born of victory over tyrants. The confidence was so strong that, to this day, no revisionists have arisen seriously to question whether World War II was a necessary war, whether the stakes were as high as then perceived, whether the devastation of war was justified at all.

In neither Europe nor America is there today quite the same clarity and confidence about the choices and stakes, about the problem to which the Alliance is the solution or about the solution.

At the most radical level, some Europeans doubt today the moral difference between "the superpowers."

John Vinocur wrote in yesterday's *New York Times Magazine* of certain German intellectuals who speak of "America as aggressor; America as polluter, nuclear terrorist and profiteer; America as-the-force-keeping-us-from-the-way-we-want-to-be." (Of course, he also described in the same piece the dramatic turnaround of French intellectuals with regard to the U.S.)

The transformations of time have dimmed old visions, eroded old ties and created at the same time new possibilities. The rulers of East Germany have reinforced the Wall, but also seem to have understood that the personal ties among Germans lead not to satiation, but to the desire for more. The longing to break barriers between the Germanies reinforces the fear of nuclear war in this front line state, creating a state of mind called neutralism—much as the sense of unnecessary vulnerability and unappreciated solidarity feeds American isolationist impulses.

Accompanying these ongoing mutual re-evaluations of moral and political character, strategy and tactics are also widely discussed. Should Europe risk becoming a battlefield in a war between superpowers? Should Americans continue to expose themselves to nuclear war to protect Western Europe?

The evidence suggests that in no country of Western Europe a majority holds that their interest would be better served outside of the NATO security guarantee. On the contrary, I believe that in many cases of constructive debates over the relative merits of NATO defense modifications, media coverage has magnified radical perceptions and prescriptions. When the die was cast, Europeans and Americans alike decided the issue of deployment in favor of an Allied response to a new European vulnerability.

Some Europeans like to believe that the American stake in Western Europe is so great that the U.S. will necessarily be involved in an attack on a NATO nation.

Some Americans, thinking radically, doubt that this is necessarily the case—providing we had neither troops nor missiles in Europe. Some Americans insist that European and American defense is divisible.

It is as tempting and mistaken to exaggerate distrust, dislocation in U.S./European relations as it is to ignore them.

Dissatisfaction with the Alliance's tactics, plans and structures surely is rooted in changing economic and military facts and relations which must be continually updated.

But much of the current "crisis mongering" is surely rooted less in changed objective realities than in changed expectations.

We have overloaded the Alliance with expectations which it was never intended to bear; then, because it does not meet these new expectations, we are surprised and view this instrument as deficient. The image of frictionless relations between allies is almost exactly analogous to the image of the frictionless marriage or the perfectly ordered house. These exist only in fantasy. The fact *is* that the relations between the United States and its NATO allies today are very good and very strong. They are based on common values, deeply related common institutions, legal systems and a very great deal of mutual respect on the part of most significant figures in all of the societies—not just governments, but societies.

The debate over the Alliance security strategies was not begun with the installation of Soviet SS-20s. It will not end when deployment of INF is completed. For many the idea that the United States would consider an attack upon Western Europe as an attack upon itself has always seemed hard to accept. We would hope that for now the absence of any authoritative discussion of reducing the level of U.S. troop strength in Europe, the rejection of proposals to renounce first-use of nuclear weapons in Europe, the improvement of theater nuclear defenses and, of course, the continued expressions of unshakeable support from Washington for U.S. commitments to European security would allow European fears to subside. But questions will and, of course, should continue. And new developments will require new modifications. The emergence of chemical weapons promises to raise new questions about the nuclear threshold to illuminate Europe's commitment to a nuclear defense, to illuminate, as well, U.S. vulnerabilities deriving from any strategy that foresees "going nuclear" as an early response.

Doubtless, too, there will be new demands for and against restructuring decision-making within the Alliance. Italian Foreign Minister Colombo suggested in a recent speech a new "Euro-American Friendship Pact and also periodic meetings between foreign ministers to coordinate their respective views . . ." and provide continuity in discussions among NATO governments.

The instrumentalities necessary for adaptation to changing realities exist. Power in the Alliance *is* shared, as former German Chancellor Helmut Schmidt noted two years ago during the controversy over NATO modifications: "The voice of the Europeans is strong enough to be heard if they so desire. There are fifteen members in the Alliance, thirteen of which are Europeans. Why don't they speak if they want to be heard?"

They do want to be heard. They do speak. The NATO system can and will respond.

Doubtless, too, there will be U.S. frustrations with the Alliance which will doubtless persist. In the U.S. government we chafe today over European failure to understand our problems outside Europe. Larry Eagleburger, a staunch and warm supporter of the Alliance, expresses his disappointment that, in a year after the Falklands, the Europeans could not restrain harsh criticism over the Grenada landing in which we moved in careful concert with the nations of the Caribbean: "At the very least could not our friends have suspended judgment until the emerging situation became clearer?"

It is not a perfect marriage, no counsellor can make it one. We have and will continue to have distinct interests and shared ones as well. "Who profits most from the Alliance—Europe or America?" Aron asked a decade ago.

The fact that the question was not easily answered then and is not easily answered today illuminates the foundations of the Alliance. This pattern of cooperation and alliance among the nations of the Atlantic area will survive generational change because it is bound on more than nostalgia. It will survive new important economic ties to the Pacific because it is bound together by more than shared economic interests. It will survive disappointments and misunderstandings because the leaders of the democracies understand, finally, that all our nations and all their freedoms, depend finally but immediately on the civilization that sustains us all.

There is no perfect alliance. There are no perfect friends, and as James Reston commented concerning this debate on NATO defense improvements, "There is no perfect security. There is only the struggle. With friends at our side doing the best we can."

The American government and the people it serves have every intention of continuing that struggle, side-by-side with our European friends.

7
Violence and Lies

THE THREAT OF INTERNATIONAL TERRORISM*

With Joe Shattan

The theme of my remarks this afternoon is the profound threat posed by international terrorism to an orderly and secure world. Before touching on this subject directly, however, I would like to address four widely-held misconceptions about terrorism which have seriously obscured the nature of the terrorist threat to the goals and ideals underlying our way of life.

The first misconception about terrorism relates to its meaning. According to a number of distinguished students of the subject, a rigorous and objective definition of terrorism is impossible. This is so, it is argued, because, "One man's terrorist is another man's freedom fighter." Hence, consensus as to what is and is not terrorism becomes impossible, and we are left in an intellectual and moral limbo. As one authority on the subject put it, "There is no satisfactory political definition of terrorism extant or forthcoming: there is similarly no common academic consensus as to the essence of terror and no common language with which to shape a model acceptable to political scientists or social psychologists. Terror appears to be a condition known implicitly to most men, but which is somehow beyond rigorous examination."

If this view is correct, if no objective definition of terrorism exists, then it seems to me that we might all throw up our hands and resign ourselves to the inevitability of further terrorist outrages. If terrorism as a political, social and moral phenomenon eludes rigorous examination and if we can-

Address before the American Society for Industrial Security, June 2, 1982.

not even articulate what we *mean* by terrorism, then how can we possibly hope to devise effective measures to counteract terrorism?

Fortunately, not everyone subscribes to the view that terrorism is undefinable. In the summer of 1979, in fact, a number of prominent academics, journalists and political figures from around the world met at the Jerusalem Conference on International Terrorism, and, *inter alia*, drew up a definition. Terrorism, they said, is "the deliberate, systematic murder, maiming and menacing of the innocent to inspire fear in order to gain political ends."

This definition is a good one. It draws our attention to what is, after all, the distinguishing characteristic of modern terrorism: its focus on noncombatants. Hijacking aircraft, exploding bombs in marketplaces and in pubs, attacking school buses and kindergartens, kidnapping businessmen and taking civilian hostages—these are, objectively speaking, terrorist acts, regardless of whether or not one is in sympathy with their ultimate political purposes. That perpetrators of terrorist acts may have been moved by motives that some would consider noble is an altogether secondary matter and has no bearing on the quality of the terrorist act itself. "By their fruits shall ye know them"—and not by their ideological bluster: that is how the Jerusalem Conference identified terrorists, and that Biblical injunction might well serve as our own guide as well.

A second misconception about terrorism is the widespread tendency to regard terrorists as "frustrated idealists," "desperate men" who turned to terrorism as an instrument of social progress only because they regretfully concluded that "the system doesn't work." Proponents of this point of view, while disassociating themselves from terrorist methods, are quite willing to praise the courage, sincerity, commitment and idealism of the terrorists themselves—provided that the terrorists openly identify with the radical Left and maintain a properly critical attitude toward "American capitalism" and all its works.

What advocates of the "frustrated idealist" school of thought fail to understand, however, is that terrorists are not at all interested in facilitating social progress. On the contrary, as James Q. Wilson has pointed out, "Terrorists will do whatever they can, make whatever alliances are necessary (including alliances with common criminals and homicidal maniacs) to prevent any 'political solution' short of the destruction of the state itself. They will thus direct their attacks chiefly against groups desirous of constructive change. The Red Brigades killed Aldo Moro, a center-liberal politician, and not some monarchist fanatic. The aim of the true terrorist is not to hasten progress, but to provoke a fascist reaction."

A third misconception about terrorism is the notion that terrorist actions have their causes in the social environment. To those who hold this view, the fact that terrorist outrages are committed against American, British, Dutch, German, Italian and Israeli nationals is an implicit indictment of American, British, Dutch, German, Italian and Israeli societies—for surely no one would engage in such outrages unless he or she had first been traumatized by severe social injustice. Until the "underlying social causes" of terrorism are adequately dealt with, until war, racism, poverty and all other political and social evils are fully eliminated, this view maintains that terrorism will remain an incurable social affliction.

The "social injustice" theory of terrorism is invalidated, however, by two rather crucial facts. In the first place, while it is certainly the case that some degree of injustice exists in all societies, the activities of international terrorist groups are hardly directed against the world's most oppressive polities—that is, against totalitarian societies. On the contrary, as the former Soviet dissident, Vladimir Bukovsky, has observed, "Where there are real tyrants, and the worst oppression, we do not see such violence." Terrorist violence is aimed almost exclusively at democratic or pro-Western regimes, while Communist and pro-Soviet regimes are left almost entirely unscathed. This can hardly be a coincidence.

Moreover, the level of training and organization that has enabled international terrorism to become an effective force capable of challenging established governments is simply beyond the reach of local, isolated terrorist groups. International terrorism is inconceivable apart from the financial support, military training and sanctuary provided to the terrorists by certain states. To look for the causes of terrorism in the behavior of societies victimized by terrorism is thus a pointless exercise. Rather, these causes are to be found in the convictions and expectations of the terrorists themselves, and in the activities of those states which find it in their interest to support international terrorism.

The fourth misconception about terrorism is the notion that democratic societies can easily cope with the challenge of terrorism. In this perspective, there is nothing to worry about. Terrorism, it is argued, is a marginal, largely irrelevant phenomenon with little or no impact on the democratic political process.

This complacent attitude that modern, democratic, industrial societies can easily cope with a handful of terrorist malcontents is profoundly mistaken. West German Chancellor Helmut Schmidt was much nearer the mark when he observed in 1976 that the revolutionary left posed the greatest challenge to German democracy since its creation. Chancellor Schmidt understood that a systematic campaign of terrorism can undermine the moral consensus which underlies any democratic political order. As a noted American political scientist, Bernard Brown, recently wrote, "Popular irritation and fear generated by disorder and chaos could well provoke a reaction by those who believe that democracy is unable to defend itself or the society. The temptation will be great to sacrifice individual liberties, and then perhaps to turn to those who will eliminate disorder by authoritarian means if necessary. The attempt by revolutionaries to overthrow parliamentary democracy could well bring about a revival of fascism in Germany and Italy. Profound authoritarian forces in both countries come to fore under conditions of sharp conflict and political violence. In Germany and Italy, small numbers of revolutionaries, disdainful of the electoral process and unable to win popular support through the ballot box in any case, have succeeded in converting the climate of opinion from one that sustains parliamentary debate into one that encourages blows and counterblows, coups and countercoups, violence and counterviolence. Parliamentary institutions require an appropriate public attitude if they are to function effectively; and that favorable, supporting public attention is breaking down."

Despite the seemingly senseless and random nature of many terrorist acts, terrorism is a carefully conceived strategy designed to bring about what is called a "revolutionary situation" where none existed beforehand. The essence of the terrorist's strategy is provocation: through persistent, murderous attacks which disrupt society and make ordinary life impossible, terrorists hope to goad the authorities into a policy of massive and reckless repression, in the expectation that such repression will polarize the society, alienate large segments of the population, undermine the legitimacy of the regime and create widespread and evergrowing havoc and discontent. Terrorists seek to transform the democratic state into an authoritarian state, and the authoritarian state into brutal and arbitrary dictatorship. Where, for example, the press is free, terrorists would like to see it muzzled; where an independent judiciary exists, terrorists would invite martial law; where police excesses are curbed, terrorists seek to provoke police brutality. Recognizing that they alone are too weak to overthrow the state, terrorists try to induce state authorities to discredit themselves by revoking precisely those freedoms upon which the entire edifice of human rights rests: freedom of speech, freedom of press and freedom of assembly.

The theory of modern terrorism was first formulated in the most famous document of the 19th century Russian revolutionary movement, *The Revolutionary Catechism*. Written in 1869 by two of Russia's most prominent revolutionaries, Mikhail Bakunin and Sergei Nechaev, *The Revolutionary Catechism* called for the establishment of a totally dedicated, tightly knit "terrorist association." This terrorist association, it declared "will use every means in its power to *foster* and *spread* those wrongs and those evils which will finally break the patience of our people and force them to a general revolt."

The history of the Russian revolutionary movement constitutes, in large measure, a vindication of the terrorist strategy developed by Bakunin and Nachaev. The first modern revolutionary-terrorist group, The People's Will, was founded in Russia in 1879. Dedicated to the destruction of the Czarist state and all its institutions, The People's Will initially consisted of no more than 30 conspirators, yet by 1881 it had succeeded in murdering Czar Alexander II along with many lesser government officials. The success of The People's Will seriously undermined the authority of the Czarist regime, and the wave of governmental repression provoked by The People's Will and its successor groups still further eroded the government's authority. As one historian of the period put it, "From 1879 onwards the Imperial government introduced a series of extremely harsh counter-measures meant to prevent terror, but which had the effect of alienating moderate groups in Russia. In the long run this made it impossible for the regime ever to secure the support of moderately conservative and liberal elements in Russian society, so it was left to fail, isolated and alone, in 1917. Terrorism in Russia thus succeeded beyond the wildest expectations of its supporters."

The lessons of the Russian revolutionary movement have not been lost on contemporary terrorist groups. Indeed, the strategy of modern day terrorism is little more than a restatement and elaboration of the principles in *The Revolutionary Catechism*. Consider, for example, the most widely-known and influential terrorist tract of the twentieth century, *The Minimanual of the Urban Guerrilla*. Written by the Brazilian Communist-turned-terrorist, Carlos Marighella, and posthumously published in 1970, the Minimanual is quite literally a strategic blueprint for terrorists the world over. Its basic ideas, however, simply echo views expressed in *The Revolutionary Catechism*. The aim of the terrorist, it explains, is to create a situation where "the government has no alternative except to intensify repression. The police roundups, house searches, arrests of innocent people and of suspects, closing off streets, make life in the city unbearable." In the wake of these repressive measures, it continues, "the general sentiment is that the government is unjust, incapable of solving problems, and resorts purely and simply to the physical liquidation of its opponents." Eventually, as repression grows, "the political situation in the country is transformed into a military situation in which the militarists appear more and more to be the ones responsible for errors and violence, while the problems in the lives of the people become truly catastrophic." During this critical period, the *Minimanual* counsels, "the urban guerrilla must become more aggressive and violent, resorting without letup to sabotage, terrorism, expropriations, assaults, kidnappings and executions, heightening the disasterous situation in which the government must act."

This brief summary of the theory of terrorism should explain why the Reagan Administration believes that international terrorism poses such a profound threat to human rights. It is not simply because terrorists frequently deprive their victims of the most fundamental human right of all—the right to life. Rather, it is because terrorists, as a matter of deliberate policy, set out to destroy the human rights of an entire society. To be sure, terrorists invite repression from the right in the expectation that it will ultimately lead to a revolution from the left—a denouement which they regard as "progressive." In the meantime, everyone's human rights are diminished and all must suffer the appalling consequences of an escalating spiral of terrorism and counterterrorism. That terrorists have provoked successful military coups against democratically-elected governments in Uruguay, Argentina and Turkey, and have also provoked an unsuccessful military coup against the democratically-elected Spanish government, only underscores the gravity of the terrorist threat to human rights.

Unfortunately, that threat has grown particularly acute since 1968. A recent book on the subject of terrorism, referring to the massive proliferation of terrorist groups and activities over the last 10 years, calls the 1970s the "Fright Decade." According to an unclassified CIA study, some 3,336 terrorist attacks attributable to groups with international connections killed or wounded almost 10,000 people—nearly all of them civilians—between 1968 and 1979. In 1980, 760 international terrorist incidents resulted in over 1,600 people killed or wounded, the highest recorded casualty level since the U.S. began keeping statistics on terrorism. Preliminary data for 1981 shows a continuation of 1980's high frequency of terrorist attacks.

The wave of terrorist attacks which swept across the democratic and pro-Western world during the "Fright Decade," and which has yet to run its full course, could not have attained its current height without the substantial support which terrorists groups receive from the Soviet Union and its allies. Recent studies by Claire Sterling and Herbert Romerstein, carefully documented and drawn entirely from unclassified sources, have proven beyond a reasonable doubt that Soviet Union, either directly or through its satellites and proxies, is deeply involved in supporting international terrorism.

Clearly, the Soviet Union and its allies all have grasped the revolutionary potential of terrorist movements, particularly in the so-called Third World. They have recognized that throughout Asia, Africa and Latin America there are more than a few weak governments with low levels of legitimacy and high levels of instability. To a degree far greater than most Americans realize, these governments are acutely vulnerable to terrorist disruptions and are therefore inviting targets for the kind of terrorist campaign of destabilization advocated by Marighella and others. In providing terrorist movements with arms, training and political support, the Soviet Union and its allies have discovered a highly "cost-effective" way of making the point that in today's world it is not at all safe for any government to be openly pro-American.

What measures, then, can be taken to protect the potential victims of international terrorism?

The first thing to be done is to pursue multilateral diplomatic efforts aimed at outlawing various aspects of international terrorism. In this connection, a significant victory in the fight against terrorism occurred on December 17, 1979, when the United Nations adopted the International Convention Against the Taking of Hostages. The basic thrust of the Hostage Convention is that those who take hostages will be subject to prosecution or extradition if they are apprehended within the jurisdiction of a state party to the Convention. States party to the Convention are also obligated to cooperate in the prevention of acts of hostage-taking by internal preventive measures and by exchanging information to prevent such acts. Other significant anti-terrorist agreements include the 1973 Convention on the Protection of Diplomats, and the Tokyo, Hague and Montreal Conventions on Interference in International Civil Aviation. These agreements are the products of long and arduous diplomatic efforts. As a government and a people committed to the rule of law in international affairs no less than in domestic affairs, we are obliged to make such efforts.

At the same time that we pursue the diplomatic route, however, it is equally necessary for public officials and private individuals to address some of the more widely-held misconceptions about terrorism.

By talking in a forthright and candid way about terrorism—about who the terrorists are, what their purposes are, and which governments support them—I think that we can help to bring the process of terrorist intimidation out of the dark shadows and into the sunlight. Hopefully, that combination of the light of day and fresh air will render the effects of the intimidators a little less intimidating, and will eventually bring the onus of international censure to bear where it belongs: the terrorists and their supporters, and not on the victims of terrorism and the opponents of terrorism.

Terrorism as War

The most difficult problem in understanding politics is to see phenomena as they are without confusion or mystification, simply to observe who does what to whom, to hear what he says about his actions, and to observe their consequences. The more simply and clearly the phenomena can be observed and described, the greater the possibility that their meaning and significance can be understood.

What the terrorist does is kill, maim, kidnap, torture. His victims may be children in the schoolroom; travelers like those held and rescued at Entebbe; or gathered in an airport as at Lod. They may be industrialists, political leaders—diplomats in Paris, London, Los Angeles—or legislators like those on whom machine guns were turned in the 1950s in Washington. The terrorist's victims may have no particular political identity—like the cafe-goers at Goldenberger's in Paris or the passers-through at Lod (now Ben Gurion Airport); or they may be political symbols, like Aldo Moro or Pope John Paul II. They may be kidnapped and held for ransom, maimed or simply blown to bits.

One defining characteristic of the terrorist is his choice of method: the terrorist chooses violence as the instrument of first resort. Yet terrorism is distinguished from violent crime. Crime, too, is unauthorized violence against persons who are not at war. How does terrorism differ from simple crime? The difference lies not in the nature of the act, but in the understanding of its perpetrator, and, however vague, of what he is doing. Terrorism is *political* in a way that crime is not; the terrorist acts in the name of some political, some public purpose. Political man, Harold Lasswell wrote, is one who projects *private* affects onto public objects and rationalizes them in the name of a conception of the public good. The members of Murder, Inc. acted for private purposes. John Hinckley attempted to kill President Reagan for essentially private reasons. But the killers who sprayed bullets into Goldenberger's, like those who attempted to murder Eden Pastora, had a public goal in view. Terrorism is a form of political war. While the conception of the actor transforms the act, and while a purpose related to a public goal makes an act political, it does not make it moral. A public purpose does not make a terrorist who has been arrested a political prisoner.

Terrorism should also be distinguished from conventional war and terrorists from soldiers who wield violence. A soldier wields violence in accor-

Address to the Jonathan Institute Conference on International Terrorism, Washington, D.C., June 25, 1984.

dance with the legal authorities of his society against enemies designated by legally constituted authorities. Soldiers use violence where a state of belligerence is recognized to exist. The terrorist engages in violence in violation of law and against persons who are not at war with him. Even in this century of total war, when civilian targets are drawn into conflict by bombing and by resistance movements, belligerency is at least a condition known to all the parties to a conflict. The Nazi occupiers patrolling the streets of Paris understood that French civilians were not only conquered but that for many, the war continued. They understood that some unknown portion of the civilian population was at war with them and had not acquiesced in the surrender signed by France's wartime government.

Terrorists use violence against people who do not understand themselves to be at war. The victims of terrorist attack are unarmed, undefended and unwary. They may be sleeping Marines on a peace-keeping mission, or an industrialist coming home from work or schoolchildren in their schoolroom. The crucial point is the victims conceive themselves as civilians. They do not understand that they are regarded, or may be regarded, by someone else as belligerents in an ongoing war. This is a reason that one study done in our government emphasized that terrorism is "politically motivitated, premeditated violence perpetrated against non-combatant targets by subnational groups or clandestine state agents."

If we listen to the terrorist, we understand that he is at war against us. Terrorism is a form of war against a society and all who embody it. War is as Clausewitz emphasized, "a real political instrument, a continuation of politics by other means." It is "an act of violence intended to compel our opponent to fulfill our will."

Terrorist war is part of a total war which sees the whole of society as the enemy, and *all* the members of a society as appropriate objects for violent action. It is absolute war because its goal is absolute destruction of a society and because it accepts annihilation of persons as an appropriate means. Terrorists are the shock troops in a war to the death against the values and institutions of a society—Western society or non-Western society—and of the people who embody it.

The terrorist does not necessarily possess a comprehensive doctrine or plan. It is only necessary that he relate his violent act to a social political goal. In our times he is likely also to be linked to an organization of others who share his understood "political" interests, and who organize and assist his violent acts and relate them to international political goals.

The affinities between terrorism and totalitarianism are multiple. Both politicize the whole of society—the totalitarian by making society, culture and personality the object of his plans, actions and powers; the terrorist by taking the whole of society as the object and enemy of his violence, his war.

Both conceive violence as an appropriate means to their political ends and use violence as an instrument of first resort aggressively. They understand that smashing a society means smashing people. Both reject basic moral principles associated with Judeo-Christian civilization, such as the value and responsibility of the individual, and also reject prohibitions against the use of offensive force in social or international affairs. "We are against everything that is good and decent," said home-grown terrorist Bernadine Dohrn.

Both terrorists and totalitarians act and see themselves as acting in the name of a new morality and on the basis of a different epistemology. Both see their violence as justified by their "higher" morality whose transcendent collective ends justify and demand violation of conventional morality and the sacrifice of people whose membership in the old society makes them "expendable." Both permit and even encourage expression of aggressive, murderous instincts whose repression, Freud correctly emphasized, is a precondition of civilization. The social relations of both to outsiders is dominated by hostile intent. The enemy is everywhere, struggle is inevitable. It is unending. It is total.

Despite the many affinities of terrorism and totalitarianism, the two need also be distinguished. Totalitarianism is the property of a certain kind of society or polity. One of the instruments of that polity is terror. Terrorism, on the other hand, may be the property of individuals, small groups or governments which do not possess total power, whose rulers may have totalitarian aspirations, but whose societies have not yet become totalitarian. Both Libya and Syria are examples of such states.

Raymond Aron described three kinds of terror as present in the Soviet experience: that used by a party or faction against parties or factions hostile to them; that which aims at eliminating class enemies, such as liquidation of the Kulaks as a class; and that which turned terror previously used against class enemies or adversaries against all those who disagreed with the ruler. This third category permitted anyone who was in any way objectionable to be classified as an "enemy of people." All these categories of terror are present in the violence of the terrorist. Totalitarian society is saturated with coercion. Nonetheless, not all coercive societies are totalitarian and not all societies that support, sponsor or harbor terrorists and terrorism are totalitarian.

The most important relations between terrorism and totalitarianism seem to me to be, first, that the most important totalitarian state of our times is also the principal supporter and sponsor of international terrorism as a form of political action; and second, that those who pursue power by terrorism aspire to found totalitarian societies. Orwell wrote: "It is not merely that 'power corrupts'; so also do the ways of attaining power. Therefore all efforts to regenerate society *by violent means* lead to the cellars of the O.G.P.U." "The essential act," he wrote also, " is the rejection of democracy—that is, of the underlying values of democracy; once you have decided upon that, Stalin—or at any rate someone *like* Stalin—is already underway."

In Nicaragua, rejection of democracy by the Sandinista junta and the choice of the method of violence has led indeed to something like Stalinism—a system that has forced Miskito Indians into internment camps or exile, has imposed prior censorship, absorbed free trade unions, controlled businessmen, repressed the church and the church leaders and sees Nicaraguans who want a voice in their own government as "enemies of the people."

It happened, too, in Grenada, where Maurice Bishop and his colleagues seized power by force and attempted to create on that tropical island a full-blown totalitarian state. It happened, of course, in Vietnam where the North imposed a "military solution" on the South and followed its victory with the establishment of totalitarian institutions which have forced hundreds of thousands of South Vietnamese into labor camps for "re-education," driven others into the sea and pressed thousands of others into the armies conducting their ongoing permanent war against Cambodia. Something like Stalinism has led to the liquidation of a nation.

The choice of method is the essential political act. It is hardly surprising that rulers who choose coercion as an instrument of government should see violence as a central instrument of government. Beginning in the late 1960s, for example, the Soviet Union and Soviet theorists began to identify the "armed road," as they called it, as the way to power in the Western hemisphere. They discovered that their own experiences could be applied elsewhere and set about applying those experiences in this hemisphere—the Bandera Roja, FARC, M-19, Sendero Luminoso, FSLN, FMLN, ERP, the Monteñeros, the Tupamaros, the MIR, to name just a few of the small bands of technicians in violence and propaganda, who found ready, external support in their effort to win power by violence over unwilling societies.

They begin with terror and seek, as the definition proposed at the last conference sponsored by the Jonathan Institute suggested, to inspire fear through the use of terror to gain political ends. Such deliberate use of terror is relied upon to produce a revolutionary situation. It has become the preferred tactic in contemporary revolutionary conflicts. This now familiar cycle is accompanied by a chorus of moral outrage from a self-designated constituency of Soviet client states. They seek to win symbolic support for the violence used in the pursuit of total war and absolute power. These "technicians in violence" and propaganda head what are called "national liberation movements." The Soviets frankly acknowledge that their support for these movements may be decisive as, for example, when they say:

> National liberation struggle is a form of war waged by peoples of colonial and dependent or formerly colonial territories in which Socialist countries become the decisive factor when peoples launch an armed struggle against internal reactionaries.

"National liberation movements" is the name given to groups supported by the Soviet Union and associated states seeking power by violence. Their acceptance as legitimate in the United Nations is a good indicator of the moral confusion which has come to surround the use of violence and the choice of violence as the method of political action.

Inside the United Nations, beginning in the 1970s, successive majorities of the General Assembly have passed resolutions asserting their support for the right of SWAPO, the PLO, and other national liberation movements "in their struggle, by all means, including armed struggle . . ." to achieve power. Inside the United Nations, the majorities, forged in blocs, many of whose overlapping members are Soviet-client states, proclaim the right of these national liberation movements to use all means including violence. The same majorities deny that their intended victims and targets have the right to defend themselves. Thus, Abu Eain, accused of planting a bomb in a teeming market area in Tiberias, Israel—a bomb that killed two boys and injured some thirty others—was treated by the General Assembly as a mere political dissident whose right to dissent and asylum should have been protected by the American courts, whose protections he made full use of for a period of years. The General Assembly denounced the various U.S. court decisions, including that of the U.S. Supreme Court, that held that Abu Eain should be extradited for trial in Israel. American courts concluded that bombing of civilians was not a political, and hence non-extraditable offense, but rather that it constituted the crimes of murder and attempted murder and that the perpetrator was subject to prosecution and punishment in the state where the crimes were committed. The United Nations General Assembly then reaffirmed, in effect, that terrorism in defense of national liberation is no crime and that the intended victims have no rights of self-defense.

In the semantics of UN majorities today, the distinction between legitimate and illegitimate use of force has not so much been blurred as stood on its head. Where traditionally states are seen as having a monopoly on the legitimate use of violence, UN majorities today see liberation movements as having a monopoly on legitimate use of force against targeted states. According to this upside-down view of terrorism, the peoples whose homes and villages are burned, whose school-children are bombed, whose crops are destroyed, whose cattle are killed, whose leaders are murdered and whose families are forcibly relocated may not be seen as victims of illegitimate violence, but rather as objects of national liberation. Only governments that seek to repress the violence of national liberation movements are cited for human rights violations. In this view, a targeted society has no rights of self-defense against the armed bands within its midst.

However, it cannot be that the Federal Republic of Germany has no right to defend itself against the Baader-Meinhof gang; that the Italian government has no right to defend itself against the Red Brigades; that the Government of Spain has no right to defend itself against Basque terrorists; that the Government of El Salvador has no right of self-defense against guerrillas who boycott its elections, attack its co-ops, murder its peasants; or that the Government of Uruguay has no right to defend itself against the Tupamaros.

The level of confusion has grown very deep and very serious. Yet we all know it cannot be that terror wreaked on a civilian population by a revolutionary movement is liberation, while violence committed by a government responding to a guerrilla threat is repression. It cannot be that national liberation movements have the right to use violence against civilians, economies, societies and governments, and that those societies have no right to defend themselves—that violence conducted in the name of revolution is legitimate, while violence used by governments and societies to defend themselves against guerrillas is illegitimate. The distinction between terror used in defense of society and terror used to destroy society is really not so difficult. Many, however, have become confused by the semantics of totalitarianism, by the specialists in propaganda.

The liberation of Grenada provided, I believe, a particularly clear-cut example of the confusion surrounding the legitimate use of force, and not only of confusion inside the United Nations. Outside that body, in some allied nations, extraordinary confusion was displayed.

There is one last affinity between terrorism and totalitarianism that I should like to mention. Both attempt to confuse as well as terrorize. Solzhenitsyn, Orwell and others have emphasized that violence is used to maintain a system of lies, and lies are used to justify relations based on violence. Violence can be used to close a society; lies can be used to veil the violence. To call open that which is closed, true that which is false, and insane he who raises questions about either is the fundamental purpose of what Solzhenitsyn termed "the lie."

Violence, as Solzhenitsyn emphasized, is the opposite of peace. It is war. Terrorists and totalitarians alike thrive on falsification and intimidation. Finding the courage to face the truth and speak about it is surely the first important step toward the defeat of those who would destroy our freedom and our world.

KAL 007: Violating the Norms of Civilized Conduct

Most of the world outside the Soviet Union has heard by now of the Korean flight 007 carrying 269 persons between New York and Seoul which strayed off course into Soviet air space, was tracked by Soviet radar, was targeted by a Soviet SU-15 whose pilot coolly, and after careful consultation, fired two air-launched missiles which destroyed the plane and, apparently, its 269 passengers and crew.

This calculated attack on a civilian airliner—unarmed, undefended, as civilian airliners always are—has shocked the world.

Only the Soviet people have still not heard about this attack on KAL 007 and death of the passengers because the Soviet government has not acknowledged firing on the Korean airliner. Indeed, not until September 5 did Soviet officials acknowledge that KAL 007 had disappeared in its icy waters.

The Soviet government has not been silent about the plane, it has merely lied.

On September 1, Foreign Minister Gromyko announced that:

> An unidentified plane coming from the direction of the Pacific Ocean, entered the air space of the Soviet Union over the Kamchatka Peninsula and then for the second time violated the Soviet air space over the Sakhalin Island. The plane did not have navigation lights, did not respond to queries and did not enter into contact with the radio control service.
>
> Fighters of the Anti-Aircraft Defense, which were sent aloft towards the intruder plane, tried to give it assistance in directing it to the nearest airfield. But the intruder plane did not react to the signals and warnings from the Soviet fighters and continued its flight in the direction of the Sea of Japan.

The next day, September 2, Tass repeated Gromyko's charge that Soviet airspace had been rudely violated by

> An unidentified plane which in violation of international regulations . . . flew

Address before the Security Council, September 6, 1983.

without navigation lights . . . Tass referred to efforts to establish contacts with the plane using generally accepted signals and to take it to the nearest airfield in the territory of the Soviet Union. Over the Sakhalin Island, a Soviet aircraft fired warning shots with tracer shells along the flying route of the plane. Soon after this the intruder plane left the limits of Soviet air space and continued its flight toward the Sea of Japan. For about ten minutes it was within the observation zone of radio location means, after which it could be observed no more . . .

Yesterday, when Soviet General Romanov finally admitted that the Korean plane had crashed killing "numerous" people he asserted, "the jetliner was flying with its lights out . . ."

This is what Tass said, but we do not have to wonder about what really happened to the airliner, or when it happened, or what Soviet officials knew about its fate. We know, because we know what the Soviet pilots who intercepted the Korean airliner over Sakhalin said to their ground controllers during the 50 minute period from 1756 to 1846 on August 31 while they tracked, discussed and destroyed the Korean airliner and its 269 passengers.

The U.S. Government in cooperation with the Government of Japan had decided to spread the evidence before this Council and the world. It is available on the video tape I am about to play. On this tape you will hear the voices of the pilots of Soviet interceptors—which included three SU-15 Flagons and one MIG-23 Flogger, including the SU-15 pilot who pulled the trigger which released the missiles that destroyed Korean Airlines flight 007. While it is obvious that the pilots are acknowledging instructions from ground controllers, those instructions are not audible. What I am about to play back for you is the intercepted tape of the actual air-to-ground reports; it is of course in Russian; on the monitor screens you will see, simultaneously, the original Russian and the English translation; through your audio system you will listen to these voices in translation into all the working languages of the United Nations. (Immediately following my presentation, Mr. President, the Russian-to-English transcript will be made available to all who may wish to study it. At the close of this session of the Security Council an audio cassette on which voices are still clearer will be provided to any interested mission.)

Nothing was cut from this tape. The recording was made on a voice-actuated recorder and, therefore, it covers only those periods of time when conversation was heard.

The transcript we have just heard, Mr. President, needs little explanation. Quite simply, it establishes that the Soviets decided to shoot down this civilian airliner, shot it down, murdering the 269 persons aboard, and lied about it.

The transcript of the pilots' cockpit conversations illuminates several key points.

- The interceptor which shot KAL 007 down had the airliner in sight for over 20 minutes before firing his missiles.
- Contrary to what the Soviets have repeatedly stated, the interceptor pilot saw the airliner's navigation lights and reported that fact to the ground on three occasions.
- Contrary to Soviet statements, the pilot makes no mention of firing any warning shots, only the firing of the missiles which he said struck the "target."
- Contrary to Soviet statements, there is no indication whatsoever that the interceptor pilot made any attempt either to communicate with the airliner, or to signal for it to land in accordance with accepted international practice. Indeed the Soviet interceptor planes may be technically incapable of communicating by radio with civilian aircraft presumably out of fear of Soviet pilot defections.
- Perhaps the most shocking fact learned from the transcript is that at no point did the pilots raise the question of the identity of the target aircraft, nor at any time did the interceptor pilots refer to it as anything other than the "target." The only activity bearing on the identity of the aircraft was a statement by the pilot of the attacking interceptor that "the target isn't responding to IFF." This means the aircraft did not respond to the electronic interrogation by which military aircraft *i*dentify *f*riends or *f*oes (IFF). But, of course, the Korean Airliner could not have responded to IFF because commercial aircraft are not equipped to do so.

We know the interceptor which shot down KAL 007 flew behind, alongside, and in front of the airliner (coming at least as close as 2 kilometers) before dropping back behind the plane and firing his missiles. At a distance of two kilometers under the conditions prevailing at that time, it was easily possible to identify a 747 passenger airliner. Either the Soviets did not know the Korean plane was a commercial airliner. Either he knew what he was firing at or he did not know his target was a civilian passenger airliner. If the latter, then he fired his deadly missiles without knowing or caring what they would hit. Though he could easily have pulled up to within some number of meters of the airliner to assure its identity, he did not bother to do so. In either case there was shocking disregard for human life and international norms.

In the days following the destruction of KAL 007, Soviet leaders and the Soviet press have said they do not understand what all the fuss is about. They began by accusing the U.S. of creating a "hulabaloo" about nothing, and more recently they have accused us of a "provocation"—implying, though never quite saying, that we "provoked" them into shooting down an airliner that strayed into their space, "provoked" them into violating the internationally agreed upon standards and practices of behavior. They have spoken as though a plane's straying off course is a crime punishable by death. They have suggested that "like any self-respecting state, [they] are doing no more than looking after [their] sovereignty which [they] shall permit no one to violate" (from the UREMYA newscast, September 4, 1983, Moscow Domestic Television Series). They have claimed still without acknowledging that they shot down the Korean Airliner that "our anti-aircraft defense has fulfilled its duty for the defense of the security of our motherland." They have suggested that they may have mistaken the Korean Airliner for an American reconnaissance plane, but *still* do not admit that they attacked and destroyed it.

But none of these lies, half lies and excuses can withstand examination. Straying off course is not recognized as a capital crime by civilized nations. And no nation has the sovereign right to shoot down any person or vehicle that may stray across its border in peacetime. There are internationally agreed upon standards for intercepting unwelcome aircraft. They call for serious efforts at identification, verification, warning, and if the case is serious, for intercepting the intruder and forcing it to land or to leave one's airspace. Sovereignty neither requires nor permits shooting down airliners in peacetime.

Recently the Soviets have implied that the KAL 007 may have been mistaken for a U.S. (aerial) reconnaissance flight. But that is no more persuasive. The Korean Boeing 747 was on a routine scheduled flight. At the time it was shot down the U.S. reconnaissance plane referred to by the Soviets had been on the ground fifteen hundred miles away for more than an hour.

Moreover, the U.S. does not fly reconnaissance missions in Soviet airspace. We do regularly operate aircraft in international airspace to monitor Soviet compliance with SALT and other arms control agreements. The Soviets know what our usual flight patterns are and can readily identify these missions.

Finally, neither the U.S. nor any other country upset about the slaughter of the 269 passengers of KAL 007 is creating a hulabaloo by exaggerating the importance of the events. We are protesting very important violations of the norms of civilized conduct on which international aviation rests, without which it will not be possible for any of us to board airliners, fly across continents and oceans without fear of being the object of a murderous attack. To a degree we rarely consider, international air travel depends on networks of mutual trust that we will not shoot down one another's airliners, kidnap, jail, or poison passengers and crews.

Why did the Soviet Union violate these norms—why have they lied about it? Two reasons are most often advanced to explain why the Soviet pilot shot down the airliner. One is that it was a mistake—the mistake of a trigger happy pilot who with his ground controller followed a philosophy of shoot now, identify later.

But if pilot error was responsible for this tragic mistake, why has the Soviet government not said so? Why has it lied, and why is it complementing the murderous attack on KAL 007 with a lying attack on the United States for provocation and aggression?

As I considered this question my mind returned to a debate that took place in this Security Council twenty-one years ago when my distinguished predecessor, Adlai Stevenson, called the attention of the Council to the "unmistakable evidence" that a series of facilities for launching offensive nuclear missiles were being installed in the Western hemisphere. Soviet Representative Zorin flatly denied the charges and, as Soviet Representatives so often do, coupled his lying denial with a vicious attack on the United States. Our calling attention to threatening Soviet behavior, Zorin asserted, only masked the United States' own aggression and piracy. But Adlai Stevenson, too, had the evidence to back up his charge—as irrefutable as the audio tapes we have today.

The fact is that violence and lies are regular instruments of Soviet policy. Soviet officials regularly behave as though truth were only a function of force and will. As if the truth were only what they said it is; as if violence were an instrument of first resort in foreign affairs. They occupy Afghanistan and accuse the U.S. of interference in internal affairs. They create massive new European vulnerabilities with their SS-20s and accuse NATO of seeking to upset the balance of power.

We think otherwise. We believe that truth is as vital to cooperation and peace among nations as among people.

It is depressing to consider seriously our global prospects if they must be built on relations devoid of truth, devoid of trust. It is depressing to consider a world in which a major nation equipped with the most powerful modern weapons believes it has a sovereign right to fire on a commercial airliner lost over its territory. These Soviet actions and claims illuminate the Soviet conception of appropriate relations among nations in peacetime. They illuminate the world in which we live and work and make policy.

Of course, some sophisticated observers believe that the destruction of flight 007 was neither the work of an isolated Strangelove, unconcerned about human life, but was instead a deliberate stroke designed to intimidate—a brutal, decisive act meant to instill fear and hesitation in all who observed its ruthless violence much as the destruction of Afghan villagers or the imprisonment of the Helsinki monitors are intended to secure compliance through terror.

Whichever the case—whether the destruction of KAL 007 and its passengers reflects only utter indifference to human life or whether it was designed to intimidate—we are dealing here not with pilot error but with decisions and priorities characteristic of a system. Not only did Soviet officials shoot down a stray commercial airliner and lie about it, they have callously refused offers of international participation in search and rescue efforts in spite of clearly stated "International Standards and Recommended Practices" of the International Civil Aviation Organization, which call on states to "grant any necessary permission for the entry of such aircraft, vessels, personnel or equipment into its territory and make necessary arrangements . . . with a view to expediting such entry."

We are reminded once again that the Soviet Union is a state based on the dual principle of callousness and mendacity. It is dedicated to the rule of force. Here is how Lenin described the "dictatorship of the proletariat" in 1920: "The scientific concept of 'dictatorship' means nothing more than unrestricted power, absolutely unimpeded by law or regulations and resting directly on force" (The Fifth Russian Edition of Lenin's Collected Works, Vol. 41, p. 383).

It is this principle of force—this mentality of force—that lies at the root of the Korean Airline tragedy. This is the reality revealed to the world by this horrible tragedy. It is a reality that we all must ponder as we consider the threats to peace and human rights that face all of us today.

The United States deeply believes that immediate steps should be taken here in the United Nations to decrease the likelihood of any repetition of the tragedy of KAL 007. We ask our colleagues to join with us in the coming days in the effort to wrest from the tragedy of KAL 007 new clarity about the changes of our world, and new efforts to render us all more secure.

SACRED SOVIET BORDERS

The issue that we have been discussing now for more than a week bears directly on the ability of all of us working together, working singly to secure and preserve peace in this world. It bears also on the readiness of member

Address before the Security Council, September 12, 1983.

states to take responsibility for achieving a civilized and peaceful international order.

Destruction of the civilian airliner, KAL 007, was a deeply shocking act. But even more disturbing than the deed itself has been the behavior of the Soviet government in the days since it shot down that plane. Had the Soviet government taken responsibility for the action, admitted that a terrible mistake had been made, offered compensation to the families for the loss of life, and in cooperation with other states, undertaken a review of the incident to ensure that such a tragedy would not recur, then the consequences of the event would have been contained and, to the degree possible, minimized. Nothing, to be sure, could reclaim the lives of 269 people. But relations among nations would not have suffered, and civilian air travel might have been rendered less vulnerable to such errors in the future.

But as we all know, the response of the Soviet Government has been quite different. Instead of admitting error, it has insisted that no error was made. Instead of taking responsibility for the act, it has lashed out with groundless accusations. Instead of taking steps to ensure against a repetition of such an incident, it has emphasized that it would do the same thing all over again.

By taking this position the Soviet Union has magnified the negative consequences of a tragic incident and has damaged anew the already tattered fabric of international relations. It has further poisoned the international atmosphere. For this, as for the incident itself, the Soviet Union must bear heavy responsibility.

During the past ten days, the Soviet Union has taken a position at once inconsistent and contradictory. It has been self-justifying and self-defeating in its statements. In its determined defense of an indefensible act, the Soviet Union has demonstrated an attitude that is as contemptuous of the truth as it is callous toward human life—an attitude underscored by its veto of the resolution before us today.

For nearly a week, the Soviet Union refused to admit it shot down flight 007. Then it admitted to having fired warning shots. Only after the public disclosure of the tape recordings in which the Soviet pilot told Soviet ground control that he had executed the order to destroy "the target," did the Soviet government announce that one of its pilots had, in fact, "stopped the flight," as they euphemistically put it.

In the ensuing days we have heard a tangle of charges from the Soviet Union. On the one hand, it has been said that flight 007 was itself on a spy mission and therefore *invited* destruction. But it has also been said that the presence, earlier in the evening, of an RC 135 reconnaissance plane, which had landed more than 1,500 miles away from the location of the incident, "caused" the Soviet pilot to mistake the two aircrafts, thus acknowledging tacitly that the Korean 747 was not on a spy mission after all.

Not surprisingly, the testimony of the Soviet pilot who shot down KAL 007 corroborates the official Soviet version of events. The Korean pilot is dead and cannot refute this testimony. But it is interesting and significant, I believe, to note in this context the testimony given to *The New York Times* by Kim Chang Kyu, the pilot of the Korean Airlines plane that strayed over Soviet airspace in 1978, thus becoming the target of a Soviet missile that sheared off nearly 15 feet of the plane's left wing and killed two of the plane's passengers. The pilot was able to regain control of the plane and was able to make an emergency landing on a frozen lake 400 miles northeast of Leningrad.

"After I was shot down," the pilot recounts, "the Russians made the same claims we're hearing now. They said, 'We tracked you for more than two hours, flew around the plane, fired tracers in front of you'—all that. It all sounds exactly the same this time."

Mr. Kim gives a different version of what actually happened. He tells us he saw the plane only once, off to the right and somewhat behind him. He thought this was strange, since international guidelines call for intercepting fighters to fly to the left of the plane, where the pilot sits. When Mr. Kim's co-pilot, who had a clearer view of the plane, reported that it bore the red Soviet star, Mr. Kim immediately slowed his speed and turned his landing lights off and on repeatedly, the recognized international signal that an aircraft will follow the interceptor's directions. In addition, Mr. Kim tried to establish contact with the Soviet craft, but the two planes' radios were on different frequencies. In any event, the next thing Mr. Kim knew a missile fired by the Soviet pilot had torn off a good part of his plane's left wing.

In light of this previous incident, and in view of the established fact that the pilot of KAL 007 made no radio transmissions indicating that he had been intercepted, one can only conclude that there was no communication with the pilot of KAL 007 in accordance with normal procedures and on normal emergency frequencies.

The fact that the tapes now show that the Soviet pilot fired "cannon bursts" six minutes before he destroyed KAL 007 does not alter this conclusion. Clearly the Korean pilot was not aware of the Soviet fighters, nor was he aware that any warning was given. If there were shots fired six minutes in advance of the fatal shot, it, therefore, seems likely that they were not tracers but regular, normal cannon rounds which are *not* visible.

Even assuming for the sake of argument that the Soviet pilot had tried to establish communication with the pilot of KAL 007, but for some reason that we do not know had failed to get through, *this would not justify shooting down a 747 civilian airliner.*

Mr. President, what conceivable harm could the plane have done, especially since it was within sixty seconds of leaving Soviet airspace, a fact that renders absurd the statement by one of the Soviet pilots that the 747 might have been carrying "a bomb that might have fallen, maybe on my house"—presumably located in the Sea of Japan.

Let us recall for a moment the incident almost two years ago when a Soviet W-class submarine penetrated deep into restricted Swedish waters near Karlskrona naval base and ran aground there. In response to the protest of the Swedish government, the Soviet government said: "It was expected, of course, that the Swedish authorities would abide by existing international norms under which if a foreign warship does not even observe the rules of a coastal state regarding passage through its territorial waters, the only thing the coastal state may do with respect to the given warship is to demand that it leave its territorial waters."

According to this unique interpretation of international law, if a Soviet warship—a *war*ship mind you—invades the territorial waters of another state, that state cannot even detain the warship but must simply escort it out of its territorial waters. But if a civilian airliner with 269 people aboard happens to stray into Soviet airspace, the Soviet Union is justified in shooting it down, even as it is about to exit that airspace. Mr. Leonid M. Zamyatin, the spokesman on the Central Committee for General Secretary Yuri Andropov, went so far as to say that Soviet air defense forces were "humane" to have waited so long before destroying KAL 007. How callous it is to talk about "humaneness" with regard to a ruthless act that resulted in 269 deaths. Is a Soviet warship entitled to more "humane" treatment than a civilian airplane?

The Soviet leadership refuses to concede the possibility that a civilian airliner, traveling a scheduled flight, with 269 people aboard, might have strayed accidentally into its airspace—despite the fact that there have been 21 recorded incidents where civilian planes with similar navigational equipment have strayed off course. Here, too, the incident of the Soviet W-class submarine offers an interesting analogy. In its statement to the Government of Sweden, the Soviet government rejected the Swedish charge that this warship was engaged in "carrying out impermissible activities," namely, spying. According to the Soviet statement, the submarine "went off course as a result of the failure of its navigational instruments and resultant mistakes in position finding" and therefore "entered unintentionally the territorial waters of Sweden. ... The Soviet side, taking into consideration the breakdown character of the incident, could rightfully expect at least a manifestation of correct attitude and objective appraisal of what happened." Instead, it charged the Swedish government with "distorting facts" and it flatly rejected the Swedish demand "to prevent the recurrence of such a gross violation," saying—and I quote—"In this concrete case this sounds like a demand to rule out the very possibility of breakdown situations occurring at sea. This demand," said the Soviet Union, "is simply out of tune with common sense."

Yet the Soviet Union finds it is inconceivable that such a "breakdown situation," to use their term, might have occurred in the case of the civilian airliner, KAL 007.

Now we come to the final Soviet argument—its ultimate line of defense. It was stated in explicit terms last week by Soviet Foreign Minister Andrei Gromyko: "We state," he said: "Soviet territory, the borders of the Soviet Union are sacred." It is on the basis of this principle that the top Soviet leadership has defended, and by so doing, has assumed responsibility for, the destruction of a civilian airliner.

In this context, we would like to ask the Soviet Union: Are the borders of the Soviet Union more sacred than, say, the borders of Sweden, not to speak of the borders of Afghanistan? Are they more sacred than the airspace of the United States, which has frequently been violated by Soviet planes flying off-route over sensitive military facilities, though these planes have not as a result of such violations been shot down? And how, may we ask, can the Soviet Union reconcile this remarkable doctrine of absolute Soviet sovereignty, according to which the Soviet Union is within its rights to shoot down a civilian airliner that strays across its sacred borders, with its doctrine of "limited sovereignty," which was propounded 15 years ago in relationship to the Soviet invasion of Czechoslovakia?

In the article in *Pravda* (September 26, 1968) where this doctrine of "limited sovereignty" was propounded, the Soviet Union not only claimed the right to invade any Soviet bloc country that threatened to deviate from the path of fealty to Moscow; it also claimed the right to intervene in the internal affairs of states that are not part of the Soviet bloc.

This same article explains how the Soviet Union reconciles the doctrine of absolute Soviet sovereignty with the doctrine of "limited sovereignty" for everyone else, as well as with the norms of international law. Accordingly, it states that "Laws and the norms of law are subordinated to the laws of the class struggle and the laws of social development ... The class approach to the matter cannot be discarded in the name of legalistic considerations. Whoever does so forfeits the only correct, class-oriented criterion for evaluating legal norms and begins to measure events with the yardsticks of bourgeois law."

In other words, there are two forms of law—"bourgeois law," which includes the Charter of the United Nations, and "the laws of the class struggle," and there is no question that in the Soviet view, the former are conditioned by and subordinate to the latter. This dual conception of international law accords to the Soviet Union absolute rights but no obligation to respect the rights of others, while it accords to all other states no rights but absolute obligations to respect the rights of the Soviet Union.

The destruction of KAL 007, and especially the manner in which the Soviet Union has defended that action, have illuminated as few events in recent years the nature of the predicament that faces us all.

Mr. President, I would like to quote from a letter written by a Soviet citizen who is surely one of the outstanding and most courageous persons of our age. I am referring to Dr. Andrei Sakharov whose letter was secretly transmitted to the outside world from within the Soviet Union where he has been internally exiled. In his letter from exile, Dr. Sakharov warns that "the world is facing very difficult times and cruel cataclysms if the West and the developing countries trying to find their place in the world do not now show the required firmness, unity and consistency in resisting the totalitarian challenge. This relates to governments, to the intelligentsia, businessmen and to all people. It is important that the common danger be fully understood—everything else will then fall into place."

If the destruction of KAL 007 helps us to understand the nature of the world in which we live and the dangers to our rights and laws therein, helps us to show the necessary clarity and firmness in defending precisely the principles of international law contained in the Charter of the United Nations—then perhaps the 269 people aboard that ill-fated airliner will not have died in vain.

In closing, Mr. President, I should like to say that there is one question which above all confronts this Council and the world in this debate, which is responded to by the resolution we have adopted, in spite of its veto. Does a nation which is not at war have the right to shoot down planes that enter their air space without authorization—that is the question with which we have been confronted. The answer to that question must be no. We do *not* believe that the protection of sovereignty of any nation gives that nation an absolute right in peace time to shoot down any plane flying any place over its territory. There are internationally agreed on procedures to take care of such problems. We believe that this view has been endorsed by a majority of this Council in the resolution we have considered this afternoon.

We stand ready to work with our colleagues to ensure greater safety for all passengers and pilots, indeed, for all people.

8
Economic and Social Policy

FREEDOM AND DEVELOPMENT*

*With Carl Gershman

As a political scientist I know that about nine out of ten American Blacks are Democrats and that during the last election, when voters of the most diverse kinds were deserting Jimmy Carter in droves, most Black voters remained loyal. I also know that politically active persons tend to have especially strong, tenacious political views. I assume, then, that I am speaking this evening to an audience most of whose members are confirmed Democrats who were not exactly pleased by the outcome of last November's elections and who are not predisposed to be enthusiastic about the policies and plans of the Reagan administration.

To persuade you of the virtues of the Reagan administration's foreign policy is probably impossible; so I propose instead a more modest goal: to convince you that our foreign policy is not as bad as you think it is.

First, however, I want to say that I am delighted to be here this evening and to have the opportunity to address this forum. I have long admired the work of the National Urban League, and I have admired also the wise leadership that has been provided by your distinguished president, Vernon Jordan. Since virtually the beginning of this century, your organization has been a leading force in the effort to eliminate racial discrimination from our society. By your efforts you have made an extraordinary contribution not only to the well-being of American Blacks but also to the strength of our society as a whole. If we are a more united and cohesive society today than we were a generation ago, this is due in no small measure to your

Address before the National Urban League, Washington, D.C., July 20, 1981.

continuing dedication to achieving racial equality in the context of a democratic society.

Since it is relevant on this occasion, I might add that your efforts have also contributed—indirectly and directly—to American foreign policy. The civil rights movement has helped keep our attention focused on this nation's fundamental commitments. Moreover, fighting Jim Crow at home has enhanced the stature of the United States in the eyes of the international community and strengthened our just claim to speak on behalf of freedom.

The civil rights movement also affected American foreign policy in a more direct way. It is surely no coincidence that this movement arose and flourished during the very period when the peoples of Africa and Asia were gaining their independence from colonialism. These movements reinforced each other. Martin Luther King, Jr., borrowed the philosophy of nonviolent struggle from Mahatma Gandhi, the great leader of the Indian independence movement. Dr. King, whose picture hangs in the office of Zambian President Kenneth Kaunda, in turn inspired the leaders of independence movements in Africa. The civil rights and independence movements alike reflected growing egalitarianism and a changing world order in which both second-class citizenship for American Blacks and colonialist subjugation of the peoples of Africa and Asia could no longer be tolerated.

I think it is fair to say that the civil rights movement, which as Gunnar Myrdal understood was rooted in the deepest principles of the American creed, also reinforced the aspects of our political culture that made us more sensitive to the concerns of the newly emerging nations. As a former colony and a new multiethnic nation, we had special reason to understand nationalism and nation building. Moreover, the enhanced political influence of American Blacks and their growing preoccupation in the post-civil rights era with international questions had an inevitable impact on the conduct of our foreign policy. It heightened our concern with Africa. The mere fact that 26 million Americans trace their ancestral roots to Africa—and that the rich influences of Africa are fixed in our national fabric—further guaranteed that we would take more than routine notice of developments on that continent.

It is also true, however, that beginning in the late 1960s and continuing into the next decade, the United States and many of the countries in the developing world became increasingly divided from one another. In an important sense, this clash was the inescapable consequence of expectations created during the independence struggle—expectations that were not, and probably could not be, quickly fulfilled. It was expected that political independence would lead quickly to economic and social development and the equalization of living standards between the developing world and the advanced industrial states. But of course it did not and could not work out that way. Here, too, there is a parallel with the experience of American Blacks, who were disappointed to find that social and economic equality did not follow automatically or easily upon the achievement of political and legal rights any more than they had followed on the achievement of national independence. That many people have become impatient, frustrated, and resentful during this period should not surprise us in the least. This new challenge is more complicated than the old.

In the United States we have entered a new period whose chief challenge for women, and for Blacks and other minorities, is to use the newly available legal and political rights to win larger shares of wealth, power, skills, status, and the other good things society has to offer. In the developing world we have entered a new period in which the less-developed nations, now freed of the last vestiges of the old colonialisms, confront the task of using their independence to achieve the greatest good for the greatest number of their citizens.

I believe this new period offers the prospect of a closer and more cooperative relationship between the United States and many of the nations of what has come to be called the third world. Such a relationship is now possible because attitudes toward development are changing, and there is a new appreciation in both the industrialized countries and the developing world of their mutual interest in economic cooperation.

I believe that the orientation and policies of the Reagan administration are peculiarly well suited to this new phase in our relations with less-developed nations. My theme for the evening is that the Urban League's concerns and commitments on foreign policy are not significantly different from those of the Reagan administration. Once the thicket of misunderstanding has been cleared away, I think you will find that our goals are entirely compatible with yours and our methods acceptable to you. My basic message is that you are going to like our policies better than you think you do.

First, however, it is necessary to dispel three misconceptions about the administration's foreign policy that have taken root and flourished in the past six months: one is the myth that the United States does not care about human rights; another is the myth that the United States does not care about the less-developed countries and does not intend to help them; and a third is the myth that the United States government views the world exclusively from the perspective of East-West conflict. These myths misrepresent the goals, perspectives, and plans of the Reagan administration. They create distrust, disapproval, and embarrassment among Americans and inhibit our capacity to be effective in the world.

First, the question of human rights: I desire to say simply that protecting, expanding, and enhancing human freedom, democracy, and the rule of law is a central commitment of this administration in foreign policy. We believe it is inextricably bound to our national interest. All of us involved in making, securing, and implementing the administration's foreign policy believe that human rights can be, should be, must be, will be taken into account by U.S. foreign policy.

How there came to be such confusion on this point is another complex story rooted in our criticisms of Carter foreign policy. My own experience is a case in point. Greatly to my surprise, I heard it said that I thought human rights should have no important role in foreign policy. The basis of this utterly mistaken view was my criticism of the specifics of the Carter human rights policy—its failure to *achieve* its goals in foreign affairs. Those goals were moderation and democracy. The results were Khomeini in Iran and the Ortega brothers in Nicaragua.

It is not useful to continue the stale debate about the past administration's policies. What is important now is what this administration proposes. I can assure you that I speak for this administration when I say that we are firmly opposed to arbitrary arrest and detention, torture, restraints on free speech, press, religion. We believe democratic government based on free, periodic, competitive elections is the best government. We plan to encourage democracy and the rule of law wherever we have the opportunity to act in a way that will leave peoples more free and governments more lawful. That goes for Africa, South America, the Middle East, Asia, wherever.

The second myth that undermines our foreign policy is that we do not care about the less-developed countries or mean to help. The notion is abroad that we in this administration don't really care about the less-developed nations because we are traumatized by East-West relations or overcome by a new isolationism and concerned only with our own national security, narrowly conceived, or because relative affluence has rendered us indifferent to the hardship of others. But, of course, none of these propositions is true.

We care about the development of the less-developed nations for both rational and moral reasons: we care because our economic, social, and political well-being are inextricably bound together with theirs; and we care because, as in the past, the American people respond with empathy and concern for the hardships of others.

The reason the theme of interdependence has increasingly come to dominate discussions in the United States of the world economy and of America's role in it is that the U.S. economy today is more than ever before intertwined with the economies of other nations. Since 1960 the combined annual export-import trade of the United States has expanded from $35 billion to $473 billion, making us the world's largest trading nation. Millions of American jobs depend on our exports to the rest of the world.

Moreover, our trade with the less-developed nations has expanded most rapidly of all—to the point where these exports now account for over 35 percent of the U.S. total. Today we sell as many manufactured goods to the less-developed countries as we do to Europe, Japan, and the Communist countries combined. Conversely, the importance to the United States of imports from developing countries—of oil and other vital raw materials and of manufactured goods as well—hardly needs restating.

In 1979, 45 percent of total U.S. imports, with a value of $95 billion, came from less-developed countries, and less than half this total reflected energy costs. I do not desire to bore you with figures, but it is significant in thinking about our relations with the developing countries that during the last five years the less-developed countries have consistently provided more than 30 percent of U.S. food imports. It is significant, too, that the United States is and has been a major source of capital for the developing countries.

Interdependence, then, is a fact of the contemporary world. So are continuing poverty, malnutrition, disease, illiteracy, and inefficiency in many societies that we call "developing." Neither the characteristic optimism of the age, nor the rising expectations of those who live there, nor public, private, or multilateral assistance has altered the fact that some twenty-nine of the world's countries still have average annual incomes of about $150 per capita, still have populations that grow faster than resources, and still remain utterly vulnerable to every natural or social disaster. More people than we can bear to think about live at the raw edge of subsistence, in societies that feature low social and geographical mobility, primitive technology, and rigid social and economic structures. And things are not necessarily getting better. The less-developed countries now expend 27 pecent of their export earnings for oil; and in 1980 one-half of the developing countries grew less than 1 percent in real per capita terms.

In many societies, life is not necessarily getting easier, and it is not necessarily getting safer. Despite the widespread assumption that democracy was rapidly replacing autocracy everywhere, dictatorships of one kind or another flourish on most continents; and despite the persistent belief that modernity would somehow render people more rational and more peaceable, fanaticism, tyranny, aggression, and violence remain the everyday reality in many parts of the world, in developing and developed countries alike, not only producing a high toll of human misery but also augmenting the steady stream of refugees that is a hallmark of the turbulent half-century just past.

The interaction and interdependence of the United States and the developing countries are not only economic. Refugees from war, revolution, population pressures, natural disasters, and just plain poverty produce their impact also on our country and our government.

Self-interest and empathy alike guarantee that we are and will remain deeply concerned with the nations of southern Africa, of the Horn of Africa and its northern tier, of the Middle East, of Southwest Asia, East Asia, Latin America, and the Caribbean—indeed, the world.

The new United States government not only cares about the less-developed areas; we are ready to help. First, we are giving direct aid, bilaterally, regionally, and through the many multilateral institutions. As I am sure you know, although the administration is seriously committed to controlling inflation, cutting expenditures, and balancing the budget, we have recommended to the Congress support for most United Nations agencies at approximately current levels. In our budget, our contributions to the United Nations system were exempt from the cuts to which most parts of the budget were subjected.

We also think we can expedite trade with the less-developed countries by opening markets and eschewing economic protectionism. This administration can and will open markets, provide access to capital markets, and otherwise work to stimulate trade and development opportunities.

We believe, moreover, that the Reagan administration is singularly well suited to help the developing countries develop—not just by giving them emergency handouts but also by providing the kind of advice and help that will culminate in self-sustaining growth. It can help make the case for a new, more realistic ideology of development, which takes account of the experience of actual countries.

The old development ideology maintained that underdevelopment was the result of exploitive policies pursued by the industrialized countries, particularly the United States. The strategy for development, therefore, centered on the need for a political struggle against the so-called neo-colonialist West, which was called upon to transfer massive amounts of resources to the third world. Development was also thought to require command economies in which an all-powerful state bureaucracy would impose sacrifices upon the population. Freedom, it was held, was a luxury that the poor could not afford. It would have to be denied, at least for the present, in order to achieve equality.

Whatever one may think of this view from a political or a moral standpoint, the fact is that it did not work as a method of development and was probably counterproductive. The countries taking this course—generally speaking, countries that are part of the Soviet bloc or that practice radical socialism—stagnated economically. Moreover, their failure could not be attributed to the absence of resource transfers from the West since during this very period the developing countries accumulated debts to the West, above and beyond the help they received in the form of grant aid, totaling some $500 billion.

At the same time, there were a number of success stories. South Korea, Taiwan, Singapore, and Hong Kong progressed so rapidly that they began to compete effectively with the economies of the West. Other countries, such as Malaysia and Brazil, followed a similar upward course. In Black Africa, the Ivory Coast, Kenya, and Malawi achieved significant growth in contrast to the poor performance of some of their neighbors.

The important point about these successes is that they were accomplished in defiance of the conventional wisdom about development. Instead of fighting against the industrialized West, these countries sought a partnership based on close cooperation and mutual advantage. Rather than impose command economies on captive peoples, they emphasized market forces, free trade, and individual initiative. Where others had sought to make the state the motor of economic development, they encouraged the private sector through tax concessions to both corporations and individuals.

The case of Sri Lanka is particularly interesting in this regard because here we have a country that abruptly altered its policies four years ago, substituting as the main force for growth the incentives of the market for the coercion of the state. In the first three years under this new approach, unemployment dropped by five percentage points, and the real rate of economic growth more than doubled—despite a number of natural disasters and the escalating price of oil.

Such models of development are a source of hope, not just because they demonstrate that success *is* possible, but also because they reaffirm the importance of freedom—the very freedom that the civil rights movement struggled to achieve and which is the core value of our nation. It is especially encouraging to note the growing awareness in the world that economic liberty, far from being an obstacle to material well-being, is a precondition for it. As the experience of the Western democracies and the newly industrialized countries has shown, wealth is a consequence of freedom. It is created by innovation and experiment, by human intellect and effort; by the activity, in other words, of free, creative individuals. Freedom is not a luxury for the rich, therefore, but a necessity above all for the poor.

Interdependence and the growing trend toward market-oriented development among the poorer nations provide a particularly solid basis for a new relationship between our country and the less-developed world. Meanwhile, the lessons of experience with development and the core convictions of President Ronald Reagan and his administration coincide almost perfectly, for just as President Reagan's vision of politics features the free individual, his approach to economics features the free individual as the source of creativity, energy, and production—the source of the wealth of nations.

This brings me to the third myth that causes many people to think ill of this administration's foreign policy: the myth that we see all other countries through the lens of East-West relations. Once again, it is surely not so, least of all in Africa.

The United States government wants in Africa precisely what Africans want for themselves—a continent composed of strong, stable, independent states that are able to articulate their own interests and promote the well-being of their populations. Our interests are entirely consistent with the hopes and aspirations expressed in the charter of the Organization of African Unity.

We are, moreover, fully committed to working to achieve peace, stability, self-determination, and democracy for all the nations of Africa. We will work for these goals in all available arenas—in our bilateral relations, through cooperation with the Organization of African Unity, and in the United Nations.

The high priority that the Reagan administration gives to its relations with the nations of Africa is reflected in our commitment of resources as well as high-level attention. In the relatively brief period since President Reagan assumed office, five very senior officials of African countries—all at the ministerial level or higher—have come to Washington for talks, and we have sent a number of key advisers to Africa on fact-finding missions. I myself have spoken with the foreign ministers of at least a dozen African countries and ambassadors from two dozen others.

With regard to the independence of Namibia, when we took office on January 20, we found a situation in which all movement toward a solution of this longstanding problem had stopped. If a free, independent, democratic Namibia was to be born, a new initiative was necessary. This we have now begun.

As a necessary step to reinvigorate the search for an internationally accepted settlement in Namibia, the administration has held discussions with front-line and other African states, with the Western Contact Group, and with the South African government. In these discussions we have stressed our commitment to work for a settlement that will promote peace, security, and stability in southern Africa and self-determination and independence for the people of Namibia. To the government of South Africa in particular, we have made clear that while this problem remains unresolved, it will be a major obstacle between our two countries.

I do not know if these new initiatives are going to succeed. The problem has lasted more than twenty-five years, and we have been in office only six months. But it is evident that the old policies of confrontation have not brought the people of Namibia closer to the independence and freedom that are their due. It's time to try something new.

Need I add that there can be no doubt about where this administration stands on the question of apartheid? We have said, and I repeat here, that we find South Africa's policies of racial separation repugnant. It is our profound hope that there will be steady progress in South Africa toward eliminating it. We have not gone through a revolution in race relations in our own country only to acquiesce in a system of racial separation practiced by others. Together with the National Urban League, we support measures designed to improve the lot of Black and Colored workers in South Africa. Such measures exemplify the policy of constructive engagement that we believe will best promote evolutionary change in that country.

We are also working on what we coonsider very practical ways to bring progress and justice to other parts of the African continent. For example, we have pledged $225 million over three years in special economic assistance to the new nation of Zimbabwe. This is concrete evidence of our willingness to work with governments in Africa to achieve their own goals. We want to see Zimbabwe succeed, and we will play our full part in helping it to do so.

There is also the heart-rending problem of refugees. In East Africa alone, there are more than a million refugees. I am proud to say that at an international conference held in Geneva last April on the plight of African refugees, we pledged $285 million to help feed, clothe, and resettle, in some cases in the United States, these destitute victims of famine, war, and revolution. Our pledge amounted to more than half the total amount pledged by all nations.

We are also committed to the peaceful resolution of other conflicts in Africa. We welcome, for example, the recent call by King Hassan of Morocco for a cease-fire and a referendum to settle the conflicts in the western Sahara. We share the profound distress, expressed publicly and privately by African leaders, over Libya's invasion of Chad and hope that the Organization of African Unity will be able to act decisively to end the Libyan occupation and restore Chad's sovereignty.

Not least, we will continue to insist upon the withdrawal of Cuban, Soviet, and East German military forces from Africa. We are concerned with East-West issues in Africa only where Soviet-sponsored violence and military adventures force them into the forefront of our attention.

The United States was never a colonial power. But just as we opposed the old colonialism, we cannot look with equanimity upon the imposition of a new colonialism, albeit one that hides its real purposes behind revolutionary slogans. We hope that the time is near when all foreign troops will be withdrawn from Africa, and we will pursue that goal.

Under the Reagan administration, American foreign policy has recovered from a period of self-doubt. Throughout the world countries recognize that America has regained its confidence and is now prepared to exercise its power with a firm and steady hand. Power, however, is not an end in itself, but is an instrument that must be used toward an end. For the United States—a great pluralist democracy—the end we seek is a world of peace, freedom, and diversity.

In order to succeed in our policies, we need the understanding, support, and participation of organizations like your own, which have helped make America internally strong and which represent values that America must stand for abroad as well as at home. Our own experience and advantages as a nation give us a special responsibility to help others achieve a better life in peace. We welcome that responsibility as well as the prospect of working with you to achieve our common goals.

A Strategy For Global Development

I have asked for permission to speak to this body this morning because I desire to state clearly on behalf of my government to this body that the United States cares deeply about poverty, hunger, human misery and intends to join with others in mapping a cooperative strategy for global development.

In an essay on the Spirit of the Age, John Stuart Mill wrote that "Mankind are, then, divided into those who are still what they were, and those who have changed: into the men of the present age, and the men of the past . . ."

Americans are men of the present. We are people who believe in progress. My country, including the city in which we now sit, was founded by people who believed in progress; who believed that human problems will yield to creative, determined action by purposeful men and women. My government shares this conviction of our forebears.

Men of the present know that while some human problems are rooted in human nature and may last as long as man does, others are rooted in technology—in our knowledge of things, in our tools, in the technology we

Address before the 36th General Assembly, November 5, 1981.

can bring to bear to solve problems. Mr. President, problems rooted in technology become socially and morally intolerable once the knowledge and technology exist that offers a prospect of their practical solution.

President Reagan said at Cancun:

> I am puzzled by suspicions that the United States might ignore the developing world. The contribution America has made to development—and will continue to make—is enormous.
>
> We have provided 57,000 million dollars to the developing countries in the last decade—43,000 million dollars in development assistance and 14,000 million dollars in contributions to the multilateral development banks. Each year, the United States provides more food assistance to the developing nations than all other nations combined. Last year we extended almost twice as much official development assistance as any other nation.
>
> Even more significant is the United States' contribution in trade. Far too little world attention has been given to the importance of trade as a key to development.
>
> The United States absorbs about one-half of all the manufactured goods that non-OPEC developing countries export to the industrialized world, even though our market is only one-third of the total industrialized world market. Last year alone, we imported 60,000 million dollars' worth of goods from non-OPEC developing countries. That is more than twice the official development assistance from all Organization for Economic Cooperation and Development (OECD) countries. Our trade and capital markets are among the most open in the world.
>
> The range and breadth of America's commitment extend far beyond concessional assistance. We believe in promoting development by maximizing every asset we have.

We care about the development of the less developed nations for both rational and moral reasons: We care because our economies and our social and political well-being are inextricably bound together with theirs; and we care because, as in the past, the American people respond with empathy and concern for the problems and misery of others.

The reason the theme of "interdependence" has increasingly come to dominate discussion in the United States of the world economy and America's role in it, is that today the United States economy is more than ever before intertwined with the economies of other nations. We know that our well-being is interdependent with that of other nations. We know that their well-being is interdependent with ours.

In the recognition of interdependence and in determination to act President Reagan took part in the Ottawa Summit and in the conference on International Development at Cancun. At Ottawa, my government agreed with the leaders of other industrialized nations to "participate in preparations for a mutually acceptable process of global negotiations in circumstances offering the prospect of meaningful progress." President Reagan's statement at Cancun carried this commitment a major step forward by outlining four broad understandings—the essential foundations, in effect, for the achievement of the "meaningful progress" we all seek.

At Cancun, President Reagan and other leaders paved the way for a problem-oriented, practical, pragmatic approach to the great human problems that face the world. Today we lump those problems under a single word: development. President Reagan and the other heads of state at Cancun recognized, as we recognize here, that the hungry must be fed; the young must be nurtured; the sick must be treated; the poor must be sustained and helped to become self-sufficient; the hopeless must be given a measure of hope that help is on the way, that their conditions will somehow be alleviated. Mr. President, the United States understands that the nations of the world must respond to these needs and these imperatives; that is why we are determined to move forward with others in seeking solutions to these urgent, tragic problems.

What, then, is to be done?

We must join together in all the arenas available to us, using all the tools available to us. And we call on all other nations interested in human misery and human progress to join us.

Feeding hungry people must have priority. Practical positive negotiations leading to world-wide cooperation provides us an opportunity to assure regular and adequate food supplies for the needs of the hungry and the malnourished.

Four challenges confront us if we are to increase world food security: food production in the developing countries must be increased; we must help bring the miracle of the second Green Revolution to farmers everywhere.

International cooperation should also extend to the area of food aid. In the short run, more pledges are needed, in cash and commodities, under the Food Aid Convention, the World Food Program, the International Emergency Food Reserve.

Meanwhile, we must all continue to search for an international grains agreement and improve the capacity of international bodies to act in the case of food emergencies resulting from natural disasters.

Turning to the area of commodities and industrialization: the United States is committed to an open world trade system which will provide all countries an opportunity to strengthen and diversify their economies. We know that trade can provide a strong engine for growth both in developed and developing countries as increased exports lead to an increase in production, employment, development and greater integration in the world trading system. The United States is committed to continue efforts designed to ensure that developing countries are more fully integrated into the international trading system and are able to derive increased benefits from it. We are ready to work closely with developed and developing country trading partners to prepare for a GATT Ministerial in 1982 and to strengthen the multilateral trading system embodied in GATT.

Regarding money and finance: recognition of greater economic interdependence among nations places a premium on all nations working together to achieve prosperity. We must all understand that the external contributions of trade, private investment and commercial capital flows responding to incentives of the marketplace are essential practical ingredients to achieve long-term, non-inflationary economic growth and development.

A smoothly functioning international monetary system is also essential to a prosperous world economy. Private financial markets, supplemented by efforts of existing international institutions and new initiatives, are indispensable and should be fully utilized in our effort to achieve desired goals.

Finally, concerning energy: the United States understands how much hardship rising energy prices have caused and continue to cause the less developed nations. We are ready to help to produce more energy for growing world economies, to promote more effective use of the energy we produce, and to increase investment in energy production and energy-efficient equipment. We are ready to join with others in working out practical solutions to the energy problems of all.

Mr. President, my delegation was at first disinclined to enter in this plenary debate—on the grounds that it was premature and because, though the principles are agreed upon, the procedures remain undecided. We felt that the debate was premature in view of the extensive consultations that are now taking place here and in capitals around the world. However, we decided that we all have the responsibility for transplanting the spirit of Cancun to all the arenas of the United Nations system. We all have an obligation to nurture this fragile new beginning. This time we must not fail; too many are counting on the success of our activities here in New York.

Let us get on with the job.

ON REFUGEES

It is a very great pleasure to receive an award, almost any award, but to receive the 1982 Liberty Award of Hebrew Immigration Aid Society (H.I.A.S.) is truly, to me, a special pleasure. In the third Book of Moses, Chapter 19, we read, "The stranger who sojourns with you shall be to you as the native among you and you shall love him as yourself; for you were strangers in the land of Egypt." For a century now H.I.A.S. has served as a beacon of hope for the stranger, a haven for the needy, and a source of employment, instruction and desperately needed relocation assistance for refugees the world over. There are, I have learned, few Jewish families in the United States today, one of whose members has not been helped in one way or another by H.I.A.S.; and I know that quite a large number of non-Jewish refugees as well, including Indochinese, Cubans and Haitians have been assisted by H.I.A.S..

Refugees are the human residue of the violent upheavals of this violent century. According to certain legal criteria and statistical estimates they number about 10 million. By other reckonings, they are much more numerous. I wish to draw attention to these millions of human beings who quite literally find themselves on alien ground, in no-man's land, searching in some insecure and unsettled middle point, between despair and hope, between death and a new life.

Obviously, refugees and the status of refugees have a special meaning for the Jewish people of our century, whose tragic search, between hope and despair, for a new life has marked our dreadful times. Obviously, refugees have a special meaning for the United States as well, since the Pilgrims who landed at Plymouth were, quite literally, refugees, half-way between despair and hope, between death and a new life, who also came searching for freedom from oppression, searching for freedom to build a new world for themselves. We are all, all of us here, the beneficiaries of those searches.

Legally speaking, a refugee is one who flees or otherwise finds him or herself outside his country of nationality and citizenship and is unable to return because of well-grounded fear of persecution on account of race, religion or political conviction. In simple terms this is the definition recognized by the United States and many other national governments through legal instruments of the United Nations and corresponding national statutes. In human terms, a refugee is one who finds life so difficult, so threatening, so unbearable, that he or she is willing to abandon all that is

Address before the Hebrew Immigration Aid Society, New York, New York, September 12, 1982.

familiar—language, job, birthplace, family—to risk the unknown in some unfamiliar world. The tidal waves of refugees passed through our century in response, above all, to its violent politics and wars. The Bolshevik and Nazi revolutions created the first mass waves of refugees in our times. In thinking about the generosity of countries who have accepted refugees, it is always important to recall the irony of the fact that, in the case of Nazi refugees, their contribution was so significant in the final defeat of that terrible movement. Refugees, as we all know, may create a blessing for the country in which they are received.

War and revolutionary terror are the prime causes for the flight of today's refugees. The Soviet military campaign against the Afghan people, for instance, has produced more than 4 million Afghan refugees, causing nearly 3 million to flee to Pakistan and something over 1 million more to seek haven in Iran. Efforts to put Communism into practice in Vietnam, Laos and Cambodia have resulted in the flight of about one and a half million citizens of those Indochinese countries to non-Communist lands, to almost any place. Half a million Ethiopians are subsisting in temporary refuge in Somalia in the wake of the terrible war between those two states.

The Americas, of course, have been the scene of some mass exoduses as well. More than a million Cubans, that is to say nearly one-ninth of the island's total population, have fled the Castro dictatorship since it came to power. Only in this past Christmas season, on the remote eastern coast of Nicaragua, when the rulers of the Sandinista junta decided that life was too dangerous for the Miskitos and burned their churches, their crops and their animals, thousands of Miskito Indians, whose Christian, communal values and whose traditional way of life do not conform to the utopian ideals were forced to flee. Some 15,000 Miskitos have taken refuge in neighboring Honduras, while thousands more have sought, and seek today, to escape into the more desirable, for them, status of refugee. There have, of course, been other thousands of refugees produced by other regimes in this hemisphere and elsewhere: some 35,000 refugees, for example, have fled the authoritarian states of the southern cone.

Last August my own life intersected with some of the more remarkable refugees of our age, the survivors of the Cambodian holocaust, along the border of Thailand and Cambodia. The setting was a partly-cleared jungle of man-made savagery difficult even to imagine. The woods were littered with booby-trapped mines designed not to kill, but only to maim. There were scores of legless children who demonstrate the effectiveness of the design. There is a hospital whose principal function is to produce and to fit and teach children to use artificial legs when their own have been blown off by these vicious booby-traps. Last August, as now, Vietnamese soldiers were clashing with the remnants of their communist rivals, the Khmer

Rouge, Pol Pot's troops, as well as with some Cambodians of more demo-cratic persuasion. Then, as now, the Vietnamese artillery occasionally would strike a refugee camp, taking the lives of persons who had suc-cessfully fled to the border, thinking they were safe there. Still, hundreds of thousands of Cambodian refugees consider this to be more hospitable than their own country.

Of the 300,000 Cambodians encamped along the Thai border or in the United Nations-sponsored camps inside Thailand, most fled the regime of Pol Pot which has already passed into history as a sort of paradigm of political murder, having killed perhaps a quarter of the Cambodian popu-lations. I think we can say with no exaggeration or distortion or trivializa-tion that, in our time, the only people who have suffered a tragedy com-parable qualitatively to the tragedy of the Jewish people under the Nazis is the Cambodian people under Pol Pot. Those who survived Pol Pot's mur-derous utopia suffered famine, brought on by the war and by deliberate starvation policies of the Khmer Rouge, and many more thousands fled. Even today, Cambodians are still making a long, perilous trip to the dan-gerous frontier in the effort to escape the tightening grip of Vietnamese occupation upon their cultural, religious, economic and political lives.

Thailand is a temporary haven too for refugees from Laos, both from the Mekong River lowlands and from the rugged mountains to the north and west. The Hmong hill tribesmen especially have been made targets of this vendetta, traceable ultimately to Moscow, carried out by the Lao and Viet-namese governments. The Hmong people's testimony and a growing body of physical evidence indicates that chemical weapons devised in the Soviet Union, outlawed by international convention, that infamous yellow rain, are being employed in attempts at genocide against these isolated, quite harmless, Hmong peoples.

The seas of Southeast Asia are now known, perhaps best of all, for the phenomenon of their strange inhabitants, the boat people from Vietnam. Harshly punitive "re-education camps," forced internal exile to ide-ologically planned "new economic zones," harsh restrictions on intellec-tual and religious freedom, have impelled hundreds of thousands of Vietnamese to set forth in fragile vessels to the neighboring inhospitable shores of Malaysia, Singapore, Thailand, Hong Kong, the Philippines, braving storms, drowning and pirates along the way.

The annals of the boat refugees who cross the Gulf of Thailand abound with accounts of rape, robbery and murder. According to United Nations statistics, more than three-quarters of the 455 refugee boats that reached Thai shores in 1981 had been attacked by pirates on the average of not once, but incredibly enough, four times. Five hundred seventy-one re-fugees were killed, to our knowledge, by pirates. Some five hundred ninety-nine were raped, most repeatedly. Some two hundred forty-three of the Gulf of Thailand refugees are known to have been abducted on the high seas in 1981, with only seventy-eight of those later rescued. Those pirates who abduct the helpless refugees in the Gulf of Thailand stand as the exact moral and social and human opposites, if I may say so, of H.I.A.S.

More than three years since the mass exodus of Vietnamese boat refugees began, nearly all of the refugees who arrive on Thai and Malaysian shores today admit that they knew in advance of setting out of the suffering, degradation, risk of loss of life that they faced. Foreign broadcasts, including the Voice of America, letters from abroad that had cleared or evaded censorship, word-of-mouth communication, had made most of the refugees aware of the menace of piracy. Nonetheless, they took to the seas.

One might say that the refugees who risk their lives and possessions to break free from unbearable conditions at home are expressing a brave belief and hope in the possibility of a more humane social order—one might say they are expressing hope in the future of civilization itself. And happily, to a large measure, the civilized world has responded to the plight of the refugees. Through personal charity and courage, through voluntary associations such as H.I.A.S., through governments and through inter-governmental associations—progress has been made in establishing, both in principle and in practice, the protection of the lives and liberties of these miserable refugees.

The United Nations system has shown itself in one of its very best aspects in its protection and provision for refugees. The United Nations convention and protocol on refugees oblige their contracting parties *never* forcibly to repatriate authentic refugees who meet the legal definition of having a well-grounded fear of persecution should they return. Moreover, the Office of the United Nations High Commissioner for Refugees, through its good efforts, has gained the cooperation of many states in providing at least temporary asylum for refugees, even though these states may not have bound themselves by international law to offer asylum.

When it works, the United Nations' legal and practical approach to the protection of refugees scarcely could make a greater contribution to the protection of human rights in the contemporary world. When presented with an individual or a mass movement of refugees, the United Nations High Commissioner for Refugees seeks first, and as a favored solution, voluntary repatriation. At the same time, the UNHCR, when it is operating according to design, vigilantly guards against involuntary repatriation of refugees. This policy, in and of itself, recognizes in the individual refugee a fundamental freedom he had lost or perhaps had never enjoyed in his country of origin. This policy indeed affirms the wisdom of the American Founders by asserting that, even though one may no longer have a country from which to claim citizenship or nationality, no one is utterly "alien." For all men have, in some sense, *inalienable* rights.

Besides the affirmation of the fundamental rights of refugees, the United Nations system makes a formidable effort at fulfilling the essential material and educational needs of millions of inhabitants of refugee camps. I have seen at first hand the UN system of relief and protection for refugees, not only in Southeast Asia on the Thai and Cambodian borders, but also in Pakistan on the Afghan border, where there is today the world's largest concentration of refugees. It is there that 3 million Afghan refugees have sought safe-haven, while the Soviet occupying troops, some 100,000, wage a brutal war against their homeland.

The United Nations High Commissioner for Refugees and other specialized agencies of the United Nations that cooperate with them are making an admirable effort at meeting the subsistence requirements of these large numbers of refugees in Pakistan, Somalia, Thailand and elsewhere. This effort was, of course, recognized in awarding the Nobel Prize to the Office of the United Nations High Commissioner for Refugees, an award which I have publicly and repeatedly applauded in many, many meetings. It was an appropriate and well-deserved award which should inspire other agencies of the United Nations to focus in similar ways on the humanitarian tasks for which the organization was created.

The UN's efforts at assisting refugees on the governmental and intergovernmental levels would fall far short of meeting those needs were it not for the contributions of self-sacrificing individuals, such as you, and of charitable institutions, such as H.I.A.S. In Thailand, for instance, no fewer than 90 private, voluntary relief agencies today assist Indochinese refugees. A broad representation of the civilized world may be seen in these organizations, including groups from Japan, West Germany, Ireland, the Philippines, France, Finland, Norway, Switzerland, the United Kingdom, the United States, and of course, Thailand itself. Many of these organizations, too, represent the charitable ministries of religious communities.

The classically American response to tyranny, cruelty and alienation has always been freedom, generosity and hospitality. We ought to take pride in the willingness of the American government, voluntary organizations such as H.I.A.S., and the American people to accept for resettlement hundreds of thousands of refugees, and to assist in that resettlement. Government and private agencies in the United States, such as H.I.A.S., have helped the recent Asian refugees meet their critical needs during the early transition years of their life in America. This year's United States governmental contribution alone to support refugees in camps overseas and in resettlement here is estimated at one and one half billion dollars. But much more significantly, the United States offers the new refugees a political environment that respects their human dignity and resourcefulness and allows them the freedom to seek fulfillment of their God-given potential.

The phenomenon of refugees very sharply demarcates what I have been calling the civilized world from those unhappy places dominated by regimes that deny their people the freedom to pursue their aspirations and build their civilizations. The extraordinary fact is that the same regimes that create refugees also deny their people the right to immigrate. There is the extraordinary inverse correlation between countries which permit their citizens to leave freely and those whose citizens desire to leave.

The Soviet Union, unfortunately, and other regimes of the Soviet Empire systematically refuse to agree to the United Nations conventions and protocols on refugees. The Soviet Union and other regimes of the Soviet Empire, unhappily and extraordinarily, contribute not one cent to the more than half a billion dollars that the United Nations High Commissioner for Refugees will administer this year in voluntary contributions from national governments. I am terribly proud, as I think most Americans are and I'm sure the Americans involved in H.I.A.S. are, that the United States contributes one-third of all the voluntary funds expended by the UNHCR, with the developed nations of the free world, the democracies that is, contributing virtually all of the remaining two-thirds. Many of the lesser developed countries of the free world, of course, make costly contributions to the support of the world's refugees by granting them asylum—often protracted asylum—on their soil.

It is important that we be clear about the responsibilities that lie behind the creation of refugees. The civilized, democratic world should never shirk its burden in caring for the needy, neither can it nor should it shirk from facing facts about how refugees are created, where they are created. Because only by facing those facts can we find a prudent, careful but persistent way to try to deal with the problem at its root—that is, to deal with the problem of a world in which too many refugees are created, too many regimes who do violence to them.

Ultimately, the problem of refugees can be dealt with only by avoiding the kinds of oppression which create refugees. Ultimately, the problem of refugees can be dealt with only by promoting effectively human rights around the world. United States foreign policy today is committed to these goals. So are the policies of the Secretary General of the United Nations. The Report of the Secretary General, by the way, is, I think, an extremely interesting and promising report, as have been his early initiatives as Secretary General. I believe that we can expect under his leadership that the United Nations will achieve new levels of effectiveness in dealing with the problem of refugees after they are created and also, perhaps, taking more effective measures to try to prevent the creation of this problem, that inside the United Nations is more and more often called the problem of mass exoduses.

Unfortunately, the problems have not been solved. H.I.A.S. will not be out of job in the near future. H.I.A.S.'s efforts, those of the United Nations, those of the United States Government and of civilized people everywhere are terribly important. They reinforce one another. We all have major contributions to make to this task. H.I.A.S. makes theirs year in and year out.

ALONG THE THAI BORDER

I visited Thailand in August for discussions with Thai leaders on matters related to this year's United Nations General Assembly, and while there was able to visit two refugee camps along the border with Kampuchea. I would like to share with you and the members of your Committee something of what I learned, and what I observed at first hand.

First, some of the dimensions of the problem. There are just under a quarter of a million Indochinese refugees in Thailand: Vietnamese, Khmer, Lao and Hmong. Thailand continues to receive the greatest number of Indochinese fleeing the grim oppression of the regimes controlling Vietnam, Kampuchea and Laos. In the nine months between October 1980 and June 1981, refugees fleeing to Thailand by land averaged 3,700 each month. Those fleeing by sea averaged 2,300 per month. In the rest of Southeast Asia, refugees from Indochina arrived at the countries of first asylum—Malaysia, Indonesia, Singapore, the Philippines, Hong Kong and Macau—at the rate of 5,700 per month.

From this we can see certain facts. First, although the international press no longer dramatizes their flight or their fate, refugees continue to pour out of Indochina at the rate of about 12,000 per month, swelling the residual population still in camps throughout the region. Second, Thailand provides first asylum for about half of this great outpouring of the victims of oppression.

It has become fashionable, I know, to refer to those who have fled recently, or are fleeing Indochina now, as "economic migrants," and to see them as something distinct from the political refugees who managed to escape in the 1970s. I believe this distinction is open to serious question. Is

Address before the House Judiciary Committee, Washington, D.C., September 29, 1981.

the family which flees Vietnam after the expropriation of its business and receipt of orders to join a collective farm leaving for economic or political reasons? One recalls that Nazi propaganda referred to Jews who fled Germany after Krystallnacht as *Wirtschaftsemigranten*—economic immigrants. There, too, businesses had been expropriated, livelihoods lost, and the world was told that those fleeing did so from motives of greed.

There are other parallels as well: the persecution of ethnic Chinese by Hanoi for the very reason of their ethnicity; and the persecution of the Roman Catholic population of Vietnam because of their religion.

I have, as I mentioned, visited the camps in Thailand. I have met families who lost everything and fled; and I have met families who intentionally abandoned everything they owned in order to flee. I do not see much difference in the two cases.

Members of both the House and Senate have visited the camps. I do not know any who have come away unaffected. I cannot believe there are any who, having seen the camps, having heard at first hand the story of what these people have endured, would not be proud of what the United States has done to help. Or would not want the United States to go on helping.

Finally, let me point out that our program of resettlement, in addition to the humane aspects, which respond to our view of ourselves as moral beings in a moral universe and to our view of the United States as the last, best hope of mankind, contains another dimension with which we must be concerned. Thailand is our most exposed ally in Southeast Asia. The economic, as well as the political and military, security of Thailand is enormously important to the United States' interests in that part of the world. And the destabilization of Thailand ranks high among the goals of our adversaries.

Our program to resettle the refugees in Thailand is as important to that country's stability as the economic and military aid we provide in more convenient ways. We have tried to allay the residual doubts among the Thai leadership as to American steadiness and resolve. We have said that we are with them for the long pull, that we can be counted upon to shoulder and to keep on shouldering our part of the joint burden. The actions that we take, the actions that this Committee and the Congress take, will, in the end, count for much more than our words, however fair.

I urge in the strongest possible terms that the United States continue to accept Indochinese refugees for resettlement up to a ceiling of 120,000 per year.

CAMBODIAN AID

The suffering of the Cambodian people continues. The annual dry season offensive waged by Vietnam against the Khmer people has, in this its sixth year, reached new levels of violence and destruction. Since the last meeting of the donors, more than 170,000 Khmer have been forced to flee for their lives, to leave their homeland and seek temporary shelter in Thailand. Their security has once more been shattered by the Vietnamese army and its weapons of modern warfare. Their homes, markets and garden plots have been destroyed and replaced by shell craters and mine fields. Suffering unprecedented dangers, they have fled across their border to seek temporary asylum in Thailand. Unprecedented dangers have been created at the borders by the presence of Vietnamese troops and artillery there.

The United States deplores these attacks, and we condemn them as we have in the past condemned Vietnamese attacks. We deplore and condemn the continuation of war against the Cambodian people. We will continue to deplore and condemn this war until Vietnam finally heeds the call of the United Nations General Assembly for withdrawal of foreign forces from Cambodia. We warmly support the efforts of the United Nations to resolve this prolonged tragedy and to return Cambodia to its own people.

Naturally, the United States is very pleased that despite the ferocity of the Vietnamese attacks since November, the number of civilian casualties has been remarkably low. For this, my government joins the international community in expressing its appreciation to those responsible for the early, rapid and efficient evacuation of most of the camps. The Royal Thai government's willingness to provide temporary safe-haven for more than 200,000 Khmer must be recognized as humanitarian assistance of the very highest order. The efforts of the UN Border Relief Operation (UNBRO) team, the International Committee of the Red Cross (ICRC) and the voluntary agencies operating on the border have been herculean. The sheer numbers of people moved, supplies provided and services rendered would be impressive under any circumstances. But when considered in light of the violence and the hazardous conditions which have existed along the border during the past four months, these accomplishments are practically unparalleled in the annals of UN humanitarian operations. We congratulate all those involved for this success. We offer our sincere appreciation for a job well done to all those who have worked so hard on behalf of the border population.

Address to the Donor's Meeting—Humanitarian Assistance to the Kampuchean People, United Nations, February 20, 1985.

Unfortunately, the demands on the Royal Government of Thailand and the UNBRO and ICRC operations have not ceased but are intensifying as the fighting continues and the evacuation sites require additional resources. It is imperative that the international community not lag in its support for these efforts at this time. Through our statements and contributions, we must signal our continued support for the Khmer people and to the international efforts to relieve their suffering.

I am pleased to report that the United States has pledged an additional $2 million to UNBRO bringing our total pledge to date during this fiscal year to $4 million. This pledge was announced earlier in Bangkok at the time of the Secretary-General's visit to Southeast Asia. We will also contribute 800 metric tons of vegetable oil to UNBRO through the World Food Program. In addition, the United States government has provided $1.5 million to the ICRC for its medical and protection programs on behalf of the border population.

We also wish to express our special appreciation to Dr. Kunugi and Mr. Salle for the report on agricultural conditions inside Cambodia. We recognize the limits of the study as outlined by Mr. Salle, but believe that the information provided can assist donors in assessing the situation. The United States continues to believe that the major responsibility for allaying the effects of any localized food shortage must remain with the Vietnamese who occupy Cambodia and with the supporters of that occupation.

Let me conclude by stating that the United States government will continue its support of those who labor to ensure that security and the basic necessities of life are provided to the Khmer who have fled to the Thai-Cambodian border. Our sympathy continues to be deep-felt for those Khmer people. We will continue to work with others in the international community to seek a peaceful resolution of this conflict as we provide the pressing needs of the people afflicted.

Assistance For African Refugees

It is my pleasure to bring you greetings from our president, Ronald Reagan. Because he is deeply moved by the suffering of Africa's refugees and desired to express in a compelling fashion the solidarity of the United

Address to the International Conference on Assistance to Refugees in Africa, Geneva, Switzerland, April 9, 1981.

States government and the American people, President Reagan had initially designated Vice President George Bush to head the U.S. Delegation. When his injury made it necessary for the Vice President to remain in the United States, President Reagan asked me to attend—less as our Permanent Representative to the United Nations than as one of the members of the U.S. Cabinet who operates in the field of foreign affairs. The President also asked me to personally express his devout hopes for a successful conference. And the Vice President requested that I express his regrets that he cannot be with you today. The President, his Vice President, and the Secretary of State are following our proceedings with great interest. I will report to them on the conference soon after I return to the United States.

To draw attention to this conference a bill of the United States Congress and a proclamation of the President have designated today, April 9th, as African Refugee Relief Day.

The United States not only has links with Africa, Africa is present in the United States. The African heritage is one of our component parts. Americans have many links with Africa; links which President Reagan's administration fully intends to reinforce and expand. Twenty-six million of our people trace their ancestral roots to Africa. The exchange of students, teachers, missionaries, businessmen, and diplomats between the United States and Africa has a long history fruitful to both sides. The rich influences of Africa in our culture and society are fixed in the national fabric.

My message today is simple: We feel deeply the suffering of Africa's millions of refugees forced by political, economic, natural catastrophes to leave their homes in the search for safety and even for survival.

We sympathize also with the countries in which refugees have sought and found asylum—with the strain that growing refugee populations put on scarce resources and difficult conditions in their host countries.

We want to help. We mean to do so.

Contrary to some reports, the government of the United States cares a great deal about our relations with the nations of Africa: this concern is reflected in the careful review of African policy and in the consultations now being carried out by our new Assistant Secretary of State, Mr. Crocker. Even more dramatic evidence of the U.S. Government's concern is found in its new budget: while deep cuts are being made in most domestic and foreign expenditures, the administration has recommended to the Congress a 30% increase in our overall aid for Africa—the first real increase in African aid in a number of years.

My administration's special concern with refugees has already been made clear. Last month some 50 million dollars in assistance was committed to the government of Zimbabwe to help in war reconstruction efforts and other activities and programs of direct benefit to the thousands of returnees in that country. Moreover, the United States has consistently and generously contributed to humanitarian programs for the relief of African refugees.

Today I am pleased to announce here that during the two years of 1981 and 1982 the United States will further make available, dependent in part on congressional authorization, a total of 285 million dollars to programs assisting African refugees.

That pledge is not only an expression of our desire to help but also of our conviction that something can be done—that the problems of the African refugees are not beyond solution.

Most tragically, the staggering number of refugees comes on top of the many burdens that Africa already bears. Most asylum countries in Africa are struggling against great odds to meet the needs of their own people. Moreover, African development needs and population growth, together with declining per capita food production, combine with Africa's refugee crises to threaten genuine disasters. OAU Secretary General Kodjo recently posed the issue in stark terms when he said "By the end of the century, Africa will either be saved or completely destroyed."

Even though the number of African refugees continues to grow—having more than doubled in the horn in 1980—we remain hopeful and for several reasons.

The first ground for hope is the generosity of the African countries themselves. The more than two dozen asylum countries have repeatedly demonstrated the time honored African tradition of hospitality to strangers—even though most asylum countries in Africa are struggling against great odds to meet the needs of their own people, they have often committed sizeable amounts from their own resources to assist refugees, permitting the newcomers to resettle permanently. Most have permitted the refugees to use arable lands and available social services. These African countries are therefore the first donors.

The second ground for hope lies in the excellent efforts of a variety of international agencies, public and private, including the International Committee of the Red Cross and the many other voluntary humanitarian organizations—many of whose representatives are present among us today. The United Nations High Commissioner for Refugees has worked valiantly to meet the staggering increase in world wide refugee needs over the past five years.

A third ground for hope is found in the growing response of the international community, and recognition of the need for a massive coordinated effort to assist the millions of uprooted, homeless Africans. There is also increasing awareness among those willing to help of the importance of tailoring the assistance to the concrete circumstances of the refugees and their host countries. We believe more systematic study of these circumstances can result in still more effective help.

A final reason for hope is the return during the past year of many thousands of former refugees to their homes in Zimbabwe and Equatorial Guinea, a movement that illustrates the possibility of reversing the trend.

Reversing the negative trends and solving the problem will not only require an intelligent, generous effort by nations outside Africa, it will also require a determination to achieve peace in Africa. An end to military adventures and violent politics is necessary and we call on all the countries of this area to find peaceful solutions to Africa's problems no matter how difficult or intractable they may appear.

If we all—in and out of Africa—work together to solve the problems of Africa's destitute millions, the result will be better lives and more hopeful futures for the refugees and greater stability for their hosts.

In this effort you can count on the United States.

African Aid

The grim images of death from starvation we have recently seen coming out of Africa have moved the compassion of people in the United States and around the world. The dimensions of Africa's immediate crisis seem almost overwhelming. In addition to the human tragedy in Ethiopia, thirty-six countries are plagued by abnormal food shortages, and an estimated 150 million are facing hunger and malnutrition. Drought has turned an already critical situation into a major crisis, overshadowing large parts of sub-Saharan Africa. This is why the Secretary-General's initiative on Africa is so timely. We applaud his efforts to focus world attention on this imperiled region of the world.

Mr. President, even as we speak, people around the world are rallying to Africa's side. In my own country, all forms of aid to Africa, and particularly to those hardest hit by repeated cycles of destructive drought, have been rising significantly in the past months. Two weeks ago, my government announced an additional $10 million in emergency food aid to Ethiopia. This raises our total aid to that country to $45 million this year, roughly double our emergency aid of last year. Only last week, President Reagan also approved an additional $45 million in emergency food assistance to

Address before the 39th General Assembly, November 6, 1984.

the drought-ravaged African nations of Kenya, Mozambique and Mali. All in all, food assistance to Africa increased by 175 percent this year, and we are still considering other emergency appeal requests. In addition, private citizens in America continue to open their hearts and pocketbooks to the devastated peoples of Africa. Private voluntary organizations and UN agencies in this country are being swamped by inquiries and contributions. The response has been an affirmation of the special compassionate bond between the peoples of Africa and the people of the United States.

Other Western countries are also responding generously to this catastrophic situation. The European Community recently announced an emergency grant of nearly $22 million for relief efforts, and other individual countries are supplementing that assistance. We applaud all these efforts.

Clearly, the current mobilization of the world community has been substantial. In fact, the surge in food shipments has begun to strain the region's transportation system. Ships are stacked up in harbors awaiting off-loading. Grain waits on the pier for trucks to transport it to refugee camps and feeding centers. Such situations dramatize the need for careful coordination of relief efforts, and they also make clear the obligation of national governments to make relief efforts their first priority. What is more reprehensible than to find relief for some regions hampered and disrupted for political reasons? What could be more discouraging to the generous impulse of people abroad than reports of corruption among customs or military officials who control the transportation of these crucial food supplies? With this in mind, we should also ask ourselves what impression this General Assembly will leave if we appropriate $75 million for a grand conference center in Addis Ababa, while millions starve for lack of food elsewhere in the country. What priorities and preoccupations are reflected in such a decision in such a year?

Though the tragic situation in East Africa has only recently focused the world's attention on Africa's economic woes, these problems are not new. They will not be washed away when the rains come once again. The United States has long been cooperating with African countries in efforts to strengthen African development against the inevitable, tragic cycles of climactic and economic change. Our support for international institutions such as the International Monetary Fund and the World Bank helps African countries meet short-term crises and lay the foundations for long-term development. We are by far the largest contributor to development efforts in the region through our bilateral aid programs, and voluntary contributions to the UN Development Program, UNICEF, ICRC and other multilateral programs. In the last four years, long-term U.S. bilateral development assistance to Africa has increased some 35 percent, averaging nearly $1 billion a year. This figure is over and above the emergency food assistance mentioned earlier. It is twice as much aid to Africa as my country gave only seven years ago. The same trend is mirrored in many other traditional donor countries. Recent years have been marked by a major increase in the share of total official development assistance (ODA) devoted to low-income, sub-Saharan countries.

Despite significant assistance flows, for over a decade African development has lagged considerably behind that of other developing regions. The recent global recession compounded these long-standing problems, and now renewed drought has driven millions of Africans further into destitution. A stark question confronts us: had African development stumbled well before drought made a terribly difficult situation desperate? State-controlled programs designed to provide a short cut to development had already resulted in a sharp decline in agricultural output. Many parts of the continent, including areas that were previously net food exporters, had become dependent on food imports. Coercion failed where market incentives might well have succeeded.

Our challenge here today is not only to express our concern for the current plight of African peoples, but also to chart a course for the future which faces and accepts the hard lessons of experience. I am pleased to note that there is a growing consensus on what sort of policies are called for. A joint ECA-African Development Bank report put it very succinctly. "Growth," it declared, "cannot come simply from increased government spending and intervention in the economic process as in the past. What is necessary at this stage is for governments to act to remove obstacles in the way of individual initiative, eliminate inappropriate prices and subsidies which discourage production, and effectively control waste and mismanagement in the public sector. This entails more reliance on efficient allocation mechanisms and more decentralization of decisions away from central authorities to individual producers and to firms." Simply put, these two regional institutions recommend that African governments put their faith in the people. They should do so, not for some ideological or political motives, but simply because it works. Market mechanisms and adequate producer incentives have proven to be the most effective engines of economic development. They worked in Europe and North America in the last century, and they are working in South and East Asia today.

Mr. President, we believe the qualities required in this crisis are those which have often served us well: qualities of compassion, realism, industry and optimism. These are the qualities that transformed the vast wilderness of the new world. We try to make them the basis of our cooperation with countries in today's world who themselves face the challenges of development. The United States is ready to put aside every consideration of politics and self-interest in the effort to remove the shadow of death and suffering from men, women and children threatened by starvation. But realism compels us to recognize that in the end the progress which alone consistently averts misery cannot be the gift of compassion. It cannot be the gift of one state to another any more than it can be the gift of an all powerful state, however enlightened. It cannot be a gift at all. Sustained development and economic growth can come only from the initiative, effort and discipline of people themselves, the work of their own hands, heads, hearts and fertile imaginations.

Director-General Saouma of FAO recently observed that "Aid will tend to flow to those who are most sincerely trying to help themselves." This principle lies at the heart of the new U.S. assistance program we call the Economic Policy Initiative (EPI) for Africa. I am pleased to be able to announce that only two weeks ago the United States Congress approved over $75 million in additional aid in FY1985 to help reinforce the efforts of those African countries we see successfully tackling their developmental problems. We hope with the successful implementation of the EPI to increase our development assistance to Africa over the next five years by an additional $500 million directly to those countries whose policies encourage the initiative and enterprise of their people.

Thus, despite the grim images, undeniable errors, failures and setbacks, we have not lost faith in Africa's destiny. We put our faith in the African people, and in the freedom which we believe can unleash their abilities and energies. We put our faith in the growing realism and determination with which many African governments are charting new and difficult courses, courses that recognize the value of this freedom. We should all recall that the desperate gloom with which some view Africa today was mirrored two decades ago by dire predictions for South Asia. Yet, though serious problems have yet to be surmounted, people there now look to the future with justifiable hope. So too can the people of Africa, if their governments have the wisdom to take down the barriers athwart the many roads to progress. The future lies in the hands of farming women, when they have incentives to grow the food that will feed their hungry nations. It lies in the ambition of small scale entrepreneurs, when a climate exists to encourage their initiative. It lies in the prudence of governments that encourage productive private investment from abroad. It lies in the wisdom of leaders who realize that no great monuments to fame are as important, as impressive or as lasting as the accomplishments of individuals who toil in freedom for a good they have freely chosen as their own.

HELP FOR ETHIOPIA

Since the middle of October, the world has witnessed an unfolding human tragedy in the ancient nation of Ethiopia. The United States along with other nations in the western world and elsewhere have responded with compassion and with unprecedented volumes of material relief aid.

During this month alone, ships from the United States, the European Economic Community, six other nations and the World Food Program will unload more than 100,000 tons of desperately needed food in the ports of Ethiopia. Aircraft from the United States helped to ferry this food from ports to feeding centers; transportation and medical experts search meanwhile for solutions to pressing logistical and disease problems.

The United States government has committed, since October 1 of this year, $135 million worth of commodities and other assistance, including 210,000 metric tons of emergency food aid, for the people of Ethiopia. Contributions from United States private citizens have exceeded $15 million. Over twenty American private voluntary organizations are actively involved in relief assistance on the ground in Ethiopia. We fully expect that the American people will continue to help the Ethiopian people through this disaster.

Experts in Ethiopia report that, despite the massive outpouring of aid, the grim effects of the drought and famine are spreading. The north is affected, the east is affected, and now the south is affected. We estimate that some one-and-one-half million tons of grain will be needed during the next fourteen months—over 100,000 tons monthly.

A month ago, we worried that this volume of assistance could not be absorbed by the three ports serving Ethiopia. Thanks to the effort of the Ethiopian government's Relief and Rehabilitation Commission, we are now assured that food can get in. It is vital that this effort be sustained. Moving the food up-country so that all needy people can benefit remains a problem, and logistical coordination and assistance are needed. In this regard, we commend the Secretary-General's appointment of a special representative to Ethiopia for donor coordination.

As important, however, is safe passage for hungry people and food supplies throughout the country. The United States government is committed to a policy of equal access of all needy people to emergency aid.

My government remains concerned that the current resettlement efforts may divert attention from the real emergency situations in the north and

Address to the Donor's Meeting for the Ethiopian Food Emergency, United Nations, December 18, 1984.

elsewhere and create new pockets of hunger among displaced persons in the south. The problem we all confront now is the pressing, urgent need of providing famine relief. Mobilization of support is needed to provide food and medical supplies to millions of people in risk of starvation. We remain concerned that preparations for a large-scale population movement and provision of the necessary infrastructure to ensure basic self-sufficiency will divert valuable resources from this fundamental task.

The United States hopes and expects that the humanitarian resources desperately needed to save the people of Ethiopia will be forthcoming. Ethiopia's famine is a challenge to the United Nations and to all of us member nations. We all know that donor pledges remain far short of the needs anticipated for the next fourteen months. Obviously, we must all do our best.

APPENDIX

This is the second of a two volume set. The List of Documents of the first volume is reproduced below.